JEWISH BOOKS IN
NORTH AFRICA

SEPHARDI AND MIZRAHI STUDIES
Harvey E. Goldberg and Matthias Lehmann, editors

JEWISH BOOKS IN NORTH AFRICA

Between the Early Modern and Modern Worlds

Noam Sienna

INDIANA UNIVERSITY PRESS

This book is a publication of

Indiana University Press
Office of Scholarly Publishing
Herman B Wells Library 350
1320 East 10th Street
Bloomington, Indiana 47405 USA

iupress.org

First Printing 2025

Cataloging information is available from the Library of Congress.
ISBN 978-0-253-07308-2 (hardback)
ISBN 978-0-253-07309-9 (paperback)
ISBN 978-0-253-07311-2 (ebook)
ISBN 978-0-253-07310-5 (web PDF)

To Ruth and Perel—even if you never read this, I hope that the love of books, and the worlds they open for us, will continue to carry you past the horizons of imagination. And if you do read this, you will have some idea of what I was working on for all those years.

To my parents, and in memory of my grandparents, with gratitude for gifting me the ink in my veins and teaching me the power of the Jewish book.

CONTENTS

Preface *ix*

Acknowledgments *xiii*

On Transliteration and Translation *xvii*

Archival Abbreviations *xix*

Introduction: The World of Maghrebi Jewish Books *1*

1. Medieval Books in Early Modern North Africa *15*
2. Scribes, Artists, and Patrons of the Handwritten Book *42*
3. Maghrebi Jews in European Printing Houses *68*
4. Elia Benamozegh and the Modern Maghrebi Jewish Book *91*
5. Landscapes of Print in the Nineteenth-Century Maghreb *115*
6. Early Modern and Modern Maghrebi Jewish Libraries *151*

Conclusion: The Ink in My Veins *193*

Notes *203*

Bibliography *283*

Index *319*

PREFACE

EXPLORING MY FAMILY'S BASEMENT ONE day as a child, I discovered a small box with half a dozen old books. The bindings were fraying; their rough covers had colorful marbled paper pasted on the inside. Their pages were yellowed and fragile, but the printed Hebrew letters were still bold and clear. Being an inquisitive and imaginative child, I was immediately captivated, dreaming that I had discovered some rare and ancient treasure. When I showed them to my parents, my father explained that he had been given these books when he had worked with the Jewish community of Morocco in the mid-1970s as a volunteer for the American Joint Distribution Committee (an international Jewish aid organization). I pored over these mysterious relics, fascinated and puzzled by them, and three questions in particular stayed with me.

First, my father told me they were from Morocco, but I saw that the title pages declared them to have been printed somewhere called "Livorno." Looking up Livorno in the tomes of the *Encyclopedia Judaica* that my parents kept on the living room shelf, I learned that Livorno, or Leghorn, was a port city in western Italy with a prominent Jewish community—but why, and how, did books from Italy end up in Morocco? The second mystery was that although I could read the printed Hebrew characters, when I sounded out the words, some were in a totally unknown language. Who was writing and reading this mysterious Jewish language that looked like Hebrew but didn't sound like it? And finally, perhaps the most intriguing mystery of all was that the books' previous owners had left traces of themselves throughout: names inscribed on the inside covers, notes squeezed in the margins, doodles scribbled on the flyleaves, and occasionally a full page or more of handwritten text in a fluid cursive script that I found impossible to decipher. Who were they? I spent many an afternoon imagining the people who had used these books, where they had lived, what they had thought, and what else they had read.

Decades later, those questions (and those books) have now returned to me. Some of my childhood curiosity can be satisfied; looking through this modest archive, I can identify the titles and dates, and I can read the Judeo-Arabic texts that once left me puzzled. I know that the books are mostly liturgical titles, although they also include Judeo-Arabic ethical literature and a collection of Hebrew stories.[1] I recognize some of the authors as scholars and intellectuals—whose work we will encounter in this book, including Avraham Ankawa (Morocco/Algeria, 1807–1891) and Shlomo Zarqa (Tunisia, d. 1876)—and the publishers as exemplars of the nineteenth-century Livornese printing houses that specialized in the Sephardi market. After years of paleographic practice, I can even make out some of the names in the handwritten inscriptions: Yuda ben Gavriel Ḥassin, Aharon Ḥalawa, Masʿud al-Qubi, and so on. But in some respects, I am still left with the same questions I had at my first encounter: What might one of these books have meant to the person who first held it? Or the person who inherited it, or doodled in it, or sold it? How had it made the long journey from a manuscript to a Livornese press and from there back to the Maghreb? How many people read it before it was consigned to the attic where my father picked it up, half a century ago? While I may not be able to answer these questions for this particular collection of books, I hope to restore the picture of their now-lost world, uncovering the social lives of Jewish books as they moved across the early modern Maghreb.

ACKNOWLEDGMENTS

IN THE FOLLOWING PAGES, I argue that books are social objects, produced and sustained through networks of connection: this book itself is no exception. It is an honor and pleasure to thank the many people whose loving assistance has brought me to this moment.

This book began as a doctoral dissertation at the University of Minnesota, and my adviser, Daniel Schroeter, was—and continues to be—a constant support. From the moment of this project's inception, he was convinced of its value and committed to helping me research and write it with suggestions, feedback, and gentle critique. Through his teaching, scholarship, and personal mentorship, he has modeled an ethics of generosity, commitment, and thoughtfulness that will remain with me for many years. I was blessed with the support of my dissertation committee and many other professors at the University of Minnesota, especially Ann Waltner, Kay Reyerson, Giancarlo Casale, Katherine Gerbner, Patricia Lorcin, Michelle Hamilton, J. B. Shank, Marguerite Ragnow, Juliette Cherbuliez, Leslie Morris, Natan Paradise, and Riv-Ellen Prell.

I am deeply grateful to the Association for Jewish Studies (AJS) for having provided an intellectual home for me for many years; the AJS Dissertation Completion Fellowship was a true blessing that allowed me to finish my research in a timely manner. I also gratefully acknowledge the support of the Jordan Schnitzer First Book Publication Award, administered by the Association for Jewish Studies. A doctoral scholarship from the Memorial Foundation for Jewish Culture funded a lengthy research trip to Israel, which led to some essential findings. I also received invaluable hands-on training in working with rare books and many essential insights into the field of book history through academic workshops at the Bodleian Library, the University of Pennsylvania's Katz Center for Advanced Judaic Studies, the University of Antwerp, and the Israel Institute for Advanced Studies. Early drafts of this material were presented in various forms at the Mediterranean Workshop; the University of Minnesota; the Society for the History of Authorship, Reading, and Publishing (SHARP); the AJS; and the National University of Ireland-Galway. I am grateful for the keen insights and feedback of all the participants.

This book could not have been written, of course, without the access to and insights about historical materials facilitated generously and professionally by the librarians, archivists, and collectors I have been privileged to work with and learn from. At the Ben-Zvi Institute, Ofra Tirosh-Becker—who has been a mentor since my undergraduate years and who first introduced me to the study of Judeo-Arabic—opened the institute's doors and shelves to me, took a serious interest in my project, and helped me work with the librarians and archivists there. At the National Library of Israel, Yoel Finkelman and Alexander Gordin showed me great kindness and hospitality and assisted me with many vexing queries. I had productive visits to the Center for Jewish History in New York, the Ariel Bension Collection at the University of Alberta, the Sterling and Beinecke Libraries at Yale University, and the Bodleian Libraries at the University of Oxford, with thanks to the librarians and archivists there. Much valuable material was acquired through the generosity of two private collectors: Paul

Dahan, at the Centre de la culture judéo-marocaine in Brussels, and William Gross in Tel Aviv. I hope my work pays tribute to their love of Jewish books and the people who made them.

Scholarly encouragement was provided in ample measure by colleagues and friends to whom I turned with general and specific queries; I am grateful for their kind assistance and useful feedback. In addition to the people already mentioned, I add my expressions of thanks, in alphabetical order, to Dotan Arad, Javier Del Barco, Yael Barouch, Dainy Bernstein, Clémence Boulouque, Francesca Bregoli, Zsófi Buda, Michelle Chesner, Yosef Chetrit, Elka Deitsch, Theodor Dunkelgrün, Yaacob Dweck, Jordan Finkin, Rahel Fronda, Matteo Giunti, David Guedj, Raphael Halff, Brad Sabin Hill, Arthur Kiron, Marjorie Lehman, Paul Love, Chen Malul, Jessica Marglin, Barbara Martinelli, César Merchan-Hamann, Sharon Mintz, Yigal Nizri, Ben Outhwaite, Vanessa Paloma, Bryan Roby, Avraham Roos, Shalom Sabar, Rachel Schine, Menahem Schmelzer z"l, Emile Schrijver, Kathryn Schwartz z"l, Jerry Schwarzbard, David Sclar, Adam Shear, Aron Sterk, Noam and Dinah Stillman, Muneeba Syed, Joshua Teplitsky, Ton Tielen, Yosef and Tsivia Tobi, Shani Tzoref, Michael Waas, and Dan Yardeni.

Above all, my family has seen me through this process with patience, humor, and love. I am deeply grateful for the support of my siblings, in-laws, and, especially, my parents, Baruch and Elyse, who shaped this book before I even knew I was going to write it. From my mother, I learned a passion for Judaism as a living tradition, a love of Jewish text, and a deep attention to voices on the margins. My father first introduced my young hands to the wonder and art form of making letters, and he has continued to inspire me through his love of Jewish text and dogged pursuit of meaning across the changing technologies of reading. My parents have followed my work with sincere curiosity and affection for many years and have kept me afloat through my personal storms and shipwrecks.

The constant support of my husband Aaron, his loving curiosity, and his gentle encouragement assured me of the value of my work and kept me focused on reaching my goals. In the primary sources I researched for this book, I can only recall coming across one example of an author thanking their spouse: Avraham ʻAyyash, an Algerian Jew living in Jerusalem, writes that he succeeded in bringing his father's book to press in Germany "by the merit of my honorable and modest wife, Hazibuena, may she be blessed, who was reason and cause and helpmate; by her good-willed consent I travelled abroad. Certainly, the reason for this book's printing lies in her hands" (Sulzbach: Aharon ben Meshulam Zalman, 1776). Aaron is my reason and my cause and my helpmate, and it was by his good-willed consent that I did my traveling abroad. Certainly, the reason for this project's success lies in his hands.

Almost all introductions in early modern Jewish books conclude with an apology by the editors and printers, using such stock phrases as "Who can be aware of all errors? Clear me of unseen faults" [Ps. 19:13] and a popular Hebrew proverb: "Just as there cannot be grain without straw, so too there cannot be books printed without mistakes." As Eliya ben Binyamin Halevi, proofreader of the *Arbaʻa ṭurim* printed in Istanbul in 1493, remarked in his colophon: "Indeed, it is in the nature of this labor, which includes copying its parts from hand to hand, that no-one involved in it can be free of errors, but only through as great an effort as possible can one reach a state of comparative perfection." This book, too, has many parts that have passed from hand to hand. I take responsibility for having made as great an effort as possible to correct the mistakes in this work, and I ask my readers to clear me of unseen faults.

Noam Sienna
Minneapolis, MN, January 2025

ON TRANSLITERATION AND TRANSLATION

AS A HISTORIAN, I AM always longing for an impossible encounter, straining to hear a forgotten melody that can never return, trying to imagine a world I will never visit. The physical book, in particular, embodies this tension: it promises a material encounter with the voices of the past, while at the same time reminding us of everything we cannot know about it and its world. I have tried in these pages, which span continents, languages, and centuries, to bring together many different stories into a single whole. My goal was to weave the diverse languages and contexts discussed here into consistent and understandable English prose, while never losing sight of our distance from their origin.

With that in mind, I have kept the use of many terms in Hebrew and Judeo-Arabic, followed the first time they are used with a gloss in square brackets. The transliterations for Arabic follow the system used in the International Journal of Middle Eastern Studies, with the omission of vowel diacritics. I have taken some liberties with colloquial Judeo-Arabic, which has numerous regional variations and idiosyncrasies. For Hebrew, I have followed the Library of Congress transliteration guidelines, with the exceptions of noting the ʻayin with a left inverted comma (ʻ) and pharyngeal letters with under-dots, as in Arabic (ṣ, ṭ, ḥ). For Yiddish words and names, I have used the YIVO romanization scheme. Arabic and Hebrew words commonly used in English are given in their standard English spellings (e.g., sultan, rabbi, Torah, Kabbalah). Common place names are given in their standard English spellings (e.g., Algiers, Fez, Cairo), while smaller locations are rendered as they are on modern maps—often, for North African places, in French orthography (e.g., Sefrou, Debdou).

Personal names present a particularly thorny challenge. In general, I have transliterated names, including biblically derived names, directly from Hebrew or Arabic (i.e., Yiṣḥaq and not Isaac), except in the cases where a specific romanization is known to have been used. In those cases, I use the historical romanization and present the transliteration in round brackets the first time a person is mentioned, for example, "Moïse Sebaoun (Moshe Sib'on)." In some cases, I combine a transliterated first name with a romanized family name, for example, "Ya'aqov Abensur (Ibn-Ṣur)." For family names derived from patronymics, I have used a capital letter and hyphen (e.g., Refael-Aharon Ben-Shim'on or Shmuel Ibn-Danan) to distinguish them from regular patronymics (e.g., Netanel ben Yehuda or Freḥa bat Avraham).

In general, I have attempted to offer a simple, consistent, and understandable system. I have preserved transliterations in quotations according to the spelling of the original author. All translations, unless otherwise noted, are my own.

ARCHIVAL ABBREVIATIONS

ISRAEL

YBZ	=	Yad Ben Zvi (Ben-Zvi Institute for the Study of Oriental Jewry), Jerusalem
NLI	=	National Library of Israel, Jerusalem
Benayahu	=	Meir Benayahu Collection, Jerusalem
Gross	=	William Gross Collection, Tel Aviv

NORTH AMERICA

JTS	=	Jewish Theological Seminary, New York
BC YR	=	Bension Collection (Yalqut Ro'im), University of Alberta
HUC	=	Hebrew Union College, Cincinnati
YUL	=	Yeshiva University Library, New York

EUROPE

CCJM	=	Centre de la culture judéo-marocaine, Paul Dahan Collection, Brussels
BNF	=	Bibliothèque nationale de France

BSB	=	Bayerische Staatsbibliothek, Berlin
NLR	=	National Library of Russia, St. Petersburg
Braginsky	=	Braginsky Collection, Zurich
BL	=	British Library, London
Bodl.	=	Bodleian Library, University of Oxford
TCD	=	Trinity College, University of Dublin
CUL	=	Cambridge University Library, Cambridge

JEWISH BOOKS IN
NORTH AFRICA

INTRODUCTION

The World of Maghrebi Jewish Books

A LIBRARY LOST

In the spring of 1955, Ukrainian-Israeli scholar Haim Zeev Hirschberg (1903–1976) arrived in the Algerian city of Oran (Wahran) looking for books. Hirschberg was on a research mission through North Africa sponsored by the Jewish Agency of Israel [*Sokhnut*] "to gather materials on the life of Jews in this area, in the past and the present day." This work would eventually result in his magisterial study, *A History of the Jews in North Africa*. In particular, he had come to North Africa "to search for *genizot*, and seek out manuscripts and old printed books, that might shed light on the history of Jews in this region."[1] Hirschberg was particularly impressed with the Great Synagogue of Oran (built in 1880 and inaugurated in 1918), observing that the synagogue not only was a place of prayer but also functioned as a central community hub, with "offices, bureaus, and school classrooms," and, most importantly, "a 'midrash,' namely a study hall, with bookcases filled with books. According to the inventory, it contains the works of the sages of the Maghreb, and rare editions from Livorno; but I did not have time to even glance at them." The community was preparing for Passover: the synagogue was frenetic with activity, and Hirschberg was whisked along to the next stop on his tour. Elsewhere on his travels, Hirschberg poked his head into Jewish libraries in Tetouan, Tangiers, Sefrou, and Fez, but none were as extensive or lavish as this one.[2]

The magnificent Jewish library of Oran, which Hirschberg regretted being unable to examine more closely, had been assembled by nineteenth-century Algerian rabbi Moïse Sebaoun (Moshe Sib'on, ca. 1806–1888).[3] At the time of Sebaoun's death, French newspapers reported that his library contained over five thousand volumes, and it was also claimed (in the words of one eulogist) that "he had a great number of them stored in his memory."[4] A surviving portrait photograph of Sebaoun shows him posed in his library with an open book of responsa in his lap and a stack of books piled almost out of the frame to his left.[5] After his death, Sebaoun's library was transformed into a communal resource, and it was housed for decades in the Great Synagogue of Oran, opposite the offices of the *tribunal rabbinique*, as it was for Hirschberg's visit.

In the early 1960s, however, some Jewish leaders in Oran feared that Jews would not be welcome in newly independent Algeria, and they started making plans to safeguard their community assets, including the Sebaoun library. By 1964, after the migration of most Algerian Jews to France, discussions regarding the transfer of the books had begun, and in 1972, three cases of Sebaoun's books arrived on the doorstep of the Consistoire israélite de Paris.[6] Comprising some 662 books, this collection certainly represented less than half of the original library and was probably only a small portion of it: as French historian Gérard Nahon indicates, the library was cataloged in the early 1950s (presumably the "inventory" that Hirschberg mentions), and the surviving books retain their cataloging numbers. The largest of these numbers is 1439, which means that the 662 surviving volumes could represent at most only 46 percent of the original collection.[7] These books were partially cataloged by Nahon in 1974, but

Figure 0.1 Rabbi Moshe Sebaoun in his library, Oran, ca. 1880. YBZ.0237.037, reproduced with the permission of the Yad Ben-Zvi Photograph Library.

the current location of this part of the collection is unclear.[8] It is also unknown where the rest of Sebaoun's library is. The books seem to have been dispersed, although individual volumes from his collection turn up occasionally at public auctions in Israel.[9]

But this glimpse (imperfect as it may be) into the lost library of a nineteenth-century Algerian rabbi raises larger questions about the significance of these books in their social context: How had each book found its way from author to printer (in some cases, a very long distance) and from there to its readers? How did these books, some in circulation for over three centuries, end up in Sebaoun's collection? Who used the library while it was in Sebaoun's possession and during the decades it stood in the study hall of the Great Synagogue of Oran—and who did not have access to it? And what is still unknown about this library and others like it—libraries that were likewise dismantled, broken up, dispersed, and never cataloged? The answers to these questions would reveal not just the history of these books but also the social world around them.

Historically, scholars often treated the Jews of North Africa as being situated on the edge of the modern Jewish world. Even Hirschberg, who was hoping to locate historical materials from what he considered the "golden period" of medieval Islam, was disappointed in the books that he found (or didn't find) in North Africa. In his two volumes of *A History of the Jews in North Africa*, he devotes little more than a few pages to the internal life of Jewish communities beyond the seventeenth century; Hirschberg portrayed the modern North African Jewish world as one of mainly anthropological value, showing little interest in the intellectual production of the preceding two centuries.[10] Earlier work on Maghrebi Jewish history drew heavily on colonial sources as well as the liberal-assimilationist views of the Franco-Jewish philanthropic organization the Alliance Israélite Universelle (AIU). Indeed, several important early historians of Maghrebi Jews were AIU graduates. Thus it was common to equate the beginning of modernity for Sephardi Jewish communities with the arrival of European colonialism, which emancipated the allegedly "primitive" Jews of the Orient and raised their intellectual and geographic horizons until they were able to join their enlightened European coreligionists.[11]

But, as we shall see, the Jewish communities of early modern North Africa were already socially diverse, internationally mobile, economically central, and intellectually vibrant well before the establishment of the European colonial administration. The relationship between North African Jews and European (or Euro-Jewish) modernity was not passive but rather interactive, as they each formulated their own distinctive expressions and responses. And while the Jews were involved, sometimes quite intimately, with French colonial officials and institutions, they did not lose their Maghrebi and Mediterranean networks and orientations and continued to interact with broader and older social landscapes (although often in increasingly parochial ways).[12] Moving away from a teleological narrative centered around the European model of modernity demonstrates how the colonial perspective may not match the realities on the ground. As primary sources in both their content and their material form, Jewish books from North Africa present an opportunity to reexamine our narratives of the past centuries and the nuances those narratives elide. The complexity of Jewish history in general, and particularly the study of material culture, has been identified as a promising avenue away from the narrowness of opposing terms like East/West, early modern/modern, Europe/Africa/Asia, and Old World/New World.[13] This book, through its engagement with the material and intellectual production of North African Jewish communities in a global context, is a contribution to that effort.

THE PEOPLE OF THE BOOKS

The centrality of books in Jewish culture has been evident for well over a millennium. In late antiquity, the Qur'an referred to Jews (and Christians) as *ahl al-kitab*, "People of the Book," a term that became a source of pride and self-identification among Jews.[14] Since the Middle Ages, Jews have celebrated their "text-centeredness," and scholars in Jewish studies have devoted many pages to tracing the evolving genealogies of Jewish texts.[15] But in recent years, the development of Jewish book history has shifted from the analysis of Jewish texts alone—with no consideration for the physical forms that carry them—toward a focus on the interactions of material and cultural dynamics that form the unique qualities of the Jewish book.[16] Jewish books are continually moving between the fuzzy boundaries of local and international traditions, between manuscript and printed forms, between Hebrew and vernacular languages, and between elite and folk culture.

The interplay of these factors demonstrates the need to study the Jewish book simultaneously as a textual, material, and social artifact and as a window into the Jewish communities that produced and used it.[17] In this book, I focus on a context that, in both its geographical and temporal scope, has been neglected as a site for the development of Jewish book culture, namely, North Africa from the end of the Middle Ages to the turn of the twentieth century. By following the material life cycle of Jewish books as they were produced and circulated in North Africa in the early modern and modern periods, we can see how North African Jews were integrated into global networks of the Jewish world while also inextricably part of their local environment. We will follow the trail of Jewish books—manuscripts and printed books—throughout North Africa and across the Mediterranean, from their authorship and production through distribution and circulation, centering the books themselves as physical, portable, commercial, and material objects.

The North African Jewish book is thus a vital source for Sephardi history. I use the term "Sephardi history" to refer to this field of study, recognizing that it is (in the words of Matthias Lehmann) "a category superimposed on a historical community by modern scholarship." It brings together groups of Jewish communities with *commonalities* (such as a relationship, real or imagined, with Iberia as a former homeland), *connectedness* (such as networks of commercial and familial ties), and *groupness* (such as the belief in a shared heritage).[18] The relationships revealed in this book are part of the "Sephardi" world, to be sure, but they are more than that: they encompass trans-Mediterranean family networks, the intellectual overlaps among Arabic-speaking North African Jews and Ladino-speaking Ottoman Sephardim, North African encounters with and responses to the Ashkenazi Haskalah, the ambivalent relationships between North African Jews and the Islamic cultural landscape around them, and more.

The study of books and their readers can reshape our understanding of North African Jewish society during the complex and turbulent transition into modernity, revealing how it balanced between its local landscape and a transnational Jewish diaspora. We will come to understand not just the texts they contain—although those, too, remain critically understudied—but also the books as physical objects that were crafted, scribed, painted and printed, shipped and carted and hawked in marketplaces, bound and rebound, marked up and discarded, or preserved pristine on shelves. Because this book sits at the intersection of two fields, Sephardi history and book history, readers will be more or less familiar with different aspects of it. Scholars of Jewish culture might consider the new insights brought by the methodologies of book history, while book historians may benefit from grounding themselves first in the specific cultural contexts of this book. In other words, readers must ask two questions: Why should we study North African Jews? And why should we care about their books?

MAPPING THE NORTH AFRICAN JEWISH WORLD

While this book about North African Jewish books has a global scope, it is grounded in a set of particularities: this geography, this people, and this network of circulation. Our setting might be imagined as a series of overlapping diasporas: the Jews of North Africa, which overlaps with the larger Sephardi diaspora, which itself overlaps with the Jewish communities of the Islamic world, all within the Jewish diaspora as a whole. The importance of this specific cultural setting is evident in the composition of

Moïse Sebaoun's library (or, at least, the surviving portion of it), in which the books of North African authors took pride of place, surrounded by the compositions of other Sephardi communities in both Europe and the Ottoman Empire, and accompanied by the larger cultural production of the Jewish world from as far away as Poland or Germany.[19] This library is not a generic Jewish library: it was shaped by the particular context of Sebaoun's experiences and those of his community in Oran, in French-occupied Algeria, and in the nineteenth-century Mediterranean. The Jews of North Africa occupy a fascinating position from which to explore the diversity of the early modern world: a community that was at once globally connected and locally rooted and that cultivated a unique voice in response to both European colonialism and European Jewish narratives of emancipation and modernization.

North Africa, also known as the Maghreb (Arabic *al-maghrib*; literally, "the West" or "the place of the setting sun") refers to the northern coast of the African continent, including the modern countries of Morocco, Algeria, Tunisia, and Libya.[20] The earliest Jewish communities of this region likely settled in the Roman provinces of Africa Proconsularis and Mauretania around the first century CE, as demonstrated by archaeological evidence.[21] By the time of the Islamic conquest, Jewish communities were found across the Maghreb, where they expanded and flourished during the Middle Ages. Urban centers, especially Kairouan (Qayrawan), Gabès (Qabis), Fez, Sijilmasa, and Constantine, produced famed Jewish scholars and attracted Jewish merchants from elsewhere in the Mediterranean region.[22] Medieval documents from the Cairo Geniza show that Jewish merchants of Maghrebi origin played a large role in international shipping and trade in areas as distant as the Malabar Coast of southwestern India.[23]

Further waves of Iberian Jewish migrants in the fourteenth through sixteenth centuries were transformative for the Jewish communities of the Maghreb. The riots of 1391 and the expulsion of 1492, in particular, prompted large and significant influxes of Jewish refugees to North Africa. These Sephardim integrated into their local Jewish communities in complex ways as part of the newly forming "double diaspora" of Sephardi Jewry, and they maintained narratives of distinction even while those boundaries were increasingly blurred or even fictionalized.[24] Many of the Sephardim in North Africa served as political and economic intermediaries between the Iberian and Maghrebi governments. They developed the mercantile and intellectual networks of a robust diaspora linking North Africa, southern Europe, Italy, the Balkans, and the Levant.[25] Subsequent migrations of Jews from Italy (of both Sephardi and Italian origins) added to the diversity of Maghrebi Jewish society. Tunis, in particular, was home to a large community of Jewish families of Livornese origin known as the Grana, or "Leghorn Jews." This group formally separated from its autochthonous Tunisian coreligionists, known as the Twansa, in 1710, although the line between Grana and Twansa families is not as clear-cut as the vocabulary might suggest.[26] Wealthy financier Nissim Shamama, for example, claimed membership in the Grana community to pursue Italian citizenship, even though the Shamama family was generally known to be Twansi.[27]

The Jewish Maghreb in the early modern period was thus centered around a network of interconnected cities (like Fez, Salé, Tunis, Algiers, and Oran) that were tied to other centers of Maghrebi Jews—and the Sephardi diaspora more broadly—across the Mediterranean (Livorno, Gibraltar, Jerusalem, Istanbul). These urban centers were both crossroads and frontiers, linked not only to the Mediterranean but also to their local inland surroundings. The *mellaḥ* [Jewish quarter] of Marrakech, for example, functioned as a permeable Jewish space: an integral part of urban life for the Marrakech residents, Jews and Muslims alike. They were inextricably tied into the regional networks of rural and trans-Saharan trade routes, beginning in the seventeenth century and continuing well into the twentieth century.[28]

This book covers the periods loosely defined as "early modern" and "modern," beginning in the sixteenth century but focusing on the eighteenth and nineteenth centuries and coming to a close at the turn of the twentieth century. This was a time of great transformation for the Mediterranean region as a whole, and for its Jewish communities in particular, although the precise nature of that change for the Jews of the Maghreb has been the subject of scholarly disagreement.[29] I write in contrast to a perception, still widespread in both scholarship and the popular imagination, that understands Jewish society in North Africa and the Middle East as stagnant and declining amid the "postclassical decay" of the early modern Islamic world until European modernization brought about the disintegration of traditional Jewish societies in the Islamic world and their "rescue" to Israel or abroad.[30] This book argues that we should consider the early modern period instead as a time of activity and innovation spurred by encounter and challenge, with North African Jews taking the stage as agents in their own history.

The "modernization" of North African Jews entailed both continuities and transformations, moving into the colonial period rather than beginning in it.[31] In the eighteenth-century economic sphere, many Jews were tied to the local governments through their status as merchants of the sultan or governor, but they also increasingly sought (and were granted) European consular protections, which had legal, social, and political effects that reverberated into the nineteenth and twentieth centuries.[32] In the nineteenth century, the course of French colonialism and the resulting social, legal, and economic changes—different for each country—placed the Jews in an uncertain position.[33] While they were increasingly separating (or being separated) from their Muslim neighbors, they also had to negotiate their relationships to colonial power amid tensions internal and external to their society: processes that reverberated in the postindependence period and the resulting exodus of Maghrebi Jews and that continue to this day in North Africa, France, and Israel.[34]

Today, the Jewish presence in the Maghreb is rapidly dwindling. As Emily Gottreich and Daniel Schroeter have observed, "Whole generations of North Africans have never even met a Jew; for these generations, the very notion of Jews as indigenous is an alien concept. Jews have become almost invisible in the Maghrib, yet for a new generation of researchers, they are everywhere part of the landscape: the objects of memory, nostalgia, and research."[35] This book participates in mapping this now-invisible world, highlighting communities that were both indigenous and diasporic, local and international, Maghrebi and Mediterranean. This context is essential for the culturally grounded analysis of book history, which considers not only the books themselves but also how they were woven into the everyday lives of individuals and communities.

THE MATERIALITY AND SOCIALITY OF BOOK CULTURE

We begin our study of the material and social book by considering its readers. Individual readers made meaning of books not only through their private reading but also by placing the physical books and their texts into cultural narratives formed through the relationships between readers. Some scholars have begun to explore how Jewish books can point to larger conceptions of regional reading communities: for example, categorizing medieval manuscripts by Jewish "geocultural areas" like Ashkenaz rather than national frameworks like "German" or "French."[36] Similarly, scholarship on Ladino journalism and rabbinic literature has shown how local authors, publishers, patrons, and reading communities were integrated into a transnational network of vernacular speakers of Judeo-Spanish, connecting writers and readers across the Mediterranean.[37] This book argues for a similar conception of the Jewish Maghreb as a coherent category, without assuming the consistency of "national" frameworks or imposing them onto the past.

By mapping more clearly the contours of these interconnected communities in the Maghreb, and the place of books within them, we see how books both helped to form and were formed by the world around them. Natalie Zemon Davis presciently argued in her first collection of essays that we must "consider a printed book not merely as a source for ideas and images, but as a carrier of relationships," and she carried this insight into much of her subsequent work.[38] Similarly, Leslie Howsam writes that studying book culture "asks questions about relationships. . . . The book is not so much a category as a process."[39] This is why I strive to study books not only in the context of their production but also in their subsequent lives as part of social communities. Where did people go to acquire books? How did they decide how to share books with friends and neighbors? Which books did they choose to keep and collect? What kinds of books were available for public reading? And how were they understood? Books are continually reshaped and reinterpreted in different contexts, through practices of translation, commentary, and material reconstruction.

In this view, books are both material and social objects since they are at the nexus of physical processes and cultural meanings. As Roger Chartier states, "There is no text apart from the physical support that offers it for reading (or hearing)."[40] Some scholars have termed this methodology the "sociology of texts" or "social codicology": an in-between space where bibliography and material analysis are combined with textual interpretation and social context.[41] I am also inspired by what Hugh Amory provocatively called "ethnobibliography," which attempts to analyze books as "entangled objects" inseparable from their cultural function and social meaning.[42] Taking as his starting point a page from an English Bible that was wrapped in cloth and buried with a young

Native girl in the Mashantucket Pequot cemetery in the late seventeenth century, Amory castigates the bibliographers who would suggest that "[this] collocation would be as meaningless as the discovery of a Bible in a trash basket, or its use as a doorstop."[43] Instead, he argues that we can only study the manifestation of this text in this particular material form if we understand the particular entanglement of cultural contexts that produced it.

After all, books can be many things. In addition to vehicles for their textual content, they can be artisanal crafts, commercial merchandise, family heirlooms, illicit contraband, religious relics, and more. A deep engagement with the materiality of books, both in the various aspects of their production (editing, copying, typesetting, illustration, binding, etc.) and in their circulation and reception (rebindings, ownership marks, annotations, etc.) brings important and unique aspects of their history to light. Beyond their status as objects, books are also nodes in a social network, part of a complex cultural system that connects people, objects, places, and ideas. Decades ago, folklorist Simon Bronner defined material culture as the interconnection of objects, people, and the society around them; as he writes, material culture is not only "tangible things crafted, shaped, altered, and used across time and space. It is inherently personal and social, mental and physical. . . . But more so, it is the weave of these objects in the everyday lives of individuals and communities."[44] Since then, historians have increasingly blurred the boundaries between "document" and "artifact," reading objects as historical documents and vice versa.

Following general trends in book history, recent studies in Jewish book history have explored the role of printing technologies in the development of modern Jewish intellectual, social, religious, and literary history in early modern Europe. These scholars have investigated the complex relationships among new technologies of bookmaking, reading practices, and social, religious, and political transformations for early modern European Jews, modeling a Jewish book history that places the books themselves—their materiality, circulation, and changing audiences—at the center of the story.[45] The majority of studies of the Jewish book in the Islamic world to date, however, have focused on bibliography: cataloging the names and locations of printers and the titles and editions of the books they produced.[46] While the landmark scholarship in the previous decades has brought many overlooked texts to light and expanded our understanding of the literary landscape of Maghrebi Jews, we still need a large-scale analysis of Jewish books in the Maghreb that highlights the intersection of the materiality and sociality of the book.

This study follows the life cycle of the Maghrebi Jewish book in three parts, beginning with production and proceeding through distribution and circulation. Part 1 explores the evolution of post-medieval Jewish manuscript culture, showing that the persistence of handwritten manuscripts was part of the vibrancy of the Maghrebi Jewish relationship with books. Part 2 challenges standard narratives of the history of Jewish printing, emphasizing the active role of North African Jews in developing, accessing, and engaging with print technologies. Part 3 maps out the physical landscape of Jewish books as they moved through North African Jewish communities, showing how bookstores, presses, and libraries served as nodes in a network of global connections and as incubators for modern intellectual, political, and literary developments. Throughout, we will attend to what Bronner described as "the weave of these objects in the everyday lives of individuals and communities": What did it mean in the early modern Maghreb to write, read, or own a Jewish book?

ONE

MEDIEVAL BOOKS IN EARLY MODERN NORTH AFRICA

INTRODUCTION: SEPHARDI BOOK CULTURE BETWEEN IBERIA AND NORTH AFRICA

In 1496, four years after the expulsion of Jews from Spain, Yiṣḥaq Ibn-Shoshan sat in the seaside port of Goletta (today La Goulette / Ḥalq al-Wadi, Tunisia); from his window, he could gaze across the Mediterranean toward the shores of his distant homeland. He was (as he later called himself) one of the *megorashei sfarad*, the "Exiles of Sepharad."[1] He comforted himself, as so many did, by writing books. In the colophon to a manuscript of a commentary on the tractate *Avot* by fourteenth-century Iberian scholar Yosef Ibn-Shoshan (presumably one of his ancestors), our scribe mournfully situated himself, physically and spiritually, in the exilic space between Spain and North Africa.

> I, the unfortunate man of sorrows, Yiṣḥaq Ibn-Shoshan, copied these commentaries on tractate *Avot* . . . while I was on the seashore of the city of Tunis, [in the place] called in the Romance vernacular *Goletta*, in the house of the outstanding sages, the pursuers of justice, Ḥayyim and Makhluf Abula'ish, in the attic room that they provided for me to stay in. May God reward their effort, amen. [I finished] on Thursday, the 30th day of the *'omer,*

> in the year "Cry out in REJOICING [5256] for Jacob, and be glad! Shout at the crossroads of nations, and sing aloud in praise, saying: Save Your people, O Lord, [save] the remnant of Israel!" (Jer. 31:7).[2] And may God say "enough!" to our troubles.[3] Just as we were exiled from the land of our birth on account of our sins, so may the Scripture be fulfilled for us, "But I will leave within you a poor and humble folk, and they shall find refuge in the name of the Lord" [Zeph. 3:12]. . . . Amen, so may it be.[4]

Ibn-Shoshan and the thousands of Iberian *megorashim* [exiles] like him who found refuge in North Africa had experienced an irrevocable and traumatic rupture, which they testified to in the pages of their books. In one incomplete manuscript that was taken out of Spain and finished in Morocco just two months after the expulsion, the scribe signs as "the one saddened at heart, anxious and bitter, whose spirit is as bitter as wormwood . . . on the 4th of the month of Tishrei, in the year 'For you were STRANGERS [5253].'"[5] In the colophon to another manuscript, copied by an Iberian exile in Fez in 1505, the scribe prefaces his signature with the phrase "the knees which did not bow to idolatry, although surrounded by the fire and kindling," perhaps a reference to having escaped the auto-da-fé of the Inquisition.[6] At the same time, the exiles held on to their cultural heritage as rooted in the Jewish life of Iberia, or Sepharad as they knew it, while they continued to produce Jewish texts, books, and other objects in their new homes. This was neither the beginning nor the end of the relationship between these two shores of the Mediterranean. The book culture of the early modern Maghreb was part of a continuous tradition linked to the medieval manuscripts of Sepharad, and it was impacted by the continued physical presence of medieval books, mostly from Iberia, which circulated in Maghrebi communities for hundreds of years.

In this chapter, I demonstrate that early modern Maghrebi book culture developed through the exchange of objects, ideas, and people across the Mediterranean, as it had since the early

Middle Ages. I first follow the movement of books and book-makers from Iberia to North Africa after the exile, showing how medieval Sephardi books and the practices surrounding them found their way to the early modern Maghreb, both in the context of manuscript culture and in the establishment of a short-lived Maghrebi Hebrew printing press. The final part of this chapter highlights how medieval books themselves continued to play a role in the life of Maghrebi Jewish communities throughout the early modern and modern periods and well into the twentieth century.

When Iberian exiles brought their books to North Africa at the end of the fifteenth century, it was not so much an introduction as a reunion. As scholars have long noted, the branch of medieval Jewish book culture termed "Sephardi" is associated most strongly with medieval Spain, but it was not unique to the Iberian Peninsula, even during the Middle Ages. The vast majority of the textual, paleographic, codicological, and artistic features that characterize medieval Sephardi books are found in books produced all across the western Mediterranean and especially in North Africa.[7] This is no surprise: throughout the Middle Ages, Iberia and North Africa were intertwined, and during the Almoravid and Almohad dynasties (eleventh through thirteenth centuries), they were part of the same political structures. Objects and people moved regularly between them, and the Jewish communities of both regions were particularly well connected. It is in this context that we must understand the development of a transregional "Sephardi" style of bookmaking.

It is clear from a variety of sources, including the booklists of the Cairo Geniza, that medieval North Africa was a center for the copying and wide distribution of Hebrew books. As one scholar puts it, "The impressive contents of the Cairo Genizah are in no small degree due to the arrival there of many Jewish refugees from Tunisia [after the conquest by the Banu Hilal in 1057] and to the transfer of the bibliographical riches of the North African communities to the Egyptian centre."[8] In fact, the earliest examples of books demonstrating a recognizable Sephardi style are not from Iberia but from the Maghreb.[9] Hebrew codicologists and paleographers still debate which aspects of Sephardi book production originated in the Maghreb and spread to al-Andalus, that is, the southern regions of Iberia under Islamic rule, and which went the other way.[10] As Malachi Beit-Arié explains in his definition of the "geocultural" type of Sephardi codicology: "Codicological traits characteristic of and unique to the Sefardic type . . . were visible already in the earlier tenth- and eleventh-century manuscripts produced in Tunisia, and in the Middle East by immigrants from the Maghreb. Accordingly, one might assume that the roots of Iberian bookcraft were in North Africa. . . . Both bookcraft and script style that had originated most probably in the Muslim Maghreb were, no doubt, further shaped and elaborated in Muslim Spain, and eventually adopted throughout the Iberian Peninsula and even beyond it."[11] It is often impossible to tell in the absence of a colophon whether a given medieval manuscript in Sephardi script originated in Iberia or North Africa.[12] This is true in the realm of book decoration as well, with many of the same artistic motifs—including micrographic patterns, architectural motifs like the horseshoe arch, spared-ground vegetal and floral ornament, and geometric tiling and interlacing—found in both medieval Maghrebi and Iberian manuscripts.[13] For all of these reasons, it is clear that Sephardi book culture comprises a family of shared techniques, styles, and aesthetics developed in the early Middle Ages through the cultural interplay between the Jewish communities of al-Andalus and the Maghreb.

The Jewish communities of the Maghreb and Iberia had also developed in unique and distinct ways, but the expulsions and subsequent dispersion of large numbers of Sephardi *megorashim* into North Africa in the fourteenth and fifteenth centuries brought these traditions into conversation and, eventually (for the most part), integration.[14] Books are one of the primary vehicles through which we can observe this process, both in their physical forms and in the associated social significance of their production and use. In this chapter, I explore how medieval books, especially from Iberia, continued to carry meanings—as objects, texts, and symbols—for early modern and modern North African Jewish communities.

BOOKS AND BOOKMAKERS ON THE MOVE

Sephardi scribes and printers in exile brought with them their books and their knowledge of bookmaking in both manuscript and print to all the regions of their dispersion in North Africa, the Ottoman Empire, Italy, and beyond, continuing their traditions and practices in new but not completely unfamiliar contexts. Many books were left behind, confiscated, or destroyed. One well-known anecdote describes how Spanish Kabbalist Avraham Saba mourned the incredible library he left in Iberia before fleeing to North Africa. Writing in al-Qṣar al-Kbir (today in northwestern Morocco) in 1499, Saba explained that he had to rewrite his work from memory since he was unable to take any of his books with him. He described his library, "the light of my eyes," as comprising "innumerable books, an unbelievable amount: books of the Zohar and Kabbalah, doubled and tripled in multiple editions, and innumerable new books of midrash and exegesis. Who could proclaim its greatness and glory!"[15] But as Saba lamented, despite fleeing from Castile to Portugal, his books were not safe there: in 1496, King Manuel I issued an edict of expulsion for all the Jews in his Kingdom of Portugal and further decreed that "all [Hebrew] books must be delivered to the Great Synagogue of Lisbon, on pain of death." Saba had already left most of his library in Porto; all that remained were the handwritten manuscripts of Saba's commentaries. These, too, he had to abandon.

> I went in fearful panic and dug into a great olive tree which had large roots in the ground. I buried there my three books which I

> had composed. . . . For these I mourn and wail, and weep day and night!. . . . [After six months,] we were taken by boat to Arzila, and there we entered the lands of Islam. I stayed in Qṣar al-Kbir, and the holy community there dressed me and tended to all my needs. . . . I stayed there a long while, ill and distressed in my heart, weeping over my children and the books I abandoned, and especially those books of my own writing.[16]

This story was surely repeated many times over.

But still, the number of books the exiles managed to transport is remarkable. Yehuda Ḥayyat, who, like Saba, left Spain for Portugal in 1492 and sailed to North Africa the following year, testifies that when he was rescued from imprisonment by the Jews of Chefchaouen, "I gave them close to two hundred books that I had in my possession [to repay them] for ransom."[17] Similar numbers of books traveled with Sephardi exiles to other parts of the Mediterranean world, including Salonica, Constantinople, Venice, and Cairo.[18] One exile from Spain, Yosef Ben-Ḥanin, who fled to Tunis in 1492, bequeathed a small library of books to his son upon arrival; as inscribed on the inside flyleaf of one of them, he testified in the presence of witnesses "to give to my son Yehuda for his possession this book [of the Torah]; the commentary of Avraham Ibn-Ezra on the Torah; the tractates of *Ketubbot* and *Giṭṭin* with commentary; the tractate of *Berakhot*; the commentary of Rabbenu Baḥya on the Torah, and the Writings with commentary, on paper; the Torah, with the Targum, on paper. . . . This was done before us, Monday, the fourth of Adar, 5252, in the city of Tunis."[19] We might wonder if some of these books specified by Ben-Ḥanin as being "on paper" are not manuscripts but rather incunabula, namely, the fruits of Iberian Hebrew presses. We certainly know that some exiles took printed incunabula with them: Moshe al-Ashkar, for example, carried his three-volume set of the Former Prophets (Leiria, 1494) with him through Tunisia on his way to Egypt in the decade after the Expulsion.[20]

Many exiles in financial straits chose to sell the precious books they had brought from Iberia, which then made their way into the Maghrebi and Mediterranean book markets. Fifteenth-century Portuguese astronomer Avraham Zacuto testified in his work of Jewish history, *Sefer yuḥasin* (completed in Tunis in 1504 after Zacuto fled from Portugal), that two volumes of a famous medieval Bible manuscript known as the Hilleli Codex "were carried, after the expulsion from Portugal, to the city of Bougia in Africa [today Béjaïa, Algeria], and sold there; they remain there today."[21] Some remnants of these sales are marked on the books themselves: a codex of the Prophets with Targum and commentaries, written in Segovia (Spain) in 1487, was inscribed with a bill of sale in Tlemcen (Algeria) in 1495 or 1500.[22] A Masoretic codex of the Torah, written in the Iberian Peninsula in 1478 for a certain Yosef b. Yiṣḥaq Kohen, likewise carries an inscription from Safi (Morocco) showing that it was sold by one Doña Dona, the widow of Don Yosef Hakohen—perhaps the original patron of the manuscript—on November 27, 1522.[23]

Iberian Christians, both "New" (i.e., conversos) and "Old," also availed themselves of the lucrative opportunity to sell Hebrew books—many of which no doubt originated from Iberian Jewish libraries confiscated during the Expulsion—in the markets of North Africa. Nuno de Freitas, the royal overseer [*feitor*] in Portuguese-occupied Safim (today Safi, Morocco), recorded fifty Hebrew books brought into the port as merchandise between 1498 and 1500.[24] Throughout the sixteenth century, Portuguese Christian merchants were disciplined by the Inquisition for trafficking in Hebrew books for the North African market. For example, a twenty-four-year-old seaman from Lisbon was questioned in 1553 for his role in bringing "Hebrew books from Venice" to the Portuguese fort of Santa Cruz do Cabo de Gué (today Agadir, Morocco) "to sell to the Jews who are there in the land of the Moors."[25] In 1562, a New Christian merchant named Melchior Vaz de Azevedo was accused of having brought to the port of Larache in northern Morocco, "twenty-six large coffers and chests of Bibles and other Hebrew books for the Jews."[26] This trade also occasionally went in the opposite direction, with conversos in Iberia testifying to the Inquisition that they had acquired Hebrew books from Jews in North Africa. Portuguese authorities were concerned about the subversive potential of the North African market in Hebrew books at least until the early seventeenth century.[27] Many of these books, as we shall see, continued to circulate in Maghrebi Jewish communities for hundreds of years.

It was not only books that traveled across the Mediterranean but bookmakers as well. Iberian scribes and printers brought their technical skills, artistic preferences, and knowledge of the Jewish library (if not the libraries themselves) to the Maghreb. We can trace the careers of several scribes or scribal families who worked in Iberia before the expulsion and in the Maghreb afterward. Among these were Yosef b. Yehoshua Frontino, who copied a miscellany of philosophical texts "in the mellaḥ of Fez" around 1495, and his two brothers Shmuel and Ya'aqov b. Yehoshua Frontino, who are documented as having copied numerous manuscripts in Seville between 1470 and 1480.[28] The most prominent trans-Mediterranean scribe is Moshe Ibn-Zabara, who is known for having copied several luxuriously illuminated Bibles in northwestern Spain between 1473 and 1477; after the expulsion, he apparently settled in Meknes, where he achieved great renown as a scribe of Torah scrolls and scholar of scribal laws.[29] While Maghrebi scribes had already developed a corpus of manuscript traditions and practices, Sephardi scribes like Frontino, Ibn-Zabara, and Yiṣḥaq Ibn-Shoshan brought new ideas and practices surrounding the production of Jewish books.

One of these new practices was using the yeshiva as a kind of scriptorium where groups of students copied manuscripts for their rabbi or other students: a practice Michael Riegler has demonstrated was prevalent in Castilian yeshivot during at least the fifteenth century and possibly earlier. But this was not the norm in most of the Jewish world, where manuscripts were generally copied by individual scribes on behalf of individual patrons.[30] This tradition appears to have been established among Sephardi exile centers in the Maghreb in the early sixteenth century. One such manuscript was copied at the yeshiva of Yiṣḥaq Nahon, a scholar of Iberian origin who settled in Fez after the expulsion: Joseph Gikatilla's Kabbalistic work *Sha'ar meshalim*, written by two different students in 1524.[31] Another group of manuscripts has been shown to have originated from a different yeshiva of a Sephardi exile in Fez, namely, the one under the leadership of Yehuda 'Uziel (d. ca. 1545). One manuscript of 'Uziel's commentary on the Torah, copied in Fez in 1514, was written for "the pleasant student Re'uven" by a group of students from "among the study circle [*ḥavura*] of the great sage, Rabbi Yehuda 'Uziel," although only one signed the colophon by name: "the small one, Shmuel Kohen."[32] Two other manuscripts were copied by Yosef Ibn-Amram, who similarly called himself "the youngest of the students among the study circle of the honorable and great sage, Rabbi Yehuda 'Uziel," in the fall of 1541 and spring of 1542.[33] To these, we might add several other manuscripts of Yehuda 'Uziel's teachings, which were copied in Fez in the first half of the sixteenth century and which may have been produced by his students.[34]

In addition to their vibrant manuscript culture, the Sephardi exiles brought the knowledge of Hebrew printing, which had flourished in Spain and Portugal for two or three decades before the expulsion.[35] In the century after 1492, Iberian Sephardim established Hebrew presses in Fez, Salonica, Constantinople, and Cairo (although most of these enterprises were relatively short-lived) and also participated actively in the burgeoning Hebrew presses of Italy, especially in Ferrara and Venice. The Hebrew press of the Nedivot family in Fez, established in the early sixteenth century, was in operation for less than a decade; nonetheless, it represents the beginning of a new relationship with books and book production that would shape the world of early modern Jewish communities across the Maghreb and beyond.

THE NEDIVOT PRESS IN FEZ

The first books to be printed with mobile type on the continent of Africa, in any language, are most likely those printed in Fez by Sephardi exiles Shmuel b. Yiṣḥaq Nedivot and his son Yiṣḥaq.[36] The similarities between their type, ornaments, and page layouts and those of Eli'ezer Toledano's press in Lisbon suggest that the father and son had been involved in printing there and that they brought their typographic equipment with them when they left Portugal for Morocco, presumably after Manuel I's Edict of Expulsion took effect in 1497. In Fez, they printed around eight to ten rabbinic works, including *Sefer abudarham*, the *Yore de'a* of the *Arba'a ṭurim* (and possibly the other three sections as well), and several Talmudic tractates, from 1515 or 1516 until around 1522.[37]

Very few complete copies of imprints from the Nedivot press have survived, and only one title with a colophon naming the place has been identified so far: the liturgical commentary of *Sefer abudarham* (Fez, 1516), which had first been printed by Toledano in Lisbon in 1487. The Nedivot imprint apparently used the Toledano edition as a copy-text, for the typography and page layout are identical. The only difference is the replacement of the details in the colophon: "[printed] in the month of Kislev, in the year 5277 [1516 CE] since the Creation, in the city of Fez, in which there is a community of scholars and heads of yeshivot . . . by Shmuel, known as Nedivot . . . and his son Yiṣḥaq."[38] The edition of tractate *'Eruvin* carries a colophon dating it to November 1521, but there is no other information. It is only through a careful typographic and bibliographic analysis that scholars have assigned it to the Nedivot press in Fez. Finally, there are fragmentary pages from printings of *Rosh ha-shana* and *Ḥullin* with

Figure 1.1 The final page of *Sefer abuhardam* (Fez: Shmuel and Yiṣḥaq Nedivot, 1516), showing the colophon and watermark. HUC-JIR Klau RBR B 2076, reproduced with the permission of the Klau Library (Cincinnati), Hebrew Union College-Jewish Institute of Religion.

no known attribution similarly assigned to this press based on typographic comparison.[39]

Unfortunately, other than these two short colophons, the surviving products of the Nedivot press offer no explicit contextual information about their production. One manuscript page may offer some clues: in 1979, Haim Zalman Dimitrovsky identified a late medieval bifolium manuscript of the Talmudic tractate *Ḥagiga* as probably coming from a printer's copy prepared for the Nedivot press in Fez.[40] This manuscript page matches the exact placement, textual layout, script styles, and size of the other tractates printed by Nedivot. As Dimitrovsky writes: "The general resemblance between them is so strong that in photographic reproduction, it is difficult to recognize that the pages of *Ḥagiga* are actually in manuscript and not printed on the same press that printed the pages of *Rosh ha-shana*." The page also carries some annotations and markings that seem to come from the correctors in the press.[41] Furthermore, Dimitrovsky observed that the manuscript text itself, both in content and in layout, seems to have been copied directly from the printed edition of the tractate produced in Guadalajara, ca. 1480.[42] Based on a close comparison of the type and page layouts used by Nedivot, Dimitrovsky reconstructed the timeline of Nedivot's press producing the tractate *Rosh ha-shana* in 1515 or 1516, followed by *Sefer abudarham* in 1516, and then the other works, including *Ḥagiga*, *'Eruvin*, and *Ḥullin*, between 1516 and 1522.

The typography and texts of the books printed by Nedivot reveal a clear relationship with Iberian book production, both in directly material ways (e.g., using Iberian printed texts as models) and in their general methods and scope; they are, in one scholar's phrase, "clearly Sephardic imprints."[43] Although we still know little about the press, its workers, and its audience, we might extrapolate from its surviving titles that these books served to strengthen and promote the continuity of Sephardi reading practices through the circulation of print. Certainly, some of these books were treasured by generations of Maghrebi readers and book collectors, as we shall see. And beyond its physical remains, the legacy of the Nedivot press was remembered, at least in some circles, with great pride; Fez-born rabbi Yedidya Monsonego (1907–1994) reported hearing in his youth about the unique *masekhtot* [Talmudic tractates] that had been printed in Fez centuries earlier.[44]

The reasons for the end of the Nedivot press in Fez have not been clearly demonstrated. Some scholars have suggested that the Spanish government prohibited the export of paper, but although this assertion has been repeated in multiple publications, there is no direct evidence for a prohibition of this kind, and, in any case, it is not clear that the press's books were ever printed on Spanish paper.[45] Others have proposed that the press's activities were disrupted due to anti-Jewish disturbances in the turbulent transition between the Waṭṭasid and Saʿadi dynasties of Morocco, although the city of Fez itself remained solidly under Waṭṭasid control until 1550.[46] It is more likely, in my opinion, that the Nedivot press simply fell prey to the same issue that plagued printing houses worldwide in the early modern period: the overwhelmingly precarious economic nature of printing as a business.

The requirement of large initial capital, especially for paper (the main expense for presses by far, until the modern period); the need for highly trained professional workers; the uncertainty of a return on investment; and the problem of unsold stock all combined to create a volatile business model. As one book historian has observed: "Most of the presses established in [sixteenth-century] France lasted only a few years, and produced only a handful of books. In the first forty years of the sixteenth century just three towns in France would sustain printing continuously," and other presses in Italy and Germany fared similarly.[47] It seems the Nedivot press was another such victim of the unsustainable nature of early printing. Another factor was likely the serious earthquake that shook southern Spain and Morocco in the autumn of 1522; one observer described it as having "completely ruined the city of Fez, and destroyed all the surrounding places for a distance of 40 leagues; most of the people living in this area died."[48] If the Nedivot press was damaged or even destroyed during this earthquake, it may well have been the final straw for an already struggling venture.

What is unusual in the case of Fez is not that the Nedivot press went bankrupt but that no other presses emerged to replace it. This was likely due to economic pressures, especially given the relatively small market for Hebrew books without the interest and support of Christian Hebraist patrons (as compared, for example, to the Hebrew presses in Italy).[49] Notwithstanding one other isolated example, to be examined in chapter 3, it would be another three centuries before the Maghreb again became a center for producing printed Jewish books. Nonetheless, the Nedivot press is an exemplar of the continuity of book culture between late medieval Iberia and the early modern Maghreb. The exiles brought with them not only books and texts but also the tools, techniques, and training that allowed them to continue their work as scribes, printers, and other artisans involved in the practices of making books, alongside their Maghrebi coreligionists. Over the coming centuries, the physical books that linked North African Jewish communities to the history of medieval Iberia remained powerful symbols of this legacy.

MEDIEVAL BOOKS, EARLY MODERN READERS, AND MODERN COLLECTORS

Medieval books continued to circulate in the Maghreb throughout the early modern period and were actively cherished as part of the intellectual and cultural heritage of Maghrebi Jewish communities. Iberian books in particular were prized as a link to the elite status of Sepharad, especially for those families who claimed descent from the *megorashim*. They were also scholarly resources in their own right, drawing on the established reputation of Sephardi books as the most accurate, reliable, and authoritative texts.[50] The Maghreb was known throughout the Jewish world as a place where medieval Iberian culture, specifically its books, was preserved. In the 1620s, Portuguese-Italian scholar Immanuel Aboab explained that "after the kings [of Iberia] banished us from their states, all the books that [the Jews] had were scattered, according to the various parts of the world where their owners lived. In particular, I understand that there are still some very perfect books which were written in Spain, now in the city of Fez in Africa, and in Salonica in Greece, and in the Holy Land."[51] One of the manuscripts used in collating the text for Joseph Athias's 1667 *Biblia Hebraica Accuratissima*, for example, was an illuminated Iberian Bible, written in Spain and decorated in Portugal. It had been purchased in Italy in 1618 by Dutch Sephardi diplomat Jacob Curiel from a certain Rossilho family, "natives of Fez."[52] Athias's Jewish editors referred to it as "this most ancient exemplary manuscript, more accurate than any other which could be found. . . . It is suitable, both on account of its age, and its exceptional purity, to be followed faithfully."[53]

North African readers, too, prized these medieval books, and many manuscripts were regularly consulted as references and used in liturgical and ritual settings. For example, the biblical volumes brought to Tunis by Yosef Ben-Ḥanin in 1492 contain notations in an eighteenth-century Maghrebi hand marking the *mishmarot* [extra-liturgical divisions], and candle drippings on the pages for the Book of Lamentations, traditionally read at night during the commemoration of the ninth of Av.[54] These material traces demonstrate how medieval Iberian manuscripts continued to have ritual lives for centuries in North African Jewish communities. They were also used in ongoing scholarship, especially among Maghrebi rabbis with extensive libraries of manuscripts and printed books. One thirteenth-century copy of Maimonides's Judeo-Arabic commentary on the Mishnah contains notes, and even interlinear Hebrew translation, from many eighteenth-century Moroccan users, including Immanu'el Serero (b. 1705).[55]

According to one witness, eighteenth-century Moroccan rabbi Ya'aqov Abensur annotated his copy of the 1661 Leusden-Athias Bible with references to a medieval Iberian *ḥumash* [Pentateuch] copied by Moshe Ibn-Zabara, which was apparently held in his library: "In the library of Refael [II] Abensur [1830–1917], I saw a very old Bible, printed in Amsterdam by Yosef Athias in 1661, and all its margins were filled with precious comments regarding the Masora . . . and at the front of the book, there was a note from Ya'aqov [I] Abensur [1673–1753] as follows: 'these notes which I have written in this book are from a *ḥumash* with the haftarot and megillot which was copied by the great scribe Moshe b. Ya'aqov Ibn-Zabara in Castile in 1472.'"[56] A manuscript of the responsa of medieval Sephardi rabbi Shlomo Ibn-Adret, copied in Fez in 1505, was similarly used in the Abensur family library for centuries.[57] It bears copious annotations in the margins, in several different hands, which comment on the text and compare the manuscript to printed editions of Ibn-Adret's responsa and other books, showing that this manuscript continued to be consulted as a reference work well into the eighteenth and perhaps even the nineteenth century. For example, on one folio, one hand has written: "I have not found this [section] in any printed book of the responsa of Ibn-Adret." On the same folio, a different hand has commented: "compare this to *Beit yosef* [of Yosef Qaro, first printed Venice, 1551], no. 266 in *Yore de'a,* and to what is written in *Bedeq ha-bayyit* [of Qaro, first printed Salonica, 1605], and see also the work *Mishne la-melekh* [of Yehuda Rosanes, first printed Constantinople, 1731], chapter 1 of the laws of circumcision, no. 10."[58]

Maghrebi Jewish libraries valued not only medieval manuscripts but also incunabula and early printed books, like the 1661 Athias Bible of Abensur, mentioned previously. We know that the Abensur family library held at least three or four incunabula in addition to rare printings of the sixteenth century, such as the titles produced by the Nedivot press and similar holdings among other families. In fact, Moshe Berdugo of Meknes (ca. 1679–1731) records a textual variant from the Fez 1521 edition of *'Eruvin,* writing: "I found [this reading] in a very ancient printing [*defus qadmon me'od*]."[59] In some cases, it was the age of the book itself that prompted wonder: in an incunable copy of Qimhi's dictionary *Sefer ha-shorashim* (Naples, 1491), which was passed down in an

Algerian rabbinic family in Tlemcen, one owner inscribed on the flyleaf that "according to certain scholars, it seems that [this book] dates to the era when the Moors ruled Spain—a rare heritage which we [received] from our venerated grandfather, Rabbi Chaloum Sultan (may his soul be bound in the bonds of eternal life)," and added his own signature on another page, dated precisely to the evening of January 25, 1887.[60]

Over the eighteenth and nineteenth centuries, some Maghrebi Jews faced difficult choices regarding their custodianship of this medieval heritage, which was becoming increasingly lucrative for European book collectors. In the late seventeenth century, scholars and bibliophiles (both Jewish and non-Jewish) had already begun seeking out antiquarian books, especially medieval manuscripts and incunabula, among the Jewish communities of North Africa and the Middle East.[61] For example, the Masoretic codex, which had been sold by Doña Dona in Safi, was acquired in the early eighteenth century along with a fourteenth-century manuscript of the Prophets written by Yehoshua' Ibn-Gaon. The buyer was a certain Irishman, "Major Clanaghan, of Gibraltar... from a Jew in Africa," who then donated them to Trinity College at the University of Dublin in 1748.[62] Several of the Iberian manuscripts that Yosef Ben-Ḥanin bequeathed to his son in Tunis in 1492 were acquired in Egypt by European scholars on a Danish mission in 1762.[63]

The magnificently illuminated manuscript known as the Kennicott Bible, written by Moshe Ibn-Zabara and decorated by Yosef Ibn-Ḥayyim in La Coruña in 1476, likewise made its way from North Africa to Gibraltar in the mid-eighteenth century, where it was purchased by a wealthy Scottish merchant, Patrick Chalmers, around 1760.[64] In 1770, Chalmers offered it to English Hebraist and librarian Benjamin Kennicott (1718–1783), who informed the trustees of the Radcliffe Library "that he [Kennicott] has now in his hand a very elegant & finely illuminated MS of the whole Heb: Bible, which is to be sold. It was, not long since, brought from Gibraltar; purchas'd there from Africa. It belongs to Mr Chalmers of Auld Bar, in Scotland."[65] The following year, the library took his suggestion and purchased the manuscript for £52 10s.[66]

Another beautifully illuminated Iberian codex in Kennicott's collection, written in Toledo in 1222, has a provenance note inscribed on the inside cover by Kennicott himself: "This manuscript was presented to me by the Rev[eren]d Mr. Isaac Netto, on the twentieth of August 1770—Mr. Netto bought it when at Tetuan in Barbary, of a boy carrying it to a box in the Sinagogue call'd [genizah—in Hebrew characters][67] where all fragments of holy writings are preserved, lest they should chance to be put to improper uses."[68] In other words, if we are to believe this account, this manuscript being carried to the genizah was finally being taken out of circulation in northern Morocco in the mid-eighteenth century, some five hundred years after it was written in Spain, presumably having been used in the community for much of that time. The manuscript itself, although incomplete (beginning at Isaiah 39:2), is still in excellent condition, and so, Kennicott's story that Nieto had "rescued" the manuscript from oblivion might be camouflaging a different kind of acquisition.

The idea of these kinds of "neglected treasures" was already a common trope in accounts of manuscript discovery in North Africa and the Middle East, and the Maghreb began to attract book dealers and collectors who were eager to uncover more.[69] While the treasures of the Cairo Geniza attracted the lion's share of attention from collectors after their publicized "discovery" and extraction from Egypt in the late nineteenth century, other areas of the Middle East and North Africa also held the promise of untold riches from Jewish history.[70] Moses Hecht, a German Jewish bookseller living in Morocco in the 1850s, sold dozens of manuscripts acquired in Morocco to European institutions like the Bodleian Library and Leiden University.[71] While most of the medieval manuscripts Hecht acquired were of Iberian or

Maghrebi origin, there were some exceptions. He found an incomplete fourteenth-century parchment codex of French biblical commentaries written in Ashkenazi semicursive but with marginal notes and comments on the text in Maghrebi cursive, confirming that it had been held and used in a Moroccan library (although its recent provenance and the evidence of this later usage was of little interest to Hecht or the Bodleian Library where he sold it).[72]

Similarly, a Polish rabbi named Eli'ezer Ashkenazi settled in Tunis in the mid-nineteenth century and spent his years there searching for and acquiring rare medieval manuscripts of Sephardi origin, which he both sold and published.[73] As Ashkenazi wrote in the introduction to one of these publications, *Sefer ha-zikaron*: "For these last ten years, it has been my pleasant duty to serve the best selection of the human race, to bring books back and forth and up and down, from many books, new and old, from Ashkenaz to Sepharad and from Sepharad to Ashkenaz. No distance was too great for me; the heat of Africa did not deter me, the cold of Europe did not scare me."[74] In addition to medieval manuscripts, he also acquired and sold early printed books, such as the two incunabula he purchased from the Abensur library (to be examined in chap. 6) or a copy of the 1521 Fez imprint of tractate *'Eruvin*, which he bought in 1849.[75]

Another rabbi and book collector of Ashkenazi origin, Jacob Soffer (1857–1930), also sold manuscripts that he had acquired while living in Oran (Algeria). In 1898, he placed an advertisement in the Hebrew journal *Ḥavaṣelet* offering five medieval manuscripts for sale, and in 1902, he corresponded with Russian rabbi Eliyahu Akiva Rabinowich about selling some medieval manuscripts from Algeria to the "Imperial Library" in Vienna (now the Österreichische Nationalbibliothek).[76] Anglo-Jewish scholar Elkan Nathan Adler (1861–1946) traveled extensively through North Africa in the late nineteenth and early twentieth centuries, acquiring such books as a thirteenth-century Iberian codex of the Prophets (purchased in Morocco); a fifteenth-century illuminated Iberian Pentateuch (purchased in Algiers); Yosef Shem-Tov's commentary on Aristotle's *Ethics,* written in Tlemcen in 1480 (and presumably purchased there); and a medieval fragment of a Hebrew–Old French glossary, reused as "the binding to a Hebrew Incunable bought in the Tunis Mellah [i.e., the Jewish quarter, usually known as the *hara*] in 1905."[77] Moroccan bibliophile Yosef Bennaim recalled witnessing two especially memorable expeditions of European Jewish book hunters visiting Morocco: first, in 1910, London-based antiquarian bookseller Jacob Lipschitz bought a number of manuscripts and early prints in Fez, including three copies of the Fez 1516 imprint of *Sefer abudarham.*[78] Second, in 1927, Vienna-based booksellers Lipa Schwager and Jacob Halpern "took away old and precious books, for which we have no substitute," including five manuscripts and "some old and rare printed books," one of which was the Fez 1516 imprint of *Yore de'a* of the *Arba'a ṭurim.*[79]

The circumstances under which Maghrebi Jews parted with these books are not clear. Writing in the early twentieth century, Yosef Bennaim expressed some ambivalence regarding the manuscripts purchased by these collectors, praising Eli'ezer Ashkenazi for "bringing those works which were sitting in gloom and exiled in darkness into the light," but also bemoaning "how many dear rarities, more precious than rubies, these manuscripts of our earlier sages, were taken from our holy community."[80] While we know little about how the Maghrebi owners were compensated, this activity was quite lucrative for the dealers. One sales contract between Ashkenazi and Moroccan rabbi Shlomo-Eliyahu Abensur (1822–1873) records some twenty-nine books purchased by Ashkenazi from the Abensur family library in January 1841. The list includes at least two incunabula (the Former and Latter Prophets with David Qimhi's commentary, printed at Leiria, 1494 and Lisbon, 1492, respectively) and over a dozen manuscripts, the oldest identifiable ones being a late fourteenth-century copy of a commentary on tractate *Avot* by Yiṣḥaq b. Shlomo of Toledo and a fifteenth-century copy of Moshe Narboni's commentary on Ibn Rushd's *Epistle of the Possibility of Conjunction,* as well as the aforementioned manuscript of Ibn-Adret's responsa from 1505, titled *Sefer ha-battim.*[81] Many of the Abensur manuscripts that can be traced from this purchase were sold by Ashkenazi to French collector Eliakim Carmoly (1802–1875), and from his collection moved to institutional libraries, including the Bibliothèque nationale de France, the Russian State Library, and Cambridge University Library.

This activity was often described by European and American Jewish collectors as salvaging, rescuing, or even discovering lost Jewish heritage. It combined antiquarianism and Orientalism with an ideology Israel Bartal calls "the project of *kinnus* (ingathering): the collection, editing, and preservation of the [Jewish] nation's cultural creative assets."[82] The *kinnus* project, which was born from the nineteenth-century Jewish intellectual movements of the Haskalah and the Wissenschaft des Judentums, as well as the rise of Zionism, applied initially to European Jewish history; it quickly grew, however, to encompass the whole of Jewish history, including Jewish life in the Islamic world.[83]

Two of the first publications of the Maskilic *Mekitze Nirdamim* (Rousers of the Slumbering) Society, based in the Prussian city of Lyck (today Ełk, Poland), were based on manuscripts from North Africa: S. D. Luzzato's edition of the *Diwan* of Yehuda Halevi (1864), based on a fourteenth-century manuscript purchased by Eli'ezer Ashkenazi in Tunis in 1839, and Salomon Buber's *Pesiqta of Rav Kahana* (1868). This second work was edited mainly from two manuscripts, one from Egypt via Italy, and another from Fez (then owned by Eliakim Carmoly).[84] Luzzato wrote approvingly of Ashkenazi that "he does a great kindness for the seekers of Torah . . . to travel the lands of Europe [Edom] and cross the seas to the lands of Islam [Yishma'el] to buy and sell books . . . and to rescue these invaluable texts from their secret burial places." Luzzato added that, at first, "[Ashkenazi] sought to buy [the *Diwan* manuscript], but they did not wish to sell it. I then hurried to tell him to return to that land without worrying about gold or silver, but endeavour to purchase it at whatever price," which he did.[85]

This "rescue mission" ideology continued into the mid-twentieth century. Ukrainian-born scholar Yiṣḥaq Ben-Zvi (1884–1963), second president of Israel and founder of the Ben-Zvi Institute for the Study of Oriental Jewry (1947), described the purpose of the Ben-Zvi Institute as saving "the many documents which could shed light on the last three hundred years, found in the hands of people who hide them in their homes. . . . The first goal of the Institute is to save these spiritual treasures of Middle Eastern Jewry, in order to present them in the correct light."[86] This view, however, ignores the fact that these manuscripts were not, in most cases, buried treasures or undiscovered relics but living texts that were cherished, referenced, and cared for by families and communities whose custodianship over the centuries was what allowed these scholars to have access to them in the first place.

Maghrebi scholars advocated for a more active preservation and custodianship of their manuscript heritage.[87] Several rabbis worked to gather and collect rare manuscripts; for example, Bennaim recorded that Refael II Abensur of Fez (1830–1917) "would collect and gather many books of Torah, out of his love for Jewish literature, in addition to those books he inherited from his family. . . . He did not ignore even a single manuscript leaf, but would gather dispersed leaves and bind them into volumes; at the time of his death he left behind many such volumes, and his library is still in the hands of his son."[88] Chapters 5 and 6 describe how Maghrebi intellectuals in the nineteenth and early twentieth centuries, such as Avner-Yisrael I Serfaty, Refael-Moshe Elbaz, Shmuel Ibn-Yuli, Refael-Aharon Ben-Shim'on, and Ya'aqov Moshe Tolédano, availed themselves of the historical resources found in North African libraries, especially the medieval manuscripts, so they could produce their own modern scholarship on Jewish texts and North African Jewish life.

Maghrebi scholars also continued to encourage the publication of medieval manuscripts held in family libraries, local collections, and even synagogue *genizot*. North African Jews had been involved in publishing texts from medieval manuscripts throughout the early modern period; toward the end of the nineteenth century, rabbis began issuing calls for a concerted effort to find and print these rare works. In the introduction to one such book of responsa published from an older manuscript, Meknessi rabbi Shalom Amar (1862–1899) emphasized the precarious fate of Maghrebi manuscript heritage: "The cruel moth joined its strength with rot, to destroy what was pleasant to the eye. . . . Great is the neglect in this country [Morocco], which has not had the enlightenment of the time touch its palaces, and the vision of printing has not spread in its regions." He urged his readers to "turn to us with a searching eye, and seek out the books of rabbis that are scattered across the cities of Morocco, to improve their situation and status, since they have not yet seen the light of print and remain in manuscript. . . . Arise, dear lords, to fulfill the Torah!"[89]

Similarly, Algerian scholar and poet Yiṣḥaq Morali (Mar'eli, 1867–1952) published a collection of medieval Sephardi piyyutim from manuscripts in the Berlin-based Maskilic journal *Koveṣ 'al yad* in 1897. In his introduction, Morali praised the foresight of his colleagues in Algiers who had recognized and preserved these manuscripts "found among the ancient books hidden in heaps of dust in the area for genizah, with scattered leaves worn out by age," but he also lamented that "it is a deep disappointment to all lovers of our ancient literature that the precious books which were composed in former centuries . . . often fall into the hands of people who do not appreciate their value, and who discard them cruelly and mercilessly as if they were empty vessels."[90] The value of the medieval Sephardi heritage to be found in the libraries and genizot of North African manuscripts had to be balanced with their precarity regarding both their physical vulnerability to decay and damage and the changing social circumstances that left them inaccessible to the scholars who would appreciate them.

The work of these historians, antiquarians, and community leaders, to be examined more fully in the coming chapters, reveals how Maghrebi Jews were deeply conscious of their role as guardians of their history. In a time of changing attitudes toward textual history, and changing technologies of book production, they strove to apply modern standards of scholarship to the preservation of the medieval books that had been read and reread, annotated and cross-referenced, carried to and from synagogues or preserved on family bookshelves, and passed down from generation to generation.

CONCLUSION

Medieval books maintained a physical presence in the book culture of early modern North Africa, representing one of the most substantial legacies of the cross-Mediterranean transfer of Sephardi Jewish communities in the late medieval period. Drawing on the long-standing connections between Jews in Iberia and North Africa, the fifteenth- and early sixteenth-century Maghreb was a site of refuge for Sephardi exiles and their books, and a place for the re-creation of libraries, scribal workshops, and printing presses that maintained and developed their traditions of bookmaking, circulation, and reading. The books of this period, both those brought from Iberia and those produced in the Maghreb, continued to circulate for centuries, serving as scholarly resources, community treasures, and family heirlooms.

These books were preserved as historical relics and also impacted the development of local book culture over the following centuries. In particular, many of these medieval books, especially biblical and liturgical manuscripts from Sepharad, were lavishly illuminated. These manuscripts shaped not only the textual landscape of Maghrebi Jewish books but also their visual forms. The work of North African scribes and artists in the eighteenth and nineteenth centuries, to be examined in chapter 2, was actively informed by their interactions with medieval manuscripts. The specific artistic and material forms of early modern Maghrebi Jewish book decoration may represent direct continuities of artistic training and the transmission of practice as well as the continued visual influence of decorated medieval manuscripts in the Maghreb.

As we saw in this chapter, these illuminated manuscripts continued to circulate in Maghrebi Jewish communities well into the early twentieth century and beyond. A medieval illuminated prayer book with liturgical poems for the High Holidays, written in Catalonia in the fourteenth century and (according to legend) brought to Algeria by Shim'on bar Ṣemaḥ Duran, was preserved by the descendants of the Duran family in Algeria and then in France until the turn of the twenty-first century.[91] One particularly striking example of the transference between Iberian and Maghrebi manuscript traditions is an illuminated Masoretic Pentateuch written in Iberia in the fifteenth century and purchased by the Bodleian Library in 1852 from Moses Hecht.[92] The first quire of the manuscript, however, is decorated in a Maghrebi style and written in a nineteenth-century Moroccan hand—in fact, the hand of the same Avner-Yisrael I Serfaty who would go on to amass one of the most important rabbinic libraries in nineteenth-century Morocco (to be examined in chap. 6).[93] A note on the first folio explains that "this book, attributed to our teacher, the honorable rabbi Moshe Zabara, of the Castilian Exile, was completed by me, Avner-Yisrael Serfaty."[94] While Serfaty's association of this manuscript with Ibn-Zabara has not been accepted by contemporary scholars, his calligraphy and decoration demonstrate a fascinating balance between a close attention to

Figure 1.2 Page added in nineteenth-century Morocco by Avner-Yisrael I Serfaty to an illuminated Masoretic Pentateuch from medieval Iberia. Bodl. Or. 614, reproduced with the permission of the Bodleian Libraries.

the original layout of the medieval manuscript and a recognizable creation of Moroccan aesthetics.

We do not know why Serfaty added this quire to the manuscript. Was this one of the manuscripts in his family's possession? And where did he copy the Masora from—perhaps another medieval manuscript in the Serfaty library (recall Abensur's reference to copying the Masora from a manuscript of Ibn-Zabara's)? Other questions relate to the manuscript's circumstances of sale.

How and from whom did Hecht acquire it? Was the young rabbi Serfaty (no older than twenty-five at the time, based on its date of acquisition) perhaps commissioned by Hecht to supply the missing pages of this manuscript in order to make it more attractive for sale? Serfaty's claim that he could complete this medieval manuscript, and his creativity in doing so, demonstrates that many Maghrebi Jews saw themselves in living continuity with the bookmaking traditions of medieval Sepharad. In the coming chapters, we investigate the development of those traditions in the early modern Maghreb.

TWO

SCRIBES, ARTISTS, AND PATRONS OF THE HANDWRITTEN BOOK

INTRODUCTION: JEWISH MANUSCRIPTS IN THE AGE OF PRINT

Thousands of Jewish manuscripts of the early modern period have survived from North Africa.[1] They range in size from small booklets to massive tomes and cover every genre of writing, from biblical and Talmudic commentaries to poetry, history, and science. Some are scrappy and plain; others are carefully scribed and lavishly decorated; some seem to have been forgotten soon after being written, while others were read and reread over the centuries until they were practically falling apart. The diversity of this corpus demonstrates the vitality and importance of handwritten books in Jewish communities throughout the modern period. In this chapter, I examine the processes of manuscript production in Maghrebi Jewish communities. I argue that manuscripts produced during this period are not static or fossilized remnants of medieval preprint culture but innovative objects that respond to and engage with Jewish book culture—including printed books—in creative ways.

This chapter begins by exploring the social position of the *sofer* (scribe) as a culturally valued role that required professional training and was connected to other positions of rabbinic authority but was also tied to popular culture. Next, I turn to the manuscripts and consider how their creation and decoration were formed in response to their textual, aesthetic, economic, and intellectual contexts. To do this, I draw on the data obtained from the examination of hundreds of the surviving Maghrebi Jewish physical and digital manuscripts of the seventeenth, eighteenth, and nineteenth centuries that are now scattered in collections around the world. While this chapter pays close attention to the material and visual aspects of manuscript-making, including decoration, it is not necessarily an art-historical analysis of decorated manuscripts as artistic objects. Rather, I aim to capture the social context of handwritten Jewish books in the Maghreb, arguing that they were created and circulated as part of a vibrant and globally connected book culture, while also responding to local aesthetics and social conventions.

According to Emile Schrijver, the majority of extant Hebrew manuscripts were produced after 1500 and thus after (or perhaps we should say alongside) the emergence of printing technology.[2] Their visual and material aspects demonstrate that Jewish scribes were not only proficient at their traditional tasks but also inventive, experimental, and receptive to contemporary aesthetics. Schrijver's examples illustrate the complex and interwoven natures of print and manuscript production in early modern Europe: luxurious Haggadot handwritten by scribes copying the typefaces of Amsterdam printed books (letters cut from an exemplar provided by a master scribe) and decorated with printed illustrations pasted onto the pages, and artists who could in a single career produce hand-painted illustrations, engraved frames for handwritten manuscripts, and title pages for Hebrew printed books.[3] Despite this focus on manuscript culture among Jewish communities in early modern Europe, the Jewish communities of the Islamic world have still languished under assumptions (often rooted in Orientalist historiography) that their manuscript culture must simply be a leftover product of their "medieval" distance from modernity.

Schrijver acknowledges that "little is known about the actual circumstances under which post-medieval Oriental manuscripts were produced. . . . Modern research on post-medieval Oriental manuscripts is therefore more than necessary."[4] Similarly, art historian Shalom Sabar writes that "despite the richness of the extant material, scholars of Jewish art have generally disregarded the field of manuscript illumination among the Jewish communities of the East during the modern era."[5] The classification of North African book culture as part of "Oriental" or "Eastern" Jewish communities shows how far we still have to go in devoting attention to the nuances of this context. No scholarship to date has focused specifically on Jewish manuscript culture anywhere in the Islamic world in the early modern period; this chapter begins to address that lacuna.

By confronting the incredible variety of early modern Maghrebi Jewish manuscripts, we see how assumed binaries of manuscript/print, private/public, and medieval/modern begin to break down. The importance of scribal publication and the circulation of manuscripts prove that handwritten books were mobile, dynamic, and integral to the intellectual and social worlds of Maghrebi Jews. The development of a unique visual tradition for Maghrebi Jewish manuscript decoration in distinct regional styles further demonstrates the vitality of manuscript culture. The interwoven visual influences of medieval Iberian illumination and early modern printed book art on this tradition emphasize the hybrid position of manuscript books as modern Maghrebi Jewish objects. Finally, the continued movement of manuscripts alongside printed books among readers and collectors illustrates the necessity of integrating manuscript books into our examination of Jewish book culture, a term that is too often assumed to be synonymous with print in a postmedieval context.

JEWISH SCRIBAL CULTURE IN NORTH AFRICA

Like medieval Jewish manuscripts, many modern Maghrebi manuscripts were user-produced.[6] In addition to works the user wanted copies of (such as biblical, liturgical, legal, exegetical, or mystical texts), almost every scholar or rabbi in North Africa tried to produce some kind of original composition in a variety of genres: *ḥiddushim* (insights into the Bible, Talmud, Kabbalah, or legal codes); *she'elot u-teshuvot* (legal responsa); *derashot* (collected sermons and homilies); and piyyutim (liturgical poetry in Hebrew and vernacular languages).[7] Some of these manuscripts were single texts copied as a single unit, sometimes even with a colophon. A Moroccan manuscript commentary on *Sefer yeṣira*, for example, concludes with the note "I, El'azar Azrad, son of Moshe Azrad, copied this book for myself, here in Meknes, and I finished writing it on Thursday, the 28th of Nisan, in the year of '*WHEN I gather you*' [= April 29, 1718]."[8]

Other user-produced manuscripts were more like commonplace books or miscellanies, with a wide variety of textual units, often added over multiple years. A certain Avraham bar Ya'aqov Charvit, for example, inscribed on the front page of a manuscript of piyyutim: "I bought this book in a city of the Tafilalt [region] for two *uqiyyot*, and I have added many new things, and copied into it piyyutim and compositions of my own."[9] In this chapter, I will focus mainly on manuscripts copied by a scribe on behalf of someone else. These might have been specifically intended for a single named patron or to circulate generally among many readers.

We know little about the institution of the sofer during this period, from the sixteenth through nineteenth centuries. In general, the scribal profession seems to have been restricted to men; I have not yet found any evidence of Maghrebi female scribes.[10] We do know that scribes began their training during their elementary schooling, and after studying the Hebrew alphabet and basic religious texts, some students went on to study calligraphy in cursive and square scripts.[11] Oral histories from the mid-twentieth century involving elderly Moroccan Jewish immigrants to France, for example, describe the educational process around the end of the nineteenth century: "The student began with a copy of the Psalms, a Talmudic text, or a piyyut. Once he had acquired some facility, he was entrusted with a notebook into which he copied the Haggadah of Pesaḥ, Pirqei Avot, or chapters of the Shulḥan Arukh or the Talmud. . . . This copying process achieved three goals at once: books were gained, the student better retained the content, and he learned the occupation of the sofer."[12]

Although we have no direct testimony from the early modern period, surviving manuscripts show that some students received scribal training as part of their education. For example, Meknessi scholar Ḥabib Toledano (1658–1716) served as a sofer for the yeshiva of his father, Ḥayyim, during his teenage years. Between 1673 and 1679, he copied into a single codex (now incomplete) a miscellany of texts, including a selection of Talmudic supercommentaries, his own insights, and correspondence relating to the yeshiva.[13] On one page, he signed his colophon with the wish that "the Holy Blessed One may grant me to copy and compose more books, brilliant as sapphires."[14] On another, he confessed: "This is as much as I found written in that quire. . . . If you desire, you may find an additional halakha in the quires of El'azar Ibn-Ḥabib, for I am now occupied with copying them, but they are sewn into the book of Almosnino's."[15] As a young adult, Toledano continued to copy books, including another anthology of Talmudic commentaries copied between 1678 and 1680, a 1679 copy of Yekhiel Mikhael Kalischer's sermons, *Sha'arei shamayyim* (only four years after it had been printed in Prague!), and at least two copies of his grandfather's biblical commentary, *Ohel ya'aqov*.[16]

Other scribes identify themselves explicitly as students copying manuscripts for their teachers; in one case, scribe Makhluf

Ben-Chitrit wrote: "I was thirteen years old when I copied this honorable manuscript" for his teacher Yosef Azrad in 1785.[17] Another manuscript, a Passover Haggadah, was copied by Moshe Ḥalawa in 1810 at the age of fifteen.[18] Yosef Bennaim testifies that he owned two manuscripts of Talmudic commentary copied by Mimoun Birdugo (1767–1824) of Meknes in his teenage years, one finished in 1782 and the other in 1787.[19]

Sofrim served as scribes for manuscripts and letters and as public notaries for legal documents (both religious and secular) such as marriage certificates, wills, sales, leases, mortgages, and contracts of partnership.[20] Some sofrim also copied Jewish ritual texts: the parchment scrolls of the mezuzah and tefillin and the parchment scroll of the Torah used for liturgical reading in the synagogue, which had to be copied according to particular guidelines dictated by halakha.[21] Other scribes specialized in writing amulets, a body of knowledge with its own set of guidelines and standard procedures.[22] Much of a sofer's work involved copying and filling out formulas from scribal manuals containing the standard texts for these documents. Many examples of these scribal manuals survive, the most important being *'Eṭ sofer*, a collection of legal formularies by Moroccan rabbi Ya'aqov Abensur (1673–1752).[23] But while these manuals provide examples of the content and form of Jewish legal documents used by Maghrebi Jews, they shed little light on the training, daily practice, and social role of scribes involved in copying books.

The profession of scribe seems to have been respected, although in some contexts, it might have been considered less prestigious than other positions connected with rabbinic authority (such as teacher, judge, or shohet—the licensed slaughterer of animals). The role of scribe was seen as a stepping stone to other professions or simply as "clerking."[24] In a letter from Ya'aqov Abensur to Shmuel Azawi in Salé, who had apparently criticized Abensur as a mere functionary, Abensur defended the scribal profession as a noble one: "I saw that you mentioned me several times with the title *sofer* in a derogatory tone, as in 'that *sofer* wrote,' 'that *sofer* did,' etc. By my life, if you were with me in this city, I would find you in the street, kiss you, and bring you to my scribal house [*bet safruti*] and copyist's room [*ḥeder lavlaruti*]; I would seat you at my right side and let you drink from the wine of my labour, and I would teach you to succeed in this blessed work, secure and arranged in all things."[25]

Some manuscript colophons include dates of the beginning and completion of the manuscript, which helps us understand how quickly or slowly the manuscripts were made. In the case of a beautifully decorated manuscript of Kabbalistic texts, for example, copied in Tunis in 1720 by Yiṣḥaq Ḥajjaj, the scribe indicates that the first 60 pages were copied over four months.[26] Another scribe, David Bensoussan (Ben-Susan) of Tetouan, was much faster: he copied two Kabbalistic manuscripts, each comprising around 150 pages, in Algiers in the summer of 1781.[27] The unnamed Tunisian scribe who copied a 152-page manuscript of *Qol be-rama* (a Kabbalistic commentary) began on October 16, 1727, and finished on January 30, 1728; he had a very fine hand and arranged the text in complicated layouts, so he may also have drawn the ornamented title page.[28] Moroccan scribe Avraham Lesri (al-'Asri) boasted in the colophon of a manuscript of laws on kosher slaughter (comprising some 94 pages): "I wrote this manuscript for my son Raḥamim, may God protect him, and from the day I started writing it until the day I finished was 21 days."[29] A large eighteenth-century mahzor of a hundred folios, with the prayers for the High Holidays according to the custom of Constantine, was copied by Faraj Bouchoucha in two months, just in time for Rosh Hashanah.[30] In fact, on one page, Bouchoucha admits that certain piyyutim "were copied after Rosh Hashanah, since the pressure of time prevented me from writing them [earlier], and so I began writing them on the Fast of Gedalya [the day after Rosh Hashanah]."[31] The speed of copying would depend on the scribe's training, the complexity of the text, the material characteristics of the manuscript (script, size, etc.), and whether or not the scribe was able to work full-time.

Some scribes were not able to work as fast as they might have wished. In the colophon to his copy of *Minḥat yehuda,* El'azar Bahlul apologized that the book "was delayed in my hands for a long time, since I could not write on consecutive days, but only on Friday afternoons, when there was a moment of leisure in the synagogue."[32] One manuscript of *Ohel ya'aqov* was copied from a printed edition in Meknes in 1865 by a group of four students.[33] The scribes—brothers Ḥayyim and David Messas, Yosef Elbaz (al-Baz), and Shmu'el Benitah (Ben-Yitaḥ)—apologized that they were only able to copy the beginning and end because the book from which they were copying belonged to a traveling Ottoman scholar who left before they could finish "since he was pressed to continue his journey."[34] This colophon also suggests that some scribes worked in teams to copy a book if only to increase their speed and coverage. For the *Ohel ya'aqov* manuscript, the different hands seem to start and stop in the middle of the page (rather than for each quire, for example, or each parashah), which might indicate that each scribe worked for as long as they could each day, and the next scribe simply picked up where they left off.

Another manuscript colophon records the plea from an anonymous Moroccan scribe that "if, Heaven forbid, some mistake is found in my copy of this honorable and noble book, let me receive no blame or complaint or curse," giving two reasons: "This copy was done as I was copying from another's mouth, that is, another person who was reading the book [aloud] and instructed me to write what he was saying: this is the first reason. The second reason is that some of the copying was done [at night] by candlelight, and thus it was like 'an error that comes from an authority' [Eccl. 10:5] and was not intentional."[35] In the book, however, the scribe made his own emendations and editorial additions, including adding three chapters "since the version of this book in print has only 35 chapters . . . but we have found a manuscript which has some additional chapters, and so we have seen fit to copy them here."[36] All of these comments and colophons demonstrate how scribes and copyists balanced between recognizing the textual precarity created by the various (often inadequate) conditions of manuscript copying and the flexibility that came with their editorial authority.

SCRIBAL PUBLICATION AND THE CIRCULATION OF MANUSCRIPT BOOKS

The term "scribal publication" was introduced to the field of book history by Harold Love, drawn from his work on manuscript circulation of seventeenth-century England. Love contended that various types of works, including political and bureaucratic documents, poetic miscellanies, musical booklets, and scholarly correspondence, were part of a common phenomenon, namely, "the publication of texts in handwritten copies within a culture which had developed sophisticated means of generating and transmitting such copies"—in other words, scribal publication.[37] The term "scribal publication" simultaneously brings to focus and undermines the stability of the automatic and assumed elision between "unpublished" and "unprinted." What does it mean for a text to be published in manuscript? Love suggested that publication is simply the "making public" of a particular text: its movement from the private sphere of authorial creativity to the public sphere of consumption. We might productively compare this to how the internet is used to circulate "prepublication" papers, which are clearly different from the private drafts and works in progress that are not meant for wide-scale distribution or discussion.[38] Similarly, a manuscript draft written by a user for their own reference is obviously different from a manuscript intended to circulate among a broader public of readers, as we shall see.

Love introduced a number of important categories for the discussion of manuscripts: initiatory and replicatory copies to distinguish between the first published copy and subsequent copies made by later readers (cautioning against judging a work's popularity or extent of circulation based on the number of surviving copies) and authorial, entrepreneurial, and individual copies—those produced by the author or a professional scribe, and those produced by a reader for their own consumption.[39] Love also advised that entrepreneurial publication was not an innovation but a continuation of established book-trade practices that existed before the advent of printing.[40] At the same time, scribes were not merely keeping alive some archaic skill. They were drawing on their contemporary training in producing handwritten correspondence, forms, contracts, and other documents for commerce, law, the church, the military, and a diversity of other arenas. This is certainly true regarding Jewish manuscripts in North Africa, where a vibrant culture of manuscript books circulated widely in the form of authorial, entrepreneurial, and individual copies. Furthermore, this manuscript culture remained fairly consistent across the seventeenth, eighteenth, and nineteenth centuries, as will be seen from the examples discussed in this chapter.

Some authors prepared their own work for circulation. A letter from Ya'aqov Abensur (Ibn-Ṣur, 1673–1753) notes that "a copy of these [piyyutim that I composed] will reach you with this letter. . . . I also sent a copy of these [piyyutim] to David Ben-Farjun, and if any other poet should wish to copy them, please instruct David Ben-Shuqrun not to prevent this, for they were made for this purpose."[41] Even authorial manuscript copies could still be prepared with an audience in mind. For example, when El'azar Bahlul copied his anthology of *ḥiddushim* and *derashot* (titled *Mar'e'enayyim*) in Meknes in 1712, he intended it to be read by others. He decorated the first page with a carefully drawn border, wrote the title in large letters, and began the book with an introduction, all of which points to an intended audience.[42] This culture of scribal publication continued to shape Maghrebi book production to the end of the nineteenth century and beyond.

One late example of a text prepared for scribal publication is a Moroccan manuscript of piyyutim written by Yaḥya ben Makhluf Dahan (1866–1957) at the end of the nineteenth century.[43] Titled *Tehillot adonai*, its title page is carefully inked, each section is introduced with a beautifully drawn headpiece, and the whole text is finely calligraphed in two columns. Although Yaḥya Dahan was the scribe (signing the introduction as "the author, the writer, and the signatory [*ha-meḥaber, ha-kotev, veha-ḥotem*]"), he clearly intended to share the book with a broad audience rather than keeping it as a private or personal manuscript.

The book begins with an introduction of the author addressed to readers. Dahan writes that when he studied as a young man with his grandfather, renowned scholar Ya'aqov Abuḥaṣira (1806–1880), in the village of Oudjan (a small settlement in the Tafilalt region), Dahan showed him "all the writings I had with me . . . and all the poems I had composed." Abuḥaṣira then "commanded me to write these things, and add to them any additional writings . . . and take care to make them composed in collections, so that they can last for many days."[44] Here, the manuscript book is assumed to be a creative, long-lasting, and accessible format, and the choice to circulate a book in manuscript is a valid, productive, and public one.

Dahan then explains to readers the structure of the book, which is divided into seven thematic sections. Each poem has a short introduction explaining the poem, the circumstances of its composition, and the melodies to which it should be sung. These features emphasize that Dahan's manuscript carried a vision of a public audience, even though Dahan likely did not intend to print it. Both the content and material form of Dahan's book make it clear that it was meant for a wider audience than just the author. Dahan might have consciously chosen to write the book in manuscript rather than print for any combination of economic, practical, and ideological reasons. Chapter 6 examines another nineteenth-century text circulated through authorial scribal publication: the chronicle of Avner-Yisrael Serfaty (Ha-ṣarfati, 1827–1884). A manuscript would have been much easier for Dahan or Serfaty to produce; at that time, Hebrew printing had just begun in northern Morocco, hundreds of miles away, and the closest Hebrew presses were across the Mediterranean in Italy. But as will be explored further in subsequent chapters, many Moroccans and other Maghrebi Jews did pursue printing, while others chose to circulate their texts in manuscript form.

Texts circulated not only in the form of authorial copies but also, as we saw earlier, as entrepreneurial copies created by professional scribes working for authors or interested readers. There were obvious benefits and drawbacks to manuscript transmission: on the one hand, it required the time and commitment of capable scribes; on the other hand, it was an easily accessible method to obtain copies of books (whether originally printed or in manuscript). Maghrebi Jewish correspondence shows that readers often wrote to each other to inquire about books (both in print and manuscript), to arrange the sending and receiving of copies, or to seek out manuscripts of difficult-to-obtain books, occasionally going to great lengths.[45]

Some scholars even went so far as to specify the precise conditions under which their manuscript was to be copied. Moroccan bibliophile Ya'aqov Abensur wrote to an emissary in Tunis, asking him to "check, as far as you are able, how much it will cost to hire the scribes to copy just *Eṣ ḥayyim* by itself, versus just *Bi'ur ha-zohar* by itself in general, and additionally, how much each volume would cost specifically, since I am sure they are not all equal in size, even if they are alike in quality." He went on to request a list of "the names of the students who will copy each of these books, and their family lineage, so that I may know how to write to them appropriately . . . and tell me which scribe among the scribes of the city [you think] is the most suitable and qualified to copy these books."[46] He also asked whether the book was "organized in gates or chapters or homilies? Please tell me the names of the chapters . . . so that I might ascertain whether it is the same as one of the works I have here, or a different one entirely. If you can, please list for me, 'Gate X, which has 26 Sections,' etc., everything laid out clearly in writing, so that I can know what they will do in their copying." He concluded with a semi-ironic apology "for burdening you [with all these requests], but when you take up your pen to answer me, first read this letter, and re-read it carefully, so that it might be a reminder for you regarding each and every detail."

A century or so later, Algerian scholar and translator Yehuda Ḍarmon of Oran wrote a similarly detailed letter commissioning a manuscript copy in 1866.[47] After opening with the usual salutations and blessings to his colleague Shlomo-Eliyahu Abensur in Fez, he gave an emotional explanation to justify his request for a specific manuscript.

> I wish to tell my master that close to nine months ago, the scholar and rabbi Raḥamim Jayani was visiting here, from the city of Sefrou.[48] One time, we were talking together about both worldly and sacred matters, and while we were talking he mentioned that in his city there was a book called *Divrei ha-yamim* in manuscript, which had stories of all the events that have happened, generation after generation, from the time of the expulsion from Castile until now.[49] My soul longed greatly to see this manuscript, and he gave me a complete promise that when he returned to his city he would personally endeavour to make me a copy. . . . But I have been waiting and expecting [it], and yet I have still not merited to see even one page from this [book], and I fear that my hopes have been disappointed. . . .
>
> If I have found favour in your eyes, please inform me about the condition of this manuscript: its size and quality, and what year it begins in, and whether it contains stories of daily events, as was told to me. If you extend your grace to me, as soon as you obtain the manuscript, please hire scribes who know to write beautifully, in Rashi script, in a manner where they will not make a single mistake. Let them copy about ten or fifteen pages from [the manuscript],

> and send them to me via our dear friend "Ṣhmuel Ibn-Ṣur". And please inform me about the price of their copying, and I will pay it all, and when these pages come to me I will examine them, and then give permission for these scribes to finish the copying. . . .
>
> I hope that my master will fulfill my desire and request, and heal this ailment which has afflicted me while waiting for Rabbi Raḥamim's promise. . . . I anxiously await the timely response of my master, may he be blessed with strength and peace.[50]

These letters not only testify to the efforts of Ḍarmon and Abensur to acquire and read the works in question and their general interest in history and rabbinic scholarship but also demonstrate the connection between the intellectual and material aspects of book production. The writers attempt to investigate the content of the manuscripts and their chronological scope and textual organization. They ask their addressees to ensure that the manuscript is copied by skilled scribes (Ḍarmon even specifies that he would prefer to read it in cursive script) and indicate that they would like to see and approve as much of the process as possible.[51] These types of requests are the product of a vibrant manuscript culture, one that connected scholars, authors, scribes, and travelers across the Maghreb and beyond, through the movement of people and books.

NORTH AFRICAN STYLES OF MANUSCRIPT DECORATION

What did these manuscripts look like? And why did they take the material and visual forms that they did? Like the scribal process in general, we know very little about the decoration of manuscripts in North Africa in the postmedieval period. In the case of medieval Jewish book arts, the decorators and illuminators sometimes signed their manuscripts and left other archival evidence testifying to their involvement. Unfinished medieval manuscripts, texts on illumination, and scientific manuscript analyses have all helped reconstruct the working processes and materials of medieval Jewish artists.[52] But for the postmedieval period, there is little evidence apart from the manuscripts themselves, which have received almost no scholarly attention. I argue that the decoration found in early modern Maghrebi manuscripts demonstrates a sophisticated engagement with a number of aesthetic styles and a conscious choice to create a visual object that was clearly recognizable as a Maghrebi book. I have divided North African decorated manuscripts into three main styles of decoration: spared-ground, northern floral, and southern geometric. The first is the oldest, most common, and most widespread style of manuscript decoration; the other two are limited to later manuscripts and are generally restricted to particular regions.

The spared-ground style is characterized by vegetal and arabesque forms outlined against a solid or shaded background (hence "spared-ground"). This type of decoration often uses the same brown or black ink as the text, but it can also be painted in colors, usually red and green. This style, while drawing on some aspects of medieval Iberian illumination, is a unique development of the early modern Maghreb and becomes characteristically developed in urban centers such as Fez, Meknes, Marrakech, Algiers, and Tunis. Found on book title pages, illuminated megillot [Esther scrolls], and ketubot, it often takes the form of a keyhole or horseshoe arch. It may also include elaborately tessellated geometric patterns, known as "Islamic geometry," which are commonly associated with North African art and architecture (especially tile work, known in Maghrebi Arabic as *zellij*). In some later examples, the background is not solid in color but shaded with hatching, closely resembling the techniques of European copperplate engravings and presumably inspired by the aesthetics of printed frontispieces.[53]

Many features of spared-ground decoration, including the white vines against a green and red background and the horseshoe-shaped arch, are clearly related to similar decorations of Jewish

Figure 2.1 Manuscript of *Shi'ur qoma*, copied in Morocco in 1789 by Rafael Elbaz. Olim Gross Family Collection MO.011.008, photograph by Ardon Bar-Hama, used with permission.

manuscripts from fourteenth- and fifteenth-century Iberia.[54] The earliest examples of this style of decoration appear in the late sixteenth century in forms that show the transition from late medieval Iberian models to the early modern Maghreb. The title page of a copy of *Ayelet ahavim*, written in 1560 in Fez, is adorned with a twelvefold star against a spared-ground panel, which is characteristic of this Maghrebi aesthetic. Its interior headword panels are decorated with Iberian-style filigree penwork.[55] Other seventeenth-century decorated books and ketubot demonstrate the development of this style for both title pages and interior panels.[56] In some cases, it is clear that this style was a conscious choice by the scribe/decorator. A copy of *Penei moshe,* written in Fez in 1696 by Mordekhai Edrei (al-Dra'i), was copied from the printed edition (Lublin, 1681), but Edrei replaced the rectangular, typographic border of the printed book with an elaborate, arch-shaped border with spared-ground arabesque vines.[57] Books, ketubot, and megillot continued to be decorated with this style until the end of the nineteenth century.[58]

The northern floral style appears to have developed in northern Morocco, especially in the cities of Tetouan and Tangiers, in the early nineteenth century. This style likely arose from the combination of Sephardi settlers in northern Morocco (who used the Judeo-Spanish dialect, *ḥaketía,* rather than Judeo-Arabic) and the influence of their proximity to Iberia, Gibraltar, Italy, and other centers of European Sephardi life.[59] This decorative scheme is characterized by bold vegetal and floral decorations with rounded lobes, outlined in brown or black and painted in colors, usually red and green. It also includes images of the ḥamsa (or *khmissa,* a stylized hand), and birds.

This northern floral style is most commonly associated with the characteristically decorated ketubot of northern Morocco, but it was also used in book decoration. A manuscript of piyyutim, for example, written in both Tetouan and Gibraltar during 1825–1838, includes three full-page decorations in this style as well as decorated headings throughout the text.[60] Sabar called this the "Tetuan style" and surmised that these artists worked primarily in ketubah decoration but also decorated books and Esther megillot in ways that show how they were "closely familiar with, and deeply involved in, the decoration of marriage contracts."[61] One fascinating example is a megilla from northern Morocco

Figure 2.2 Scroll of Esther, copied in Essaouira ca. 1750–1850. Gross Family Collection 081.012.024, photograph by Ardon Bar-Hama, used with permisssion.

originally done in the late eighteenth or early nineteenth century. The first panel, however, was damaged and repaired sometime in the mid-nineteenth century. The style of the original panels more closely resembles the older spared-ground style, whereas the new panel, which is structured in the layout of a ketubah, clearly shows the innovations of this floral style.[62]

The third style, which I term southern geometric, developed in southern Morocco, especially in the regions of Marrakech and Tafilalt.[63] Some elements of this style may have originated from medieval Iberia (Sabar suggested that "such elements were better preserved in the Tafilalt region because, in contrast with the large towns, it was rather isolated and thus less exposed to new modes and foreign influences"), but it is also clearly informed by local aesthetic traditions, especially Amazigh crafts.[64] This style was usually created using only black or brown ink, although it was occasionally painted. Typically structured as a rectangular or arch-shaped frame, southern geometric style is characterized by panels of geometric line drawings, including knotwork or pointed braids, tessellations of eight- and four-pointed stars, and repeated diamond or square patterns (often with small flowers inside); it also occasionally includes spared-ground vine work within the geometric divisions. Like the other two styles of book decoration, this style can be found adorning single-page works like ketubot as well as manuscript books, which indicates that the same artists (or artist-scribes) worked in a variety of genres.[65] While some southern geometric works were done in a very fine hand, there are others—more than spared-ground or northern floral—that were drawn in a rough or untrained hand with slanted or crooked lines (as opposed to the geometric designs incorporated into the spared-ground decorations of urban manuscripts, which were usually very carefully done, such as in fig. 2.1).

One unique genre of decorated manuscripts, found only in southern geometric style, is the decorated Passover Haggadah, which usually included an associated collection of piyyutim, liturgical readings, and translations known as the *ḍahir*—a term that means "Sultanic decree" or "certificate" in Moroccan (Muslim) Arabic, but in Moroccan Judeo-Arabic, it referred to any document containing instructions and thus to the Passover liturgy.[66] Over a hundred ḍahirs decorated in the southern geometric style (some painted in color; others simply drawn in ink), survive from the Tafilalt region of southern Morocco but none have been found in any other region of North Africa.[67] The oldest dated examples appeared in the late seventeenth century, and the tradition of the decorated ḍahir continued well into the twentieth century.[68]

Although the ḍahirs vary in how they are illustrated, there are consistent design elements that include panels for the various sections; archways (often double) framing pages or sections of text; and, unusually, some figural illustrations in a folk style. These illustrations typically include some of the Passover ritual

Figure 2.3 Illustrated *ḍahir* from Morocco, ca. 1800. Bayerische Staatsbibliothek Cod.hebr. 455.

foods, especially matzah (*maṣa*) and bitter greens (maror), and other table objects (especially teapots); some even include illustrations of stylized people and animals.[69] Several ḍahirs conclude with an illustration of a comb framed by two *tizerzai* (fibulae-style clasp), the triangular brooches characteristically worn by Amazigh women.[70] These manuscripts are part of a shared aesthetic tradition, one that developed in southern Morocco during the eighteenth and nineteenth centuries. The similar style and layout of the illustrations across different manuscripts suggest that artists were familiar with this visual tradition or able to reference other manuscripts; many of the ḍahirs indicate through their colophons that they were created on commission, emphasizing the important role of (semi) professional production.[71]

Unfortunately, while we can reconstruct the processes of apprenticeship and artisan work by Maghrebi Jews in a variety of other crafts, we still know very little about how and why book decoration was done and who performed this craft. Some of the decorations were likely done by the scribes themselves since they integrate drawings and script using the same hand and ink as the text. This is the case for a Kabbalistic anthology copied in Tunis in 1720 by Yiṣḥaq Ḥajjaj, who must have also drawn the elaborately decorated title pages.[72] Some manuscripts include decorations not only on the title page but also for headings throughout the text, such as the volume of poetry by Yaḥya Dahan, which were clearly done alongside the writing of the text.[73] In many other cases, however, the decorations appear to have been done separately. Often, the text of the title page is squeezed into a frame that is too small, or it is stretched out to fill a frame that is too large. One manuscript, written in Morocco in 1785, includes a page with a predrawn border for a title that was never filled in.[74] Another manuscript has two title pages with the same outlined frame; one has been partially filled in (with no title), and the other, with a similar design, has been filled in completely and has a short title on the top.[75] This might be the result of an artist trying out different ideas or working on multiple commissions at the same time.[76] It may also indicate that scribes worked with other artists to provide predrawn decorations for their manuscripts, which they did not always use as planned.

At least one case demonstrates that scribes and artists were aware of these differing regional styles of decoration. A short booklet of scribal formularies is prefaced by two decorated title pages in two different styles: the first page, with no title, declares that it was "written for the wise sage . . . Avraham Kohen, may God protect him, here in the city of Essaouira."[77] The decoration, an elaborate vegetal border with scrolling vines, combines characteristics of the spared-ground and northern floral styles. The second page, which appears to be done by the same hand and with the same ink, is titled *Ḥesed le-avraham* and is also inscribed to "Avraham Kohen" but is attributed to "here, in the city of Tinzert, Tagadirt, may God protect it."[78] This page is decorated with a geometric border in the style of southern Morocco. The presence of these two title pages in their context as part of a book of scribal formularies suggests that these may have been trials, artistic experiments, or perhaps even models that could be shown to prospective clients to demonstrate examples of the scribe's facility in lettering and decoration in different styles. Such an idea offers a tantalizing window into how scribes and artists marketed their work to patrons.

These three styles of book decoration—spared-ground, northern floral, and southern geometric—all draw on the local aesthetics of Maghrebi crafts and artistry. Scholars have long noted the important role that Jewish communities played in the development of crafts, especially textiles and jewelry, in North Africa.[79] The layouts, motifs, and symbols found in decorated books are part of a familiar material landscape, as are jewelry, clothing, tile work, and other household objects. The varying regional styles further relate these books to the specificities of local visual culture. Moreover, I contend that the very act of creating a decorated title page for a North African manuscript, whether copied from a printed book or as an independent text, was a way of shaping the book into a visual form recognizable as a product of the Maghrebi Jewish world.

The presence of a title page should also be seen as a response to the frontispieces of printed books, since the title page is not itself a medieval tradition but rather a feature of early modern printing.[80] As with illuminated manuscripts, Maghrebi scribes and artists were undoubtedly familiar with the artistic aspects of the printed books in their libraries, and the engraved decorations of Hebrew printed books contributed generally to the aesthetic development of Maghrebi Jewish book art. The tradition of decorated title pages in Maghrebi manuscripts, therefore, is a hybrid form. These styles of manuscript decoration are not mere continuations of "preprint" practices with some local color. They are, in fact, innovative creations of early modern Maghrebi Jewish communities, combining medieval Iberian traditions of manuscript illumination, the aesthetics of contemporary North African material culture, and the stylistic influences of printed books.

CONCLUSION: DID THIS KILL THAT?

In her landmark study of printing in early modern Europe, Elisabeth Eisenstein posited that printing transformed European intellectual life as well as our patterns of thought, claiming that "the gulf that separates our experience from that of literate elites who relied exclusively on hand-copied texts is much more difficult to fathom. There is nothing analogous in our experience or in that of any living creature within the Western world at present."[81] This massive shift, she argued, is the result of the key features that defined print as a medium against the manuscript: the heavily increased output and accessibility of textual material, the standardization and new fixity of textual (and visual) materials, the opportunity for large-scale collaboration and feedback, and the new possibilities for cataloging and referencing. Drawing on a scene from Victor Hugo's *Hunchback of Notre-Dame*, Eisenstein transposed Claude Frollo's memorable aphorism *Ceci tuera cela*—"this [book] will kill that [cathedral]"—to refer to how the world of the manuscript was ineluctably and irreversibly destroyed to make way for the world of print.[82] The scribal culture described in this chapter, however, does not suggest a world apart from, distinct from, inferior to, or subsumed into the new world represented by print; rather, it is engaged, complementary, and responsive.

Although now challenged and refined by decades of scholarship in the field of book history generally, Eisenstein's model of the conclusive "rupture" of printing continues to shape some discussions about Jewish books, including in the Islamic world.[83] Zeev Gries justified the decision to focus his study of "the book in the Jewish world" entirely on Europe by casting the Islamic world as having "paid a heavy price for rejecting printing . . . and in point of fact, the entire world is still suffering, because for all those years millions of people failed to benefit from the development, and the spread of knowledge, characteristic of those countries where printing took root."[84] Jews in the Islamic world did not engage with printing, Gries suggests, and therefore they have no modern Jewish book history to speak of. Scholars of Islamic book history have repeatedly refuted the binary of "print or manuscript" and the simplistic assumption that the Islamic world "rejected" printing and thereby trapped itself in a static manuscript culture.[85] Instead, we now understand that both manuscript and printed books in the Islamic world were mobile and active forms of conversation and knowledge transmission.

A useful (although perhaps unexpected) example might be the case of Iceland, which Robert Darnton admits "contradicts everything" in the standard narrative of early modern book history.[86] He explains:

> Iceland had a printing press nearly a century before the Pilgrim Fathers set foot on Plymouth Rock. But it turned out nothing but liturgies and other ecclesiastical works required by the bishops in Skálholt and Hólar. Secular printing did not begin until 1773, and even then it was confined to a small shop in Hrappsey. . . . Iceland never had any bookshops between the sixteenth century and the mid-nineteenth. It also had no schools. Yet by the end of the eighteenth century the population was almost entirely literate. . . . For three and a half centuries, it had a highly literate population given to reading books, yet it had virtually no printing presses, no bookshops, no libraries, and no schools. An aberration? Perhaps,

> but the experience of the Icelanders may tell us something about the nature of literary culture throughout Scandinavia and even in other parts of the world, especially in remote rural areas where oral and scribal cultures reinforced each other beyond the range of the printed word.[87]

Of course, this is not an exact parallel with the Jews in the Maghreb, most of whom lived not in "remote rural areas" but in cosmopolitan urban centers; they had numerous schools and no long, cold months of darkness. But Darnton's observations about Iceland prove surprisingly fruitful when considering the Jewish communities of North Africa in the early modern period. They, too, were "a highly literate population given to reading books," but they had no local printing presses and few bookshops until the nineteenth century. Darnton's exhortation to consider how the transmission of texts in oral and scribal form shaped and reinforced the development of literary culture alongside printed books is equally relevant in the North African context. The more we examine cases like North Africa or Iceland not as "aberrations" from the "standard" European model but as alternative formulations of book culture, the richer our understanding of the meaning of the book becomes. Manuscripts and print appear as complementary forms, not in opposition: the relationship between the past and the present is not one of rupture but reconfiguration.[88] The forms of scribal publication and circulation that we saw in early modern North African manuscripts show how the conscious choice to create a manuscript book allowed the maker to shape its textual and visual contents in conversation with both its manuscript precedents and its printed contemporaries.

In the magnificent eighteenth-century mahzor copied in Constantine by Faraj Bouchoucha, the scribe notes at one point that "the custom of earlier [generations], who ordered their prayers according to the order of manuscript [prayer books], was to say these poems [at this point in the service] . . . but I order them [otherwise]."[89] Later on, he returns to harmonizing the differing liturgical orders of manuscript and printed prayer books, instructing the prayer leader:

> If he ordered the prayer service according to the order of print [*seder ha-defus*, i.e. the order in a printed liturgy], now he should recite [the following prayers] . . . but if he is ordering the prayer service according to the order of manuscripts, namely that he recites these poems and confessions during the service, he should [follow a different order] . . . I believe that even those who have this custom of praying [according to the manuscript order] should not recite [this prayer until all have reached that point] . . . and so those who are ordering their prayers according to the print [liturgy] should recite [this prayer] and finish their prayers according to the printed order.[90]

In other words, a High Holiday worshipper in the eighteenth-century synagogue of Constantine would encounter others with a variety of book traditions, some based in manuscript prayer books, others in printed liturgies, and still others in manuscripts responding to those printed prayer books, all attempting to pray together.

The vitality of Jewish manuscript culture in modern North Africa presents a challenge to narratives that uncritically apply models developed in a European context, positing an inherent link between the development of printing and modernity (or the lack thereof), to Africa and the Middle East. The existence of the corpus of modern manuscripts alone demonstrates that printing did not kill the manuscript—far from it!—and the analysis presented in this chapter has shown the inner workings of modern Jewish manuscript culture. In the following chapters, I explore how North African Jews encountered printing in the eighteenth and nineteenth centuries: not as a replacement for manuscripts but as a complementary technology alongside manuscript culture, first through their patronage of European and Ottoman presses and then through the establishment of a Jewish printing industry in North Africa.

THREE

MAGHREBI JEWS IN EUROPEAN PRINTING HOUSES

INTRODUCTION: MAGHREBI JEWS AND TRANSNATIONAL PRINT CULTURE

One sunny day in 1761, in the Mediterranean port of Tunis, a young Algerian Jewish merchant named Ḥayyim Yona Duran finished writing his book.[1] To be clear, he did not "write a book" in the contemporary sense of the term, which would indicate that he authored a book of his own composition. The book in question, *Qiṣṣur zekher ṣaddiq,* had been written centuries earlier by a Castilian rabbi named Yosef Ben-Ṣaddiq in 1467.[2] But Duran also did not "write a book" in the sense described in chapter 2: copying a book to read himself or circulate it as an accessible representation of the original text. Rather, Duran wrote this book explicitly as part of the printing process, as he explained in his note on the final page of the manuscript he consulted: "In the year 1761 I copied this [book] here, in the city of Tunis (may God protect it) while on my journey by ship across the heart of the sea, to find an opportunity to print it, along with the book *Magen avot*. . . . May God help me and answer all my heart's desires for good, amen."[3] In other words, Duran took a manuscript book, copied it into another manuscript, put that new manuscript in a bag with at least one other manuscript book, and boarded a ship across the Mediterranean to find a Hebrew printing house.

Duran was only partially successful in this endeavor. Although he did not find a way to print Ben-Ṣaddiq's book, he did have *Magen avot* (written by his ancestor Shim'on bar Ṣemaḥ Duran in the early fifteenth century) printed in Livorno in 1762 at the press of Moses Attias.[4] I begin with this story because it illustrates the many complex ways that a book can move through different contexts, not only geographically but also materially and socially. These types of movements were a crucial part of a book's coming into being. In this chapter, I turn to Maghrebi involvement in the larger world of Jewish printing in the Mediterranean. Maghrebi Jews were active participants in the economic and intellectual networks of Jewish printing in Europe, even though they did not develop a robust printing industry in North Africa until the nineteenth century. In the first section of this chapter, I examine the social, material, and economic dynamics involved in bringing a Maghrebi Jewish book to press in the early modern period, especially the eighteenth and early nineteenth centuries. In the final section, I focus on the rise of Italy, and specifically Livorno, as a center for Maghrebi Jewish printing, beginning in the second half of the eighteenth century.

I argue that in some ways, the Livornese printing houses represented a continuity in the mobility of Maghrebi Jews during the bookmaking process and their involvement in the multicultural world of Jewish printing houses. In other ways, however, the transition from the eighteenth to the nineteenth century illustrates what Daniel Schroeter has called "the end of the Sephardic world order": an increasingly localized Maghrebi Jewish community moving away from its ties to Sephardi Jewry in Western Europe (like Amsterdam or London) and toward the specificity of the Judeo-Arabic world of the central Mediterranean, between North Africa and the North African diaspora in Italy.[5] As outlined in the introduction, I advocate for an approach that considers the deliberate practices that go into creating local cultural histories of print.

Choosing to print a Maghrebi book in the eighteenth and early nineteenth centuries would have required travel from North Africa to a Jewish printing house or a printing house that could produce Jewish texts. The standard explanation for why Maghrebi Jews traveled abroad to print books is that there were no printing houses in North Africa until the mid-nineteenth century (with one exception, to be discussed later in this chapter).[6] The reverse, however, might be true: there were no Hebrew printing houses in North Africa because Maghrebi Jews preferred to travel abroad to print their books. As we shall see, Maghrebi Jews continued to patronize foreign printing houses even after the establishment of a local printing industry in the second half of the nineteenth century. In fact, some of the very same figures who were involved in running Jewish presses in North Africa also published their own books at European and Ottoman Jewish presses at the same time.

The Jewish presses of the Ottoman Empire challenge another common supposition, namely, that there was some force inherently opposed to printing in the "Islamic environment" of Maghrebi Jews that prevented the establishment of printing presses.[7] The Ottoman Empire, also an Islamic environment, supported a variety of Jewish, Armenian, and Greek printing houses, starting in the late fifteenth century for Hebrew and in the sixteenth century for other languages.[8] Ottoman rulers resisted the wide-scale establishment of Arabic-character printing not because it was a technological innovation but because of social concerns (not unfounded!) regarding its potential to undermine the legitimizing relationship between Islamic religious and political authorities.[9]

Orlin Sabev argues that print culture in the Islamic world should be understood as an "evolutionary" rather than "revolutionary" process: "Is the existence of a printing press in itself enough to enable us to speak of print culture? . . . The formation of print culture must be considered a long-term process, which took more or less time, depending on various sociocultural contexts."[10] In his work on Armenian printing, Sebouh Aslanian has shown that the evolution of early modern Armenian print culture is intrinsically linked to the Armenian integration into networks of mobility, especially their transnational presence in port cities—also a characteristic of Maghrebi Jewish communities during this period—even though printing did not develop in the historic Armenian heartland itself.[11] In this chapter, I suggest that Maghrebi Jews were likewise able to participate in a developing print culture even with no local printing industry and even as they continued to engage with the norms of a still-evolving scribal culture.

Furthermore, there was an eighteenth-century attempt to establish a Hebrew press in North Africa: the press of Yeshu'a Kohen Tanuji, who printed one book in Tunis in 1768. As we shall see, this press did not face any local opposition to "print culture," political or otherwise—in fact, quite the opposite—but it failed to overcome other social and economic factors. The short-lived existence of this press raises the larger question of why Hebrew presses generally flourished in some Islamic environments, including Anatolia, the Levant, and the Ottoman Balkans, and in Europe, but not in the Maghreb. The robust and self-perpetuating system of overlapping networks that supported the production of Jewish books, mapped out in this chapter, might provide one explanation. Jews looking to print books traveled from the Maghreb to sites where they had well-established commercial and social ties and where Hebrew printing already flourished (Salonica, Jerusalem, Constantinople, Livorno, Amsterdam). The constant flow of people to these presses, in turn, reinforced those links that had brought them there. This aligns with the observations of scholars such as Evelyne Oliel-Grausz, who emphasized that histories of "port Jews" must focus not just on the nodes themselves but also on "communication, relations, connections, conflicts and more generally circulation between the various poles and port Jewries."[12]

Why might a Maghrebi Jew have chosen to travel abroad to print books? The journey could be long and expensive; Meir Crescas spent six years traveling from Algiers to Amsterdam to print *Sefer ha-tashbeṣ* and almost ran out of money at several points.[13] It could also be hazardous to traveler and book alike, as shown by the following story about the book *Beit yehuda* by Yehuda ʿAyyash (printed in Livorno in 1746), which was recorded by nineteenth-century Tunisian scholar Eliyahu Ḥai Guedj:

> They sent it [i.e., the manuscript] on a ship to the city of Livorno in order to print it, but as the ship was sailing in the ocean, a great storm came, and because of this storm much water came into the ship, such that this book was almost lost entirely, for [the manuscript] had soaked in the water, and the letters flew away. They rescued what was left from the ocean and printed it. Therefore, you might find in it some jumbled letters, and many customs which have been unfortunately lost, and you might also find some phrases that seem to be missing some words, or some spaces that have been boxed out: this is for the reason mentioned above.[14]

There are similar stories about other Maghrebi manuscripts getting damaged or lost in the water on the way to Livorno; clearly, this was a common concern.[15] This story highlights not just the specific dangers of the North Africa-Livorno trip but also the fragility of books—even printed books—in their materiality. Books were precarious objects that relied on social networks of trust and responsibility and that were subject to risks and contingencies. As discussed in chapter 2, earlier generations of book historians proposed that the "revolutionary" nature of printing was in establishing the stability and dependability of the texts in printed books as opposed to the variable and impermanent nature of manuscript transmission.[16] But Guedj's story presents printed books as even more unstable than the manuscript tradition, implying that the printed versions of Beit Yehuda are not trustworthy precisely because of the material conditions of printing it!

Yet there was immense social value placed on the continued movement of Maghrebi Jewish books from manuscript to print (even as books moved in the opposite direction as well—printed books copied into manuscripts—as discussed in chap. 2). Despite the many obstacles and anxieties just described regarding the unreliability of printed books, Maghrebi Jews continued to spend time and effort to bring books to print throughout the eighteenth and nineteenth centuries. Many Maghrebi scholars feared that rabbinic works kept only in manuscript were vulnerable to both destruction and oblivion, and they appreciated the wide audience and longevity of printed books.[17] In the introduction to one of his books, Moroccan rabbi Yosef Knafo (1823–1900) describes a speech that he claims to have given to a group of supporters in Essaouira urging them to support the printing costs of his book and listing the advantages of printing.[18] He explains that the commandment to write one's own Torah applies

> in our time specifically to the printing of books since one who writes a Torah scroll [in manuscript] has created a unique copy, whereas printed books exist in thousands of copies. . . . Furthermore, the holy Torah scroll is read only occasionally [during synagogue services], whereas printed books are found in the study houses, where anyone who wishes can learn from them, day and night. . . . And finally, the radiance of the Torah scroll grows dim over the years as it becomes worn out, and the letters fade [until it must be buried]. But printed books, however, are found in great numbers, so that even if one copy is ripped, it can be replaced, and thus they will last for many years.[19]

In addition to publishing their own works, Maghrebi scholars worked hard to print old and rare manuscripts. A deceased rabbi's writings were frequently brought to press by his children or grandchildren, and bibliophiles searched in the libraries and genizot of scholarly families to find old manuscripts to bring to print.[20] This dynamic became especially pronounced in the nineteenth century; Yigal Nizri found that over half of the works of Moroccan rabbis published during this period were printed between 50 and 150 years after the author's death.[21]

The ability to work with a Hebrew press outside of North Africa, however, was not accessible to everyone, and many works of Maghrebi rabbis were never published due to lack of funds. Even in the twentieth century, Yosef Bennaim (Ben-Na'im, 1882–1960), the great bibliographer of Moroccan rabbinic writing, lamented: "See how great is the merit of Rabbi Vidal Serfaty, that his books escaped from Morocco, and saw the light of publication in print, and were not forgotten. Almost all the rabbis of Morocco composed books, so that they would be remembered in the world, but because of our poverty, we have lost them . . . since the press was not found in Morocco, and the economic lack was great."[22] The economic pressures are also evident in the importance of the patrons and subscribers who sponsored the printing of Jewish books and who are so often lavishly thanked in the introductions and even on the title pages.[23] Nissim Shamama (1805–1873), the wealthy Tunisian *qa'id* [secular head of the Jewish community], financed the printing of close to twenty different books published between 1837 and 1888 at presses in Livorno, Jerusalem, and Paris.[24]

After a safe landing, the labor of book production began in earnest. The person transporting the manuscript had to find and choose a printing house, convince the printer to take on the project, and pay for the book's printing, which was often a considerable amount. In most cases, the person bringing the book to the press (whom we might term the "publisher") stayed in the area throughout the printing and was often physically involved in the book's production, as we shall see. Then the books had to be transported from the printing house back to North Africa, distributed to the subscribers, and sold to other buyers and booksellers. An example is given in the *pinqas* [record book] of David Attias, an emissary from Meknes who left in 1821 to raise funds in Western Europe and North America. Among his records of expenses and donations, he also recorded three lists of books he was bringing back to Morocco: two lists of "the books which I have in storage, which I brought from Livorno to Gibraltar through Mr. Aharon Qardozo," and another list of "the books which I have among my books at the lodging house, at the Custom House [*fi kastam-haws*] of London, which I bought in Amsterdam."[25] The sixty-one books listed by Attias include several multivolume sets of the Tanakh, prayer books of various sizes, and a number of books in Judeo-Spanish (although Attias spoke Judeo-Arabic), which confirms that he was transporting books on behalf of others or intending to sell them to communities throughout Morocco. Attias's books traveled along the routes of powerful cultural and commercial systems and were supported by the networks that linked the Maghreb to Jewish communities in Italy, the Ottoman Empire, and even farther afield.

THE LABOR OF MEDITERRANEAN BOOKMAKING

Throughout the development of printing in early modern Europe, Maghrebi Jews participated in the process of bookmaking as "print professionals" (to use a term from Anthony Grafton); they served as editors, correctors, typesetters, and other press workers.[26] Already in the early sixteenth century, Maghrebi Jews had found employment in Italian printing houses: Tunisian Jewish scholar Ya'aqov ben Ḥayyim Ibn-Adoniyyahu served as an editor for the famed Venetian press of Daniel Bomberg after "the vicissitudes of time forced me to wander from the lands of the Maghreb, and pushed me to Venice," working alongside Italian and Ashkenazi Jews to produce some of Bomberg's most influential editions, including the Jerusalem Talmud (1523) and the Second Rabbinic Bible (1525).[27] Some Maghrebi Jewish travelers had the specific goal of bringing a book to press, while others took part in the material labor of Jewish book production, even when not traveling with the intention of printing. For example, Moroccan scholar Shmuel Ḥagiz composed a book of sermons "in exile, wandering from one end of the horizon to the other" between North Africa and Italy, and printed it in Venice in 1596.[28] Over the following two years, while staying in Venice, Ḥagiz also printed a book of his commentary on *Devarim rabba*; brought to press a book of sermons by his Algerian colleague Shlomo b. Ṣemaḥ Duran (as he writes, "I received a letter from [Duran] requesting me to labor in the work of bringing this book to press, and I girded my loins to do it, since I remembered well the great kindnesses he showed me when I had stayed with him [in Algiers]"); and edited a mahzor according to the minhag of Algiers at the bequest of two brothers from that city.[29]

The first Maghrebi Jew to travel to a press with a specific manuscript for printing was likely Aharon Ibn-Ḥayyim, who left his native Fez in the early seventeenth century to bring his manuscripts to print in Venice. He modestly wrote that "since so many books [of biblical commentary] have already been printed, I said that there was no need to print another book [of my own], except what I have seen fit to add with their assistance."[30] While in Venice, Ibn-Ḥayyim also wrote at least one *haskama* [approbation] recommending another work for publication.[31] Italy was one of the primary destinations for printing Maghrebi manuscripts in the early modern period, but they were also brought to press in other European centers like Amsterdam and Sulzbach, and the Ottoman Empire, especially Istanbul (Constantinople), İzmir, Thessaloniki (Salonica), and Jerusalem.[32] The movement of *shadarim*, peripatetic rabbinic emissaries from the Land of Israel, was also essential to bringing manuscripts to print in the Mediterranean, including from North Africa, throughout the seventeenth to nineteenth centuries.[33]

To illustrate the importance of the labor performed by Maghrebi Jewish print professionals, I highlight an aspect that may seem minor but that had a significant impact on book production: the issue of handwriting. Since the beginning of the early modern period, scholars, printers, and editors have lamented the incomprehensibility of the Maghrebi Hebrew cursive script to European Jews.[34] Avraham Sasportas, the son of Algerian rabbi Ya'aqov Sasportas (1610–1698), wrote that when he attempted to print his father's manuscripts, none of the local Dutch scholars could read his father's handwriting, which was "written quickly, with broken cursive letters, which they are not accustomed to in these places."[35] Finally, he managed to obtain the help of Portuguese Sephardi scholar David ben Raphael Meldola, who "lifted the barrier, and connected the letters that were scattered and dispersed and erased and hanging between the lines of words upon words."[36]

But even with the assistance from Sephardi scholars in reading Maghrebi script, the typesetters and workers in the print houses, who were mainly Ashkenazi, still struggled. The printers' copy of Shim'on bar Ṣemaḥ Duran's *Sefer ha-tashbeṣ*, brought to press by Naftali Herz Levi Rofe in Amsterdam in 1738–1739, shows numerous headings in Maghrebi script crossed out and rewritten in Ashkenazi script.[37] In *Yavin shmu'a* (Livorno, 1744), another work of Duran's printed from an Algerian manuscript, editor Moshe ben Raphael Meldola (David Meldola's brother), apologizes for any mistakes in the printing, writing that "the handwriting of the manuscript was entirely in Arabic handwriting [*mikhtav 'aravi*] and the workers cannot recognize these letters at all."[38] His other brother, printer Abraham Meldola, also explains that any mistakes "are not malicious or purposeful, but because the manuscript copy was worn out, very old, and in Arabic script which no-one could understand or recognize the letters, for they seem strange [to us]. . . . It was only towards the end of the work that my dear brother, the delightful youth Moshe Meldola, came to me and recopied the manuscript in his own handwriting."[39] When a work of Algerian rabbi Yehuda 'Ayyash, *Ve-zot li-yhuda*, was brought to a press in 1776 by his son Avraham, the German printer almost gave up hope of reading it.

> He [Avraham 'Ayyash] brought us the manuscript of the great sage [Yehuda 'Ayyash], written in his own hand, in the script and letters of the people of the Barbary State. . . . But since it was entirely written in those strange and unfamiliar letters, it was hidden and untouched for much time. . . . I examined it carefully with my own eyes, but I myself could not understand that script, and it seemed very difficult to me; I could only make out the titles of the chapters which were written in square script. . . . I was convinced of the great merit for whoever could bring the book of this saintly scholar to print; it just needed to be copied into our script so that it would be easy for the eyes of the typesetters. . . . I lifted my eyes to heaven and exclaimed, "Master, please help me, and send a learned man who can reveal this script and these letters, so that I may print [this book]!" Just as I was speaking, I learnt of the arrival of a certain Sephardi from there to here . . . and just as I imagined, so did he do; may God repay him in full.[40]

Thus North African Jews often found themselves pressed into work as typesetters and editors at European printing houses dealing with Maghrebi manuscripts. The manuscript of *Magen avot* brought by Ḥayyim Yona Duran from Algiers and printed in Livorno in 1762 was edited for printing by Tunisian scholar Ḥayyim ben Mas'ud al-Fasi; whether he was living in Livorno or just traveling through is unknown.[41] The typesetting of *Shufre de-ya'aqov* by Tunisian scholar Ya'aqov Ma'arek was overseen by one of his colleagues, Yehuda Najjar, who was in Livorno arranging for the printing of his own book *Limudei ha-shem*—both books were printed at the Livorno press of Castello and Saadun in 1787. Shmuel Adawi of Tunis, who printed his *Sefer bnei shmuel* in Livorno in 1759, thanked Tunisian noble Yosef Naṭaf "who today resides in Livorno" for financially supporting the printing and also mentioned that he "additionally worked as the editor for my book and cleared it of mistakes."[42] Naṭaf acknowledged that "it was only due to the pleading of the author, and his great love, that I left my zone [of comfort] and entered an area not my own."[43] Wandering Moroccan Kabbalist Moses Edrehi (Moshe al-Dra'i, ca. 1760–1840) happened to be in Amsterdam in 1807 when a group of Jews from Meknes arrived with a manuscript of liturgical poetry for printing. In his introduction to the resulting printed volume, Edrehi explained that he was tasked with editing it "and the heavy labor was mine alone, for there was no-one else who was able to read this script besides myself, since it is the script of my homeland."[44] All these examples demonstrate how the physical and material labor of book production, and the process of typesetting and proofreading in particular, could be shaped by conditions as seemingly incidental as one's style of handwriting.

The "heavy labor" of reading and editing the manuscript might have been Edrehi's alone, but he was far from the only person working in the printing house. Scholars of early modern European printing have reconstructed the environment of the printing house as a workplace that was noisy, crowded, fast-paced, perhaps even frenetic; Jewish printing houses were no exception.[45] David Meldola offers a vivid picture of the bustling workers at Naftali Herz Levi Rofe's press in Amsterdam, writing that "many times, after the text was all ordered and fixed for the hour of printing, because [the room] was crowded and [the workers] would bump into each other, the letters would jump out from their place, and shift from line to line and from forme to forme, but the workers would not pay attention to return them to their proper place."[46] Moshe Meldola similarly describes the atmosphere of his brother Abraham's Livornese printing house in 1744 as follows:

> Even after the pages were printed, I had to go over the text and carefully check each word, once or twice or even three times, so that everything would be correct. But even so, I knew it was impossible that mistakes would not remain, because of the running of the hurried workers, saying "quickly, speed up," and they do not leave any room to correct calmly and thoughtfully.

> Sometimes I would fix a mistake and give it to the workers to reprint, but they would skip it from absentmindedness. And aside from this, letters would stick out from the forme and cling to the ink, but they do not pay attention to return them to their place, as is well-known to those expert in the labor of printing.[47]

Printing was demanding work that relied on speed, flexibility, and, above all, cooperation among different workers of a variety of backgrounds. An example of this diversity of the Jewish labor force is evident at the Livornese press of Castello and Saadun. The names of the workers as given in the paratexts of their published books from 1780 to 1790 (some twenty-three individuals in total) reveal a diverse group of Italian, Ottoman, Ashkenazi, Sephardi, and Maghrebi origins.[48] Their titles include manager [*niṣav ʿal ha-mel'akha*], editor/corrector [*magiah*], publisher [*mevi le-veit ha-defus*], typesetter [*mesader/mefazer otiyyot*], pressman [*poʿel ba-mikhbash*], and apprentice [*ṣaʿir*]. Most of them surely spoke Italian to some degree, although some were native speakers of Portuguese, and others grew up speaking Judeo-Spanish, Judeo-Arabic, or maybe even Yiddish. Some were lifelong residents of Livorno, while others moved back and forth between Italy and North Africa or the Ottoman Empire, and some had come to Livorno specifically in search of a publishing house. It was the shared labor of bookmaking, and the site of Livorno as a heartland of Jewish printing, that brought them all together. But before we turn to the emergence of Livorno's printing industry, we must first consider a singular Hebrew book that was printed in eighteenth-century North Africa.

A MEDITERRANEAN PRESS IN THE MAGHREB: *ZERAʿ YIṢḤAQ* (TUNIS, 1768)

It is reasonable to imagine that some of these Maghrebi scholars working with overseas presses and growing more familiar with the mechanics of the printing process, must have wondered why they could not print Jewish books in North Africa. In the middle of the eighteenth century, there was a brief effort to establish a Jewish printing house in Tunis, which yielded one book printed there: *Zera' yiṣḥaq*. This work of Talmudic supercommentary was authored by Yiṣḥaq Lombroso, a rabbi of the Grana community of Tunis.[49] After Lombroso died in 1752, his students attempted to have his work published posthumously, but, according to legend, Lombroso had offended another local rabbi, who cursed him, saying that his work should never be read in print. Thus the manuscript was sent twice to Livorno to be printed there, but twice the boat carrying it was shipwrecked.[50] Finally, the wealthy *qa'id* Yeshu'a Kohen Tanuji decided in 1768 to bring a full press with all the necessary type and equipment (which had previously belonged to Ottoman printer Yehuda Ḥazzan) from İzmir to Tunis.[51]

As Lombroso's son writes in his dedicatory preface: "[I thank] Yeshu'a [Kohen Tanuji], may he live long . . . who spent much money from his own pocket, covering all expenses of the workers, great or small. And even more importantly, he brought a press which he purchased from the city of İzmir, may God protect it; before this, there had been no such [press] in our land, as our elders have told us, from time immemorial."[52] Indeed, this was not only the first book printed in Tunisia but the only Jewish book printed anywhere in North Africa from the time of the Nedivot press in the early sixteenth century until the mid-nineteenth century. But why did this press not continue its work beyond printing this single book?

One answer is that the local Jewish population may have lacked the skills to operate the press and produce books efficiently. *Zera' yiṣḥaq* includes an apologetic introduction by the editor, David Bela'ish, who laments the many mistakes in the print, complaining that the press was "a new thing which no eye had seen before in our city of Tunis . . . and the equipment for the work was old and worn-out, and these stupid fools,

Figure 3.1 Title page of *Zera' yiṣḥaq* (Tunis: Yeshu'a Kohen Tanuji, 1768). Gross Family Collection B.759, photograph by Ardon Bar-Hama, used with permission.

empty and useless, had no knowledge of the principles of this type of labor."[53] Indeed, many scholars have observed that the typography is of very poor quality (see fig. 3.1). One early twentieth-century French bibliographer concluded by sarcastically reflecting on the legendary curse that the book should never be read in print, writing that "the Lord, taking into consideration the merits of Lumbroso [*sic*] and the effort of Cohen-Tanugi [*sic*], finally allowed the book to be printed; but since it was impossible not to take into account the curse of a character of such sanctity, God made it so that the edition could not be read except with the eyes of faith."[54]

But *Zera' yiṣḥaq* was not quite as unreadable as it was rumored to be. It is quoted frequently, for example, in a commentary from Livornese Sephardi scholar Ya'aqov Nunes-Vais, which was published only fifteen years later.[55] Moreover, while modern scholars might focus on its historical and bibliographic significance as the first book printed in Tunisia, it appears that *Zera' yiṣḥaq* was not received that way at the time. Although the rabbinic emissary (and bibliophile) Ḥayyim Yosef David Azulai (known as the ḤIDA) stayed with Yeshu'a Kohen Tanuji while visiting Tunis in 1774, he does not spend much time describing the existence of the press, only recording tersely that "the rabbi Yiṣḥaq Lombroso was the author of *Zera' yiṣḥaq*, which was printed in Tunis," and spending far more time praising the scholarly reputation of Lombroso and his many students.[56] In 1793, Yehuda Najjar included additional writings of Yiṣḥaq Lombroso as an appendix to the book he was printing in Livorno; he described this new material simply as "that which was not included in [Lombroso's] shining book *Zera' yiṣḥaq*, which is well-known. . . . Happy is he, since he merited to have his work printed at the hands of the great sage and royal servant, Yeshu'a Kohen Tanuji."[57] Nothing indicates that its contemporaries saw *Zera' yiṣḥaq* as exceptional, neither as a historic achievement nor as a catastrophic failure.

Rather, it was a printed book like any other, except that its production was perhaps not as smooth, efficient, or high-quality as the easily accessible printing houses of Livorno. We should recall that Yeshu'a Kohen Tanuji had apparently ordered the printing materials from an Ottoman Jewish press only after failing twice to have the book printed in Italy, and he was unsuccessful or uninterested in building up the necessary knowledge and competency to support a local print industry beyond this single book. Like the Fez press of the Nedivot brothers examined in chapter 1, the short lifespan of this press is not unusual and testifies to the strength of Mediterranean Jewish book culture and its dependence on transnational networks.[58] Within just a few years of publishing *Zera' yiṣḥaq,* Tunisian scholars were already back in Livorno working with presses there. From the perspective of a narrowly nationalist bibliography, *Zera' yiṣḥaq* is exceptional, but if we look at the early modern Mediterranean region as a whole, it is simply one of many North African works that merited being brought into print, one way or another.

Maghrebi Jews thus found themselves enmeshed in networks of print, which both relied on and reinforced the movement of people, materials, and texts from community to community. While Jewish presses in the eastern Ottoman Empire (İzmir, Constantinople, Salonica) might have been closer culturally or politically to some North African communities, Italy was closer geographically and also had a more developed and proficient Hebrew printing industry, which became even stronger throughout the eighteenth century. Thus, for a combination of social and economic reasons, Tuscany became the heart of Maghrebi Jewish book production and remained a central force in Hebrew printing until the early twentieth century. I conclude this chapter with an examination of Livorno's rise to prominence in Hebrew printing and its role in fostering connections among Maghrebi Jews around the Mediterranean.

BOOKMAKING AND THE MAGHREBI DIASPORA IN LIVORNO

Starting in the 1740s, one Italian site in particular emerged as a world center for Jewish book production: the port city of Livorno (Leghorn) in western Tuscany. Livorno became a center of Sephardi life in the late sixteenth century when Ferdinand I de' Medici, the grand duke of Tuscany, encouraged Jewish settlement in the port. He granted Jews a charter of special privileges (known as the *Livornina*) and encouraged trade with North

Africa and the Ottoman Empire.[59] By declaring Livorno a "free port," Ferdinand hoped to turn Livorno into a thriving commercial center and economic hub—which he did—particularly by attracting Sephardi Jews (including Spanish and Portuguese "New Christians" as well as Jews of Iberian origin living across the Mediterranean) renowned for their mercantile prowess.

Livorno was the only site in Italy where the Jewish community was not required to live in a ghetto, and by the turn of the eighteenth century, the Sephardim of Livorno formed the second-largest Sephardi settlement in Western Europe (after Amsterdam) and the single-largest group of the mercantile class in the city. Although exact population numbers are difficult to come by, estimates indicate that the Sephardim of Livorno made up about 10–15 percent of the city's population during this period.[60] Livornese families maintained long-standing economic and personal ties throughout northern and southern Europe, the Levant, North Africa, and even South Asia; clusters of diaspora Livornese communities were especially prominent in Tunis, Algiers, Tetouan, Alexandria, Salonica, Aleppo, and İzmir.[61] There was also, importantly for this book, a very large Maghrebi diaspora in Livorno. By the end of the eighteenth century, North African Jews made up some 13 percent of the city's Jewish community and 43 percent of its Jewish commercial firms.[62] The 1841 census of Livorno shows that close to 10 percent of Livornese Jewish households were still headed by someone born in the Maghreb, along with many more families of second-generation Maghrebi immigrants.[63] Settling in Livorno, even for a temporary period of residence, was especially attractive to Maghrebi Jewish merchants; if they could be admitted to the Livornese *nazione ebrea* ("Hebrew Nation," i.e. resident Jewish community), they would then be eligible to receive consular protection to trade in the Ottoman Empire as subjects of the French or Tuscan consuls.[64]

In addition to international commerce, another factor that drew Jews from across the Maghreb to Livorno was the importance of the Hebrew printing industry there. The first Hebrew press was established in Livorno in 1650 by Yedidya ben Yiṣḥaq Gabbai, but it lasted less than a decade before closing.[65] Hebrew printing reemerged in Livorno only in 1740 through the partnership of Abraham Meldola, scholar and businessman, and Livornese paper merchant and entrepreneur Clemente Ricci.[66] Livorno's prominence in Sephardi Jewish commercial networks was an essential part of its rise in the Hebrew publishing industry. By the end of the eighteenth century, Livorno had become one of the largest and most important centers for the publication and distribution of Hebrew books in the Mediterranean market (aided, no doubt, by the Livornese Jews' exemption from customs duties). North African Jews soon made up a large portion of clients commissioning and bringing to print Hebrew books in Livorno, and several Livornese printing firms began to focus their marketing attention on North African communities.

Some sixteen Hebrew publishing houses operated in Livorno between 1763 and 1870, and many of them worked with Maghrebi clients. The presses of Castello and Saadun, Israel Costa, and Salomone Belforte produced large numbers of books destined for the North African and Sephardi markets not only in Hebrew but also in Judeo-Spanish and Judeo-Arabic.[67] In some cases, these printers seemed to understand that they were the access point for printing among North African communities. In the introduction to *Tosfei ha-rosh* (a Talmudic commentary by medieval rabbi Asher ben Yeḥiel, known as the "Rosh"), the editor describes how medieval manuscripts were unable to be printed until they were brought to Italy:

> The books that they brought with them to the city of Fez, in that first generation of the exiles from Castile . . . were all manuscripts from Castile, for they did not have printing presses. And behold, we merited to have [other] books of the Rosh's decisions and his responsa published, in the cities of printing [*be-ʿarei ha-defus*], and their wisdom spread throughout the Jewish world. But this book,

> the *Tosfei ha-rosh,* stayed in the city of Fez, and the printers of Torah did not know of it; it was kept by the rabbis of the Serero family in their *estudyo* [library] . . . until it came to this city, Livorno, and [now] its teaching can be spread to light up the world. For through being printed, its wellsprings can scatter outward, and in houses of study all over the world many [students] can delve into it and increase knowledge.[68]

The competition among Livornese Jewish booksellers vying for the North African market could turn antagonistic, as in the case of Ya'aqov Sornaga, Yiṣḥaq Akhris, and Avraham Attias. Attias (a Livornese merchant) had entrusted Sornaga (a rabbinic emissary from Jerusalem) with a case of books to sell in North Africa, but Sornaga was traveling on the same ship as Akhris (another Livornese merchant), who was also shipping books to the Maghreb; he insisted that Sornaga be prohibited from bringing his case onboard. In the end, Akhris agreed to allow Sornaga to board with the books, but then he confiscated them when the ship arrived in North Africa, prompting Attias to complain to the Livornese Jewish court. In 1766, Sornaga's crate was returned to Livorno empty of books (and money), and Attias sued Akhris for the cost of his lost books.[69] The movement of these Hebrew books was embedded in the relational networks of economics and communal ties that linked North Africa, Italy, and the Ottoman Empire.

Over the course of the nineteenth century, the production of printed books played an increasingly central role in shaping a distinctive Maghrebi identity. Maghrebi Jews traveled to Livorno to publish the books that were created by and for their own communities, expressing their unique liturgical needs, intellectual traditions, and social circumstances. Increasingly aware of their place in the global Jewish world, Maghrebi Jews defined themselves through their books. For example, in a Judeo-Arabic preface to a translation of the daily prayer book *Tfila be-khol lashon* (1883) by Tunisian rabbi Eliyahu Ḥai Guedj (1830–1904), a group of Algerian rabbis praise his book as "fitting for all of Africa, since its language is how we speak in Arabic. And when there are some words which are different in other countries, [Guedj] has given two versions, both our form and others, and set off those [other] words in brackets, so that those in other lands might also understand."[70] Involvement in bookmaking linked Maghrebi Jews to Jews of other communities and to the Maghreb itself.

It seems that in some cases, Livorno served as something of an incubator for the training of Maghrebi authors, editors, and other print professionals who would go on to apply their skills in the burgeoning Jewish presses of nineteenth-century North Africa. For example, let us look at Eliyahu Ḥai Guedj and his family's involvement in printing houses in Livorno. Born in Tunis, Guedj's first involvement with Livornese publishing was as a young man when he and his brother Ben-Sion edited his father's commentary on the Passover Haggadah, published by Moshe Yeshuʿa Tubiana as *Pi ha-medaber* (Livorno, 1854). Over the following three decades, Guedj published or edited nine books, all printed in Livorno by Tubiana or Israel Costa. Guedj traveled back and forth between Livorno, Tunis, and Algiers; some books were his own compositions or those of his family, while others were works of colleagues that he assisted in bringing to press.[71] In addition to his Judeo-Arabic translation of the daily prayer book, Guedj's works include a book of Judeo-Arabic stories, a collection of Hebrew and Judeo-Arabic liturgical poetry, his grandfather's Talmudic commentary, his father's commentary on the medieval mystical text of the Zohar, his own Judeo-Arabic translation of the Haggadah (reprinted many times over the following decades), and his Judeo-Arabic translation and commentary on Proverbs (edited by his son-in-law, Yaʿaqov al-Haʾik).[72] Eliyahu Ḥai Guedj and his son Yaʿaqov Guedj returned permanently to North Africa in the mid-1880s, having learned enough about the printing industry to run their own publishing house; they served as leaders of Judeo-Arabic printing in Algiers and Tunis until the first decades of the twentieth century, as will be discussed further in chapter 5.

The printing houses in Livorno thus helped the Maghrebi diaspora living there to stay connected to their compatriots and family in North Africa through the creation of books. As we saw earlier in this chapter, many of the Maghrebi books printed in Livorno were financed by North Africans living there who also assisted with editing and proofreading. In some cases, these Livornese-Maghrebi books were explicitly framed as the link between Italy and North Africa, as, for example, in a Judeo-Arabic manual on slaughter prepared in 1873 by two Tunisians in Livorno, Yehuda Sitruk (Shitrug) and Yosef Shamama, and published by Israel Costa.[73] In their introduction, they declare:

> [Even though] we are living now in a foreign country, happy and successful, among a united nation which is wise and knowledgeable, and which follows straight paths, under an upright and faithful king—our eyes are raised to our ancestral land, where we were born and where our ancestors are buried, where the elders who taught us the straight paths to follow still dwell, where the friends and loved ones with whom we grew up live. . . . To show everyone that we have not forgotten them and we have not deserted their covenant, we decided to undertake this matter [and print this book] for the benefit of our brethren, especially those who do not speak Hebrew but [only] Arabic. . . . We will conclude by saying to you, our dear brethren, that even if we are far from you, our hearts still cling to you, and we rejoice and thank God whenever we hear glad tidings from you.[74]

There were many differences—linguistic, cultural, religious, and political—separating Yehuda Sitruk and Yosef Shamama in the newly unified Kingdom of Italy from their friends and family in the Ottoman Beylik of Tunis. But from their perspective, based on the books they were making and reading, they saw themselves as part of the same community. Undertaking the labor to create Jewish books in Livorno (and elsewhere), Maghrebi Jewish print professionals asserted that although they were in a foreign country, they still belonged to the Maghreb.

Barring the particularly litigious episode of Attias and Akhris, it seems that Livornese booksellers and printers generally did a brisk business providing books to the North African market. Bregoli estimates that for the eighteenth century, close to a quarter of all Hebrew books produced in Livorno were destined for North Africa, and this seems to hold true for the nineteenth century.[75] From the Maghrebi side, Livorno became the foremost destination for Maghrebi authors looking to print books. For example, Eliyahu Refael Marṣiano lists 132 books written by Algerian scholars that were printed outside of Algeria between 1600 and 1900: of these, 75 percent were printed in Livorno.[76] This statistic is even more impressive when one considers that the Hebrew printing industry in Livorno was only active for half of this period! One nineteenth-century Livornese firm not only was a major supplier of Maghrebi Jewish books but was founded by a publisher of Maghrebi origin: the press of Elia Benamozegh (Eliyahu Ben-Amozig), which is the subject of chapter 4.

FOUR

ELIA BENAMOZEGH AND THE MODERN MAGHREBI JEWISH BOOK

INTRODUCTION: ELIA BENAMOZEGH BETWEEN MOROCCO AND LIVORNO

As we saw in chapter 3, the port city of Livorno emerged as a center of both Sephardi community and Jewish book production in the second half of the eighteenth century. North African Jews increasingly relied on the quality and accessibility of Livornese presses to print their books. Several Livornese presses, such as those of Castello and Saadun, the Tubiana family (who were of Algerian origin and whose press was later purchased by Israel Costa), and Salomone Belforte, worked extensively with Maghrebi clients and produced books destined for the North African and Sephardi markets. Among these, the press of Elia Benamozegh (1823–1900) is notable for the centrality of its Maghrebi orientation and its unique vision of Sephardi Jewish modernity. Benamozegh's work as a printer, while not explicitly articulated as a modernizing project, should be understood as an application of the ideological commitments that drove his life's work as well as a reflection of the larger trends that were reshaping Jewish communities in North Africa, the Mediterranean Basin, and beyond.

Benamozegh has already attracted scholarly attention for his innovative works of philosophy and Jewish thought, including controversial biblical commentaries using non-Jewish sources, and promotions of a universalist and humanitarian understanding of modern Judaism.[1] Some scholars view his work as a shift from his Maghrebi roots toward an Enlightenment-style European Jewish modernity. Alessandro Guetta, for example, wrote that Benamozegh "travelled the immense distance from North African Jewish culture—impregnated with traditional *pietas* and Kabbalah—to the most sophisticated philosophy then being advanced in Europe."[2] Clémence Boulouque, however, has recently argued that Benamozegh's philosophy was inextricably shaped by his interest in the mystical texts and "traditional pietas" of his Maghrebi background; moreover, his publishing endeavors demonstrate how embedded he was in the Sephardi world, suggesting a more nuanced connection among his North African roots, his professional work, and his intellectual concerns.[3]

Besides Benamozegh's own writings, the work of his press sheds light on his position as an Italian Jew of Moroccan descent as well as the variety of ideological debates and stances among the Jewish communities of the Arabic-speaking world.[4] In this chapter, I first provide some background on Benamozegh's biography and his overlapping community affiliations between Morocco and Livorno. I then examine the work of his press, focusing on three works in his catalog: one of his first publications, a Judeo-Arabic translation of the Torah, *Or ne'erav* (1854); a modernizing novel, *Zikhron yerushalayim* (1874); and a group of secular publications in Judeo-Arabic, all published around 1884–1886. These examples, which span Benamozegh's career as a publisher, highlight how his search for "alternative paths to reconcile religion with his time" arose from his traditional roots in North Africa and aimed to benefit that same world.[5]

Elia Benamozegh was born in Livorno in 1823 to Moroccan parents. As Benamozegh wrote in his only surviving autobiographical account: "Our family's roots, and the roots of our ancestors, are in the Inner Maghreb (Morocco), the birthplace of my parents of blessed memory."[6] Benamozegh's father, Avraham, was from Fez; he was seventy-one when his son was born, and he died three years later. The unusual name Ben-Amozig ("son of the Amazigh one") might suggest a connection to Amazigh communities in southern Morocco, but the family is recorded in Fez as far back as the seventeenth century.[7] Benamozegh's mother, Clara Coriat, was born in Tetouan to an illustrious Sephardi family with branches throughout northern Morocco. After her husband's death, Clara raised her son with the help of her brother Yehuda Coriat, who frequently traveled between Italy and Morocco. Benamozegh began his career as an apprentice to Tunisian-Livornese Jewish merchant Abram Enriques at nineteen; he spent only several miserable years there before abandoning mercantile pursuits for the world of the yeshiva in 1846.[8]

Benamozegh's Maghrebi upbringing shaped the contours of his intellectual, social, and professional life, in both general and particular ways. His attitude toward the Kabbalah and musar was certainly rooted in his intellectual training under Maghrebi scholars like Yehuda Coriat, and his Moroccan identity was apparent in minor ways. Writing to his friend, Italian Jewish scholar Samuel David Luzzatto (1800–1865), Benamozegh explained: "Thanks ever so much for your observations on my calligraphy. . . . My calligraphy is African because I learned the Hebraic rudiments from the good soul of my maternal uncle, one of the honorable Coriat."[9] The ability to read and write in the cursive Hebrew script common in the Maghreb was not incidental but rather an essential element of Benamozegh's cultural competency.[10] Recalling the importance of Maghrebi handwriting discussed in earlier chapters, Benamozegh's involvement in the work of Maghrebi Jewish book production and his ability to support it were tied not only to his intellectual orientation but also to the specific material conditions of printing, such as the ability to read and transcribe Maghrebi manuscripts.

Benamozegh's first involvement in the world of Livornese printing was a preface to his uncle Yehuda Coriat's book of Kabbalistic essays, *Ma'or va-shemesh,* authored when Benamozegh was only sixteen. In the preface, Benamozegh praises his uncle's book and thanks him for raising him and teaching him after his father's death.[11] In 1851, Benamozegh helped produce an edition of the Zohar that was published at the press of Salomone Belforte, one of the largest Hebrew presses of Livorno. Alessandro Guetta argues that Benamozegh's contributions (which included preparing appendices and indices of cross-references among the Zohar, the Hebrew Bible, and the Talmud) foreshadowed some of his later philosophical goals, especially that of bridging the worlds of traditional rabbinic esotericism and universal scholarship.[12] A year later, just before opening his own press, Benamozegh edited a compilation of laws for Passover at the press of Salomone Belforte.[13]

Benamozegh established his own printing house in 1854 and managed it until his death in 1900. This was one of the most prolific Hebrew presses in Livorno, producing some 163 titles—a tenth of all Hebrew books published in Livorno between the seventeenth and twentieth centuries.[14] The majority of the titles produced by his press were either scholarly works by Maghrebi and Sephardi rabbis or liturgical works aimed at a Maghrebi audience. I am aware of two extant catalogs of Benamozegh's press—one produced during his lifetime, probably around 1890, and the other, shortly after his death in 1900.[15] The opening description of both catalogs emphasizes the material superiority of Benamozegh's products, something that was a key part of Livorno's dominance in the Hebrew printing industry in general: "These are the books available at the press of the sage Eliyahu Ben-Amozig and his sons, with their prices on the side, with binding: generally a half binding, namely the spine in leather with the name of the book in gold, and the rest in multicolored paper, done with beauty and elegance."[16] From these inventories, we can see that the products of Benamozegh's press were embedded in the Sephardi world and oriented in particular toward North Africa. Of the 143 titles described in these two catalogs, twenty books are explicitly identified as written in (or containing) Judeo-Arabic, and four in Judeo-Spanish. There are also eight titles identified with specific places, for example, "a Judeo-Arabic translation of Psalms according to the tradition of Tunis," six of which are associated with North Africa (the other two are Aleppo and Italy). Indeed, even after Benamozegh's death, his son Emmanuel categorized his father's press as "une imprimerie et librairie arabe et hebraïque" (an Arabic and Hebrew press and bookstore), emphasizing that the unique quality of their books was well known "especially to our Jewish brethren in the cities of Asia and Africa."[17]

Benamozegh did not include lengthy descriptions of his publishing philosophy in his writings, nor did he explain why he chose to publish the works that he did. Because of these omissions, later scholarship has sometimes ignored his press as tangential to his intellectual achievements. But for Benamozegh, his publishing house was integral to his larger vision and in particular to his relationship with his Maghrebi roots. In a paratext published in 1855, just after opening his press, he declared proudly: "In the short time since the day that we opened our publishing house, letters and requests have poured in from every corner and every direction to know what books we are printing. . . . Many worthy scholars and nobles of our nation in every city, and in particular those in the lands of the Maghreb and North Africa, desire to publish the manuscripts of great Jewish sages, which have lain hidden among them, with us."[18]

In this chapter, I assert that Benamozegh's intellectual project for modern Judaism, which he expressed largely through his French and Italian writings, was adapted for Maghrebi audiences through his work as a printer. Benamozegh advocated for a Judaism that was rooted in tradition but open to change, that balanced science and mysticism, and that would be able to take its place alongside other faiths in a modern world. He was convinced that "recentering the Orient," in Boulouque's words, held the potential for a "philosophical regeneration."[19] By supporting a network of publications that upheld these beliefs, Benamozegh promoted a like-minded Mediterranean Sephardi intellectual world and, in particular, one oriented toward North Africa. It is true that Benamozegh also published works from his Italian colleagues; from Jewish scholars in Egypt, Iraq, India, and Syria (at least until the banning of Benamozegh's controversial biblical commentary *Em la-miqra* in Aleppo in 1865); Judeo-Spanish books aimed at Sephardim in the Ottoman Empire; and even books for Ashkenazim.[20] But the majority of Benamozegh's clients and colleagues belonged to Maghrebi communities across North Africa and beyond, and it was North Africa that was clearly the focus of Benamozegh's printing enterprise.

As noted previously, Benamozegh was far from the only publisher in Livorno printing books for Jewish communities in the Islamic world. In fact, within a few years of opening his press, he became embroiled in a legal struggle over book distribution in Yemen with his colleague and competitor, Moisè (Moshe) Tubiana, who described his own business as producing "mainly religious books, highly sought after in the Orient."[21] In Benamozegh's written defense, he strongly implied that the disagreement arose because Tubiana resented his encroaching on the market by opening his press (which Benamozegh sarcastically called "my original sin").[22] But the prevalence of Maghrebi books in Benamozegh's press catalog was neither coincidence nor merely economic convenience. A close analysis of the works published by Benamozegh demonstrates how he worked to articulate a shared vision of a Sephardi, Mediterranean, Judeo-Arabic modernity through his work as a publisher.

BENAMOZEGH AND MAGHREBI JEWISH READERS: *OR NE'ERAV* (1854)

One of Benamozegh's first publications was *Or ne'erav*, a Judeo-Arabic translation of the Torah produced by and for the North African market, appearing in 1854. The translator was a Moroccan rabbi named Mikhael Makhluf 'Allun (1795–1857), who was born in Marrakech and trained as a rabbi, *sofer*, and shohet; he had served as a rabbinic emissary in Italy since 1817.[23] We do not know whether the initiative for *Or ne'erav* came from newly established publisher Benamozegh or veteran scholar 'Allun, who had already spent decades in Italy working as a scribe and artist and attempting (unsuccessfully) to have his own books published there.[24] In his preface, 'Allun claims that he "was instructed to prepare [this translation] by the publisher, the great sage Elia Benamozegh," but this may be a standard declaration of modesty, as was common for authors and translators in this context.[25] In either case, it was an ambitious project that demonstrates the guiding principles of Benamozegh's new press (not to mention its technical prowess).

For centuries, Judeo-Arabic translations of biblical texts were widespread in the local traditions of vernacular renderings. Known as *sharḥ* (pl. *shuruḥ*), they differed from country to country and even from city to city.[26] Some Maghrebi *sharḥ* texts had been brought into print, such as the Tunisian *sharḥ* of the Ten Commandments (first brought to press in Amsterdam in the eighteenth century and reprinted in Livorno in 1815) and Moroccan and Tunisian *shuruḥ* for the liturgical readings of Passover.[27] Benamozegh would go on to print Maghrebi *shuruḥ*, such as a small volume of the *sharḥ* of Oran for a selection of biblical passages, which he published in 1866.[28]

But *Or ne'erav* was something different. 'Allun wrote that he spent two and a half years working on *Or ne'erav*. He was specifically interested in creating a clear translation that could serve to educate young Jews across the Arabic-speaking world "since we have seen now that there are many in the Arab world whose tongues thirst for nourishment, but their language goes from land to land . . . with this one speaking this way, that one speaking that way, and the land is churned up, each one reading according to their own custom."[29] This translation, therefore, aimed to establish a new, standardized rendering, to replace the variety of local *sharḥ* traditions. This initiative of ʿAllun and Benamozegh could be compared to the "Jewish German" championed by Maskilim like Moses Mendelssohn and Joel Brill as an enlightened replacement for the debased *zhargon* (jargon) of Yiddish.[30]

As chapter 5 will explore further, Judeo-Arabic was seen by many during this period—including its own speakers—as imperfect and faulty, inferior to both the historically universal Jewish language of Hebrew and the evidently modern languages of Europe. An Algerian Jewish writer who published a vernacular Judeo-Arabic biblical translation in Algiers the same year as *Or neʿerav* apologized for writing in "this corrupted Arabic language [*had l-lisan l-ʿarabi al-meshubash*]," explaining that he did so only to ensure that "anyone who reads it can understand it."[31] But ʿAllun, as he explained in his introduction to *Or neʿerav*, was aiming to create a new kind of Judeo-Arabic, a language that could encompass this innovative, modern, and even scientific endeavor. This project can be seen as similar to the proposed reforms of this same time for the standardization and modernization of the Arabic language generally, although it is unlikely that ʿAllun or Benamozegh were aware specifically of this work.[32]

ʿAllun emphasized that he took care to establish a consistent spelling convention and to translate the text word by word, providing alternate translations in brackets where necessary. While ʿAllun attempted to standardize and modernize the Torah's Judeo-Arabic renderings, he also considered his native Maghrebi Arabic to be the closest to the oldest and most authoritative form of (Judeo-)Arabic. At the end of one volume, he noted that the language he used is "according to the clarity [*ṣaḥut*] of the Arabic language, and following the translation of our master Saʿadia Gaon," with the addition of variant readings that follow the different Arabic dialects "so that this [translation] may find favor for all our Jewish brethren, whether living in the Levant (Egypt and Syria), or in the Maghreb (Tunisia, Algeria, and Morocco)"—in other words, that his translation is formal, historical, and universal.[33] He then explained that he has followed the orthographic system "established according to the language and writing of the Muslims, which are the basis of the Arabic language; this is how the ancient Jews in Arab lands would write, as anyone can see in the old manuscripts which I have, and which is still followed to this day in the lands of Morocco, and the lands of Algiers and its surroundings."[34] *Or neʿerav* thus attempts to find a balance between its universalizing reach and repudiation of local *shuruḥ* and its emergence from (and rootedness in) the North African tradition.

This project was aimed at a broad audience across North Africa and the Levant and was distributed accordingly. The archives of the Jewish community of Livorno preserve a postpublication agreement between ʿAllun and Benamozegh in which it is noted that copies of *Or neʿerav* had been sent to Algiers, Oran, Tunis, Alexandria, Syria, and Morocco (via Gibraltar).[35] Benamozegh's commitment to taking on this project as one of his first publications shows his interest not only in supporting Maghrebi reading communities but also in promoting a particular kind of reading: one that bridges traditional religious practice with modern scholarship and connects Jewish communities across national and regional boundaries.

A few years later, Benamozegh requested permission from the Livornese authorities to publish a Hebrew newspaper. Titled *Hamevasser* [*The Messenger*], it was to be "no more than two printed sheets, to be sent to our coreligionists of Egypt, Persia, and Barbary, who have expressed the desire to learn [the news]."[36]

Although the permission was granted, the project stalled; only one issue appears to have been produced, in 1860.[37] Nonetheless, this early vision for his newspaper project, like *Or ne'erav*, demonstrates that Benamozegh was attentive to the needs and interests of Jewish communities across the Mediterranean, and he invested in maintaining links of solidarity and connection among the Jewish communities of Italy, North Africa, and the larger Islamic world.

In the first decade of Benamozegh's press, his initial publishing efforts focused heavily on liturgical imprints for North African communities. Apart from *Or ne'erav*, the majority of his first publications were prayer books for weekly services and holidays following the North African rite, many of which were brought to Benamozegh by Maghrebi Jews to have them published, as he testified in 1855.[38] Others were published on Benamozegh's initiative: writing to his colleague Samuel David Luzzatto in Padua in 1858, Benamozegh confessed that "regarding African mahzors, I won't deny that I was in tense negotiations in order to publish that of Tlemcen. . . . I wrote just yesterday to one of my friends in Constantine about manuscripts to know whether there would be some over there."[39]

In other words, Benamozegh consciously sought out liturgical manuscripts that could be added to his catalog of printed books for the Maghrebi market, and he maintained ties with friends and family in North Africa that could supply him with such books. Interestingly, in Benamozegh's 1856 agreement with 'Allun, he stipulated that 'Allun return to him a copy of "an Arabic Bible" that he had borrowed; it might have been a manuscript from Benamozegh's collection that 'Allun had consulted while preparing his translation.[40] Beyond liturgical and biblical books, however, *Or Ne'erav* also represented a new kind of book: an articulation, even if somewhat tentative, of an Arabophone Jewish modernity. In the following decades, Benamozegh's press served as a mouthpiece for a number of Sephardi and Maghrebi intellectuals who were composing contemporary responses to the changing world around them.

BENAMOZEGH AND SEPHARDI RESPONSES TO MODERNITY: *ZIKHRON YERUSHALAYIM* (1874)

Through his press, Benamozegh cultivated extended relationships with many North African rabbis and scholars, corresponding with them and publishing their books over years and even decades. These figures included Abraham Coriat (Avraham Koriat, Benamozegh's maternal cousin) and Coriat's student Yosef Knafo in Essaouira; Abraham Ankawa (Avraham al-Naqawa) in Mascara; Isaac Bengualid (Yiṣḥaq Ben-Walid) in Tetouan; Mimoun Abou (Maimon ʿAbbo) in Mostaganem; and Jacob Raccah (Yaʿaqov Raqqaḥ) in Tripoli. Benamozegh also had close ties to Tunisian financier Nissim Shamama, who sponsored several books printed at Benamozegh's press and whose relatives called on Benamozegh to testify in the transnational dispute over the validity of Shamama's will.[41] But while many of the books published by Benamozegh belong to standard genres of traditional rabbinic literature (like sermons, exegeses, and Talmudic commentaries), others represent attempts to find innovative ways to synthesize an openness to modernity with respect for Jewish tradition: an issue that was central to Benamozegh's philosophical work.

In these books, Maghrebi writers like Bengualid, Knafo, and Abou—alongside others, like Shlomo Bekhor Huṣin of Baghdad—grappled with the social significance of secular education, civil marriage, and the impact of electricity, railroads, and other new technologies, as well as with ideological and theological questions about interreligious contact, rabbinic authority, Zionism, and the relationship between religion and science.[42] Bengualid, for example, advocated for the instruction of foreign European languages in Moroccan and Gibraltarian schools, particularly since this would help Jewish employment in the colonial economy, although he emphasized maintaining the distinction between secular and Jewish studies.[43] Of these works of Sephardi intellectual constructions of modernity, one of the most creative examples is Eliyahu Bekhor Ḥazzan's novel *Zikhron yerushalayim* (*The Remembrance of Jerusalem*, henceforth *ZY*), which Benamozegh published in 1874 with a lengthy French introduction of his own composition.

Ḥazzan's life, especially his later rabbinic career in Tripoli and Egypt and his work as a halakhic thinker, has been fruitfully explored by others.[44] I highlight here two points: first, the importance of *ZY*'s Maghrebi context, and second, how *ZY* as an intellectual project fits in the oeuvre of work that Benamozegh wanted to support and participate in. Although Ḥazzan was not of Maghrebi origin himself, his work and, especially, *ZY*, were rooted in his relationships with the Jewish communities of North Africa.

Ḥazzan was born around 1846 in İzmir to a well-respected Sephardi rabbinic family; as a child, he moved to Ottoman Palestine with his grandfather Ḥayyim David Ḥazzan, chief rabbi of Jerusalem from 1861 to 1869.[45] Ḥazzan first worked with Benamozegh as an editor for the legal commentary of his cousin, which Benamozegh printed in 1869.[46] In 1870, Ḥazzan left Jerusalem as a rabbinic emissary to Western Europe where he met with leaders and officials in Italy, France, and England.[47] Following this trip, he traveled for two years in North Africa, spending time in Annaba (Bône), Constantine, Tunis, and Tripoli, where he was asked to serve as chief rabbi following the death of Avraham Adadi (1801–1874). It was this trip and Ḥazzan's encounters with Maghrebi Jews that inspired him to write *ZY*. He traveled to Livorno to publish the novel in 1874 and then returned to Tripoli, remaining there until 1888.[48] In that year, Ḥazzan was called to Alexandria to serve as chief rabbi, a post he held until his death in 1908.

ZY has been variously described as a novel, a play, and a work of philosophy. It is set in Tunis and presents a series of conversations between two main characters: the Foreigner [*ger*], a rabbinic emissary from Jerusalem (representing Ḥazzan), and the Local [*ezraḥ*], a Tunisian Jewish leader. The Local's wife and children and various other characters appear throughout the sixteen acts. The work was financially sponsored by two of Ḥazzan's Algerian acquaintances from Annaba: Yehuda Mas'ud Seyman (1838–1913), a wealthy scholar, and another local merchant-rabbi, Fraji Dar'i (1838–1902); they are thanked lavishly on the title page as well as in Benamozegh's French introduction.[49] In addition to naming Seyman on the cover, Ḥazzan also portrays him in *ZY* as the President [*nasi*], one of the characters who accompanies the Local. It is likely, although not indicated explicitly, that the character of the Local is modeled after Ḥazzan's other sponsor, Dar'i.

The changing political circumstances of Maghrebi Jews, and the growing influence of French culture, are evident throughout. *ZY* opens with the Local welcoming the Foreigner to his "salon de visite," where they are waited on by attendants. Another character receives a telegram (*dillug-rav*) inviting him to join the conversation. The title of *ZY* does not appear until the final scene when the Local's son, the Prince, asks the Foreigner to pose for a photograph before he leaves "that it might be a token of love for me and a remembrance of Jerusalem."[50] At one point, Ḥazzan indicates that the local characters "switch into speaking French, in the belief that [the Foreigner] will not understand it."[51]

But this is not a simple portrait of a family abandoning traditional values in favor of French assimilation: the subsequent conversations make clear that Ḥazzan is highly skeptical of what he calls "the children of this time, the generation of freedom and liberty," who are found even in the "glorious city of Tunis . . . and her companions in the lands of Africa (*Algerie*)."[52] At one point, an Italian representative sadly reports on what he sees as the failures of emancipation: "Our brethren who live in the enlightened lands of the cities of Europe, whom God has granted favor in the eyes of kings and rulers, are treated equally with citizens and residents, Jews and Christians alike, with one law for them all. But this freedom has led them to grow close to the Gentile nations . . . without feeling shame for abandoning their holy faith, its customs, and its laws."[53] The play presents us with a vision of a complex and spirited intellectual encounter, bringing together North African, Ottoman, and European Jews to create the best form of modern Judaism—faithful to its roots but also engaged with the transformations of modernity.

In the second half of the play, the Foreigner and the President convene an international gathering of scholars and representatives of different ideologies (a reformist, a "Talmudist," a philosopher, etc.) to appeal for Jewish unity (as Ḥazzan writes: "No longer will we say, 'Sephardi, Ashkenazi, Mizrahi, Maghrebi,' but rather that one God has created us all").[54] The gathering attempts to solve the philosophical issues that were dividing Jewish communities around the world—in Zvi Zohar's words, to "set a course for traditional Judaism to follow in dealing with modernism."[55] Ḥazzan himself later served as one of the leaders of such a rabbinic gathering in Kraków in 1903, which was initiated by his Ashkenazi colleague in Cairo, Aharon Mendl Hakohen (1866–1927).[56] At the fictional gathering in *ZY*, the Foreigner makes an impassioned plea for a dynamic, evolving, innovative approach to Judaism, declaring:

> Since the Holy Torah was given to physical human beings, who are subject to change according to the shifts of time and history, of rulers and decrees, of natures and climates, and of countries and realms: therefore, the words of Torah came hidden in profound wisdom [*setuma ba-ḥokhma nifla'a*], and they can take on any true interpretation in each moment and time. . . . As each new generation arises with its own leaders, they will see that the community cannot continue with the decrees [of the previous generation]; they have the authority to add and remove,

> to destroy and shatter, to cancel and to fulfill, according to how their spirit is moved by the awe of God, any day! But indeed, the Torah of truth, inscribed by God's finger and engraved upon the Tablets, will never change and never be renewed.[57]

Later, there is a discussion about whether Jews should study secular philosophy and science. In this context, Ḥazzan has another character argue that "it is the obligation of every person blessed with wisdom to study and search out whatever wisdom is necessary for their time, in order to demonstrate that our Torah is complete and more valuable than pearls."[58] In *ZY*, Ḥazzan models a vibrant Judaism that is easily capable of meeting the challenges of the modern world and that balances between ideological extremes.

Throughout *ZY*, the participants engage in lively debate, examining contemporary legal, theological, and social issues: civil marriage, secular education, biblical criticism, scientific astronomy, the belief in the Messianic resurrection of the dead, the relationship between Jews in the Diaspora and in the Land of Israel, and the role of women in Jewish society.[59] These dialogues, while clearly fictionalized, did not appear from nowhere; they arose from Ḥazzan's perceptions of the debates taking place around him in the Mediterranean Jewish world. Some scenes may well be retellings of actual conversations that Ḥazzan had in North Africa, especially in Algeria, where the Jewish community was reckoning with the social transformations of French colonialism and the French citizenship granted by the Crémieux Decree just a few years earlier.[60]

Here is one example: In the summer of 1870, Mas'ud Seyman—Ḥazzan's host in Annaba, the dedicatee of *ZY*, and the model for one of its characters—was involved in a lengthy legal dispute with his siblings regarding whether the "personal status" of Jewish law or the *état civil* of French law should be applied in distributing their father's inheritance. The responding attorney on this case was none other than Adolphe Crémieux, just months away from introducing the proposal to settle the matter by unilaterally extending French citizenship to the Jews of Algeria.[61] Ḥazzan surely discussed this episode and other similar struggles with Seyman. In general, the boundaries between truth and fiction in Ḥazzan's work are blurred; during one of the dialogues on civil marriage in *ZY*, Ḥazzan breaks the fourth wall by inserting into the narrative his halakhic correspondence with the French rabbi of Constantine, Abraham Cahen, which he wrote while staying with Seyman in the summer of 1873. In his concluding responsum, presented within the text of *ZY*, Ḥazzan concludes that a religious marriage must be considered invalid unless it is followed by a civil ceremony.[62] Similarly, *ZY*'s discussion of the place of the secular sciences in Jewish education mirrors a later real-life conflict about the value of secular education between Seyman, Dar'i, and the consistoire-appointed rabbi of Annaba, Joseph Stora.[63] This context thus unites Hazzan's narrative explorations of modernity in the Sephardi Jewish world with the immediate circumstances of Maghrebi Jews under French colonialism.

Ḥazzan's work offers a sharp critique for adherents of the European Haskalah as overzealous and assimilationist, as well as for traditionalist rabbis of his milieu as close minded and unreasonably unaccommodating. Noam Stillman summarizes Ḥazzan's view as understanding "that the modern era was a time of fundamental change, that it provided an unprecedented existential situation that required creative Jewish responses . . . not a temporary phenomenon that had merely to be waited out."[64] This approach, which has often been identified as distinctively Sephardi, is one that resonated with Benamozegh; he says as much in his French preface, which treats Ḥazzan as an admired colleague and intellectual interlocutor.[65] Benamozegh begins by emphasizing the "Oriental" context of *ZY*, declaring that "enlightened religion [*la religion éclairée*], which takes into account the state of science, and which attempts not just to have partisan support but to persuade, is all the more pleasant when it comes to us from the country from which everything came to us, from Palestine, from our holy and sacred mother Jerusalem."[66] Benamozegh praises Ḥazzan's writing for the "science, method, style, enlightened religion, and tolerance" displayed in *ZY* and concludes that Ḥazzan "proves, at least, that true orthodoxy is not the blind enemy of all innovation which one might believe; the greatest freedom and breadth of views prevail in its decisions."[67]

Benamozegh believed deeply in the possibility of this "enlightened religion" and "true orthodoxy" and sought out other Jewish thinkers who seemed to share these commitments. Benamozegh's professional role as a publisher and his reputation as a purveyor of the finest religious texts for the Jewish communities of North Africa allowed him further opportunities to broaden the audience for these debates. Some of the same Maghrebi intellectuals, whose ideas first took shape on the pages of Benamozegh's books, would soon use his press as a stepping stone to launch their own initiatives in Maghrebi Jewish publishing.

BENAMOZEGH AND THE BEGINNINGS OF MODERN JUDEO-ARABIC LITERATURE (1884–1886)

In addition to liturgical works and rabbinic literature, Benamozegh produced nonreligious Judeo-Arabic reading material later in his career. Although he had some familiarity with Judeo-Arabic, all of his own surviving compositions are in Hebrew, French, or Italian.[68] But, as previously shown regarding his work on *Or ne'erav,* Benamozegh was committed to providing books for Judeo-Arabic speakers in North Africa. During the latter part of Benamozegh's career, his press not only produced liturgical Judeo-Arabic texts but was also at the forefront of the emerging field of popular Judeo-Arabic printed literature, alongside Benamozegh's colleague Israel Costa.[69] Benamozegh also returned to the goals of his proposed newspaper *Ha-mevasser* to produce material that would bring his "coreligionists in Barbary" the latest news and modern understandings of science, philosophy, and history.[70] In this section, I highlight Benamozegh's collaborative work with two pioneers of Judeo-Arabic publishing: Tunisian Eli'ezer Farḥi (1851–1930) and Iraqi-Algerian Shalom Bekache (Bekhash, 1848–1927).

Between 1884 and 1885, Benamozegh published a monthly journal in Tunisian Judeo-Arabic edited by Eli'ezer Farḥi, titled *Ha-mevasser / al-Mubashir* (a title perhaps inspired by his own project from decades earlier). Farḥi, whom Eusèbe Vassel called "the founder of [Tunisian] popular literature," went on to play a significant role in the development of the Judeo-Arabic press in Tunis, but his entry into the world of Judeo-Arabic publishing was through his work with Benamozegh.[71] Unfortunately, no surviving copies have yet been identified, but the monthly issues of *al-Mubashir* apparently included articles on world news, political analysis (in 1907, Vassel wrote that "by some very vague traces of socialism, it is said that *al-Mubashir* scandalized the Jews of the old school, who considered it too bold; it would rather be considered timid, I think, in the eyes of the new generation"[72]), and a serialized feuilleton: an adaptation of the classical Arabic *sira* [chivalric legend] of 'Anqa, daughter of Bahram Gur, which was later published as a stand-alone volume by Costa.[73]

In 1885, Benamozegh also published *Anis al-wujud*, a collection of short stories from Jewish history in Tunisian Judeo-Arabic, produced with Farḥi and Moshe Shamama (who had translated *Qanun al-dawla al-tunisiyya*, printed in Tunis in 1861, to be examined in chap. 5). Most of the stories were translated from the compilation of *'Ose fele* by Yosef Shabbetai Farḥi (Elie'ezer Farḥi's uncle, with whom he lived in Livorno), and others from the sixteenth-century work *Sheveṭ yehuda* by Shlomo Ibn-Verga. These stories were intended to inspire reflection on moral and educational principles. As Farḥi explained: "We have seen that most people delight in hearing stories, but they are seduced by the stories in foreign books, which are just false tales that did not take place. . . . Therefore I arose and struggled and gathered stories which really happened in ancient times, including the wondrous and powerful things that happened to the sages, our masters (peace be upon them). We selected stories from which one could learn ethics [*al-adab*] and governance [*al-siyasa*]."[74] This drive to reclaim the pedagogical potential of history may also have been the impetus for a Judeo-Arabic translation of *Sefer Yosippon* (a medieval chronicle of Jewish history) titled *Ye'etayu ḥashmanim*, which Benamozegh commissioned Algerian rabbi Mas'ud al-Dahan to translate and which he published in 1886.[75] Rachel Schine describes Eli'ezer Farḥi's work in publishing the *sirat* as "navigating a problem that pervaded the non-European politics of his era, namely, whether one could be modern—that is, whether one could perform the knowledge required to participate as an informed and ethical actor in the institutions and norms of his time—without being Eurocentric."[76] For these intellectuals, creating this corpus of historical and ethical literature in Judeo-Arabic could demonstrate to their community how to balance their admiration of European Enlightenment values with a rootedness in Jewish (and Arab) tradition. Like *Zikhron yerushalayim*, this was part of the conversation that Benamozegh aimed to inspire among the Jewish communities of North Africa.

At the same time, another scholar from the Maghreb had started working with the Livornese presses of Benamozegh, Costa, and Belforte. Shalom Bekache, an Indian-Baghdadi rabbi and advocate of the Haskalah movement, had moved to Algeria in 1878. He worked as a rabbi, shoḥet, and preacher first in Thanyat al-Ḥad (Théniet El Had) and then in the city of Algiers. In 1884, Bekache published *Mevasser ṭov* (with the Livornese press of Salomone Belforte), a collection of Judeo-Arabic essays and stories. Like Farḥi, Bekache intended his work to inspire contemporary moral and ethical values. In his lengthy introduction, Bekache addressed the balance that he believed the Jews of his day must find between the Jewish tradition and "the freedom [*liberta*] that the Christians have recently granted us." He wrote that this book would show that "our sages were wise philosophers before the Christians were, and before all other nations in the world, and that still to this day there are great philosophers among us Jews, just as the Christians."[77] Already in his first publication, Bekache expressed himself in colloquial Algerian Judeo-Arabic, emphasizing his concern for creating an accessible intervention into the Algerian Jewish culture of his day.[78]

In 1886, Bekache asked Benamozegh to publish issues of his Judeo-Arabic bulletin *Or ha-levana* (the first two issues were published by Belforte). He was also working with Benamozegh to publish two liturgical books: piyyutim for the holiday of Shavuot, with Judeo-Arabic translation, and a mahzor for the High Holidays according to the Algerian rite.[79] *Or ha-levana* shared stories of geography and history from Jewish and non-Jewish communities around the world; the third issue, for instance, featured a long translation of a story from Ibn-Verga's *Shevet̩ yehuda*, articles on the Jewish communities of China and Singapore, and even a description of the Dalai Lama! Here, too, Bekache's intentions are clearly focused on broadening the horizons of his contemporaries, encouraging their cultural and educational development, and strengthening the availability of worthy reading material in Judeo-Arabic.

We know little about how involved Farḥi and Bekache were with the publishing process at Benamozegh's press (or Costa or Belforte's, for that matter), but it is clear that their time in Livorno was an important part of their developing careers in the world of Jewish books, to be examined in chapter 5. After working in Livorno, both Farḥi and Bekache went on to participate actively in creating a Judeo-Arabic publishing industry in the Maghreb. Once *Anis al-wujud* was printed in 1885, Farḥi returned to Tunis where he attempted to purchase a press. Although he did not succeed in opening his own publishing house until 1901, he did immediately become involved with Judeo-Arabic printing at the press of Uzan and Castro, which had opened in 1885, publishing *Shomer piv,* a booklet of Judeo-Arabic prayers, in the autumn of that same year.[80] Farḥi continued to print works in both Tunis and Livorno (with the press of Israel Costa) for the next several years until he shifted to focus exclusively on his publishing in Tunis. Meanwhile, in 1887, Bekache returned permanently to Algiers and joined in partnership with the Algerian press established by Seror and Boukabza in 1885.

Benamozegh's dedication to Judeo-Arabic literature, which extended across his entire career, might be seen as part of his ideological commitment to his vision of Jewish modernity. During this period, Benamozegh published a number of Judeo-Arabic texts that are closer to the traditionalist side of the spectrum: *Shuva yisrael,* a moralizing, antiassimilation essay by Tunisian rabbi Yehuda Jarmon (1812–1912), and *'Et la-ledet qol sasson,* a collection of religious Judeo-Arabic stories and liturgical poetry by Algerian rabbi Eliyahu Allouche ('Allush, 1812–1892).[81] Of course, we cannot know whether Benamozegh specifically chose to publish these works or whether they were simply paying projects; to some extent, what gets published is always subject to economic considerations.

But taken all together, these works point to a growing Maghrebi Jewish readership for Judeo-Arabic material and an ongoing conversation, mediated through print, about the relationship between Jewish society and modernity. In response to this demand, Benamozegh chose to support a number of projects that fit with his general stance, expressed elsewhere through his own writing, of reconciling Jewish tradition with science, emancipation, and modernity. Intentionally or not, Benamozegh also contributed to the professional growth of Maghrebi writers and publishers like Farḥi and Bekache, who would continue the conversation through the establishment of printing houses in North Africa, as chapter 5 will explore.

CONCLUSION: FROM THE MAGHREB TO ITALY AND BACK AGAIN

Elia Benamozegh was thoroughly rooted in the Italian and Sephardi Jewish communities of Livorno—indeed, he rarely left the city and never traveled farther than Florence or Pisa—but through his press, he participated in and fostered a community of Jewish readers, connected across national and imperial boundaries. The works he produced in his printing press and sold in his bookstore point toward what Clémence Boulouque calls the "distinct personality" of his work: "deeply anchored in a Sephardic or Maghrebi heritage, but at the same time . . . not averse to an understanding of Jewish tradition that would make space for scientific discoveries or other practices typically held to represent modernity."[82] The intellectual links that Benamozegh fostered through his publications map out a series of active connections between Sephardi communities in North Africa, Italy, and the Ottoman Empire.

In 1869, Benamozegh wrote to his friend, Livorno-born American rabbi Sabato Morais, offering to supply American Sephardi communities with mahzors for "whichever rite they follow" and biblical books and haggadot in Judeo-Spanish and Judeo-Arabic.[83] While Morais did not take up this offer, Benamozegh's gesture is indicative of how he balanced his commitments to a universalist, modernist, and humanitarian understanding of Judaism; solidarity and connection among the Jewish communities of Italy, North Africa, and the larger Sephardi world; and articulating a unique Mediterranean Sephardi perspective on modernity. Benamozegh's rootedness in his Moroccan identity was also reflected in how he was perceived by other Maghrebi Jews, with North African scholars clearly relating to him as a compatriot. Avner-Yisrael Serfaty, for example, mentions him with pride in his historiographical work on the Jewish community of Fez, *Yaḥas fes* (1879).[84] In a letter to Benamozegh from the rabbinic court of Fez requesting his assistance with a threat to their community, the writers—addressing him as "beloved master of the city"—plead that "the graves of your ancestors are in crisis. . . . [By helping us] you will bring honor to your parents, since you will have saved the city of their birth from the jaws of destruction."[85] Benamozegh's relationship with the Maghreb, and Morocco in particular, was shaped not only by history but also by responsibility and reciprocity.

In Benamozegh's lifetime, the market for Maghrebi Jewish books was rapidly expanding, especially as a local printing industry emerged in North Africa: the first Hebrew books printed in the modern Maghreb appeared in Algiers in 1853, Oran in 1856, Tunis in 1861, and Tangiers in 1893. The work of Benamozegh's press used the resources of the established printing industry in Livorno to respond to a near-constant demand for Maghrebi liturgical books and Judeo-Arabic imprints, drawing on the strengths of the communal, intellectual, social, and commercial ties that connected Maghrebi Jews across the shores of the Mediterranean while also supporting the intellectual ties among Mediterranean Sephardi thinkers grappling with Jewish perspectives on modernity. The work of Benamozegh's press also highlights the complex relationship between manuscript and print, showing that each continued to rely on the other. His work depended on the steady stream of manuscripts (some produced explicitly for the purposes of printing them) from Sephardi communities in North Africa and the Ottoman Empire and on the linguistic and cultural knowledge necessary to transcribe and edit them. Above all, the publications of Benamozegh demonstrate that Maghrebi Jews were actively engaged in thinking and writing about their experiences with modernity within a larger circle of Sephardi intellectuals.

Rather than waiting passively for the arrival of the printing press, as has sometimes been portrayed in earlier historiography, Jews in the Maghreb were consciously involved in the creation of a vibrant and dynamic local culture of the book. Benamozegh's life is occasionally portrayed as something of a philosophical failure because it was met with indifference from his European colleagues and virulent criticism from traditionalist rabbinic authorities.[86] But through his work as a publisher for Maghrebi and Sephardi communities, Benamozegh played an essential role in a transnational conversation about the evolution of Jewish society in modern times, which brought together scholars and intellectuals from around the Mediterranean and which continued in North Africa and elsewhere long after his death.

The second half of the nineteenth century was a time of large-scale transformation for the Jewish communities of North Africa. In the wake of French colonial occupation, Jewish presses began to emerge in North Africa, further expanding the genres of Hebrew, Judeo-Spanish, and Judeo-Arabic literature that had developed over the previous centuries through the patronage of Maghrebi Jews at European and Ottoman presses. In the following chapter, we explore the establishment of these presses in North Africa and the shifts in Maghrebi book culture that emerged in their wake.

FIVE

LANDSCAPES OF PRINT IN THE NINETEENTH-CENTURY MAGHREB

INTRODUCTION: PRINTED BOOKS IN COLONIAL NORTH AFRICA

In the autumn of 1853, readers of the French Algerian newspaper *L'Akhbar* (a privately owned journal established in 1839) were treated to a brief but optimistic note on the development of Jewish printing in Algiers under the column heading of "Miscellaneous Happenings in Algiers."

> Mr. J. Cohen-Solal, a Jew of Algiers, has now gifted to the library of that city two works printed here in Hebrew [characters], of which he is the editor. The first is a new Jewish liturgy, or prayers for children on the occasion of the New Year and the Great Fast [of Yom Kippur]; the second is a liturgy for the ceremony of Saturday [evenings], concluding with a recitation of the life of Sidi Khader (the prophet Elijah), written in Arabic with Hebrew characters. The type which was used for this double printing, he said, was cut and cast in Algiers by a Polish Jew. This is the beginning of an industry which proposes to compete with the presses of Livorno, which currently control the supply of Hebrew books for the numerous Jewish communities of North Africa. In fact, the central position of our city in this region, and the rapidity and the surety of communications, whether by land or by sea,

> constitute a set of favorable circumstances which promise success for this new enterprise.[1]

In this report, Auguste Bourget, editor of *L'Akhbar,* incorporated the press of Cohen-Solal into a larger story of the success of the French colonial project, just over two decades old at this point, which hoped to "revitalize" the productivity of North African societies through modern industry.[2] The description of the press encourages a sense of pride in the fact that "a Jew of Algiers" had set in motion the creation of a new industry, pointing toward Algerian self-sufficiency as well as competition with the established industries of Europe. However, Cohen-Solal's printing endeavors should not be seen as a straightforward expression of French colonial expansion. The language and content of these books are rooted not in French modernist ideology but in the traditional Hebrew and Judeo-Arabic culture of Jewish integration in Algeria. And while the relationship of Maghrebi Jews with the Livorno presses did change during this period, it was certainly not a simple replacement of one site of industry with another but rather a more complex renegotiation of how Maghrebi Jewish communities saw themselves in the context of global Jewry.

Chapters 3 and 4 explored how books mapped out the deep integration of Maghrebi Jews into the commercial and intellectual networks of the Mediterranean world through their relationships with the Jewish presses of Europe and the Ottoman Empire. This chapter investigates the development of a local industry of Jewish printing in North Africa, and in particular, how the production of Jewish books was affected by the changing linguistic and political dynamics of Maghrebi Jewish communities after the establishment of the French colonial presence in North Africa, and the relationship among the Judeo-Arabic, Hebrew, and French languages. I begin by outlining the historical development of Jewish printing in the Maghreb, focusing on the movement of printers and presses across the Maghreb (and throughout the

Mediterranean). I then explore the functioning of Jewish presses and bookstores as community hubs and sites of local conversation through the landscape of ephemera. Finally, I look at the different genres of literature produced by these presses, and the contested linguistic landscape of Maghrebi Jews, arguing that their work sheds light on the social transformations in the second half of the nineteenth century, a time of great change for Jewish communities in the Maghreb.

As other scholars have noted, the history of the book in Africa is a "colorful and complicated area of study," which combines the long history of manuscript book production and especially the medieval and early modern trans-Saharan book trade, the production and circulation of printed books in missionary and colonial contexts (dating back to at least the Portuguese presence in the Kongo kingdom in the sixteenth century), and the development of indigenous networks of authorship and readership.[3] In the Maghrebi context, the few studies of book history in North Africa begin their narratives with the introduction of typographic or lithographic printing presses (usually in colonial contexts) in the mid-nineteenth century.[4] As Arthur Asseraf has argued, the absence of serious local engagement with print technology before then and the lackluster reception to European-style printing in North Africa has puzzled scholars and observers looking for the kinds of transformative effects that print is often asserted to have had in early modern Europe.[5]

It is important to remember that the establishment of printing presses in the colonial period is not equivalent to the "introduction" of printing to North African communities, especially for Jews. Asseraf writes that "early modern North Africans were print-aware, even if they did not print themselves," pointing out that printed European texts were being used pragmatically in the Maghreb as a source of information about Europeans, especially by merchants, interpreters, diplomats, and politicians.[6] Some earlier sources hint at possible Maghrebi encounters with printing that have been lost to history. In 1771, for example, English printer Philip Luckombe asserted that for "those remote parts of Africa called Abyssinia, and even those which are nearer, as Morocco, Fez, &c. 'tis certain they received the art [of printing] early from their neighbors, the Spaniards or Portuguese, and encouraged it for a considerable time; yet whatever be the reason, scarce any footsteps of it now remain."[7] If printing was "encouraged for a considerable time" anywhere in the Maghreb, it seems to have left no trace beyond the works already examined in previous chapters, namely, the sixteenth-century Nedivot press in Fez and the 1768 printing of *Zera' Yiṣḥaq* in Tunis, among Jews or otherwise. Nonetheless, the previous chapters of this book have highlighted the ongoing relationship of Maghrebi Jews with the labor of printing outside of the Maghreb. The production of printed Jewish books in the Maghreb is part of a longer history, in which the "introduction" of printing in the second half of the nineteenth century is a continuity rather than a beginning ex nihilo.

But for both Muslims and Jews across North Africa, the mid-nineteenth century presented a new set of questions for book production: whether books intended for publication should be printed locally or abroad. Moroccan diplomat Muḥammad al-Ṣaffar commented with wonder on the French printing presses he saw during his trip to Paris in 1845–1846, and in 1860, Moroccan ambassador Idris al-Amrawi recommended that Sultan Sidi Muḥammad IV (r. 1859–1873) "acquire a printing press and thus improve our country," noting that "it helps to increase the number of books and to disseminate knowledge of the sciences to the public.... [It] has been used in every [other] Muslim country and the famed 'ulama are delighted about it."[8] This was eventually achieved when the sultan confiscated the newly imported lithographic press of Muḥammad al-Ṭayyib al-Rudani in 1864 and repurposed it as a tool of national authority.[9] Lithographic Arabic printing had begun in Tunisia in 1845, and the Bey of Tunis authorized the first typographic Arabic presses there in 1860.[10]

Algerian Muslims similarly wrestled with how to produce and control their narratives and texts in the face of the Arabic-language material produced by French authorities since 1832.[11] Fawzi Abdulrazak concludes that the first decades of Arabic printing in Morocco were characterized by its regulation, censorship, and even its use as governmental propaganda.[12] The publications and printing houses examined in this chapter offer another perspective on the history of printing in North Africa: the complicated position of Maghrebi Jews balancing their ties to their local environment, the pull of their emancipated coreligionists in Europe, and their entanglement with colonial authority.

THE BEGINNINGS OF JEWISH PRINTING IN THE MODERN MAGHREB

The two brief experiments with Hebrew printing of the sixteenth and eighteenth centuries notwithstanding, the title of "first modern Jewish book printed in the Maghreb" might be assigned to the play *Nazahat al-Mushtaq* (*The Entertainment of the Enamoured*) by Abraham Daninos (1797–1872), which was printed in lithographic Arabic characters in Algiers in 1847.[13] However, the fact that it was printed in Arabic characters suggests that it was intended for a Muslim audience since the lithographic technology could have reproduced Hebrew characters just as easily; indeed, several examples of lithographic Hebrew ephemera survive from nineteenth-century North Africa (to be examined later in this chapter). Therefore, we will focus our attention on books printed in Hebrew characters and thus aimed explicitly at Jewish audiences.

The first printer to produce books in Hebrew characters in the Maghreb in the modern period was a *shaliaḥ* [rabbinic emissary] named Ḥayyim Ze'ev Ashkenazi, who traveled from Jerusalem to the Maghreb around 1843 and arrived in Algiers in 1849. He had previously spent some time in Salonica where he printed at least one book, a Passover Haggadah with Ladino translation, in 1842.[14] Whether establishing Hebrew presses was part of his mission is not clear, but it seems likely that this was a way to raise finances as well as support from the local community.

Ashkenazi's first Maghrebi imprint was *Yedei david,* a commentary on the Talmudic tractate *Nazir* by local rabbi David Mu'aṭṭi, printed in Algiers in 1853. Later that same year, Ashkenazi printed another two or three books: a translation of the Havdalah service in Judeo-Arabic; a passage from the Zohar, the *Idra zuta,* accompanied by piyyutim in Hebrew and Judeo-Arabic; and, if the report in *L'Akhbar* is to be trusted, a mahzor for the High Holidays. Ashkenazi oversaw the production along with two brothers from Algiers who served as editors, Haim and Jacob Cohen-Solal (Ḥayyim and Ya'aqov Kohen Shulal); the typesetting was done by Algerian Jews Moshe Ḥaddad and Yosef Dahan, and the printing took place at a French-owned press, Imprimerie de Gueymard.[15]

Avraham Attal compared the letters and decorations of *Yedei david* with those printed in Salonica during this period and suggests that Ashkenazi brought the type from there. However, Yosef Tobi believes that Ashkenazi brought the letters with him from Jerusalem, and the French report previously quoted suggests that the type was cast in Algiers.[16] Further research is needed to clarify Ashkenazi's work process and relationship with local and international Jewish (and non-Jewish) communities. In Algiers, Ashkenazi also produced a sheet depicting the holy sites of the Land of Israel, an "itinerarium" with woodcut illustrations and typeset Hebrew labels. A small label at the bottom reads "Whoever gazes on this image of the Holy Temple receives the merit as if it will be rebuilt in his days; may it be Your will that it is rebuilt speedily, amen."[17] Exactly where and how he printed this sheet is unknown.

Ashkenazi's Hebrew type and printing equipment were purchased at the end of 1854 by Haim and Jacob Cohen-Solal, who immediately opened their own press in Algiers and continued printing books in Hebrew and Judeo-Arabic. These included a Judeo-Arabic translation of *Dat yehudit*, a guide to household laws for women (originally written in Judeo-Spanish by Moroccan-Gibraltarian rabbis Avraham Laredo and Yishaq Halevi and first published in Livorno in 1827); an edition of the Passover Haggadah, accompanied by Judeo-Arabic translation; and the first volume of *Shay la-mora*, a biblical commentary on Genesis in vernacular Judeo-Arabic by Algerian rabbis Shlomo Zarqa and Yehuda Ḍarmon.[18] This last book was also typeset by Moshe Ḥaddad, who had previously worked with Ashkenazi on *Yedei david*; clearly, Ashkenazi did not just transfer the type to the Solal brothers but also spent time training local workers in printing techniques.

While the Cohen-Solal brothers were opening their press in Algiers, Ashkenazi moved to Oran, where he printed a collection of liturgical poems titled *Shivḥei elohim* in 1856, again working with Jewish workers and a non-Jewish press. In this case, the typesetting was done by Nissim Karsenty (Crescente), and the printing at the press of François Adolphe Perrier.[19] As he did in Algiers, Ashkenazi soon transferred his work and materials to a local family: Nissim Karsenty and his cousin Eliyahu (Elie) Karsenty, whose press became the major Jewish publisher in Oran until the end of the nineteenth century.[20] Ashkenazi then moved from Algeria to Tunisia where he opened his third Hebrew press in Tunis. He had apparently left one set of type in Algiers and another in Oran, so it is not clear if he managed to bring three full sets of Hebrew type (in both square and semicursive, or Rashi characters) to the Maghreb, if he was ordering them from abroad as needed, or if he had them cast by local foundries.

In 1861, Ashkenazi printed his only book in Tunis: a Judeo-Arabic translation of the *'Ahd al-aman*, or "Fundamental Pact" of 1857, and its successor, the first formal Tunisian constitution, *Qanun al-Dawla al-Tunisiyya*. As I hope to argue elsewhere, the fact that Ashkenazi's first printing project in Tunis was not a rabbinic or liturgical book, as in Algiers or Oran, but explicitly a juridical text demonstrates how Ashkenazi and his Tunisian collaborators were responding to their political moment as Jews in the rapidly changing Maghrebi and Ottoman world.[21] The translation of the Fundamental Pact and the Constitution was done by Moshe (Bishi) Shamama, and included an explanation on the title page: *Kitab qanun al-dawla al-tunisiyya: had al-kitab fiha sharh ʻahd al-aman*: "The Book of the Constitution of the Tunisian State: this book contains a translation of the Fundamental Pact."[22]

According to Eusèbe Vassel, Moshe Shamama was highly educated in classical Arabic and served not only as an Arabic instructor but also as *wakil,* or legal agent, in the civil court [*ouzara*] of the Bey of Tunis. He also later collaborated with Eliʻezer Farḥi to publish literary texts in Judeo-Arabic.[23] This was highly unusual for Maghrebi Jews, who were generally proficient only in vernacular Judeo-Arabic (alongside any European languages). Moshe Shamama explained that he "saw that the language [of the *ʻAhd al-aman* and the *Qanun*] was difficult to understand, especially for our Jewish brethren, many of whom cannot read Arabic characters. . . . For this reason, I had to translate it into the Barbary Arabic that is commonly spoken among the people, so that all our Jewish brethren will be able to understand and know the rules of this Fundamental Pact."[24] In translating the *ʻAhd al-aman* and the *Qanun,* Shamama engaged with how Jews can learn to be modern Tunisian citizens and understand both their new duties and their new rights as citizens of this new modern state.

In general, Ashkenazi's work in Tunis followed the same pattern as in Algiers and Oran: the use of Hebrew type under the auspices of a non-Jewish press with the involvement of local Jewish scholars and press workers. After his work in Tunis, Ashkenazi disappeared from the historical record; presumably, he returned to Jerusalem, but whether he continued to work in printing is unknown. The Algerian presses established in the mid-nineteenth century with the help of Ashkenazi—those of

Cohen-Solal in Algiers and Karsenty in Oran—continued to publish works in Hebrew characters, including books, pamphlets, serials, newspapers, and other ephemera, although no more Hebrew books were printed in Tunis, as far as is currently known, until the 1880s.

But surviving materials point to a broader print landscape than has previously been imagined: for example, two lithographed sheets produced by an otherwise unknown artist and *shaliaḥ*, Reuven Gabbai of Jerusalem, were printed in Algiers in 1864. Printed at the French lithographic press of A. Bouyer, the first is a hand-drawn and handwritten copy of Ashkenazi's itinerarium from almost a decade earlier; the second is an amulet for a newborn child.[25] Where do these items fit in the social landscape of Maghrebi Jewish book culture? Most bibliographies of Maghrebi Jewish printing, like print bibliographies in general, have focused on those works that can most easily be classified as books; however, as we have seen, printers collaborated with authors, artists, and other clients to produce a wide variety of reading material, much of it ephemeral, and little of which has survived. As more Jewish presses opened across the Maghreb in the final decades of the nineteenth century, the printing house and bookshop became a community hub and a site for the development of local reading communities.

MAGHREBI JEWISH BOOKSTORES, EPHEMERA, AND THE GROWTH OF A VERNACULAR PRINT INDUSTRY

In 1884, a Tunisian-born rabbi named Avraham Boukabza (Bukhobza) opened a bookstore and printing house in Algiers, collaborating with Shalom Bekache, who had been bringing Judeo-Arabic works to press in Livorno, and an Algerian rabbi, Mordekhai Seror (Ṣrur). In the first book Boukabza published, *Qol sasson* (1884), a collection of short stories in Judeo-Arabic adapted by Seror from various sources, he announced:

> Dear community, welcome! I inform you that we have many new books for sale, including: the parashah with haftarot and Shabbat prayers, in five volumes; the parashah with Rashi and Targum, and Shabbat prayers, in five volumes; the parashah with Rashi and Targum, and Shabbat prayers, in one volume; prayerbooks of every kind, large, small, and medium. . . . And some other books: books of sermons, like *Bina le-ʿitim, Yaʿarot devash, ʿOlelot efraim,* etc. etc.[26] We also have *Yosippon;* and *She'erit yisrael,* which is the continuation of *Yosippon* until Crémieux and Moses Montefiore; *Sefer ha-yashar; Sefer ḥasidim; Reshit ḥokhma; Shevet yehuda,* etc. etc.[27] We also have a Haggadah with sharḥ [i.e., Judeo-Arabic translation], and the laws [of Passover] in Arabic, illustrated and gilded, for only one franc.[28]
>
> Anyone who wants any books, whether mentioned here or not, should come to my [store] and they will find all they desire. And the community living in other areas should write to me directly, or by the bank, and they will receive all they desire through the post. And this is my address: [in French characters] *Abraham Boukabza, rabbin. Rue Pavy Nr. 2, Alger.*[29]

At the same time, Boukabza was also working with the Livornese printing house of Israel Costa, where he was publishing a prayer book for the High Holidays, a havdalah liturgy, and a Passover Haggadah with French translation by Mordekhai Seror, all released in 1886.[30] That same year, Boukabza also published a catalog of his press and bookstore, which I have unfortunately been unable to locate, but through surviving advertisements, I have been able to reconstruct approximately a quarter of Boukabza's inventory from 1885 to 1887.[31] He sold many liturgical books: a variety of Bibles and prayer books in large and small editions, works of classical rabbinic law and commentary, and unnamed Hebrew "books of the Haskalah." He also sold a great deal of vernacular Judeo-Arabic material, including religious digests (such as *Patshegen Ha-ktav,* a Judeo-Arabic translation of the *Meʿam loʿez*); books of folktales (*maʿasiyyot*) and divination manuals; and the secular Judeo-Arabic journals, pamphlets, and serialized novellas produced by his colleague and business partner Shalom Bekache (to which we will return later in this chapter), printed first in Livorno and then in Algiers by Bekache and Boukabza. Finally, Boukabza sold items of ritual Judaica like *ṭallitot* (prayer shawls), tefillin, and mezuzot, as well as printed ephemera, including "gilded birth amulets," which from surviving examples appear to have been printed lithographically by Boukabza.[32]

This dizzying array of mixed genres and goods was typical for many bookstores of the period across the Arab world.[33] In the final two decades of the nineteenth century, Jewish printers and publishers across Morocco, Algeria, and Tunisia produced hundreds of books, booklets, journals, and paper ephemera, most of which were sold directly through stores attached to the presses. The hybrid press-bookstore was thus an active site of textual creation and consumption.

While some of the books they produced were similar to those that Maghrebi Jews had brought to press over the previous centuries abroad—collections of rabbinic responsa, sermons, commentaries, and liturgy—many of them represented new genres of Maghrebi Jewish publications: journalism, literature, drama, and science. In addition, the availability of a local print industry made it possible to print small-scale ephemeral material, like wedding invitations, pamphlets, song booklets, and more.[34] One of the frustrating aspects of studying ephemera is that they survive at an inverse proportion to their prevalence; the popular leaflets and brochures, which in most cases served as the economic backbone for any given press, were read and discarded or used until they fell apart, while the larger and more expensive books sat preserved on bookshelves. As Andrew Pettegree observes, "Early printed books that survive in large numbers do so essentially because they were destined for libraries. . . . The sorts of works that delivered steady profits were usually the unregarded pamphlets, broadsheets and printed ephemera that were never intended to dignify the shelves of a library. They were intended for use: and that of course impacted in a negative way on their chances of surviving through to the present day."[35] Our attempts to understand the Jewish publishing world of the modern Maghreb must contend with the invisibility of the majority of its products.

A center for Hebrew and Judeo-Arabic publishing had begun to emerge in Tunis in the 1880s, eventually overtaking Algiers and even Livorno. The first Hebrew press in Tunis belonged to Vittorio Finzi, the Tunis-born son of a Livornese émigré, who received a license from the Bey of Tunis in 1880.[36] Another important press was opened there by Ṣiyyon (Sion) Uzan and Joseph Castro, Imprimerie Uzan et Castro, which printed large numbers of popular Judeo-Arabic booklets of folklore, newspapers, and serialized novels, starting in 1885.[37] Additionally, one of the workers trained by Bekache in Algiers, a Tunisian Jew named Ya'aqov Guedj, opened a press there. He then moved back to Tunis with his father, Eliyahu Ḥai Guedj, in 1895 and reopened his press in Tunis where he continued to print until the mid-twentieth century.[38]

The following three decades saw an explosion of Jewish books published in Tunis, mostly small booklets of popular literature in vernacular Judeo-Arabic, often called *al-'arabiyya al-barbariyya* (Barbary Arabic) or simply *al-yahud* (Jewish). In his 1907 catalog of Tunisian Jewish publishing, French scholar Eusèbe Vassel lists over five hundred such bibliographic items, all printed since 1880.[39] These included translations of European literary works into Judeo-Arabic, such as Alexandre Dumas's *Le Comte de Monte Cristo* and Daniel Defoe's *Robinson Crusoe,* and original compositions in Judeo-Arabic, such as Eli'ezer Farḥi's novel *Sirat zin al-tammam,* which was published in Tunis in 1888.[40] While some works were large volumes, there were many small booklets of folktales and popular songs as well as works of geography, history, folk medicine, and dream interpretation. The Jewish presses of Tunis also produced many posters, amulets, and other loose-leaf pieces with Hebrew and Judeo-Arabic text. Tunisian Jewish writers contributed to a large number of Judeo-Arabic journals, many of which included serialized novels as feuilletons. For example, a translation of Avraham Mapu's Hebrew novel *Ahavat ṣiyyon* (1853) by Messaoud Maarech (Mas'ud Ma'arek, 1861–1941) titled *Kitab al-ḥub wa'l-waṭan* first appeared as a feuilleton in the journal *El-Boustan* in the summer and fall of 1890. At the end of the year, it was published as a stand-alone book in three volumes by Uzan and Castro.[41]

This period also saw the emergence of Hebrew-character printing in northern Morocco. Jews in Tetouan and Tangiers were heavily involved in the establishment of newspapers and journals, most of which were in French or Spanish, but some included Judeo-Spanish and Judeo-Arabic.[42] The presses that printed them, while focused on journalism, also produced a wide variety of other materials. An 1883 advertisement, printed in Judeo-Spanish (in Hebrew characters) in a Spanish-language newspaper of Tangiers, *Al-Moghreb al-Aksa* (run by a Catholic Gibraltarian, Gregorio T. Abrines), announced: "Bills of exchange, invoices, accounts, circulars, paper and stamped envelopes, cards, invitations, programs, and all kinds of printed works with Hebrew type: at the press of Abrines, Tangiers."[43] In 1892, Abrines's press published a broadside in Judeo-Arabic, announcing a forthcoming Judeo-Arabic newspaper for the Jewish community of Tangiers under the editorial command of a certain Moshe di Avraham Kohen, to be titled *Ṣafnat paneaḥ*.[44] The newspaper promised to be written in clear Arabic and to report on local and international news, business, and politics; it also announced a raffle for the first subscribers to the newspaper, the prize to be "four books—one of daily prayers, one of holiday prayers, and two for the High Holidays—as well as a ṭallit of silk or wool." Unfortunately, no issues of this newspaper, if it was ever published, have survived.

In 1891, the first Jewish-owned press in Morocco was established in Tangiers by Salomon Benaïoun (Shlomo Ben-Ḥayyun, 1867–1921), who was born in Oran and studied printing there. In

Oran, Benaïoun had edited a short-lived Judeo-Arabic newspaper, *Ṭov le-yisrael* (1889), and served as the typesetter for the book *Musar melakhim* (Oran: A. Dupont, 1889). In 1890, he moved to Tangiers. According to Jamaâ Baïda, he was invited there by the banker Haïm Benchimol, who had purchased the newspaper *Le Reveil du Maroc* (founded in 1883 by Abraham Lévy-Cohen).[45] In Tangiers, he printed two short-lived Judeo-Arabic newspapers, *Qol yisrael* (1891) and *Mevasser ṭov* (1894), at least one form for a ketubah and, in 1893, a booklet on the calendar, *Yareaḥ le-mo'adim*. According to Eliyahu Refael Marṣiano, this was the first Jewish book printed in modern Morocco.[46] He continued to print in Judeo-Arabic, Hebrew, French, and Spanish, until his death in 1921.

Ephemera play a central role in understanding the landscape of printing and book culture, both from the side of the presses producing it and from the side of the consumers. We can see the importance of ephemera and "job printing" for Maghrebi printing in the advertisements for Abrines and Boukabza mentioned previously, and other presses and bookstores similarly promoted the range of their products with an emphasis on ephemera. Ya'aqov Guedj's Algerian press, for example, boasted in 1888: "We produce books in Judeo-Arabic [*bil-yahud*] and in Ladino, in French, and in Muslim Arabic [*bil-muslimin*], and our work is clean and our prices are low. [We serve] anyone who needs to print any books or journals, or letters, envelopes, business cards, address cards, leaflets, or brochures. . . . Write to us at our address, and the request will be answered with pleasure."[47] Advertisements and booklists for the stores and presses of Boukabza and Bekache in Algiers, Elie Karsenty in Oran, and Eli'ezer Farḥi in Tunis similarly highlight the importance of these ephemeral products in supporting these presses financially.[48] But ephemera were not only economic filler to support more expensive books; they also provided clients with personalized printed material (such as cards, invitations, and stationery), with the ability to share news and community announcements widely, and with cheap, plentiful, and constantly changing reading material in the form of pamphlets, song booklets, and feuilletons.

Booklists testify to some ephemera that have otherwise completely disappeared. Moroccan-Israeli rabbi and historian Ya'aqov Moshe Tolédano (1880–1960) recorded seeing an otherwise unknown broadside from nineteenth-century Algeria: "One page on the matter of a child born in Algiers, with the sign of some letters written on his placenta and on his nose, and his parents wished to dedicate him as a nazir, etc., printed in Algiers in 1857."[49] A description of the products for sale at the press of Shalom Bekache in Algiers in 1892 includes "[a poster of] the alphabet for children" and a number of amulets and calligraphic sheets, such as "an image of Queen Esther, written from the entirety of the book of Esther [in micrography]; and ditto, an image of the Temple, written from the entirety of the books of Psalms."[50] The micrographic image of Esther can be identified as a lithographic print by Jacob Soffer (1857–1930), a rabbi, artist, and book collector of Ashkenazi origin who lived in Oran. Three other micrographic works of Soffer survive, but there is no known micrographic image of the Jerusalem Temple as described by Bekache.[51] The alphabet poster is even harder to identify, and whether it was drawn by a local artist, typeset in Bekache's press, or produced elsewhere is unknown.

These records of lost ephemera, as frustrating as they are, expand our knowledge of the printed materials produced at particular presses. Meanwhile, surviving ephemera can present their own challenge, namely, extant testimonies to Jewish print culture (and printshops) in unknown circumstances. A number of these were produced in lithograph; earlier in this chapter, we mentioned the lithographed itinerarium of Reuven Gabbai, printed in Algiers in 1864 at the French press of Bouyer, and the lithographed amulets and calligraphic sheets sold by Boukabza and Bekache. Another mysterious lithograph is a Judeo-Arabic certificate from the Meshibat Nefesh society (founded in Essaouira in 1874 to help provide aid for the sick), recording a charitable donation presented on March 14, 1887—years before any Hebrew press was operating in Morocco.[52] We might suppose that this was printed at a French lithographic press in Essaouira or nearby. How many similar projects have vanished without a trace? These few examples suggest that even without Jewish printing houses, North African Jews turned to lithography to produce Hebrew and Judeo-Arabic ephemera meant to circulate in small numbers.

Even more perplexing are examples of printed ephemera in Hebrew type from contexts where bibliographers have not yet documented the existence of a Jewish press (or even a non-Jewish press that used Hebrew type, such as that of Gregorio Abrines in Tangiers). In some cases, we can surmise that these ephemera were printed elsewhere on commission at a known press. One such example is a blank certificate for recording a charitable donation to the ʿAmalei Torah society in Tunis (founded by Eliyahu Ḥai Burjil), dated 1874.[53] No Hebrew press is known to have operated in Tunis between 1861 and 1880, but the fine letters and typographic ornaments resemble those of Livorno, and Burjil and his circle are known to have worked with Livornese Hebrew presses around this time.[54] It is possible, therefore, that Burjil commissioned these certificates from a colleague who was working in Livorno and had them brought back to be distributed in Tunis.

But other examples of Maghrebi ephemera cannot be so clearly explained. A Judeo-Arabic wedding invitation, printed in green ink, announced the marriage of Shlomo Ben al-Dahan and Zahra Ben al-Dahan in Essaouira on May 27, 1898.[55] Where was this printed? The only Hebrew presses in Morocco known during that period were in Tangiers. Did the Ben al-Dahan family travel to Tangiers (or even farther abroad) to have a hundred or so wedding invitations printed? Another example is a small printed card in Judeo-Arabic that invited the reader to the circumcision of

Nissim al-Siqsiq in Tlemcen on November 11, 1888.[56] There was no known Hebrew press in Tlemcen at that time, and it is hard to imagine Nissim's father traveling all the way to Oran or Algiers during the week of his son's birth to print invitations to the circumcision (and since it includes the date and the child's name, it certainly could not have been prepared before his birth).

And what are we to make of the multilingual stationery of Moroccan merchants, emblazoned with their names and addresses in both Hebrew and Latin type, from the decades before Hebrew presses were operating in most of Morocco?[57] Was this done with Hebrew type found in non-Jewish presses, such as was advertised by Abrines in Tangiers? Or is it possible that there were presses or short-lived printing workshops that produced only ephemera and did not ever print a formal book, and thus have not been recorded in the bibliographies of Maghrebi Jewish printing? Either way, these ephemeral hints make clear that engagement with Hebrew printing extended far beyond the production of Jewish books at Jewish presses.

Adding these examples to the surviving ephemera from known presses in the Maghreb reveals a vibrant landscape of small-scale local printing. These ephemeral sheets and cards were important financial supports that allowed Jewish presses to take risks in printing larger projects, including serialized pamphlets, newspapers, and books, and they attracted customers to the shops and presses that sold them. These printing houses and bookstores carried a wide variety of products that combined imported books and locally produced books, booklets, and journals in Hebrew and Judeo-Arabic, covering literature, science, and history, as well as religious and liturgical texts, ephemera, and other household items. Invitations to weddings and circumcisions, calling cards and personalized stationery, broadsides and community announcements, amulets and alphabet posters: all were part of a culture of printing and reading made possible by the increasing presence of Jewish printing and Jewish presses across North Africa.

LANGUAGE POLITICS AND MAGHREBI JEWISH MODERNITY

In the nineteenth-century Maghreb, perspectives toward language use were complex and constantly shifting. Judeo-Arabic was the vernacular of the common people, and it was also developing a new body of modern literature. While some Maghrebi proponents of the Haskalah saw Hebrew as a language of transnational Jewish unity, others emphasized that Judeo-Arabic, too, could serve as a vehicle toward a Jewish modernity.[58] As the French presence grew stronger, some community leaders began advocating for the use of Judeo-Arabic as an essential element of Jewish identity, one that could reach the masses and bring them back toward the heart of traditional Jewish morality and away from the temptations of secular culture. Others, however, advocated for the universalized Jewish modernity promised by the Hebrew Haskalah movement. The French language was also linked to the power and prestige of European modernity; some Maghrebi Jews, including some of the same individuals who lauded the value of Judeo-Arabic over French, also pursued the social and intellectual advantages that the French language could bring. All of these choices were played out on the pages of the books, journals, and pamphlets produced across the Maghreb during the second half of the nineteenth century. Printers, booksellers, authors, and translators (sometimes all one person!) contributed to a transnational conversation about Jewish modernity, emphasizing the importance of balance between European modernity and traditional Maghrebi society.

Certainly, some who published in Judeo-Arabic did so simply because it was the common vernacular. Shlomo Zarqa and Yehuda Ḍarmon, authors of *Shay la-mora* (Algiers, 1854), explained in their preface that they chose to write the book not in the classical Judeo-Arabic of Sa'adia Gaon or Maimonides but "in the Arabic language spoken in our time, in order to benefit the masses . . .

so that any person whom the Exalted One has not enabled to read books in the Holy Tongue can read this book, and understand much, and take pride in our precious faith. . . . Thus we have written this book in this corrupted Arabic language [*had l-lisan l-'arabi al-meshubash*], so that anyone who reads it can understand it."[59] They apologized for having to work in what they saw as an inferior and corrupted language and one that was regionally specific—unlike the universalizing standard Arabic, for example, that Mikhael Makhluf 'Allun attempted to achieve in *Or ne'erav*, examined in chapter 4. This use of Judeo-Arabic as a regional vernacular continued until the end of the nineteenth century: Bekache declared on the front page of one of his translations: "I have printed these stories in the Arabic language used throughout all the regions of Africa: Algiers, Oran, Constantine, Tunis, Tripoli, and Morocco."[60]

But many writers saw Judeo-Arabic publishing not only as working in the shared language of Maghrebi Jews but also as part of creating a modern Judeo-Arabic-reading public, a project that had begun decades earlier with Maghrebi writers working with Jewish presses in Livorno, as examined in chapter 4. In 1870, Nessim Benisti of Algiers published the first Maghrebi Jewish newspaper, a short-lived bilingual French and Judeo-Arabic journal titled *Adziri (L'Israélite Algérien)*. The paper described itself as "a commercial, industrial, agricultural, maritime, literary, scientific, judicial, and advertising journal," and its first Judeo-Arabic headline declared "Reform, Emancipation, Progress."[61] The Judeo-Arabic language here is promoted as a potential equal to French in expressing the needs of modernity in all of its commercial, industrial, agricultural, maritime, literary, and scientific facets, although its writers still felt its deficiencies when measured against French. Much of the Judeo-Arabic writing in *Adziri* contained transliterated French words, and the editor acknowledged: "We Algerians must be initiated into this path [of modernization] *gradually;* we must first accustom ourselves to understanding some basic ideals in this *Jewish-Arabic* language, which despite being our mother tongue has neither rules of grammar, nor any systematic organization. This is a dialect mixed from Arabic, Hebrew, and French, and until now it has only served for our commercial needs; it is still difficult to express any sort of deep idea with it."[62]

Other Judeo-Arabic writers and publishers felt the need to strengthen the textual presence of Judeo-Arabic not as a gradual evolution toward French but rather as a bulwark against it. The introduction to Mordekhai Seror's collection of stories in Algerian Judeo-Arabic, *Qol sasson* (1884), for example, demonstrates that he was explicitly concerned with changing patterns of readership.

> Our masters of blessed memory said that it is obligatory for everyone to read the Torah according to the state of his knowledge: if he knows [how to read] Mishnah he should read Mishnah, and if he knows Gemara he should read Gemara [cf. BT Sanhedrin 101a].... But because of our many sins, people today do not do this, but now they say, "I do not understand what I am reading, so I will not read." And in order to expand their minds, they buy the books of the stories of the Christians (*Roman*), and the many people who buy the journals do so not to see the news in them, but so that they can read the stories in them (*Feuilleton*).[63]
>
> Therefore I have merited to make this book in Arabic, so that everyone can study the stories of the miracles and wonders that the Holy Blessed One has done for our ancestors in every generation; even if he only learns from it the lesson of fearing the Holy Blessed One, he will still have a good reward from studying them.... Also, it is good in the winter days, when the nights are long, for a man to sit and study these stories with his family, so that all the women too will know the power of the Holy Blessed One.[64]

In other words, the issue is not necessarily with the content of the reading material but with the cultural implications of abandoning Hebrew and Judeo-Arabic in favor of French. Seror's work, including his partnership with Boukabza and Bekache in the development of Judeo-Arabic printing in Algiers, expressed the belief that a Jewish idiom is just as capable as French of articulating modern science, art, and intellectual achievement. In this work, these writers and printers claimed participation in the intellectual and literary modernity of their Francophone peers and yet aimed to transmit it in a purely Jewish idiom.

At the end of 1886, Bekache joined the partnership of Boukabza and Seror, and Bekache's son Yosef Ḥayyim began working with them as an editor and typesetter. By 1890, Bekache had seemingly taken over the press completely. Bekache's press published a weekly Judeo-Arabic periodical, *Beit yisrael* (*Le Peuple d'Israel*), with news from Jewish communities around the world, along with a variety of Judeo-Arabic books, including liturgy and ethics, adapted works of modern science and geography, and translations of stories from Jewish history ranging from local Jewish saints to miracle-working rabbis of eastern Europe. The cover of *Sippurei ha-ṭeva'* (1892), for example, promised "histories[65] of the things which happened in the world in ancient times, and the things of the natural world, which many people do not understand. Anyone who reads this book will take great pleasure . . . and learn many things about nature they did not previously understand, since I have copied them from the books of learned scientists."[66] Like the work he had begun with Benamozegh in Livorno, Bekache's publications in Algeria represent a local articulation of global Jewish solidarity and an attempt to create and promote literature for modern Jewish readers.

As we saw in chapter 4 regarding the work of Benamozegh and Ḥazzan, these writers and publishers attempted to balance their work between a forward-thinking modernism inspired by European models and their emphasis on a local identity rooted in its Jewish, Arabic, and Maghrebi contexts. Their Judeo-Arabic compositions (both original works and translations) on history and geography testify to the wide horizons of interest for Maghrebi Jews and the worldwide scope of their social and political relationships: a diaspora that stretched across the Mediterranean and beyond, and an interest in (and solidarity with) Jewish communities around the world. The variety of literary material, including classical Arabic folktales, original Judeo-Arabic compositions, and translations of literary and scientific works from Hebrew and European languages, demonstrates the cultural vitality of a Judeo-Arabic reading public and their engagement with the cultural questions of the time.

The fact that these same presses—and some of the same writers—also published books of Hebrew and Judeo-Arabic liturgy and halakha and Judeo-Arabic works of morality and Jewish ideology aimed at combating Jewish assimilation and participation in French secular society speaks to the complex position of Maghrebi Jewish thinkers, writers, and printers negotiating their path to a Judeo-Arabic modernity. As Joseph Chetrit writes, "The products of this journalistic and literary effervescence outline an original intellectual adventure . . . adapting [the principles of the Haskalah] to the conditions of their community."[67] The development of this popular, vernacular Judeo-Arabic literature can be seen as an attempt to articulate a vision of modernity—whether in its secular European flavor or the Jewish ideology of the Haskalah—in a distinctly North African form.

By the late nineteenth century, Maghrebi Maskilim, or scholars sympathetic to the Haskalah, could be found in many major North African cities. Bekache, for example, considered himself a participating member of the Haskalah; he subscribed to and occasionally wrote for the European Hebrew journals *Ha-meliṣ, Ha-maggid,* and *Ha-ṣefira,* and his own Judeo-Arabic compositions show that he was deeply interested in the experience of Jewish communities around the world, "to open the minds of his coreligionists to subjects that were not part of traditional Jewish education and to broaden their knowledge of the world around them."[68] At the same time, Bekache was a community rabbi who was invested in traditional Jewish spirituality, as demonstrated by his production of books of piyyutim, liturgical compilations, and even booklets of practical magic.

This is one of the major aspects that distinguishes the form of modernizing Jewish movements like the Haskalah in North Africa from their expression in Europe. Rather than a largely secular and even antireligious movement, the figures in North Africa and the Middle East who promoted the Maskilic ideals of modernization and emancipation were also invested in supporting Jewish communal and religious identity, and they were often religious leaders themselves.[69] Several figures involved in Maghrebi Judeo-Arabic publishing, including Avraham Boukabza, Eli'ezer Farḥi, Ya'aqov Chemla, and Ṣemaḥ Levi, held roles in Jewish religious and communal leadership alongside their commitments to the social and political implications of vernacular and even secular Judeo-Arabic literature.[70] Other Maskilim focused on the universalizing potential of the Hebrew language to bring North African Jews into a global community.

Books, newspapers, and publishing houses played a major role in the Haskalah movement, both in the "heartland" of central Europe and farther abroad.[71] For example, the 1866 membership list of the Mekitze Nirdamim Society, founded in 1861 in the Prussian city of Lyck (today Ełk, Poland), contains some forty-three Maghrebi subscribers who supported the society's mission to publish scholarly editions of medieval Hebrew texts. This book has already discussed several of these members in their roles as scholars, authors, and publishers, including Mimoun Abou in Mostaganem; Moïse Sebaoun, Yehuda Ḍarmon, and Nissim Karsenty in Oran; and others in Tunis and Tangiers.[72] Although these forty-three subscribers made up only 4 percent of the society's membership, they were significant intellectuals and religious leaders in their own communities.

Inspired by groups like Mekitze Nirdamim, Maghrebi Maskilim established similar initiatives that encouraged the shared research, publication, and distribution of Hebrew texts.

In 1865, Algerian scholar and author Yehuda Ḍarmon placed an advertisement in the Hebrew Maskilic newspaper *Ha-maggid* informing "all Jewish booksellers, and especially those in Prussia and Germany, who would like to sell their books to the Jewish communities of Africa" that he would serve as a distributor since he was "very active in selling many books among the Jewish communities here in the lands of Africa."[73] In 1889, Tunisian author and journalist Messaoud Maarech (Mas'ud Ma'arek) published a similar announcement in *Ha-maggid*: "Here in Tunis we have founded a society to open a library where Jewish youth can come to read Jewish newspapers in Hebrew and French," and he asked for the assistance of the readers of *Ha-maggid* in collecting the appropriate journals.[74] In 1890, Haïm Bliah of Tlemcen led an initiative to gather an association of "lovers of the Hebrew language" and create a lending library of Hebrew books and journals.[75] It was also around this time that journalist, translator, and educator Chalom Flah (Shalom Falaḥ, 1855–1936) pioneered modern Hebrew-language education in Tunis, opening a Hebrew school and publishing a series of textbooks that advocated for a Maskilic immersion pedagogy of *Ivrit be-'ivrit* (Hebrew in Hebrew), emphasizing the use of Hebrew as a natural, living language.[76]

As I have observed, these scholars not only consumed the products of European Hebrew presses but also contributed to them: nineteenth-century Hebrew Maskilic journals carried articles and sometimes a regular series of reports from Maghrebi Jews across Morocco, Tunisia, and Algeria.[77] It should be noted that European Maskilim themselves acknowledged their debt to their North African coreligionists in inspiring the project of reviving Hebrew as a living language of Jewish life and literature, in which the Sephardi heritage and even the Sephardi pronunciation took center stage. Eli'ezer Ben-Yehuda, perhaps the most influential advocate of modern Hebrew revival, testified that the Hebrew conversations he participated in during a therapeutic stay in Algiers in 1880 were the source of his belief in the modern possibilities of the Hebrew language: "It was in Algiers that for the first time I spoke Hebrew not for the sake of speaking Hebrew but out of actual necessity. . . . The days that I spent in Algiers bore double blessings. The African sun healed my body, and my Hebrew conversations with the elders of the Israelite community and its scholars improved my Hebrew speech proficiency. . . . Their [Sephardic] pronunciation left a very strong impression on me."[78]

Maghrebi Maskilim also took up the call to recover and publish medieval Hebrew texts, as was discussed in chapter 1. This was the case with Yiṣḥaq Morali's quest for manuscripts of medieval poetry, which culminated in his publication of medieval Sephardi piyyuṭim in the Berlin-based Maskilic journal *Koveṣ 'al yad* in 1897.[79] His colleague in Mostaganem, Haïm Bliah, even published a commentary by fifteenth-century Algerian rabbi Ephraim Ankawa (al-Naqawa) from a manuscript in the Bodleian Library! Bliah, who learned of the manuscript's existence after inquiring of Salomon Buber as to the whereabouts of Ankawa's compositions, requested a photographic facsimile from the librarian of Oxford University to be sent by mail to Mostaganem. He then edited the manuscript for publication in Tunis, and it was released by the press of Uzan and Castro in 1902.[80] These interconnected networks, bringing together scholars in Europe and North Africa, represent an intellectual mapping of what Lital Levy has called the "Global Haskalah."[81]

Perhaps the most significant of these Hebrew-book-based associations in the Maghreb was that of Ḥevrat Dovevei Siftei Yeshenim, "The Society of Moving the Lips of the Sleeping," which was established in Fez in the summer of 1890.[82] Its founder, Refael-Aharon Ben-Shim'on (1847–1928), was born in Morocco and raised in Ottoman Palestine by his father David, a scholar, community activist, and bookseller. In 1891, Ben-Shim'on was appointed chief rabbi of Cairo, where he would serve for the following three decades, which included his famed encounter with

Solomon Schechter during the excavation of the Cairo Geniza in 1896–1897.[83] In 1888 and again in 1890, Ben-Shim'on returned to Morocco as a rabbinic emissary. On his first trip, he encountered a manuscript prayer book of the liturgy of the Jews of Fez, which he immediately urged the community to have printed and which he published the following year in Jerusalem under the title *Ahavat qadmonim*. In his introduction, Ben-Shim'on laments that the lack of printing in Morocco had threatened Jewish intellectual heritage.

> I asked the leaders of the community [in Fez] . . . "why do you not send your manuscripts to be printed in one of the cities of print, in another country? What will you do if this hidden treasure in your hands decays from old age? Will not the heritage of your ancestors thus be lost? This would be an immeasurable loss." They answered me fairly that the art of printing was completely unknown, from one end of the Maghreb to the other, and for other countries, there is no price that could persuade them to accept this work! I therefore vowed to devote myself to this work, with the help of Heaven, and I immediately brought the manuscript to copyists to copy it for me, for it was not in the form needed for printing.[84]

Ben-Shim'on does not blame the lack of Moroccan printing on ignorance of its value or some inherently "Oriental" opposition to its technology; rather, his belief in the historical value of print was shared by the local community, and it was his transnational connections to printing houses in the Ottoman Levant that overcame the financial and geographic barriers that had previously hindered publication. His knowledge of Jewish manuscript culture and his concern for the preservation of its historical value were also central in his choice (in his role as chief rabbi of Cairo) to grant access to the Cairo Genizah for Solomon Schechter. He was not, as portrayed in some accounts, a passive and disinterested traditionalist whom Schechter had to "woo" or even fool to gain access to the Genizah.[85] As Yigal Nizri has argued,

Ben-Shim'on's intellectual oeuvre represents a Maghrebi articulation of the Haskalah, combining "an awareness of new globalized maskilic ideologies and practices . . . a model of organizing local knowledge in light of broader European forms of organized knowledge . . . [and] an act of debt and indebtedness to the local Jewish communities, and to an idea of a shared past."[86] His involvement in the world of Jewish bookmaking and his efforts to promote the value of Maghrebi intellectual and religious history are examples of this commitment.

Upon his return to Morocco in 1890, Ben-Shim'on organized the Dovevei Siftei Yeshenim Society, which was to be devoted to the identification and publication of Moroccan manuscripts, especially works of responsa, liturgy, and sermons. While most of its members were from the city of Fez, its published lists of subscribers show supporters also in Debdou, Meknes, and Tangiers, as well as several in Egypt.[87] Between 1890 and 1903, Ben-Shim'on and the society brought another four works to print in Alexandria, all of which were authored by members of the Abensur family (and they almost certainly originated in the Abensur family library, which will be examined in chap. 6).[88] While the society was rooted in its Maghrebi context—Ben-Shim'on writes at length of the society's connections to the desecration of the Jewish cemetery in Fez in 1888, a flood in Sefrou in 1890, the death of Sultan Mulay al-Ḥassan I in 1894, and, in general, the social and political landscape of Morocco—its members also saw themselves as a learned organization in the international maskilic model.[89]

When another organization, founded in the Austro-Hungarian Empire in 1901, claimed the same name, Ben-Shim'on wrote amicably that "another Society, in the Galician city of Husiatyn, has emerged, and its goal is like the goal of our Society—to publish the hidden treasures of past scholars still in manuscript—and its name is also Dovevei Siftei Yeshenim. . . . As a sign of our joy, several of the leaders of our Society enrolled themselves in the Husiatyn Society as well, to receive their books and pay their annual membership."[90] Describing how the two societies attempted to merge but found the international distance too difficult to bridge, he concluded that "even if our countries are far apart, our hearts embrace one another."[91] The recovery, publication, and circulation of Hebrew books was part of the revival of a national Jewish consciousness, one that could connect (if not fully unite) Jewish communities worldwide. Through their participation in Hebrew modernity, Maghrebi Jews were attempting to articulate their place and their attachment to tradition in the context of a global Judaism.

The French language, however, was making rapid inroads among the Jewish communities of the Maghreb in the second half of the nineteenth century. French merchants and diplomats had maintained a presence in North Africa, along with Italian, Spanish, British, American, and other representatives of imperial powers, for centuries. But the most important European languages for North African Jews, both socially and economically, had been Italian (in Tunisia) and Spanish (in Algeria and northern Morocco). It was only after the French conquest of Algiers in 1830 and the subsequent expansion of French colonialism in the Maghreb over the following century that the French language grew to dominate the linguistic world of Maghrebi Jews.[92]

While the economic and political pull of the French colonial establishment was an important factor in Jewish linguistic Gallicization, the most powerful force in this shift by far was the Franco-Jewish philanthropic organization Alliance Israélite Universelle (AIU). Founded in 1860 by Adolphe Crémieux and a committee of French Jewish intellectuals and politicians, the AIU devoted the majority of its efforts to educating Jews in the Islamic world to participate in French culture and society.[93] Through its educational programs, as Susan Miller writes, the AIU created a cadre of modernizing Francophone Jewish intellectuals—"teachers, journalists, poets, agents for foreign countries, interpreters, and go-betweens whose livelihoods depended on their ability to negotiate across languages and cultures"—and distributed its members throughout North Africa and the Levant.[94]

The AIU's emphasis on education for girls, including the opening of girls' schools in Tetouan in 1868, Tunis in 1882, and Tangiers in 1883, had an especially strong effect on literacy in French among Maghrebi Jewish women.[95] By contrast, there is little direct evidence that Maghrebi Jewish women in this period were literate in Hebrew or Judeo-Arabic. Some Maghrebi Judeo-Arabic books were aimed at women with the expectation that their husbands would buy them and read them aloud in the house. For example, a Judeo-Arabic translation of the household manual *Dat yehudit*, printed in Algiers by Cohen-Solal in 1855 (and reprinted there by Guedj in 1894), instructs its readers "to read these laws at all times, and especially women. But since women do not know how to read, and even many men also do not know the Holy Tongue, we have thought to make these [laws] in the Arabic language, so that every man can have it in their house, and can read it to their household at all times."[96] Many sources of the period emphasize the importance of this nexus of textuality and orality, with families and other mixed-gender groups listening to Judeo-Arabic texts that were read or recited aloud.[97]

In the Judeo-Spanish-speaking areas of northern Morocco, by contrast, there is testimony that some girls were able to read the local Judeo-Spanish dialect (*ḥaketía*). The first edition of *Dat yehudit*, written in *ḥaketía* by Avraham Laredo and Yiṣḥaq Halevi, was intended for women to read themselves—as they write, "since these women cannot read [in the Hebrew language], they have missed many laws, from generation to generation. . . . Therefore women with understanding will merit to read this small book [in *haketía*]"—and its *ḥaketía* introduction was addressed directly to its female readers [*lo'azot*]: "Ladies, daughters of Israel, open your eyes to understanding."[98] The expectation that *Dat yehudit* would be read aloud by husbands to their wives emerged only with its 1855 translation into Algerian Judeo-Arabic. Haïm

Zafrani records that in the late nineteenth century, there were women's reading groups in northern Morocco devoted to the *Me'am lo'ez*, a Judeo-Spanish commentary on the Torah.[99] Zafrani describes these reading groups as meeting regularly on Shabbat afternoons or weeknight evenings, adding that "the copy of the *Me'am lo'ez* that we have in our hands was presented in 1875 to the wife of Haim Pinto, born Gimol Larédo, a gift very appreciated at the time. Like other ladies of her era, she read it fluently and diligently, surrounded by a few friends who liked to learn about Judaism, be informed about specific points of law or custom, or simply listen to the recounting of historical events or wondrous stories."[100]

But for the majority of Jewish women in North Africa, namely, those who spoke Judeo-Arabic, it seems that the education they received in the French schools of the AIU (or, in Algeria, those run directly by the French government) was a transformative factor in creating a reading population of women literate in French. For example, an 1887 advertisement for a Passover Haggadah with French translation published by Abraham Boukabza in Algiers explains: "We have printed a new Haggadah for Passover, translated into French . . . since women are obligated in the reading of the Haggadah, but the women of our time do not know how to read [in the Hebrew alphabet], and so we have done it all in French. . . . We hope that everyone who buys this Haggadah takes great pleasure on the night of seder, whether he understands it all or whether it is his sons or daughters who know how to read in French."[101] Although Maghrebi Jewish women did not publish their own writing until the early twentieth century, when they did, those first literary efforts were in French.[102]

The irresistible pull of the French language spread among almost all sectors of Maghrebi Jewish society. Chalom Flah bemoaned the dominance of French-language education from the Alliance schools in Tunis, writing in 1888:

> The goal [of the AIU school] is only to make our children into complete Frenchmen. . . . Almost all their pedagogical methods have no effect, and the only thing that remains is the French language, in which the students rise higher and higher. Do not blame me, dear reader, saying to yourselves: "How prejudiced he is against the French, for he complains bitterly for students who excel in the French language." I beg you, dear reader, do not accuse me so harshly. I love all languages and peoples, and the spirit of fanaticism has never blown across me: but I also love my own people and language. For I am a Hebrew, I am a Hebrew and I worship the God of Israel! . . . The French language and its literature have filled up all the space of the students' brains, and how could Hebrew reading find favour with them?[103]

Others attempted to reach something of a compromise. Mordekhai Seror, the very same rabbi who had lambasted Algerian Jews for buying French feuilletons in his collection of Judeo-Arabic moralistic stories, *Qol sasson* (Algiers, 1884), published his own French translation of the Passover Haggadah just two years later—his name was Gallicized on the title page as "Martin Seror, rabbin"—and printed in Livorno but sponsored by his Algerian business partner Avraham Boukabza.[104] Of course, the religious content of a Passover Haggadah obviously differs from the secular, non-Jewish temptations of the feuilletons that Seror feared; but Seror's ability to integrate his commitment to traditional Jewish practice, his support of Judeo-Arabic publishing, and the newfound advantages of the French language suggest he saw the possibility of standing in both Jewish and French worlds simultaneously.

The reverse was also true, with some French officials supporting the work of local rabbis and the Judeo-Arabic press. In 1888, Alsatian rabbi Isaac Bloch (1848–1925), who was serving as chief consistory rabbi in Algiers, wrote an approbation for a prayer book of the rite of Algiers with Judeo-Arabic commentary by Eliyahu Ḥai Guedj, praising its importance in "collecting all the customs practiced here in our city, which previously were preserved orally or written haphazardly among some individuals in imperfect and different versions" and urging all Algerian Jews to avail themselves of Guedj's book.[105] The same year, Bloch also published his own book: an academic study of tombstones in the Jewish cemetery of Algiers, *Inscriptions tumulaires des anciens cimetières israélites d'Alger,* which was given a glowing review in the *Revue Africaine* by the president of the Société Historique Algérienne, Henri-Delmas de Grammont.[106] These two books by Guedj and Bloch use different languages, emerged from different sources of knowledge, and represent different approaches to a modern Jewish identity. At the same time, they are linked through the Maghrebi context they emerged from and the shared conversations between the people who made them.

In *Neṣaḥ yisrael,* a collection of moralistic Judeo-Arabic essays printed in Tunis in 1888, the authors glorified a vision of the harmonious integration of "rationality," symbolized by the "living language" of French, and "faith," symbolized by "Israelite knowledge and its language."

> We must raise our children upon the riding-camels of knowledge drawn from two sources, harmoniously composed of "rationality and faith." The basis of that is Israelite knowledge and its language which is a key to every door. . . . Likewise our law does not prohibit us from learning living languages by which our knowledge is perfected, as we see that many authors of the Talmud and some of the [rabbinic] masters among our ancestors knew living languages. Therefore we come to know that rationality and faith are not enemies to one another, but rather they are brothers of a single mother.[107]

Thus the work of educators, writers, and printers was to articulate a modern, integrated Jewish identity that drew on all its roots in Hebrew, Judeo-Arabic, and French, all "brothers of a single mother."[108] This dynamic illustrates the larger social transformation for Jewish communities in colonial North Africa who found themselves increasingly working (and often struggling) to balance their ties to their local Muslim Arab surroundings and their orientation toward France.

Some scholars have suggested that the growth of the Jewish printing industry in North Africa was itself a product of French colonialism. In 1893, Moroccan Jewish historian, AIU educator, and bibliographer David Cazès wrote that "it would have to wait until the establishment of the French Protectorate in Tunisia to see a Hebrew press established in Tunis, publishing many works that had remained until then in manuscript."[109] To be sure, the timeline of Jewish presses in North Africa does follow the general spread of French colonialism: Algeria in the mid-nineteenth century, Tunisia in the late nineteenth century, and Morocco around the turn of the century. And as we have seen, many of the first Jewish presses and printers began their work in collaboration with local French presses. But Jewish printing in North Africa was far from a passive instrument of European colonialism or a tool of Gallicization. The books, booklets, pamphlets, newspapers, and journals that were published in Hebrew and Judeo-Arabic in North Africa in the second half of the nineteenth century testify to the vibrancy of Maghrebi Jewish engagement with their social and political milieu and their active adaptation of the medium of print technology for their various aims.

CONCLUSION: WHITHER THE MAGHREBI JEWISH BOOK?

All these trends and forces continued in the first decades of the twentieth century. The Judeo-Arabic presses of Tunis grew more prolific, but they were soon overtaken by the presses on the Tunisian island of Djerba as it became the center for Hebrew and Judeo-Arabic publishing, beginning with the press established by Djerban rabbi David ʿIdan in 1912.[110] After the First World War, Morocco emerged to dominate the Maghrebi Jewish printing industry, starting with the press of Moshe ʿAmar and Shalom Elbaz in Casablanca in 1919, and followed in quick succession by those of Ephraim Elkeslassy in Marrakech in 1921, Shlomo Ḥadida in Essaouira in 1925, and Mas'ud Cherbit (Sharvit) and 'Amram Ḥazzan in Fez, also in 1925.[111] During the 1920s and 1930s, while Jewish presses continued to operate in Algiers and Oran, other small presses also emerged in Tlemcen, Constantine, and Aïn Beïda.[112] Judeo-Arabic writers across North Africa continued to produce works of journalism, translation, and original literary creativity.[113]

At the same time, however, the power of the French language was overtaking the Jewish communities of the Maghreb. In 1903, Moroccan-born AIU educator Moïse Nahon (1870–1928) lamented the loss of the once-great intellectual life of the Sephardi exiles to North Africa amid the centuries of Jewish deterioration in their Arab environment: "With time, the newcomers degenerated, forgot (except on the banks of the Strait) the Castilian language, adopted the surrounding language and culture."[114] Nahon uses the classic language of French Jewish philanthropy to revive and regenerate the Jewish communities of the Orient whose spiritual and intellectual lives were shriveled under centuries of neglect.[115] He suggests that "one should start by 'Frenchifying' the religion, and chasing Arabic out of the study house and synagogue. Once this evolution has begun, the French rabbi will be welcomed to direct and hasten it."[116] This recommendation, and hundreds of others like it, was part of the ideology that encouraged and supported the adoption of the French language among Maghrebi Jews, along with other cultural symbols like clothing and food.

In 1910, Nahum Slouschz noted that "the Gallicizing process has gone forward rapidly . . . [and] the new generation, industrious and very much alive, is rapidly throwing off the Arab influence . . . [although] most of the older people still cling to their Judeo-Arab literature."[117] French linguist Marcel Cohen, who spent five months in Algiers in 1908–1909, noted a similar disappearance of

Judeo-Arabic texts and speech patterns in favor of French.[118] In some areas, like Tunis, printers began to produce Judeo-Arabic works accompanied by a transliteration in Latin letters, indicating that some Jews were still able to understand Judeo-Arabic but were not comfortable reading it in Hebrew script.[119] Many of the Jewish presses began producing numerous works in French, and the number of Judeo-Arabic publications continued to decline as the number of Maghrebi Jewish intellectuals writing in French increased. Some presses operated well into the twentieth century, although the bulk of their production shifted to French and Hebrew. Tobi mentions Michel Uzan's Judeo-Arabic novel *Bayn ḥuyuṭ tunis*, first published in Tunis in 1926, as an example; it was reprinted by Uzan in 1956 as a French translation, *Entre les murs de Tunis*.[120]

The market for Maghrebi Jewish books was further impacted by the mass departure of Jewish communities from the Maghreb, beginning with the establishment of the State of Israel in 1948 and continuing after the various battles for national independence (concluding for Morocco and Tunisia in 1956, and Algeria in 1962).[121] Some Jewish presses even migrated with Maghrebi Jews to Israel and continued publishing there (such as the Lugassy press, which moved from Casablanca to Jerusalem in the 1950s), although they, too, found it necessary to make the switch to Hebrew. On the whole, the nineteenth-century promise of a modern Judeo-Arabic literary and intellectual world in North Africa was never fully realized.

The movement of North African Jewish communities to Europe, Israel, and North America included books along with people; few, if any, Jewish libraries remain in North Africa today. Now scattered among archives, libraries, and private collections across the world, Maghrebi Jewish books stand today as an essential window into the cultures that produced them. Yosef and Tsivia Tobi describe modern Judeo-Arabic literature as "a mirror of important social and cultural changes taking place in modern times [and] a powerful influence in shaping the spiritual portrait of the North African Jew."[122] Indeed, through both their content and the material processes of their production, these books demonstrate how Jewish communities both shaped and were shaped by their encounter with French colonial policy and society and with the larger processes of emancipation and transformation in European Jewish communities. In chapter 6, I reconstruct the social landscape of Maghrebi Jewish libraries before their dispersal then conclude with a reflection on the continuing power of the Jewish book.

SIX

EARLY MODERN AND MODERN MAGHREBI JEWISH LIBRARIES

INTRODUCTION: TWO LIBRARIES, BOTH ALIKE IN DIGNITY

In 1728, a Jewish scholar in Meknes named Shlomo Tapiero needed some books. He was composing an anthology of the best sermons, commentary, and responsa of Sephardi sages, which he compiled into a manuscript titled *Miqve ha-mayyim*. In the introduction, he describes his research visit to a book collection, which allowed him to gather the material for his anthology: "Let us celebrate my pure-hearted, beloved colleague . . . El'azar Bahlul, who helped me immensely, showing me his entire treasure-house filled with many respected books and codices; I investigated every place that my hands could reach in his palatial chambers, in all the books that he had. He fulfilled my desires etc. and did not withhold from me anything that my soul desired to copy from him."[1]

If we are to call Bahlul's book collection a "library," we must first describe how it differs from other libraries that might be more familiar to us. The library might be imagined as a spectrum of possibilities, from the public holdings of an institutional, municipal, or collegiate library on one end to an individual's collection of books for personal use on the other. In the middle of that spectrum, we would find library configurations that might be termed "semipublic" (collections closed to certain classes of the public, such as women or enslaved people) and others referred to as "semiprivate" or "proprietary" (collections open to all members of a particular group, such as a professional association, guild, or exclusive club).[2] It is these intermediate types of libraries that are most characteristic of scholarly Jewish society in North Africa. This chapter explores the collections of two Maghrebi Jewish bibliophiles, what kinds of books they owned, how they were acquired, and how their libraries were used (and by whom).

As books moved from their places of production into Maghrebi Jewish libraries, they became symbols of intellectual authority and entry points into a global conversation. This chapter looks at the Maghrebi Jewish library in the eighteenth and nineteenth centuries, focusing on two specific libraries that can be reconstructed with some degree of certainty; they share several characteristics but also differ in significant ways to be explored later in this chapter. I argue that the library epitomizes the understanding that has anchored this study: that books, as material and social forms of texts, represent the intersection of individual and communal worlds, the intellectual and the commercial, the private and the public. As Joshua Teplitsky observes regarding the library of David Oppenheim (1664–1736), chief rabbi of Prague from 1703 until his death, we gain an unparalleled window into "premodern Jewish life, politics, and intellectual culture through an exploration of a book collection, the man who assembled it, and the circles of individuals who brought it into being and made use of it."[3] The study of the library as a space that connects the individual collector with a community of readers allows us to see books in the context of their usage: who bought and sold them, who owned and borrowed them, who read and copied them. An examination of North African Jewish libraries reveals a world of books that was globally connected, intellectually vibrant, and culturally distinct.

As described previously, these libraries functioned as semi-public spaces: while they were mainly developed by individuals and held in private family ownership, they were open to scholars, students, and other intellectuals who consulted the books held there, often for many generations in succession. We also know that many individuals gave money to support communal libraries or donated books to that end. An inventory of the library of the "Eṣ Ḥayyim" yeshiva in Tunis, conducted during the first decade of the twentieth century, shows that in addition to the 129 volumes owned by the yeshiva, the library also housed some fifteen private collections belonging to individuals. These were kept in the yeshiva "in order for students to learn from them."[4] In another example, Avraham Ankawa (1810–1890) recorded a halakhic query regarding a pair of scholars who studied in a library sponsored by a wealthy local merchant, who enjoyed the prestige of supporting this scholarly enterprise.

> I was asked by David Buenos-Ombres[5] on the matter of a certain "Reuven" who had a close friendship with a certain "Shimʿon," and they had studied together for many years.[6] Because of the scarcity of books, a certain nobleman from their city was moved to create a *yeshiva* in his home, and bought them many books, and brought Reuven to study there. Reuven attracted many students; but now Reuven and Shimʿon have renewed their bond, and signed a contract that they will each pay a defined sum to buy for themselves a set of the Talmud, and they will return to studying together [independent of this yeshiva], as they did before. When this nobleman heard, he was greatly saddened, for if Reuven were not in his yeshiva, students would not come to fill it. Therefore, many friends of Reuven have urged him to annul his contract [with Shimʿon], and now he has come to ask if it is permitted [to do so].[7]

As we shall see, these were not static collections. They were constantly being expanded and consulted, serving as places of conversation and invitations into the global world of books. Books were borrowed and lent, referenced and corrected, copied and composed. The library was both the repository of textual heritage and the birthplace of new textual creation. One term Maghrebi Jews used for a library during this period was *estudyo,* an adapted borrowing from Spanish or Italian that emphasizes the library's role as a place of study.[8] When Algerian rabbi Ya'aqov Sasportas (1610–1698) discussed the case of a widow in Salé, around 1660, who claimed possession of her husband's library, he ruled that if the books were held "in the area of the house where she lived while her husband was alive," then she could claim them as joint property, but "if the books were kept in a special place by this scholar who would regularly consult them there, and learn Torah, without the widow having any use for that place which we call in our vernacular [*la'az*] the *estudyo,*" then she had no claim to them.[9]

From its meaning as the "special place" where one consulted books, the term came to refer specifically to a collection of books. In an eighteenth-century Italian edition of a medieval Talmudic commentary, printed from a Moroccan manuscript, an unnamed (but probably Moroccan) editor described how the manuscript "came [from Castile] to the city of Fez . . . [and] was kept by the rabbis of the Serero family in their *estudyo.*"[10] Ya'aqov Abensur refers to his library as an *estudyo* in a 1713 letter to his colleague in Sefrou, Avraham 'Abo, describing how he had written a list of his desired books "in the register [of Barukh Toledano], while you were sitting with us in my *estudyo.*"[11] The estudyo was a place of gathering and conversation, a place where books were suspended in the networks of intellectual, commercial, and familial connections among people.

Unfortunately, no Maghrebi Jewish estudyo or book collection from before the twentieth century has yet been found preserved intact.[12] I therefore have used a variety of items, including booklists, catalogs, letters, and "footprints" to reconstruct both the general place of the library in Maghrebi Jewish society and the particular workings of two specific libraries.[13] I have chosen two collections of North African Jewish books, both of which coalesced in the Moroccan city of Fez, notable for its scholarship in both Jewish and Islamic traditions. For each library, I outline what can be reconstructed of its provenance, the scope of its contents, and how it was used. First, I examine the library of the Abensur (Ibn-Ṣur) family, with the core of its collection attributed to Ya'aqov Abensur (1673–1753), sometimes called the Ya'aveṣ. While it was expanded over the following generations, this library is a good example of an early eighteenth-century collection. The second library belonged to the Serfaty (Ha-ṣarfati) family, with its core originating in the book collection of Avner-Yisrael Serfaty (1827–1884); thus, I consider this library a nineteenth-century collection. The differences between the two libraries, discussed toward the end of this chapter, played a large role in the types of books that were found in each one.

JEWISH AND ISLAMIC LIBRARIES IN THE EARLY MODERN WORLD

Jewish libraries in the early modern Islamic world have received little attention to date. The Jewish libraries of medieval Egypt have been well documented, thanks to the Cairo Geniza, as have those of al-Andalus and the late medieval Sephardi world.[14] However, the scholarship on Jewish book culture after the fifteenth century, with few exceptions, has focused on Europe. For example, a number of studies on Jewish libraries in Italy have documented the flourishing culture of book collection and the establishment of community libraries by Jews across the Italian peninsula, termed by one scholar as "the cradle of Jewish libraries."[15] Joshua Teplitsky's pioneering study of David Oppenheim's library demonstrates how Jewish book collecting in early modern Europe served to cultivate scholarly expertise, communal authority, and political influence.[16] The libraries of Western Sephardim in Amsterdam similarly played a central role in what Avriel Bar-Levav has termed "the development of a new stage in Jewish library awareness, and the inception of a Jewish, traditional republic of letters."[17] The development of the Jewish library as a modern institution took hold in Europe, America, and Palestine in the second half of the nineteenth century with the establishment of public collections large and small, many of which form the core of institutional collections to this day.[18] But the Jewish bookshelves of North Africa, while rich in scope, have been left relatively unexplored.

Islamic libraries from the medieval and early modern periods—both those assembled by individuals and those attached to royal courts or religious institutions—provide ample evidence of the vibrancy of local book cultures in North Africa and the Middle East.[19] The analysis of the surviving books of Syrian scholar Aḥmad al-Rabbat (d. ca. 1836), for example, displays similar proportions of genres to the Jewish libraries discussed later in this chapter, and the notes left in the books show an extensive and active readership from both "popular" and "elite" classes of eighteenth- and nineteenth-century Syrian society, including Christian and Jewish readers.[20] However, with rare exceptions (one of which is examined in the later discussion of Serfaty's library), there seems to be little overlap or contact between Jewish and Islamic libraries in North Africa in terms of both their patrons and the books.

It is particularly instructive to compare the Maghrebi Jewish libraries discussed in this chapter with the booklist of Muḥammad b. 'Abd al-Salam Bannani (1671–1750). The list represents a private library established by a Moroccan family of Islamic scholars in Fez over three generations; it is thus both analogous and contemporary to the library of Ya'aqov Abensur.[21] The library was established as a family *waqf* [endowment] by the daughters of Muḥammad Bannani sometime between 1769 and 1775. It was eventually dispersed, and only a fragmentary portion survives in the Qarawiyyin Library in Fez today. At its height, the Bannani library comprised some eighty-three titles (including a number of multitext volumes whose exact contents are unknown), which is considered "a library of a respectable size for the standards of the time."[22] Some of the books, all in manuscript, were acquired in Morocco, others were acquired abroad (especially in Egypt and Mecca), and some were even copied by members of the Bannani family.

The library of Ya'aqov Abensur, Bannani's Jewish neighbor, shares some similarities with the Bannani library: the importance of family inheritance, the centrality of the genres of exegesis and religious law, and the continued vitality of manuscript copying as a source of book production. But there are also significant differences: Abensur's library was much larger and more diverse, and it drew on a wider and broader field of book production, integrating manuscript and print and including works produced not only in the Maghreb and the Ottoman lands but also as far afield as Poland and Lithuania. The library of Avner-Yisrael Serfaty moves even further from this model, exemplifying as it does the transformations in Maghrebi Jewish life in the second half of the nineteenth century and the increasingly distinct social and intellectual spheres for Jews and Muslims in that context.

I should emphasize that these two libraries are neither unique cases nor fully representative of Maghrebi Jewish libraries in general. As in almost every Jewish community around the world, a large library was expected for any rabbi or scholar of high social standing. To find a book collection built up over many generations and including books from a broad range of genres, formats, and places of publication is not at all surprising. At the same time, I do not claim that these two libraries are typical examples of the Jewish encounter with books across North Africa. The particular libraries that examined here were assembled by some of the most prominent and prestigious rabbinic scholars of their time in a major urban center with access to flourishing international networks of trade; these collections were certainly larger and more comprehensive than those of some of their neighbors.[23] They also emerge from the distinctive world of traditional rabbinic scholarship, offering little insight into the reading and book-collecting habits of other Jews, such as merchants, doctors, magicians, or storytellers. But they are what we have, for now. Let us enter the library.

CASE STUDY ONE: THE ABENSUR ESTUDYO

Rabbi Yaʿaqov Abensur (Ibn-Ṣur), hereafter Yaʿaqov I, was born in 1673 in Meknes to a family of distinguished scholars of Sephardi origin.[24] Considered by many to be one of the most influential Moroccan Jewish scholars of the early modern period, Yaʿaqov I was a renowned *dayyan* [jurist], halakhic authority, poet, and Talmudic scholar. As a young man, he moved to Fez, where he spent most of his life, with sojourns in Meknes and Tetouan. He began his career as a scribe and notary [*sofer*] for the rabbinic court, and over the course of his life, he assembled his letters and legal documents into a collection of epistolary models he titled *Leshon limmudim* and a manual of scribal formularies titled *ʿEṭ sofer*, both of which circulated widely in manuscript. Only one of his children survived past the age of twenty-five, his son Refael-ʿOved Abensur (1706–1769). In the following generations, however, the Abensur family flourished and continued to serve as spiritual leaders until the mid-twentieth century.

The library of the Abensur family appears to have been largely accumulated in two stages: first, the core of the collection was assembled around 1700–1750 by Yaʿaqov I Abensur and his son. It seems to have been essentially preserved in the family for the next century and then was actively reorganized (with both additions and removals) in the second half of the nineteenth century by Yaʿaqov I's great-great-grandson Shlomo-Eliyahu Abensur, and then his cousins Shlomo I and Refael II Abensur. Many books bear ownership marks and stamps from several different Abensurs, as well as other owners and readers, although it is not always clear when a specific book entered the collection—or whether clear boundaries can be established between "the Abensur library" and the books that circulated among Moroccan Jewish scholars and intellectuals of the period.

While Ya'aqov I was renowned as a bibliophile, no catalog or booklist survives from his library, and it is difficult to estimate its full extent at any point in its history. Several letters and documents reference a *pinqas* [register], which seems to have included both a list of books currently in the library and desired titles, but no such register has been located.[25] Gathering the scraps of available documentary evidence, I compiled a list of over 150 specific titles known to have been held in the library at some point. For comparison, Yitzhak Zuzot published a list of some 182 books cited directly by Refael Berdugo of Meknes (1747–1821), which Zuzot believed were likely in Berdugo's library.[26] But these numbers are a conservative estimate and represent only the very lower limit of the collection, probably a quarter or less of its true size. Moroccan-born scholar Yosef Messas (1892–1974) recalled his visits in the early twentieth century to the library of the Serero family in Fez, which he claimed "contained 2400 books, manuscripts of medieval scholars, full of wisdom—all burnt in 1912 by the armies of [Sultan] Abd al-Hafid."[27] Even if this report is slightly exaggerated, recall that the library of Moïse Sebaoun (discussed in the introduction to this book) comprised somewhere between 1500 and 5000 volumes. If the same is true for the Abensur library, we are left with a record of barely a tenth of its original size.

Some of the oldest books in the collection were likely inherited from Ya'aqov I's ancestors and possibly even carried from Spain by their oldest-known patriarch (according to family legend), a fifteenth-century Iberian scholar named Moshe-Avraham

Abensur. Other books were added to the family library over the sixteenth and seventeenth centuries; in a copy of the Mishnah printed in Riva di Trento in 1559, for example, Ya'aqov I inscribed that it was "purchased by my father of blessed memory here in Fez [in] 1683" when Ya'aqov I was ten years old.[28] Ya'aqov I also mentions owning a manuscript codex of his father's sermons, written before his father's premature death in 1684.[29] Shortly afterward, it appears that Ya'aqov I was already involved in the world of books: he copied a manuscript of Yehuda Ibn-Attar's *Minḥat yehuda* in 1687 at the age of fourteen.[30]

Copying continued to serve Ya'aqov I throughout his life as a tool for expanding his access to books, a tendency no doubt strengthened by his work as a scribe and notary. In 1693, Ya'aqov I began copying a collection of the *taqqanot* [community ordinances] of the Castilian exiles in Fez, explaining that "since the Lord has brought into my hands booklets [*qundrisim*] of the *taqqanot* of the sages [of that generation], the exiles from Castile . . . and as I saw that little by little, they were being lost to the ravages of time, I spurred myself to copy them into a [new] book, on fine and strong paper, in clear script, so that they may last for many years."[31] In 1719, Ya'aqov I wrote in a manuscript colophon that he had not brought his copy of this book when he moved to Meknes but had "left it with the majority of my books in my library [estudyo] in Fez," and therefore had written out another copy "to use in a time of need."[32] Another time, he wrote that while journeying to Meknes, he "happened upon a printed book called *Qilorit la-'ayin* [by Shlomo al-Gazi, printed in İzmir in 1660], and seeing this booklet in print, I desired greatly to copy it for myself . . . but I feared lest my caravan return to my home in Fez without my being able to copy it fully . . . so I decided to copy some parts and omit some parts," although, as he records, his caravan was delayed through a miracle, and he was able to finish the copying.[33]

Manuscripts were also commissioned specifically by Ya'aqov I and members of his family. In one manuscript, Ya'aqov I left a note to "compare [this] to the book *Oṣrot Ḥayyim* which was copied for me in Tetouan."[34] In a letter (discussed in chap. 2) to the *shadar* Moshe Yisrael of Safed, who was in Tunis at the time, Ya'aqov I gave detailed instructions for copies that he requested of two Kabbalistic works, including asking for the names and family lineage of the scribes.[35] One surviving manuscript of the Abensur library, a copy of the Kabbalistic commentary of Meir Poppers, was written by David Serfaty on behalf of Ya'aqov I's son Reuven Abensur (1717–1742) and was "copied for the price of 12 *perutot*[36] per every four leaves."[37] Ya'aqov I's other son Refael-'Oved also copied a large number of books both for his father and for himself, which subsequently entered the library.[38]

Ya'aqov I was known as a great collector, acquiring books in what one scholar has called "an almost obsessive fashion."[39] Many of his surviving books are marked with notations indicating that he had acquired them from the estate [*'izavon*] of other scholars or from the inheritors of a deceased colleague.[40] He also purchased books from sellers in other regions and asked colleagues to acquire books for him. One of his contemporaries, Shmuel De Avila, wrote to him from Jerusalem to complain that "from the day I arrived here from the city of Salé, the booksellers have been sending me letters asking for the money [owed them] for the books [I purchased for you], and it has been already a month and a half that I have paid these debts from my own pocket.... Therefore, when this letter arrives, please give me the required sums."[41] In a letter to a Moroccan colleague, Ya'aqov I described with great drama and literary flourish his disappointment when an edition of Yoel Sirkis's *Bayyit ḥadash* arrived missing one of the promised four volumes.

> I recently purchased the book *Bayyit ḥadash* from [you], Avraham Halevi Ibn-Safet, but you sent me only three [of its] volumes.... These recent days have been filled with pain: I have been wondering, shouting, languishing, shrivelling, yearning to see [the fourth volume]! My eyes are lifted in hope but I have

> not seen it until now. . . . And the three volumes sit together in my house, and the [fourth] one alone is left by itself. . . . Each one of the three volumes is worrying, crying like a bird caught in a trap, calling out, "I seek my brother!" I despair of nourishment and cannot eat. . . . Only this would comfort me: how good and pleasant it would be for brothers to dwell together! . . . Therefore, please hurry to quickly open the gates of "Ingathering the Exiles" for us, without delay or deferral, and send [the book] to satisfy our desire.[42]

We can only hope that the fourth volume was able to join its siblings in the library nest. Another time, Ya'aqov I lost a volume of *Leḥem setarim* (perhaps by lending it out) and was so distressed that he wrote to his colleagues in Meknes and Sefrou with a lengthy description of the book, asking them to "please make an announcement about it in the synagogues" in the hopes that it might be returned to him.[43]

Ya'aqov I acquired numerous books from relatives and colleagues in other areas, including parts of Morocco, Algeria, Tunisia, Egypt, and especially Ottoman Palestine. To his nephew in Salé, he wrote that he had heard a rumor "that this book [*Knesset ha-gedola*] has been bundled together with its other parts, destined to be sold all together: please hurry to purchase them for me!"[44] The movement of traveling *shadarim*—emissaries of the Holy Land sent to Diaspora communities to raise funds for the Jewish people of Ottoman Palestine—was a primary network for the circulation of books from Europe and the eastern Mediterranean into the Maghreb for generations of North African scholars.[45] A letter from one *shadar* from Jerusalem, Yom-Tov Krispo (Crespo), described his search for books on Ya'aqov I's behalf.

> I am now on my way to Alexandria via Tunis, one leg on land and one in the sea. From my great desire to serve this holy mission, I have been searching for new books since I passed through Algiers, although I did not find any. But just now, God brought to my hand the responsa of [Yoel Sirkis], and also the book *Ginnat*

> *veradim* of the rabbi Avraham Halevi. I purchased both of them for two and a half *riyal*. . . . They should reach you by the hand of the emissary Ḥayyim Ya'aqov, and with God's help I will send [whatever else] comes to my hands through another trustworthy traveller. October 28, 1721.[46]

Indeed, Ḥayyim Yaaqov is mentioned in one of Ya'aqov I's responsa as having brought books from Jerusalem for him to consult.[47] Krispo also purchased a third book for Ya'aqov I on his journey, namely, the second volume of Hayyim Benveniste's commentary on the Shulhan 'arukh (printed in Constantinople in 1717), which he inscribed: "I bought this on behalf of the outstanding scholar, Ya'aqov Abensur, for the price of one and a half *uqiyya,* here in Alexandria, July 10, 1722."[48] In a letter to *shadar* Moshe Yisrael, Ya'aqov I described how he had advanced money for book purchases to his colleague Barukh Toledano, and with Toledano's recent death, he wished to have the money redistributed accordingly. He counseled Yisrael that "since this [money] was sent for the performance of a commandment, namely the buying of books, and especially since [these books] are not to be found in all the Maghreb . . . therefore when you reach Egypt, you may open the letter I sent to Barukh Toledano, and [use the money] to buy for me the books described in it."[49]

While limited information is available about the range of book prices, it seems that older and larger books were generally more expensive, at least in this period. On the flyleaf of one sixteenth-century printed book in his library, Ya'aqov I indicated that he purchased it for forty uqiyya, and the 1559 Mishnah mentioned earlier was purchased by his father for fifty uqiyya.[50] Ya'aqov I sent twenty-six uqiyya to Meir De Avila for "a valuable book, more precious than gems."[51] Meanwhile, the manuscript his son commissioned came to only three and a half uqiyya, and the new printed book purchased by Krispo in Alexandria was one and a half uqiyya, while the other two books he bought for Ya'aqov I were two and a half *riyal,* or twenty-five uqiyya each. To a colleague in Algiers, Ya'aqov I sent four riyal to purchase nine books, writing that "if that is not sufficient, loan the remainder to me and I will pay it."[52] More research may be able to link these book prices with other data to assess the position of books within the larger mercantile economy of early modern North Africa.

Little is known about the immediate fate of the library in the decades after the death of Refael-'Oved Abensur in 1769, although it was surely maintained by the family in Fez. The library entered its second major phase in the mid-nineteenth century when it was managed by Shlomo-Eliyahu Abensur (1822–1873), his cousin Shlomo I Abensur (1805–1843), and Shlomo I's son Refael II Abensur (1830–1917). Many letters addressed to these Abensurs regarding books and the Abensur library have survived, spanning some fifty years in the middle of the nineteenth century.[53] These letters demonstrate that the library was actively being expanded during this period, particularly through the purchase of new printed books from abroad, while also being culled at the same time, as we shall see.

One of Shlomo I's frequent correspondents was Shmuel Halevi Ibn-Yuli, who acted as a kind of book scout for the Abensur library; he was also involved in book collecting, especially manuscripts, and he published a biblical commentary in Livorno from a medieval manuscript.[54] In the 1860s–1880s, Refael II Abensur acquired many books from sellers in Jerusalem, including a certain Yosef Sassoon and especially David Ben-Shim'on (1826–1879), a Moroccan educator and scholar who went by the pen name Ṣuf Devash ("Honeycomb").[55] These letters indicate that the books were to be sent from Jerusalem to Gibraltar and imported from there to Morocco, and they named a variety of family members and colleagues who were to transport them. From this correspondence, and its frequent discussion of prices, it is obvious that the Abensurs and their network of scholars and booksellers paid careful attention to the value of books and their fluctuating market.

While the main focus of the Abensur collection seems to have been on rabbinic scholarship related to the Bible and Talmud, occasional mention is made of works outside those traditional genres. In a letter from 1829, for example, Ibn-Yuli offers Shlomo I a copy of Pinhas Eliyahu Hurwitz's scientific encyclopedia *Sefer ha-brit,* first published in 1797, calling it "a wonderful book about all matters of plants and rocks, birds and animals, and the climate."[56] It seems that Shlomo I took him up on this offer because, in the following letter, Ibn-Yuli mentions that Meir Toledano would be bringing *Sefer ha-brit,* along with a manuscript of Yehoshua Ibn-Shu'aib's commentary. The scope of the library, however, especially in its earlier years, seems to have been focused largely on the main genres of medieval and early modern rabbinic literature.

It was especially rich in medieval and early modern books: as described in chapter 1, dozens of medieval manuscripts and at least three or four incunabula can be traced to the Abensur collection.[57] Combining the various titles mentioned in letters and lists and the surviving volumes of the Abensur library—including some thirty printed books and manuscripts currently in the Lubavitch-Schneerson Collection and forty-nine manuscripts from the Abensur library purchased in Fez by David Klagsbald in the 1960s—reveals a library rich in biblical and Talmudic exegesis, halakhic literature (including many manuscript volumes of the responsa of Moroccan rabbis), and philosophy and Kabbalah, spanning some five centuries of Jewish textual creativity.[58]

As noted previously, the Abensur collection was a site of active learning and use. Many of the surviving Abensur books carry extensive annotations, often from multiple generations of users. Ya'aqov I was known for filling the margins of his books with notes, and, in one *haskama,* he begged printers "not to print books on paper that is weak and soft, such that when one comes to fix a mistake in pen, or to add some note or comment on the book in ink . . . the ink spreads out in all directions and bleeds through to the other side. . . . My advice is to print on clean white paper, strong and sturdy, so that it will last for a long time and anyone will be able to correct its errors and write notes in its margins."[59] In one case, Ya'aqov I inserted an entire blank quire at the beginning of a manuscript book for his reference, explaining that these notes related to "the manuscript I own, copied by the scholar Yosef Gabison of blessed memory; but I did not dare to write my own notes in the margins of that book, since I feel myself to be insufficiently learned in these serious matters."[60] Ya'aqov I also prepared freestanding indexes to his books; at least one such manuscript has survived, comprising his index for *Midrash shmuel*, Shmuel de Uçeda's commentary on *Pirqei avot* (Venice, 1585).[61]

This activity enhanced the library's function as a resource for Ya'aqov I in preparing his scholarship, homiletics, and legal judgments. As described in chapter 1, he annotated his copy of the 1661 Leusden-Athias Bible "with precious comments regarding the masora" from a fifteenth-century Iberian ḥumash apparently copied by Moshe Ibn-Zabara in Castile, and this was not a unique case. In one of his responsa, he explains that "I checked [a particular reading] in the responsa of Asher b. Yeḥiel both in a printed edition and in a manuscript . . . and I found that the text [in the manuscript] has a variant reading."[62] A surviving manuscript miscellany of eulogies, sermons, and exegetical commentaries, written by Ya'aqov I during the 1690s, includes a wide variety of material copied from other manuscripts and printed books: the books *Shtei yadot* (Venice, 1618) by Menahem Lonzano and *Urim veha-tummim* (Amsterdam, 1653) by Avraham-Aharon Bacharach, "the booklets" [*qundrisim*] of Hiyya Dayyan, a *shadar* from Jerusalem, and even several texts labeled "I found this written [in another manuscript] but I do not know the author."[63] These excerpts are frequently labeled or annotated for Ya'aqov I's use, for example, as passages appropriate for the eulogy of an elder or a rabbi's wife, a blessing at a circumcision, or sermons on the weekly parashah.

Other users of the library similarly took up their pens to add their voices to the textual conversation, often literally. For example, in a copy of a manuscript of *Minḥat qana'ut*, Yona Bahlul's defense of Maimonides (which was owned by the Abensur family), one of its readers corrected the meter of some of the poems and drafted suggested verses in the margins.[64] A sixteenth-century manuscript of Shlomo Ibn-Adret from the Abensur library (discussed in chap. 1) contains numerous eighteenth- and nineteenth-century marginalia comparing its text to printed editions of Ibn-Adret's responsa and other books.[65] Through these notated pages, the users of the library took an active role in the textual conversation, offering corrections and additions, cross-references to other books, and commentary on the contents.

This conversation also extended beyond the library itself. Letters exchanged among scholars frequently reference books found in their colleagues' libraries or ask whether particular titles are to be found there.[66] Chapter 2 discussed the process of commissioning a manuscript, such as Yehuda Ḍarmon's request of Shlomo-Eliyahu Abensur to locate and copy for him the Judeo-Arabic chronicle of *Divrei ha-yamim*.[67] In another letter, Moshe Ben-Hamou of Sefrou (ca. 1620–1707) wrote to his colleague in Fez, Menahem I Serero (ca. 1628–1701), asking him to ask a certain Yehoshua'—presumably Menahem I's son, Yehoshua' I Serero (1670–1740)—"to please check in his library [*al-estudyo*], may God expand it, to see if he can find a copy of the tractate *Niddah*; even if it is an old one, please send it to me, for one of my students has borrowed mine, and I also lent out the two others I had with me."[68] He explained that he taught a group of some twenty students who met nightly, and, "therefore, I hope your grace will extend to send me [a copy of] the Gemara of the tractate *Niddah*."

Tapiero's account of Bahlul's library, which began this chapter, emphasizes its function as a place of active research, and Bahlul traveled to Fez several times to consult the libraries of his colleagues there, almost certainly including the Abensur library: "I was in the city of Fez twice or three times, in 1710 and 1712, and I searched in the heaps of books of previous scholars... and I did not restrain myself from copying everything I heard and saw and found, each and every day."[69] His description of copying everything that he "heard and saw and found" suggests that his research included conversations and collaborative research. Libraries served not only as sites of individual reading but also as places of encounter, discussion, and expansion.

The books of the Abensur library, like other collections, were lent out both for reading and for scholars to create their own copies from them. In the colophon to a manuscript copy of *Minḥat yehuda* from 1708, Bahlul acknowledged that "this book was written and copied through the generosity of my dear colleague Ya'aqov Abensur, who showed me grace and favor by placing this book in my hands," and he apologized that it took him so long to copy it.[70] Three years later, according to a record in the court register of Fez, Bahlul formally pledged to return four books he had borrowed from Yehoshua' I Serero (1670–1740) to copy. Perhaps thinking of Bahlul's tardiness in copying *Minḥat yehuda,* Serero indicates explicitly that the books are expected to be returned promptly within the next two months.[71] After Ya'aqov I's death, a group of rabbis from Tetouan wrote a letter of condolence to his son, concluding with a postscript asking what to do "regarding the matter of the books [of your father's] which are stored with me" and if they should be returned to Refael-'Oved.[72] Several Maghrebi manuscripts preserve lists of books lent out, with the names of their borrowers to be crossed out once the books were returned.[73]

In some cases, even individual quires of the books could be removed if only particular sections were of interest. In a manuscript from the Serero family library, a note on the first page indicates that "Barukh Toledano [1738–1817] borrowed one quire [*qunṭres*] from the end of this book, and when he returns it, he will return it to its proper place, with God's help."[74] In the mid-nineteenth century, Ibn-Yuli wrote to Shlomo I Abensur to inform him that a certain Eliyahu Azrad would be returning *Sefer ha-malkhut*[75] to the Abensur library and that "there are some six small leaves [of Azrad's notes] placed within the book," which he hoped could be returned.[76] The boundaries of the library were thus expanded through the movement of books, in whole and in part, among communities of readers. Books were taken apart and put back together, borrowed and returned, copied and recopied. Books begat more books in the context of communal use, which involved reading, writing, learning, and teaching.

At the same time, improper use of the library's liberal borrowing policies was a concern. Ya'aqov I Abensur wrote to Meir De Avila asking him to bring him a new book in stealth, explaining that "since in this area, when people find out that a scholar has some new book, they immediately come to borrow it, great and small, and soon it is torn into twelve pieces and its quires are scattered about. Therefore please bring it to me with the greatest secrecy!"[77] Similarly, amid a controversy regarding Shmuel De Avila's book *Keter torah* (Amsterdam: Proops, 1725), Ya'aqov I counseled Yehuda Ibn-Attar that "if they ask you [to borrow this book]," he should tell them that he had "only one or two copies, and that they have already been put away," so that the controversy would not spread.[78] In another instance from the nineteenth century, Ibn-Yuli discreetly informed Shlomo I Abensur that a certain manuscript had been taken from the Abensur library "around a year ago" without permission and that he himself would take the blame until it was safely returned.

> The person who took it adjured me severely and made me swear that I would not reveal the matter until he had finished copying it, and that then he would give it to me to return it to its place without disturbance. He swore that he had only borrowed it with the intention of returning it when he had finished copying it, and that it should not be thought that he had stolen it. . . . Furthermore, I ask that you not reveal this to anyone, especially your

> uncle [Ya'aqov II Abensur], and that if he asks you [where the manuscript is], tell him that I had borrowed it and that you had forgotten that you lent it to me. . . . And please, for the sake of our friendship, burn this letter once it has arrived.[79]

The correspondence of Ibn-Yuli, whom we know to have been an antiquarian and scholar of medieval manuscripts, shows that he frequently availed himself of the historical resources of the Abensur collection. In 1836, he wrote to Shlomo I, asking

> whether you have, in the collection of all your precious treasures, a copy of the Gemara of the tractate *Kallah*, for I now have found an old manuscript, written on parchment, containing several texts—some already printed, and some only in manuscript—and among them is the Gemara of the tractate *Kallah*, and I have found that it has some textual variants, some inclusions and deletions, and therefore I ask you that if you have [a copy] to please send it to me as soon as possible. . . . I have already heard a rumour that this Gemara was to be found in manuscript among [the books of] Immanu'el Serero.[80]

And again, later that same year, Ibn-Yuli requested Shlomo I "to inform me whether you have any commentaries on the Talmud from the *rishonim*[81] in manuscript, such as Avraham b. David, or Moshe b. Naḥman, or Shlomo Ibn-Adret . . . for I now have an old manuscript from them in my hand, and it is deficient in many places."[82] Thus the Abensur library served not only as a repository but also as a laboratory for the modern work of textual criticism, checking manuscripts against each other and determining the compositional history of a text.

The Abensur library played an active role as a hub of scholarship for over two centuries. There was likely a continued association between the library and Ya'aqov I for many years: in 1824, Ḥabib Toledano consulted a sixteenth-century Kabbalistic manuscript and noted on its flyleaf that he had found it "in the library [*estudyo*] of the Ya'aveṣ of blessed memory."[83] In the second half of the nineteenth century, as we have seen,

Shlomo-Eliyahu Abensur and his cousin Shlomo I Abensur took responsibility for the library and expanded it through numerous acquisitions. Shlomo I's son Refael II Abensur (1830–1917) and grandson Shlomo II Abensur (1859–1941) followed in his footsteps, and many of the surviving books from the Abensur library bear their personal stamp imprints.[84] Yosef Bennaim recorded that Refael II "would collect and gather many books of Torah, in addition to those he inherited from his family. . . . He did not ignore even a single manuscript leaf, but would gather dispersed leaves and bind them into volumes; at the time of his death he left behind many such volumes."[85] Two volumes of ephemera collected by Refael II are currently in the National Library of Israel, one bearing the notation "[Volume] No. Sixteen, containing 280 leaves" on the inside flyleaf in Refael II's hand.[86] Their diverse contents, which range from letters, homilies, and legal records to amulets, calendrical charts, and even quires from other books, demonstrate the flexibility of what might be considered a "book" for the Abensur library and also testify to the value these documents held for generations of the Abensur family and their colleagues.

It was also during this period, however, that books began to leave the library permanently. A sixteenth-century mahzor of the Fez rite bears an ownership inscription from Ya'aqov I Abensur, but it also features an ornamental title page added by Shmuel b. Yisrael-Ya'aqov Serfaty (ca. 1790–1885), so it probably left the Abensur collection sometime during the early nineteenth century.[87] Chapter 1 examined the 1841 sale of twenty-nine manuscripts and early printed books to Eli'ezer Ashkenazi, approved by Shlomo-Eliyahu Abensur. Sometime in the early twentieth century, another large group of manuscripts and early printed books from the Abensur library was sold to Sephardi scholar and collector Ariel Bension (1880–1932), presumably by Shlomo II Abensur (1859–1941).[88] It was also around this time that the two dozen printed books of the Abensur library in the

Figure 6.1a *Left*: Stamp of Shlomo (Salamon) II Abensur (1859–1941). Gross Family Collection 041.002.001, photograph by Ardon Bar-Hama, used with permission.

Lubavitch-Schneerson Collection were acquired, as several of them carry the library stamp of Refael II.

In his biobibliographical encyclopedia *Malkhei rabbanan* (Jerusalem: Ha-ma'arav Press, 1931), Moroccan scholar Yosef Bennaim (1882–1951) refers respectfully to the Abensur library and indicates in several places that it contained many valuable books and manuscripts that he had consulted or hoped to consult.[89] By his time, however, the library Finally, in depleted of some of its greatest treasures. Finally, in 1967, Shlomo II Abensur's children sold forty-nine manuscripts to Polish-Dutch scholar David Klagsbald and his son Victor. The remainder of the books seem to have been dispersed into private hands, and books and documents from the Abensur library continue to surface at auctions.[90] For over two centuries, the estudyo of the

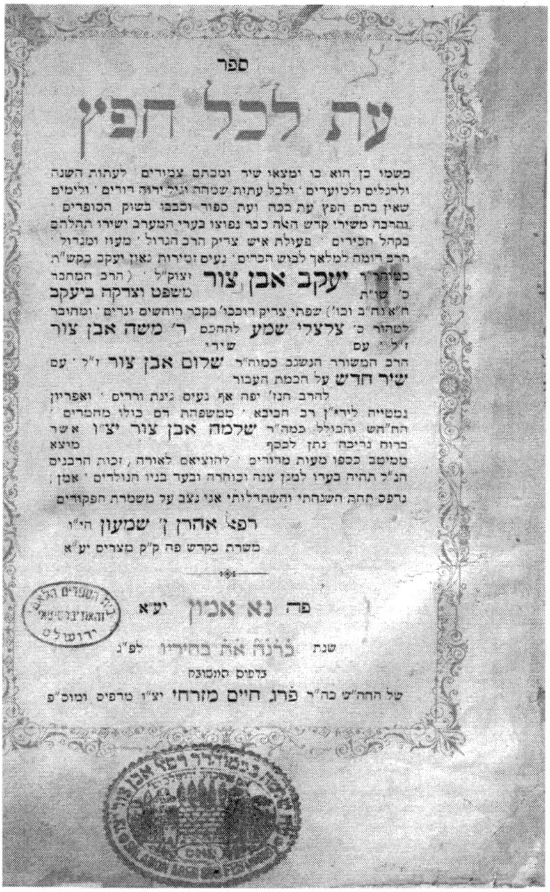

ספר

עת לכל חפץ

כשמו כן הוא כו ימצאו שיר ומכתם צמורים לעתות השנה
ולרגלים ולמועדים ולכל עתות שמחה וגיל ירגה דודים ולימים
שאין בהם חפץ עת בכה ועת ספוד וכבבו בשוק הסופרים
והרבה משירי קדש האלה כבר נפוצו בערי המערב ישירו תהלתם
בקהל חסידים פעולת איש צדיק הרב הגדול מעוז ומגדול
הרב רומה למלאך לבוש הבדים נעים זמירות גאון יעקב בקש"ת
כמוהר"ר יעקב אבן צור וצוק"ל (הרב המחבר
כ' שו"ת משפט וצדקה ביעקב
ח"א נח"ב וכו') שפתי צדיק רוכבו בקבר רוחשים וגרים ומחובר
לטהור כ' צלצלי שמע להחכם ר' משה אבן צור
ז"ל עם שירי
הרב המשורר הנשגב כמוה"ר שלום אבן צור ז"ל עם
שיר חדש על חכמת העבור
להרב הנז' יפה אף נעים גינת ורדים ואפריון
נמטייה לידי"ן רב חביבא ממשפחת רם כולו מחמדים
החו"ש והכולל כמה"ר שלמה אבן צור יצ"ו אשר
ברוח נדיבה נתן לכסף מוצא
ממיטב כספו מעות מרובים להוציאם לאורה, זכות הרבנים
הנ"ל תהיה בעדו למגן צנה וסוחרה ובעד בניו הנולדים אמן;
נדפס תחת השגחתי והשתדלותי אני נצב על משמרת הפקודים
רפאל אהרן ן' שמעון הי"ו
משרת בקדש פה ק"ק מצרים יע"א

פה נא אמון יע"א
שנת ברנה את בחיריו לפ"ג
בדפוס המשובח
של החה"ש כה"ר פרג חיים מזרחי יצ"ו מדפיס ומוכ"ס

Figure 6.1b *Right: 'Et le-khol ḥefeṣ* (Alexandria: Farag Mizrahi, 1893), with stamp of Shlomo (Salamon) II Abensur. NLI R.1025 (formerly Valmadonna 9483).

Abensur family had been a meeting place for rabbis and scholars, students and teachers, scribes and booksellers. It provided a space where books were collected, interpreted, and produced. Bringing together books from across the Jewish world, from medieval manuscripts to the latest printed volumes, the Abensur library demonstrates the vibrancy of Jewish book culture that was available in a Maghrebi library.

CASE STUDY TWO: THE SERFATY COLLECTION AND *YAḤAS FES* (1879)

The second library this chapter examines is the collection of the Serfaty family of Fez, focusing on the books of Avner-Yisrael Serfaty (1827–1884), hereafter Avner-Yisrael I.[91] This library, like that of the Abensur family, has not survived in its entirety and therefore must be reconstructed through other means. As we shall see, it shares some significant characteristics with the Abensur collection while bringing to light the changing dynamics of Jewish book culture and Maghrebi Jewish intellectuals in the second half of the nineteenth century. Because this library reflects the unique character of its collector, we must first consider the life and times of Avner-Yisrael I and how his intellectual interests shaped the books he owned, read, and wrote.

Avner-Yisrael I Serfaty was a member of an illustrious rabbinic family that, like the Abensurs, Berdugos, Sereros, and so many of his colleagues, traced its ancestry to medieval Spain.[92] He served as the chief rabbi of Fez and head of its rabbinic court for decades and was considered one of the leading scholars of the city, well respected by Jews, Muslims, and Christians alike. He advocated on behalf of the Jewish community with the Makhzan and Muslim authorities when necessary, as when, in 1877, for example, Sultan Moulay Hassan I attempted to appropriate a plot of land belonging to the Jewish cemetery of Fez.[93] A few years later, he appealed to the British ambassador to Morocco, Sir John Hay Drummond Hay, to intercede with the sultan and abolish the requirement that Jews must go barefoot outside the *mellaḥ*.[94] French Catholic geographer Charles de Foucauld, who generally held a low opinion of Moroccan Jews, grudgingly conceded that Avner-Yisrael I was "an example of virtue. . . . He was, even in the eyes of Muslims, one of the most honest men of his time. But these models are scarce, and rarely imitated."[95] Avner-Yisrael I promoted the work of the Alliance Israélite Universelle (AIU), which established a boys' school in Fez under the leadership of Shlomo Benoliel in 1883; Avner-Yisrael I's son Vidal V continued to lend his support to the AIU school.[96]

In addition to his roles as a rabbinic authority and community leader, Avner-Yisrael I was also a scholar who engaged deeply with a number of "secular" sciences, including history, geography, and astronomy as well as the literature of the Haskalah (as we shall see from his books), even if he may not have considered himself a Maskil. Bennaim described him in 1931 as "a great and famous scholar, who cultivated the knowledge of all schools of wisdom; he excelled in every wisdom and science which he investigated, not merely skimming it superficially but delving into its depths," adding that "on occasion he even debated matters of philosophy with Islamic scholars, who were impressed by the scope of his knowledge" (and indeed, Serfaty's contacts with his Muslim colleagues are discussed later in this chapter).[97] Serfaty's most important scholarly contribution is probably *Yaḥas fes,* a historical study of the Jewish community of Fez, which he wrote in 1879. Colette Zytnicki describes it as "a bridge between ancient memorial traditions, rabbinic genealogies, and modern intellectual curiosity."[98] Interestingly, Serfaty chose not to publish *Yaḥas fes* in print but circulated it in manuscript—three copies in his hand as well as half a dozen copies from the late nineteenth and early twentieth centuries survive.[99]

A glowing obituary notice for Avner-Yisrael I in the Anglo-Jewish newspaper the *Jewish Chronicle* claimed that "with his enlightened and penetrating mind, he combined a love of benevolence and a probity which won for him all hearts. . . . Mahomedans rivalled Jews in the deference they paid him, and it was not rare to see Moors coming to him in order that he might settle their disputes."[100] Already in 1900, less than two decades after his death, a French anthropologist described him as one of the venerated "Jewish saints" of the city.[101] His grave in the Jewish cemetery of Fez became a place of regular pilgrimage and was believed to have healing powers. Moroccan Jews were also known to swear by his name or call out for his protection in moments of need, crying: "O Rabbi Abner Serfati!"[102] Yomtob Sémach, an Ottoman-born educator for the AIU, praised him in 1933 as "one of the finest figures of the rabbinic lineage which illustrated Fez in the past." In particular, Sémach mentioned his magnificent library, noting that "he was equally interested in modern studies [and in traditional rabbinic literature], and collected new Hebrew books which were printed in Europe."[103] It is to his library that we now turn.

Some of the oldest books in Avner-Yisrael I's library were almost certainly inherited through the generations of the Serfaty family; his ancestor Vidal I Serfaty (1545–ca. 1619) was said to have left behind a large collection of books.[104] In 1718, Vidal I's grandson Aharon Serfaty of Salé (1665–ca. 1740) published a collection of Vidal I's biblical commentaries from manuscript, explaining: "I searched and sought in the storehouse of his collection [*beit genazav*], the collection of his treasures, and found these manuscripts [there], written in his own hand in the year 5326 [1566 CE]."[105] Presumably, at least part of the Serfaty library was drawn from this "storehouse" of books. Avner-Yisrael I may also have inherited books from the collections of the Serero family, another prominent family of noted scholars and rabbis in Fez. The Serero family was closely linked to the Serfaty family by marriage, and in fact Avner-Yisrael I was linked to the Serero family on both his maternal and paternal lines.[106] Chapter 1 discussed the fifteenth-century illuminated Iberian Pentateuch that Avner-Yisrael I examined and completed around 1850, which may certainly have come from one of these family collections. A sixteenth-century mahzor of the Fez rite, with an ornamental title page added by Shmuel b. Yisrael-Ya'aqov Serfaty (Avner-Yisrael I's great-uncle, ca. 1790–1885), may also have been part of the family's library; these two manuscripts were purchased by Moses Hecht, perhaps at the same time.[107] According to Yosef Tedghi, at least part of the Serfaty family library was stored in the synagogue associated with Avner-Yisrael I's great-great-grandfather, Eliyahu I Serfaty (1715–1805), which was known as *Ṣla d-l-ḥakham*, "the Synagogue of the Rabbi."[108]

The bulk of the Serfaty library, however, at least as it was documented by Avner-Yisrael I, seems to have been assembled by Avner-Yisrael I himself. Although there is little surviving correspondence from him—unlike the Abensur family—he is occasionally mentioned in other letters, indicating that he was in contact with booksellers abroad who kept him abreast of the latest publications and supplied him with books. In one letter, for example, Jerusalem-based dealer Yosef Sassoon wrote to Refael II Abensur in 1880 with a list of books being brought to Morocco by Moshe Suzin, including five for Refael II and two for Avner-Yisrael I.[109] Avner-Yisrael I also indicates that he was a correspondent of David Ben-Shim'on (1826–1879), the Moroccan scholar in Jerusalem who also regularly supplied Refael II Abensur.[110] Although some of the books listed in the Serfaty catalog (to be discussed in the following section) date from the sixteenth to eighteenth centuries, a significant proportion were actually published during Avner-Yisrael I's lifetime, demonstrating that his collection was actively and continually expanding to include contemporary works of rabbinic scholarship and modern Hebrew literature.

Remarkably, a full catalog prepared by Avner-Yisrael I has survived in manuscript.[111] Part of this catalog was bound with two later catalogs of the library, apparently copied by his grandson Avner-Yisrael II (1885–1933), around 1930–1932, but there is no doubt that the first inventory is in Avner-Yisrael I's hand and was prepared toward the end of his life, sometime between 1880 and his death in 1884. It is therefore the closest representation of the completed library that he was able to establish in his lifetime, some 724 books. It is likely that Avner-Yisrael I intended this index to cover only those books he had personally acquired, leaving out the manuscripts and other books inherited through his family; perhaps those books were the ones held separately in the *Ṣla d-l-ḥakham* Synagogue. It is notable, for example, that this list describes only seven books as specifically being in manuscript, which suggests that he was not cataloging the family's historical collection—which most likely contained many more—but only his own acquisitions. The list also does not include any of the printed books authored by his Serfaty ancestors, which again would certainly have been in the family's collection. This is further supported by the title of the catalog, which reads "An index of the sacred books granted to me by the Gracious One," a phrase commonly used in book dedications when describing one's purchases.

The inventory presents the books by theme, divided into the following ten categories: Bibles and biblical commentaries, collections of sermons and midrashim, Kabbalah, Hebrew grammar, Talmud and Talmudic commentaries, halakha and legal compilations, responsa, science, "miscellaneous"—mostly history and literature, and prayer books and liturgy. The books are generally given only by title, although the author is sometimes indicated; in rare cases, the age of the book is referenced (e.g., books numbered 710–714 are "an old [edition of] *Ḥoq le-yisrael*," while 462–466 are "a new [edition of] *Ḥoq le-yisrael*"), and a number of books are specified as being in manuscript.

Each book was also given an inventory number, which was tied to how they were arranged in the library. At the end of the catalog, Avner-Yisrael I describes the physical layout of the library and the book numbers to be found on each shelf, such that we are able to actually reconstruct the physical layout of the library and the distribution of its books as he arranged them. This cataloging system emphasizes the nature of this collection as a working library and the importance of this inventory as a tool of reference and organization. However, while the catalog carefully organized the books into thematic categories, the structure of the library's layout is less clear. For example, Serfaty had two full sets of the Babylonian Talmud, one that was on Shelf Ten, on the western side of the library, and the other on Shelf Nineteen, on the opposite side. Was one for lending, and one for reference? Perhaps one was an older edition kept for its historical value, and the other a newer edition for regular consultation? The book numbers assigned in the catalog move sequentially across the library—for example, Shelf One contains books numbered 1–58; Shelf Two, 59–126; Shelf Three, 127–197, and so on—indicating that the physical organization of the library came first, and then the books were numbered in the order that they were already arranged in. But it is difficult to extrapolate Avner-Yisrael I's logic in deciding which books to put next to each other solely from their listing in the catalog.

Shelf Nine, for instance, contained forty-five books (with some volumes including two or three works bound together), comprising in total four works of historical literature, seven works of geography, three works of liturgy, twelve works of Kabbalah and musar, three works of astronomy and calendrical calculations, seven works of halakha, two works of Talmudic commentary, four works of sermons and philosophical treatises, and five works of biblical commentary. The oldest book on the shelf (as far as I can ascertain) was the calendrical treatise *Tiqqun yissakhar* (Constantinople: Shlomo Ya'aveṣ, 1564), and the newest was *Shir mikhtam* (Warsaw: Natan Schriftgisser, 1880), Yehuda Ibn-Attar's compendium of the laws of shehita (kosher slaughter). This shelf even included a critical edition and English translation of Avraham bar Ḥiyya's astronomical work *Sefer ha-'ibbur*, prepared by Herschell Filipowski (London: H. Filipowski, 1851). The collection of books on this shelf seems to lack any discernible pattern, and it is possible that the grouping may be unrelated to content: perhaps by size, order of acquisition, or frequency of reference. The Serfaty inventory may be compared to another library of the same period, the collection of the Eṣ Ḥayyim yeshiva in Tunis, which was largely formed during the second half of the nineteenth century and inventoried around 1905 by Ya'aqov al-Ha'ik (1846–1914).[112] The catalog of this library organizes the books into collections—those books purchased directly by the yeshiva, and those donated by individuals—and then numbers them within each collection by their order on the shelves, which seems to be roughly according to their date of acquisition.[113]

A close look at his catalog reveals the incredible breadth of Avner-Yisrael I's reading practices. His collection of rabbinic literature in all its subfields is impressive but not surprising: a rabbi of Avner-Yisrael I's prominence could not have pursued his work without the textual support of halakhic reference works, collections of responsa, and Talmudic commentaries, which, according to Avner-Yisrael I's inventory, formed just over half of his collection. Another quarter of his library was made up of Bibles and biblical commentaries, anthologies of midrashim and sermons, liturgical texts, and works of Kabbalah and mysticism. While most of these could typically be found in any rabbinic library, some were more controversial. For example, he owned the five volumes of Elia Benamozegh's *Em la-miqra* (Livorno, 1862–1865), a modern biblical commentary that drew on contemporary findings in archaeology, Semitic philology, and even the natural sciences. It had been vociferously condemned at the time of its publication by the rabbinic establishment in Jerusalem and Damascus.[114]

The proportions of these sections of Avner-Yisrael I's library may be compared to the collection of the Eṣ Ḥayyim yeshiva: out of the yeshiva's 741 books, works of Talmud, responsa, and halakha formed 80 percent of its collection, with the remainder largely consisting of books on the Bible, Kabbalah, and midrashim (*Em la-miqra* not among them).[115] What is unusual about Serfaty's library is the significant place held by the sections labeled in his catalog as "Physics, Astronomy, Calendar, Mathematics, and Natural Sciences," "Grammar," and "Miscellaneous

Books" (mostly historical and literary texts), comprising in total over a hundred titles. Many of these books are Hebrew textbooks of science, philosophical treatises by European Hebrew writers of the Haskalah, and examples of modern Hebrew literature. For comparison, the Eṣ Ḥayyim yeshiva held only nine books in these categories, including several Hebrew dictionaries and concordances, two works of Jewish chronology and bibliography (Yehiel Heilprin's *Seder ha-dorot* and Ḥayyim Yosef David Azulai's *Shem ha-gedolim*, both also represented in the Serfaty collection), and only one book of science or mathematics: a manuscript of Ḥayyim Vital's treatise on astronomy, *Sefer ha-tekhuna* (also found in the Serfaty library in the printed edition, Jerusalem: Israel Bak, 1866).[116]

The modern sciences in Avner-Yisrael I's collection are mostly represented by works of geography, mathematics, and physics, printed in Warsaw, Vilna, and other major cities of eastern Europe. For example, he owned the four volumes of *Yesodei ḥokhmat ha-ṭeva ha-klalit* (Vilna: Fine-Rosenkrantz and the Widow Romm, 1867–1876), an illustrated scientific encyclopedia arranged by the Lithuanian science writer Zvi Hirsh Rabinowitz (1832–1889), and the first volume of a Hebrew textbook on zoology, *Toldot ha-ṭeva'* (Leipzig: Mordekhai Yellin, 1862), adapted from a German work by Sholem-Yankev Abramovitsh (1835–1917, who was more famous for his fiction written under the pen name Mendele Moykher-Sforim). The works of geography in the Serfaty collection ranged from medieval and early modern travelogues (such as the *Sibuv* of Rabbi Petaḥya of Regensburg and Avraham Farissol's Renaissance geography book *Iggeret orḥot 'olam*) to half a dozen modern works on Europe, the Land of Israel, and the Americas. Unfortunately, without the books themselves, it is difficult to determine the extent to which they were read and used actively, although Avner-Yisrael I's *Yaḥas fes* clearly demonstrates his scholarly engagement with geography and astronomy, as we shall see. At least one testimony survives to the circulation of a book from his scientific collection: Refael-Moshe Elbaz dedicated one of his riddle poems to Avner-Yisrael I "on the occasion when he promised to send me a copy of the book *Even ha-sho'evet* [the fourth volume of Rabinowitz's *Ḥokhmat ha-ṭeva*], while he was here in Sefrou."[117]

Interestingly, Avner-Yisrael I also included works of philosophy under the category of "Physics, Astronomy, Calendar, Mathematics, and Natural Sciences," so it seems he considered philosophy to be a school of *ḥokhma* [wisdom/science] as much as physics or astronomy. His library included classic works of medieval and early modern Jewish thought, such as Sa'adya Gaon's *Sefer emunot ve-de'ot* and Maimonides's *More nevukhim*, alongside contemporary works debating the development of Jewish religious thought in modern times: Serfaty's collection contained Isaac Samuel Reggio's *Iggerot yashar* (Vienna, 1834–1836), Isaac Baer Levinsohn's *Beit yehuda* (first printed in Vilna, 1839), and Nachman Krochmal's *More nevukhei ha-zman* (first printed in Lemberg, 1851). These books articulated some of the central principles of the Haskalah, arguing that Judaism was not just Talmudic law or Hasidic mysticism but also a national civilization and that the path toward Jewish modernity lay in a reform of Jewish education and an adoption of Enlightenment principles. One can only wonder whether any of these works helped Avner-Yisrael I prepare for his philosophical debates with Islamic scholars and, perhaps, with some of his rabbinic colleagues as well.

In literature, too, the Serfaty library reveals its eclectic tastes. Its shelves carried many of the classics of medieval Jewish writers: Avraham Ibn-Ḥasdai's *Ben ha-melekh veha-nazir*, Yehuda al-Ḥarizi's *Taḥkemoni*, and Immanuel of Rome's *Maḥberot 'immanuel*. It also held some of the fruits of the Maskilic revitalization of Hebrew literature, such as Naphtali Hirz Wessely's poetry cycle on the Exodus, *Shirei tiferet*; and two of Avraham Mapu's historical romance novels, *Ahavat ṣiyyon* and *Ashmat shomron*. Avner-Yisrael I was noted for his love of Jewish literature and the Hebrew language, and his own compositions were admired for their elegance of language and the beauty of his calligraphic script.[118]

In addition to the many historical works of rabbinic literature, Serfaty's library contained some works explicitly focused on Jewish history, such as Heilprin's aforementioned *Seder ha-dorot* (first published in Karlsruhe in 1769). But these works deal mostly with the Jews of Europe; at that time, there was little scholarship on postmedieval Jewish life in the Islamic world in Hebrew or any other language. Compiling and synthesizing his knowledge of the Jews of Fez with the collected resources of his library was Serfaty's contribution to the historiography of Maghrebi Jewish life, resulting in the composition of *Yaḥas fes* (1879). This work, beyond its value as a source for Moroccan Jewish history, also provides a window into Avner-Yisrael I Serfaty's self-conception as a scholar and his working process in his library and beyond.

The story of *Yaḥas fes* begins with an encounter between Moroccan and European Jews: in 1878, two rabbis from Fez, Ḥayyim Yamin Hakohen and Ya'aqov Benzimra, went on a fundraising trip to Jewish centers in western Europe. There, they met Isidore Loeb, president of the AIU, and Abraham Halevy, president of the Agudath Ahim of London. Both men plied the visiting rabbis with questions about the Jewish community of Fez. Unable to provide answers, the rabbis decided upon their return to ask Avner-Yisrael I to compose a work that would satisfy the curiosity of these European Jewish leaders, who had supplied them with written questionnaires.[119] The result of Avner-Yisrael I's research, *Yaḥas fes*, was completed the following year; it was copied in manuscript and sent to London and Paris, and it was also circulated and recopied among various readers in Morocco and beyond.

Avner-Yisrael I begins the work by noting modestly: "I only managed to spare a few moments to compose this amid the yoke of [my responsibilities to] the community; therefore some things are not in order, or the language not quite right. Sometimes, I dictated to a scribe who wrote, but the matter was changed between the mouth and the ear."[120] But it is clear that *Yaḥas fes* is the result of considerable effort not only in research but also in synthesis and organization, creating an elegant narrative that draws on multiple sources of knowledge. Avner-Yisrael I cites many of the books from his library, including works of history and bibliography (including, for example, Heilprin's *Seder ha-dorot*, Azulai's *Shem ha-gedolim*, Shlomo Ibn-Verga's *Shevet yehuda*, Samson Bloch's *Shevilei 'olam*, and more), but he also carefully mined the texts and paratexts of rabbinic commentaries for their historical value.

He noticed, for instance, that "in the leaf printed at the end of the book *Mikhlal yofi*" (Amsterdam, 1661), author Shlomo Ibn-Melekh called Fez his city of birth.[121] Similarly, Avner-Yisrael I observed: "I saw at the beginning of some title pages attached to old printings of Rabbi Yishaq Alfasi that his name was written *Rab al-fas*," namely, "the rabbi of Fez."[122] Newer books, too, held valuable insights; Solomon Judah Löb Rapoport's introduction to the scholarly edition of Shlomo Ibn-Parhon's dictionary *Maḥberet ha-'arukh* provided a discussion of ninth-century grammarian Yehuda Ibn-Quraysh in Fez, which Avner-Yisrael I cited as the earliest-known reference to the Jewish presence in the city.[123] He also subjected these books to his own critical evaluation; noting, for example, that the birthplace of Alfasi (Qal'at Hammad) was written mistakenly in some printings as Qal'at Hamman or Hammak, "and this is clearly the aforementioned place, but the printer erred in confusing the similar letters."[124]

He also recognized the historical value of manuscript books, and he often referred to manuscripts in his possession, such as the works of his ancestor Eliyahu I Serfaty or the Judeo-Arabic chronicle of the Ibn-Danan family.[125] Additionally, he sought out and consulted manuscripts held in other collections, looking especially for inscriptions and marginal notations (what some book historians today term "footprints") with historical information.

Avner-Yisrael I found one medieval biblical manuscript on parchment with a note written at the end regarding the expulsion of the Jews from Fez in 1438; in another manuscript, there was an inscription "in the hand of Rabbi Sa'adya Ibn-Danan" (d. ca. 1493).[126] A drought and famine in 1779 were recorded on the flyleaf of a manuscript of sermons by Avraham Monsano (1719–1781), and in a manuscript of sermons by eighteenth-century scholar Daniel Ben-Sultan: "I found written that there was a plague in the year 1799."[127]

Although indebted to Avner-Yisrael I's personal efforts, the composition of *Yaḥas fes* was in some ways a communal one. Avner-Yisrael I reported many observations that he had learned from personal conversations, and in some cases, he enlisted colleagues in his research, especially regarding the Jewish communities in the villages of the Fez region, including Sefrou and Debdou. In several places, he acknowledged a notary [*sofer*] "whom I sent for and instructed to copy the family lineages of [Debdou] from the register of *ketubbot* . . . and certain liturgical poems" from older manuscripts.[128]

Yaḥas fes also demonstrates in several places that Avner-Yisrael I's scholarly endeavors extended across religious boundaries to include his Muslim colleagues and their knowledge of Islamic literature: a rare experience in nineteenth-century Morocco. As he wrote in one passage regarding the history of Fez: "I asked two Muslim scholars who happened to be with me whether they had any clear knowledge of the founding of Old Fez. One of them brought a copy of their book which is called *Qirṭas* and read it to me."[129] The Arabic text alluded to, *Rawḍ al-qirṭas,* is a popular Arabic chronicle of the history of Morocco, attributed to fourteenth-century scholar Abu al-Ḥassan 'Ali Ibn-Abi-Zar 'al-Fassi.[130] The identities of these scholars and the nature of their previous relationship with Avner-Yisrael I is not known. But his description of the encounter indicates that his interest in intellectual collaboration was a shared pursuit and that the reading and writing of books united scholars who connected beyond the boundaries of family, locality, and even religious community.

Avner-Yisrael I's Muslim colleagues (likely the same ones who read to him from *Rawḍ al-qirṭas*) appear again in another remarkable passage of *Yaḥas fes*. He expressed regret that his work could not include some scientific measurements on the model of the geographic texts he had read in his library because of a lack of instruments. However, he went on to credit "Muslim scholars" with knowledge of this science, who were able to supply their own measurements, even as he maintained his desire to "measure this precisely" himself.

> Joseph Schwartz wrote [in *Divrei yosef*, printed in Jerusalem, 1843–1862] that it is of great benefit to know the degrees [of latitude and longitude] for the place where one dwells. But I am not able to research the degrees of our land, since at the moment I do not have the instruments—the quadrant illustrated in *Neḥmad ve-na'im*, or the parallactic ruler of Ptolemy, illustrated in *Yeshu'a be-yisrael*, so that I might measure our distance from the north pole.[131] Furthermore, I have little respite from the duties of the community, and so time does not permit me to construct such an instrument to satisfy this desire, by means of the techniques laid out in Schwartz' book. However, the Muslim scholars who are knowledgeable in this science have told me that Fez is located on the fourth degree of longitude . . . although I do not have the instruments to measure this precisely. Regarding the degrees of latitude, these same Muslim scholars have told me that Fez is located 25 degrees from the Spanish coast.[132]

Yaḥas fes thus combines Avner-Yisrael I's literary erudition, his embeddedness in the local geography, and his collaborative work with other scholars. His completed work shows him participating in a conversation across time and space, with both the intellectual history represented in his book collection and the colleagues and community around him.

The Serfaty library, like the Abensur library, emerges from its fragmentary records as a site of encounter and scholarly discussion and a place that sparked conversations beyond the library walls. Avner-Yisrael I's promise to send his copy of *Even ha-sho'evet* to his colleague in Sefrou was mentioned previously; another letter mentions "the book of Refael-Moshe Elbaz from Sefrou that he sent to the scholar Avner-Yisrael I Serfaty in the city of Fez," seemingly dealing with a halakhic matter.[133] Books and ideas went back and forth, centered in the library space but not confined to it. His conversations with Muslim colleagues, while not as well documented, similarly illustrate his commitment to collaborative scholarship. His description of having the *Qirṭas* read aloud suggests that he was not fully literate in Arabic script—although his library did include one Hebrew textbook of Arabic grammar—but that he valued a diversity of sources of knowledge, including those from outside the Jewish world, and this episode points us to the possibilities of oral conversation and discussion that these reading sessions may have entailed.[134] Indeed, his contemporaries, as we saw previously, credit him with earning the respect of his Muslim colleagues through his mastery of philosophy, theology, and law.

Avner-Yisrael I Serfaty died in September 1884, the week after Rosh Hashanah, at the age of fifty-seven. After his death, his library stayed in his family's possession and was maintained (and expanded) by his son Vidal V Serfaty (1862–1921). A rare glimpse into the continued active life of the library comes from the final leaf of the Benayahu manuscript of the Serfaty inventory, which holds a record of books loaned out from the collection. This list, dated to 1892, records some thirty-six readers and the titles of the books they borrowed (crossed out when the book was returned).[135] Interestingly, several borrowers are specifically noted as being from Sefrou, indicating that the regional connections developed by Avner-Yisrael I with scholars in other cities continued for at least several decades.

The books borrowed include not only the classics of rabbinic literature but also some of Avner-Yisrael I's scientific and Maskilic books: Yiṣḥaq Ibn-Danan, for example, borrowed and returned two books of astronomy, Avraham bar Ḥiyya's *Ṣurat ha-areṣ* (Offenbach, 1720) and Yonatan ben Yosef's commentary on it, *Yeshu'a be-yisrael* (Frankfurt, 1720). Meanwhile, Yishaq Maymaran borrowed and returned three works of rabbinic literature along with a book on geography, "one of the books of the Haskalah," and a medical book that he still had checked out at the time the list was last updated; another reader had just returned Mapu's *Ahavat ṣiyyon*.[136] Avner-Yisrael I's *Yaḥas fes* was apparently borrowed at least four times by different readers.[137] Refael-Aharon Ben-Shim'on, although not listed among them, similarly mentions consulting *Yaḥas fes* on his visit through the city in 1888, "among the wonderful books of [Avner-Yisrael I's] writings which he left after him, a blessing in the hands of [his son] Vidal V Serfaty."[138]

The library continued to be a scholarly resource throughout the beginning of the twentieth century. In 1910, Moroccan scholar Ya'aqov Moshe Tolédano (married to Avner-Yisrael I's granddaughter, Messouda) consulted the Serfaty library while researching his work on Moroccan Jewish history, *Ner ha-ma'arav*. He thanks Vidal V and Avner-Yisrael II Serfaty for providing him with manuscripts, including a copy of *Yaḥas fes*, from the family's library.[139] In the 1920s, Yosef Bennaim drew on the Serfaty library, along with the Abensur library and others, while researching his biobibliographical encyclopedia *Malkhei rabbanan*. He writes that "to this day, this library is still preserved by his descendants in its original place in our city."[140] In a beautiful moment of meta-bibliography, the inventory conducted by Avner-Yisrael II Serfaty in the 1930s reveals that copies of both *Ner ha-ma'arav* and *Malkhei rabbanan* had been deposited in the family library.[141] As for *Yaḥas fes*, it was circulated in manuscript and first published in 1930 by Simha Assaf in the journal of Moroccan-Palestinian educator Abraham Elmaleh (al-Maliaḥ), *Mizrah Oumaarav*; four years later, as noted previously, an abbreviated French translation was published by AIU educator Yomtob Sémach.[142]

Unfortunately, it seems that in later years, the Serfaty library was not actively used and fell into neglect. In 1969, after much of Moroccan Jewry had already begun to immigrate to Israel or France, two members of the Serfaty family in Fez found the library in poor condition. They salvaged what books they could and distributed them among the family members; some were then donated to Bar-Ilan University.[143] At least two manuscripts from the Serfaty catalog can be found in other collections today: a manuscript of sermons by Shem-Tov Ben-Amozeg, copied in 1728, which was originally Serfaty number 204, and a manuscript mahzor of liturgical poetry for the High Holidays, originally Serfaty number 721.[144] A number of printed books from the Serfaty library have also surfaced at auctions in recent years, including those that have been deaccessioned from the Bar-Ilan library and those without a Bar-Ilan stamp, suggesting that some of the descendants have sold their books, and the rest may remain in private collections.[145]

The library of Avner-Yisrael I Serfaty, as documented in his inventory and visible through *Yaḥas fes*, was both a storehouse of history and a place of collaborative scholarship. His book collection paints a portrait of a scholar who is deeply fascinated by the world and the place of Jewish people in it—someone who understands themselves to belong both to modernity and to traditional Judaism, perhaps someone who does not perceive those two modalities as being necessarily oppositional. He was not alone in integrating his interest in the Haskalah into a Maghrebi context, as we have seen: other scholars and writers, like Algerian rabbi Mimoun Abou (Maymun ʿAbo, 1820–1890) or Essaouiran merchant Yiṣḥaq Ben-Yaʿis Halewi (ca. 1850–1895), participated in reading and writing for the Maskilic newspapers *Ha-ṣefira, Ha-levanon,* and *Ha-maggid.*[146] The publishers, booksellers, and translators discussed in chapter 5, like Shalom Bekache (1848–1927) and Elieʿzer Farḥi (1851–1930), promoted the transnational circulation of books between Europe and North Africa and experimented with translating the Haskalah, both literally and figuratively, into Judeo-Arabic.[147]

Taking a broader view of the larger context of the Sephardi Mediterranean, Avner-Yisrael I might be seen as a peer to Ottoman Jewish intellectuals who produced "a wide-ranging body of serious scholarship on the history and traditions of their own communities."[148] Although Avner-Yisrael I did not leave any extensive reflections on the meaning of his library, his use of books as scholarly resources in their own right demonstrates his historiographic consciousness. In *Yaḥas fes*, Avner-Yisrael I draws on centuries of Moroccan Jewish book history while engaging in the practices of modern scholarship, such as material bibliography, textual criticism, and manuscript collation. Synthesizing his vast reading in many genres, he brought together traditional citations with modern techniques of research to center the Jewish community of Fez (and Morocco, more generally) as a valid and valuable subject of historical inquiry. In contradiction to narratives that portrayed Maghrebi Jews as frozen in tradition, disinterested in both social change and historical inquiry—in 1892, for example, an English journalist from Tangiers claimed that Moroccan Jews "themselves have no intelligent idea of their past"—*Yaḥas fes* offers a Maghrebi Jewish vision of modernity, rooted in its own history and looking toward its future.[149] Avner-Yisrael I's book collection illuminates the wide-ranging intellectual horizons of this remarkable nineteenth-century scholar, whose shelves contained five centuries of collected Jewish knowledge. Avner-Yisrael I Serfaty, to my knowledge, never left the borders of Morocco, but through his library, he could travel the world.

CONCLUSION: READING THE MAGHREBI JEWISH LIBRARY

The two Maghrebi Jewish libraries surveyed here share some core similarities. Assembled by members of elite Sephardi rabbinic families in the city of Fez whose leadership positions were passed on from generation to generation, they represent the pinnacle of achievement in the intellectual and spiritual worlds of early modern Judaism. They also testify to the global world of early modern Jewish books, with texts, materials, techniques, and books themselves traveling throughout Europe, North Africa, and the Ottoman Empire. These libraries served not only as symbols of intellectual prestige but also as active sites of learning. Consulted by scholars, expanded through new acquisitions in manuscript and print, and disseminated through correspondence and a robust culture of both lending and copying books, these libraries were hubs of activity.

It is difficult to make extensive comparisons with the few existing records, but those that are available seem roughly representative of rabbinic libraries generally in North Africa. For example, an analysis of the surviving pre-1800 imprints (some 282 books) of the library of Moïse Sebaoun of Oran shows a very similar picture to the Abensurs: this collection was also well stocked with important rabbinic works produced at Hebrew presses in Italy, the Ottoman Empire, Germany, France, the Netherlands, and Poland, with thirty-five cities represented in total; its oldest books dated as far back as 1518. These books were also well read; many of them carried additional notes and commentary, and over a dozen contained "extensive handwritten annotations."[150] Over 50 percent of the books in the surviving Sebaoun collection were authored by Sephardi scholars from North Africa and the Ottoman Empire, with another 15 percent contributed by European Sephardi authors, such as those from Italy or Amsterdam. These proportions hold for the other libraries documented from Morocco and Tunisia, emphasizing the intellectual centrality of the Sephardi world, especially in the context of halakhic jurisprudence.

At the same time, the differences between the Abensur and Serfaty libraries highlight the changing nature of North African

Jewish society over the eighteenth and nineteenth centuries. The Abensur library, the culmination of generations of rabbinic leadership, represented an unparalleled resource for the legal rulings and rabbinic writings of Ya'aqov I Abensur and his descendants. Its collected holdings of five centuries of Jewish textual creativity in biblical and Talmudic exegesis, halakhic literature, and philosophy and Kabbalah served for generations as a symbol of Sephardi and Maghrebi spiritual authority, giving particular pride of place to the unique heritage of Moroccan Jewry. The Serfaty library, on the other hand, is a testament to the seemingly insatiable passion of its creator, combining the textual heritage of Moroccan Jewry with the burgeoning Hebrew literature of the Global Haskalah. Its collection of Maskilic books, in particular, demonstrates Serfaty's appreciation of the revival of the Hebrew language into a fully competent idiom, able to articulate modern philosophy and science alongside its historical literature. The Serfaty library was also the catalyst for the creation of new texts that embodied this intermediary position between the Maghreb and the larger Jewish world. But for all their differences, both of these libraries testify above all to the power of books and the Jewish tradition they represent: their movement as material objects, across borders, between communities, and within families, and their importance as social objects, embedded in the lives of Jewish communities in North Africa.

CONCLUSION

The Ink in My Veins

WHEN I WAS A CHILD, my grandmother often found me with my nose in a book; in fact, this was usually the way she found me. She would laugh and say, "It figures! You know, in our family we have ink in our veins, not blood." She was thinking of her parents, especially her father, Samuel (Shmuel) Polisky, who was born in 1880 in the small city of Mogilev, today in eastern Belarus. My great-grandfather Sam moved to Canada in 1904, where he met and married my great-grandmother, Katie (Gitl) Blumenthal, also an Ashkenazi immigrant, from the town of Parczew in eastern Poland.

Sam and Katie loved books, especially Jewish books. My grandmother remembered clearing out her mother's library after her death and boxing up volume after volume of Shakespeare in Yiddish, Freud in Yiddish — even Rousseau in Yiddish, she once proclaimed and so on. She also recalled sitting at the table after dinner as a child and hearing her father read the great works of Yiddish literature aloud, while my great-grandmother Katie washed the dishes to the sounds of Sholom Aleichem, Y. L. Peretz, and Mendele Moykher-Sforim. Sam and Katie were founding members of the local Yiddish Bundist school, known as the Yehoash Folkshule, and subscribers to the Canadian Yiddish journal *Der Keneder Adler*; they were also active members of the Yiddish Literary and Dramatic Society of Ottawa.[1]

But my great-grandfather was not a figure of Yiddish literary or dramatic history; he was not an author, journalist, playwright, or poet. The ink that flowed from his veins to my grandmother, and from her to my father and then to me, was the ink not of a writer but of a printer. More specifically, as he proudly inscribed on his Canadian naturalization certificate, he was a pressman.[2]

Although Sam lived in a Yiddish-speaking world, he worked in English-speaking presses in Canada. Family legend recalls that he first learned to read English from the backward type in the press house, reading it from right to left, as he was accustomed to doing in Yiddish. I imagine him studying English from a phrase book such as Alexander Harkavy's *Der Amerikanisher Lehrer—The American Teacher,* first published in 1897, which helped working-class Yiddish-speaking immigrants navigate North American workplaces and industries.[3] In Harkavy's section on printing [*druk-kunst*], Sam Polisky could find English terms like "type-cases" [*shrift-kastens*], "ink rollers" [*farb-valkes*], or "composing stick" [*zetser-haken*] and practice sounding out English phrases transcribed in Yiddish such as *Ay vish to loyrn dhi art av prin-ting* or *Ay naw dhi art av prin-ting veri vel.*[4] Unfortunately, I have no records or family stories that document precisely how Sam learned "the art of printing," but he learned it very well indeed.

By the late nineteenth century, the art of printing had become far more industrialized than the hand-operated presses of the early modern period, but, still, my great-grandfather's profession demanded a high degree of technical skill as well as physical labor.[5] American printer William Kelly, in his 1902 book *Presswork: A Practical Handbook for the Use of Pressmen and Their Apprentices,* includes among the duties of the turn-of-the-century pressman the following: cleaning the press; arranging the tympans; "make-ready"—adjustments to ensure a tight lock-up and a uniform printing surface by preparing any underlying paper or board; packing the cylinder to roll smoothly over the bed; mixing the inks to the correct consistency and color, and inking the press cylinders; clearing the paper of static electricity and wetting it appropriately; running an impression through to be checked before printing; feeding the paper in and gathering the sheets; washing off the rollers; troubleshooting any mechanical issues with the printing process; navigating the vagaries of cold, hot, or damp weather; and dealing with any unusual requirements, such as deckled papers, gold leaf, or vignetted illustrations.[6] In other words, the pressman was responsible for the mastery of the many specialized mechanics of the technology of book printing.

Upon arriving for work at the Dominion Printing Bureau in Ottawa, my great-grandfather repeated this whole process hundreds of times a day, five or six days a week, for forty-three years, until his death. In 1900, the trade journal *The American Pressman* reported that the main pressroom of the Government Printing Office in Washington, DC, employed forty-nine pressmen who turned out seven thousand impressions a day from the flatbed presses and ten thousand daily impressions from the presses with automatic feeding attachments.[7] In his four decades of work as a pressman, my great-grandfather must have participated in the making of tens of thousands of books. And yet, not a single one of those books bears his name. A few years ago, I stood in the vault of the Yiddish Book Center in Amherst, Massachusetts, where my grandmother had donated her parents' Yiddish book collection decades ago. Surrounded by over a million Yiddish books, I wondered if any of them were my great-grandfather's, either of his library or his work; perhaps a book that was shaped by his hands was right there on the shelf in front of me.

It is this unrecognized labor, albeit from a very different historical context, that I hope to have honored in this study: not only the work of the people who wrote books but also the work of the people who made books, who scribed and decorated them, who edited and printed and bound them, along with the people who bought and sold them, and the people who read them. Bookmaking—and book history—includes the many hands through which the book passed, even if their names were not attached to it. The study of the movement of books also points us to the movement of people like my great-grandparents, who crossed borders and oceans, who learned new languages and alphabets, and who used books to define and redefine their relationships with others. While the pressmen of Livorno or Oran may seem far removed from Mahilyow or Ottawa, they were all awash in similar crosscurrents of modern Jewish history.[8] As Moroccan rabbi Ben-Shim'on wrote from his adopted Cairo of his Ashkenazi book-loving comrades in Austro-Hungary: "Even if our countries are far apart, our hearts embrace one another."[9]

Throughout the preceding chapters, I have argued that books are both material and social objects. They are brought into being through social processes, through networks of connection; they live within the communities who read, circulate, and collect them. Their lives, like ours, are shaped by many factors, great and small, and, like us, they form relationships with others who came before and after. Perhaps books can even die when they no longer play any social role and are discarded, destroyed, or left to crumble on abandoned bookshelves. When I speak of the "death" of a book, it should be remembered that in North Africa, as in other Jewish communities around the world, Jewish books that were worn out from use or damaged beyond repair were traditionally collected in a storage place known as a genizah, which was regularly emptied and buried in the Jewish cemetery alongside the other deceased members of the community.[10] As we have seen, this practice, which encompassed not only sacred texts like Bibles and prayer books but all kinds of reading material as well, was continued well into the twentieth century in the Maghreb and is still practiced to this day.[11] Even in their death, Jewish books maintained their meaning as culturally entangled objects.

In his first Panizzi Lecture of 1985, book historian and bibliographer D. F. McKenzie laid out his approach to "the book as an expressive form."[12] Arguing that bibliography should move from "a feebly digressive book list" toward a broader study of "the sociology of texts," McKenzie emphasized that book historians must concern themselves with the variety of material forms taken by texts, the range of social realities they serve, and the various types of interactions and encounters involved in their production, transmission, and consumption.[13] This book has demonstrated the rich insights gained by following the book as a material and social object, in our case, through the interconnected worlds of Maghrebi Jews from the end of the medieval period until the turn of the twentieth century.

The neat chronological boundaries implied by the division between "premodern" (or "early modern") and "modern" history are not so easily determined here. The sociology of Maghrebi Jewish books demonstrates how the "premodern" and the "modern" are constantly in dialogue with each other through relationships in both material form and social function. These books also highlight the overlapping yet distinct position of Maghrebi Jews within the larger context of Sephardi history over the course of this period. In some ways, they reflect features common across the Sephardi world: for example, the centrality of sites like Livorno and Jerusalem as hubs of publishing, the importance of vernacular journalism for local readership, and the growing influence of the Alliance Israélite Universelle in the Gallicization of the Sephardi world. The work of intellectuals and scholars like Shalom Bekache and Avner-Yisrael Serfaty, as we saw, paralleled that of Ottoman Sephardi Maskilim attempting to articulate their vision for Jewish modernity.

In other ways, however, our study of Maghrebi books demonstrates the unique paths of Maghrebi Jewry. For example, while the Judeo-Arabic world of North Africa did produce some examples of secular vernacular literature, it never developed nearly as robust a popular literary culture as existed in Ladino (not to mention Yiddish). Furthermore, the differing degrees of social integration between local Jewish and non-Jewish communities across the Maghrebi and Sephardi worlds, particularly in the nineteenth century, led to increasingly divergent ways of making and interacting with books. Over the centuries, the distinguishing cultural, linguistic, and historical commonalities of Maghrebi Jewish communities were both reflected in and shaped by the world of book culture in which they found themselves.

As Simon Eliot and Jonathan Rose succinctly observe: "The history of the book . . . is based on two apparently simple premises, which have inspired some strikingly original work in the humanities. The first is that books make history. . . . Conversely, books are made by history: that is, they are shaped by economic, political, social, and cultural forces."[14] This history, both of and for the book, is still being made today. Digital technologies have reshaped every aspect of book production, distribution, and consumption, changing how books are both made and read. This book was made possible by the vast number of digitized primary sources, including Hebrew manuscripts and printed books, available online through sites like hebrewbooks.org and KTIV, and by the secondary scholarship made available through JSTOR, Google Scholar, and other sites. Despite regular jeremiads about the death of the book, books are not dying but rather are transforming and adapting, just as they have done through the other technological innovations and social upheavals of the past two millennia.[15] And as scholars like Bridget Whearty have reminded us, human labor (often unacknowledged) is at the heart of the production and circulation of digital books, too, just as it was in the scriptoria and printshops of previous centuries.[16]

I will close with one final encounter with the Jewish book in North Africa, recorded on a tattered scrap of paper now held at Yale University.[17] In the winter of 1879, a Moroccan Jewish woman named Nuna, the widow of Yehuda Hakohen Adibe, purchased a set of the Babylonian Talmud for the benefit of her local community in Debdou. To be more precise, she dedicated the sum of thirty duros for the purpose and appointed scholar Moshe ben Shlomo Barmalil to travel to Oran to acquire the books.[18] This is already unusual: as noted in earlier chapters, the majority of Maghrebi Jewish women in this period were not literate in Hebrew and had little engagement with the world of rabbinic literature epitomized by the Talmud.

Nuna's late husband was from a well-respected scholarly family, and Nuna was likely known for her piety and learning. Another legal document from Debdou, dated 1893, records a sum lent to a different member of the Barmalil family, with a notation at the bottom: "from the *heqdesh* [dedicated property fund] of Nuna [daughter] of Jamila," which almost certainly refers to the same woman.[19] While many Moroccan Jewish women created and dedicated ritual items to synagogues, it is remarkable to find a woman involved in the purchasing and dedication of rabbinic books, even if she had no intention of reading the books or lacked the ability to do so.[20] In the rare cases when Maghrebi women donated money for yeshivot, they typically did so as a general donation to be dispersed after their death, leaving it up to the male scholars to arrange the purchasing of the sacred books; only occasionally do women appear in the lists of sponsors for the printing of Maghrebi rabbinic books, especially independently of their husbands.[21] But whatever her relationship was to these books, it is clear that Nuna was centrally involved in and possibly the leader of this scholarly initiative.

Our document does not specify why the books were purchased in Oran, but they were certainly not produced there; no edition of the Talmud was ever printed in Algeria (I am assuming that the volumes of the Talmud described here are in print; if we are speaking of a manuscript Talmud, there is even less reason to travel to Oran, when it could be produced locally).[22] One especially intriguing possibility is that Nuna and her friends were aware of the recently announced printing of the famed "Vilna Shas" edition printed by the press of the Widow and Brothers Romm, with a call to subscribers released widely in the fall of 1879 and the first volumes appearing in early 1880.[23] It is also possible, of course, that Barmalil was tasked with purchasing whatever volumes he could find and that he bought an older edition of the Talmud in Oran, perhaps even one previously used. In any case, the journey of these books from Oran to Debdou was only the last leg of a voyage that had certainly begun thousands of miles away, and—if Barmalil was purchasing second-hand books—perhaps decades or even centuries before.

In the legal document that was drawn up at the time, it is specified that the majority of the volumes would be held in Nuna's physical possession and that priority access to the books would be granted to the brothers of her deceased husband and their children; to Moshe Barmalil, Moshe's brother Ya'aqov, and their children; and their inheritors after them, to study these books, *'ad sof kol ha-dorot*: "until the end of all generations."[24] It is not clear whether these volumes of Nuna's were part of a personal or family collection or whether they were simply stored at her house for practical reasons: either way, this was an exceptional circumstance for Maghrebi Jewish women.

I cannot know whether Nuna's stipulation that these books be studied by her family for future generations has continued to be fulfilled through all the dislocations and peregrinations of Maghrebi Jews and their books over the last century and half; in fact, it is almost certain that it has not. In any case, this modest *estudyo* of Nuna's is a far cry from the celebrated library of her contemporary, Rabbi Moïse Sebaoun of Oran, with its thousands of ancient and modern volumes, which opened this book; it has more in common with the invisible and dispersed library of my great-grandfather, the pressman. But for all the differences between Sebaoun and Nuna, these two encounters with the Jewish book in North Africa nonetheless tell a very similar story: a story about the movement of books as material objects, across borders, between communities, and within families, and a story about the power of books as social objects, embedded in the lives of Jewish communities in North Africa, and connecting us across time and space, until the end of all generations to come.

NOTES

PREFACE

1. The titles are *Seder arba' ta'aniyyot* (Livorno: Moses Tubiana, 1847), *Sefer marpe la-nefesh* (Livorno: Salomone Belforte, 1861), *Qol ha-shem teḥina* (Livorno: Salomone Belforte, 1875), *Sefer rina vi-yshua'* (Livorno: Salomone Belforte, 1856), and *Sefer 'ose* (Livorno: Israel Costa, 1870).

INTRODUCTION

1. Haim Zeev Hirschberg, *Me-ereṣ mevo ha-shemesh: 'im yehudei afriqa ha-ṣfonit be-arṣotehem* (Jerusalem: Jewish Agency, 1957), 5–6. Haim Zeev Hirschberg was born Joachim Wilhelm Hirschberg in Tarnopol [Ternopil, Ukraine], in 1903. After studying Oriental languages at the University of Vienna and receiving rabbinic ordination from the Israelitisch-Theologische Lehranstalt, he immigrated to Palestine in 1943. In 1955, just before Moroccan and Tunisian gained independence, he undertook a research trip to North Africa to look for historical documents on Maghrebi Jews and to gather data in support of their possible future immigration to Israel. See Eliezer Bashan, "Prof. Ḥ. Z. Hirshberg z"l," *Cathedra* 2 (1976): 173–175, and Daniel Schroeter, "Moroccan Jewish Studies in Israel," *Hésperis-Tamuda* 51, no. 2 (2016): 84–85. Hirschberg's full historical study was first published in Hebrew: Haim Zeev Hirschberg, *Toldot ha-yehudim be-afriqa ha-ṣfonit* (Jerusalem: Bialik, 1965), and then in English: Haim Zeev Hirschberg, *A History of the Jews in North Africa*, Vol. 1 (Leiden: Brill, 1974) and Vol. 2 (Leiden: Brill, 1981).

2. Hirschberg, *Me-ereṣ mevo ha-shemesh*, 54. On the Moroccan Jewish libraries he visited, see 74–77, 94, 133, 194–196, 205, and 208.

3. Sebaoun had served as president of the *tribunal rabbinique d'Oran*, the rabbinic court [*bet din*], which in later years in Algeria became the *Conseil supérieur rabbinique*. See Valérie Assan, *Les consistoires israélites d'Algérie au XIXe siècle: l'alliance de la civilisation et la religion* (Paris: Armand Colin, 2012), and Richard Ayoun, "Le grand rabbin d'Algérie David Askénazi," *Revue Européenne des Études Hébraïques* 7 (2002): 103–108.

4. Anonymous, "Les obsèques du grand rabbin Seboun," *L'Univers Israélite* 44 (1889): 173–176.

5. "Rabbi Moshe Sebaoun, Algiers," YBZ Photographs 0237.037. This portrait has been reproduced in varying forms and qualities in hagiographic publications on the rabbinic scholars of Algeria, e.g., Eliyahu Refael Marṣiano, *Sefer malkhei yeshurun* (Jerusalem: Mekhon haRaShaM, 1999), 176.

6. Gérard Nahon, "Livres anciens du Tribunal rabbinique d'Oran," in *Présence juive au Maghreb: hommage à Haïm Zafrani*, ed. Joseph Tedghi and Nicole Serfaty (Saint-Denis: Éditions Bouchene, 2004), 143–146, and cf. his original report: Gérard Nahon, "D'où venaient les livres hebreux étudiés dans les communautés juives d'Algérie au XVIIe et au XVIIIe siècle?," in *International Conference on Jewish Communities in Muslim Lands* (Jerusalem: Ben-Zvi Institute, 1974).

7. Nahon, "Livres anciens," 146.

8. Nahon's indication that he would publish an analysis of the 380 books printed after 1800 "in a later study," unfortunately, did not come to fruition before his death in 2018. I was unable to verify with the Consistoire whether the 662 books studied by Nahon remain in the library today.

9. See, for example, the copy of *Tiqqunei ha-zohar* (Livorno, 1854), with a custom gilt binding reading "Moshe Sebaoun," sold by Refaeli Auctions: Auction 31.1 (October 26, 2022), lot 154, now in the author's personal collection.

10. In his preface, Hirschberg writes that "the *genizot*—to the extent that they existed—had long ago been emptied; the manuscripts were sold and disappeared; and the few rare prints that I was able to acquire were lost in transit. Thus the goal which I had originally thought of as secondary—to observe the common people, Jews and non-Jews, and learn about the past from the present—was what comforted me from this disappointment": Hirschberg, *Me-ereṣ mevo ha-shemesh*, 6. See also Emily Gottreich and Daniel Schroeter, "Introduction: Rethinking Jewish Culture and

Society in North Africa," in *Jewish Culture and Society in North Africa*, ed. Emily Gottreich and Daniel Schroeter (Bloomington: Indiana University Press, 2011), 7; Ammiel Alcalay, "Intellectual Life," in *The Jews of the Middle East and North Africa in Modern Times*, ed. Reeva Spector Simon, Michael Menachem Laskier, and Sara Reguer (New York: Columbia University Press, 2002), 85–112; and Harvey Goldberg, "Some Cautionary Tales from an Anthropological Romance with Jews from Libya," in *Serendipity in Anthropological Research: The Nomadic Turn*, ed. Haim Hazan and Esther Hertzog (London: Routledge, 2012), 109–122.

11. One need only recall the title of Chouraqui's first book, *Les juifs de l'Afrique du Nord: Marche vers l'occident* (1952), for a sense of this perspective. See also Colette Zytnicki, *Les Juifs du Maghreb: naissance d'une historiographie coloniale* (Paris: Presses de l'Universite Paris-Sorbonne, 2011).

12. Joshua Schreier, *The Merchants of Oran: A Jewish Port at the Dawn of Empire* (Redwood City, CA: Stanford University Press, 2017).

13. Alexander Bevilacqua, "Beyond East and West," in *New Horizons for Early Modern European Scholarship*, ed. Ann Blair and Nicholas Popper (Baltimore: Johns Hopkins University Press, 2021), 72–92.

14. Georges Vajda, "Ahl al-Kitab," *Encyclopaedia of Islam*, 2nd ed. (Leiden: Brill, 1960).

15. For a classic and foundational example, see Moshe Halbertal, *People of the Book: Canon, Meaning, and Authority* (Cambridge, MA: Harvard University Press, 1997); for a more recent example, see Talya Fishman, *Becoming the People of the Talmud: Oral Torah as Written Tradition in Medieval Jewish Cultures* (Philadelphia: University of Pennsylvania Press, 2011).

16. See the excellent overview in Emile Schrijver, "Jewish Book Culture Since the Invention of Printing," in *The Cambridge History of Judaism: Volume 7, The Early Modern World, 1500–1815* (Cambridge: Cambridge University Press, 2017), 291–315. Some recent studies have exemplified this methodology: Amnon Raz-Krakotzkin, *The Censor, the Editor, and the Text: The Catholic Church and the Shaping of the Jewish Canon in the Sixteenth Century* (Philadelphia: University of Pennsylvania Press, 2007); Marc Michael Epstein, ed., *Skies of Parchment, Seas of Ink: Jewish Illuminated Manuscripts* (Princeton, NJ: Princeton University Press, 2015); David Stern, *The Jewish Bible: A Material History* (Seattle: University of Washington Press, 2017); Joshua Teplitsky, *Prince of the Press: How One Collector Built History's Most Enduring and Remarkable Jewish Library* (New Haven, CT: Yale University Press, 2019).

17. Schrijver, "Jewish Book Culture," 291–292; Stern, *The Jewish Bible*, 5.

18. See Matthias Lehmann, "Introduction: Sephardi Identities," *Jewish Social Studies* 15, no. 1 (2008): 1–9, and the essays that follow in that special issue.

19. Nahon, "Livres anciens," 143–146.

20. While geographically and politically part of the Maghreb, Libya also shares many linguistic and cultural features with Egypt and the larger Levantine world, and its historical trajectory differs considerably from that of other Maghrebi countries; it will figure in this book only occasionally. Mauritania is also often included in studies of the Maghreb, but since it lacked a significant local Jewish population, it will not be discussed here. For general studies of the historiography of the Maghreb, see Michel Le Gall and Kenneth Perkins, eds., *The Maghrib in Question: Essays in History and Historiography* (Austin: University of Texas Press, 1997), and Abdelmajid Hannoum, *The Invention of the Maghreb: Between Africa and the Middle East* (Cambridge: Cambridge University Press, 2021).

21. The history of Maghrebi Jews in antiquity was a topic of particular concern for early scholars of North African Jewry: see Abraham Cahen, *Les juifs dans l'Afrique septentrionale* (Constantine: L. Arnolet, 1867); Nahum Slouschz, "Études sur l'histoire des Juifs au Maroc," *Archives Marocaines* 4 (1905): 345–411, and 5 (1906): 1–167; Hirschberg, *A History of the Jews in North Africa* (Leiden: Brill, 1974). A good contemporary overview is Karen Stern, *Inscribing Devotion and Death: Archaeological Evidence for Jewish Populations of North Africa* (Leiden: Brill, 2008). As Daniel Schroeter points out, narratives and myths about the ancient or medieval origins of Maghrebi Jews continue to serve a variety of contemporary ideologies: Daniel Schroeter, "The Shifting Boundaries of Moroccan Jewish Identities," *Jewish Social Studies* 15, no. 1 (2008): 145–164.

22. There are also some focused studies on medieval Jewish communities in the Maghreb, although much remains to be written; see, inter alia: Jacob Oliel, *Les Juifs au Sahara: le Touat au moyen âge* (Paris: CNRS Éditions, 1994); Menahem Ben-Sasson, *Ṣemiḥat ha-qehila ha-yehudit be-arṣot ha-islam: Qayrawan 800–1057* (Jerusalem: Magnes, 1996); Mabrouk Mansouri, "The Image of the Jews among Ibadi Imazighen in North Africa before the Tenth Century," in *Jewish Culture and Society in North Africa*, ed. Emily Gottreich and Daniel Schroeter (Bloomington: Indiana University Press, 2011), 45–58.

23. Hmida Toukabri, *Les Juifs dans la Tunisie médiévale, 909–1057: d'après les documents de la Geniza de Caire* (Paris: Romillat, 2002). The

Maghreb is featured prominently throughout S. D. Goitein's study of the Cairo Geniza, *A Mediterranean Society: The Jewish Communities of the Arab World as Portrayed in the Documents of the Cairo Geniza* (Oakland: University of California Press, 1967–1993). For a focused study of one such trader of Tunisian (Ifriqiyyan) origin, Avraham Ben-Yiju, see Elizabeth Lambourn, *Abraham's Luggage: A Social Life of Things in the Medieval Indian Ocean World* (Cambridge: Cambridge University Press, 2018).

24. Jonathan Ray, *After Expulsion: 1492 and the Making of Sephardic Jewry* (New York: New York University Press, 2013); David Wacks, *Double Diaspora in Sephardic Literature: Jewish Cultural Production Before and After 1492* (Bloomington: Indiana University Press, 2015).

25. Emily Gottreich, *Jewish Morocco: A History from Pre-Islamic to Postcolonial Times* (London: I.B. Tauris, 2020), 77–99; Jane Gerber, "Refuge in Morocco after 1492," in *Jews and Muslims in Morocco: Their Intersecting Worlds*, ed. Joseph Chetrit, Jane Gerber, and Drora Arussy (Lanham, MD: Lexington Books, 2021), 15–38.

26. Jacques Taïeb, "Les juifs Livournais de 1600 à 1881," in *Histoire communautaire, histoire plurielle: La communauté juive de Tunisie*, ed. Abdelhamid Larguèche (Tunis: Centre de publication universitaire, 1999), 153–164; Yaron Tsur, "Haskala in a Sectional Colonial Society: Mahdia (Tunisia) 1884," in *Sephardi and Middle Eastern Jewries: History and Culture in the Modern Era*, ed. Harvey E. Goldberg (Bloomington: Indiana University Press, 1996), 146–167.

27. Jessica Marglin, *The Shamama Case: Contesting Citizenship across the Modern Mediterranean* (Princeton, NJ: Princeton University Press, 2022), esp. 70–71, 119–136.

28. Emily Gottreich, *The Mellah of Marrakech: Jewish and Muslim Space in Morocco's Red City* (Bloomington: Indiana University Press, 2007), esp. 132–137.

29. Compare, for example, Shlomo Deshen, who identified the eighteenth century in Moroccan Jewish history as a period of great creative and intellectual productivity, with Jane Gerber, who argues that "1700, or thereabouts, also marked the end of an era . . . [leading] to the abject poverty, social humiliation, and intellectual stagnation which have characterized Moroccan Jewry in the modern era": Shlomo Deshen, *The Mellah Society: Jewish Community Life in Sherifian Morocco* (Chicago: University of Chicago Press, 1989), 8–10; Jane Gerber, *Jewish Society in Fez 1450–1700: Studies in Communal and Economic Life* (Leiden: Brill, 1980), 6.

30. Daniel Schroeter, "From Sephardi to Oriental: The 'Decline' Theory of Jewish Civilization in the Middle East and North Africa," in *The Jewish Contribution to Civilization: Reassessing an Idea*, ed. Richard Cohen and Jeremy Cohen (Liverpool: Littman Library of Jewish Civilization, 2007), 125–148.

31. Emily Gottreich, "Of Messiahs and Sultans: Shabbetai Zevi and Early Modernity in Morocco," *Journal of Modern Jewish Studies* 12, no. 2 (2013): 184–209.

32. Daniel Schroeter, *Merchants of Essaouira: Urban Society and Imperialism in Southwestern Morocco, 1844–1886* (Cambridge: Cambridge University Press, 1988), 21–29; Gottreich, *Jewish Morocco*, 102–127; Sarah Abrevaya Stein, *Extraterritorial Dreams: European Citizenship, Sephardi Jews, and the Ottoman Twentieth Century* (Chicago: University of Chicago Press, 2016), 1–23; Julie Kalman, *The Kings of Algiers: How Two Jewish Families Shaped the Mediterranean World During the Napoleonic Wars and Beyond* (Princeton, NJ: Princeton University Press, 2023).

33. Daniel Schroeter and Joseph Chetrit, "Emancipation and Its Discontents: Jews at the Formative Period of Colonial Rule in Morocco," *Jewish Social Studies* 13, no. 1 (2006); Jessica Marglin, *Across Legal Lines: Jews and Muslims in Modern Morocco* (New Haven, CT: Yale University Press, 2016).

34. Aomar Boum, *Memories of Absence: How Muslims Remember Jews in Morocco* (Redwood City, CA: Stanford University Press, 2013); Maud Mandel, *Muslims and Jews in France: History of a Conflict* (Princeton, NJ: Princeton University Press, 2014); Kimberly Arkin, *Rhinestones, Religion, and the Republic: Fashioning Jewishness in France* (Redwood City, CA: Stanford University Press, 2014); Ethan Katz, *The Burdens of Brotherhood: Jews and Muslims from North Africa to France* (Cambridge, MA: Harvard University Press, 2015); Alma Heckman, *The Sultan's Communists: Moroccan Jews and the Politics of Belonging* (Redwood City, CA: Stanford University Press, 2020).

35. Gottreich and Schroeter, "Rethinking Jewish Culture and Society," 12.

36. Epstein, *Skies of Parchment, Seas of Ink*, 47–48.

37. Sarah Abrevaya Stein, *Making Jews Modern: The Yiddish and Ladino Press in the Russian and Ottoman Empires* (Bloomington: Indiana University Press, 2004); Matthias Lehmann, *Ladino Rabbinic Literature and Ottoman Sephardic Culture* (Bloomington: Indiana University Press, 2005); Olga Borovaya, *Modern Ladino Culture: Press, Belles Lettres, and Theater in the Late Ottoman Empire* (Bloomington: Indiana University Press, 2012).

38. Natalie Zemon Davis, "Printing and the People," in *Society and Culture in Early Modern France* (Redwood City, CA: Stanford University Press, 1975), 192; compare, for example, her work on Leo Africanus: Natalie Zemon Davis, *Trickster Travels: A Sixteenth-Century Muslim between Worlds* (New York: Macmillan, 2007).

39. Leslie Howsam, *Old Books and New Histories: An Orientation to Studies in Book and Print Culture* (Toronto: University of Toronto Press, 2006), 5, and see also her essay "The Study of Book History," in *The Cambridge Companion to the History of the Book*, ed. Leslie Howsam (Cambridge: Cambridge University Press, 2015), 1–16.

40. Roger Chartier, *The Order of Books: Readers, Authors, and Libraries in Europe between the Fourteenth and Eighteenth Centuries* (Redwood City, CA: Stanford University Press, 1994), 9.

41. D. F. McKenzie, *Bibliography and the Sociology of Texts* (Cambridge: Cambridge University Press, 1999). See also Harold Love, "Early Modern Print Culture: Assessing the Models," *Parergon* 20, no. 1 (2003): 45–64; Roger Chartier and Peter Stallybrass, "What Is a Book?," in *The Cambridge Companion to Textual Scholarship*, ed. Neil Fraistat and Julia Flanders (Cambridge: Cambridge University Press, 2015), 188–204; and Daniel Bellingradt and Jeroen Salman, "Books and Book History in Motion: Materiality, Sociality, and Spatiality," in *Books in Motion in Early Modern Europe: Beyond Production, Circulation and Consumption*, ed. Daniel Bellingradt, Paul Nelles, and Jeroen Salman (London: Palgrave Macmillan, 2017), 1–14; and, for "social codicology," see Olly Akkerman, *A Neo-Fatimid Treasury of Books: Arabic Manuscripts among the Alawi Bohras of South Asia* (Edinburgh: Edinburgh University Press, 2022).

42. Hugh Amory, "The Trout and the Milk: An Ethnobibliographical Talk," *Harvard Library Bulletin* 7 (1996): 51–65.

43. Amory, "The Trout and the Milk," 51.

44. Simon Bronner, *American Material Culture and Folklife* (Ann Arbor: University of Michigan Research Press, 1985), 129.

45. Iris Parush, *Reading Jewish Women: Marginality and Modernization in Nineteenth-Century Eastern European Jewish Society* (Waltham, MA: Brandeis University Press, 2004); Stern, *The Jewish Bible*; Teplitsky, *Prince of the Press*; Yakov Z. Meir, *Editio Princeps: The 1523 Venice Edition of the Palestinian Talmud and the Beginning of Hebrew Printing* (Jerusalem: Magnes, 2022); Joseph Skloot, *First Impressions: Sefer Hasidim and Early Modern Hebrew Printing* (Waltham, MA: Brandeis University Press, 2023).

46. For early studies, see David Cazès, *Notes bibliographiques sur la littérature juive-tunisienne* (Tunis: Imprimerie internationale, 1893); Eusèbe Vassel, *La littérature populaire des israélites tunisiens* (Paris: Leroux, 1907); Avraham Ya'ari, *Ha-defus ha-'ivri be-arṣot ha-mizraḥ* (Jerusalem: Hebrew University, 1936); Daniel Ḥagège, *Intishar al-ktayib al-yahudiyya al-barbariyya al-tunisiyya* (Sousse: Makhlouf Nadjar, 1939). These were followed by, inter alia: Avraham Attal, "'Al ha-defus ha-'ivri ba-magreb," *Mi-mizraḥ umi-ma'arav* 2 (1980): 121–129; Jacqueline Fraenkel, *L'Imprimerie Hébraique à Djerba* (PhD diss., University of Paris, 1982); Eliyahu Refael Marṣiano, *Sefer bnei melakhim: ve-hu toldot ha-sefer ha-'ivri ba-maroqo mi-shnat 5277 'ad shnat 5749* (Jerusalem: Mekhon haRaShaM, 1989); Yosef (Joseph) Tedghi, *Ha-sefer veha-defus ha-'ivri be-fas* (Jerusalem: Ben-Zvi Institute, 1994); Yosef Tobi and Tsivia Tobi, *Judeo-Arabic Literature in Tunisia, 1850–1950* (Detroit: Wayne State University Press, 2014).

1. MEDIEVAL BOOKS IN EARLY MODERN NORTH AFRICA

1. In another colophon, he describes himself as "the afflicted near death, Yiṣḥaq Ibn-Shoshan of the Exile of Sepharad [*mi-gerush sfarad*]," in a copy of the Kabbalistic work *Sefer ha-qane* that he copied ca. 1500 for a certain Moshe Halevi in Safed: Bodl. Opp. 548.

2. The date is equivalent to May 7, 1496.

3. The phrase "may God say 'enough!' to our troubles" is a rabbinic expression, originating in the midrash (*Tanḥuma* Miqeṣ 10 and *Bereshit rabba* 92:1, and cf. Rashi on Gen. 43:14, s.v. *El shaddai*).

4. BnF Héb. 769 (ancien fonds 272). On Yosef Ibn-Shoshan (ca. 1310–1380) and his commentary on *Avot*, see Michael Shmidman, "Radical Theology in Defense of the Faith: A Fourteenth-Century Example," *Tradition: A Journal of Orthodox Jewish Thought* 41, no. 2 (2008): 245–255. Yiṣḥaq Ibn-Shoshan eventually moved from Tunis to Safed where he continued to work as a scribe (as evidenced by another manuscript he copied, Bodl. Opp. 548). According to the eighteenth-century catalog of the Bibliothèque du Roi (now the Bibliothèque nationale de France), the manuscript now BnF Héb. 769 had "recently been brought to the library from Constantinople": *Catalogus codicum manuscriptorum Bibliothecae Regiae* Vol. I (Paris, 1739), 27.

5. BnF Héb. 855. The date is equivalent to October 5, 1492. See Michael Riegler, "Ma'atiqei sefarim mi-megorashei sfarad ve-hemshekh pe'ilotam

be-arṣot qeliṭatam," in *Hevra ve-tarbut: yehudei sfarad le-aḥar ha-gerush*, ed. Michael Abitbol, Galit Hasan-Rokem, and Yom-Tov Assis (Jerusalem: Misgav Yerushalayim, 1997), 188–201.

6. Bodl. Opp. Add. fol. 49, 256r. The phrase "the knees which did not bow to idolatry" is adapted from I Kings 19:18.

7. Malachi Beit-Arié, "Introduction," in *Specimens of Mediaeval Hebrew Scripts, Vol. II: Sefardic Script*, ed. Malachi Beit-Arié and Edna Engel (Jerusalem: Israel Academy of Sciences and Humanities, 2002), 9–20.

8. Stefan Reif, "A Centennial Assessment of Genizah Studies," in *The Cambridge Genizah Collections: Their Contents and Significance* (Cambridge: Cambridge University Press, 2002), 1–35.

9. For example, NLR Evr. II B 124, which Beit-Arié calls "the earliest dated extant manuscript from the zone of Sefardic book production," written in Qayrawan (today Kairouan, Tunisia) ca. 941–1039 CE: Malachi Beit-Arié, *Hebrew Codicology: Historical and Comparative Typology of Medieval Hebrew Codices* (Jerusalem: Israel Academy of Sciences and Humanities, 2021), 377, passim. See also Michael Riegler, "The Distribution of the Jewish Communities in North Africa according to the Medieval Hebrew Manuscripts Copied There," in *Progress and Tradition: Creativity, Leadership and Acculturation Processes among the Jews of North Africa*, ed. Moises Orfali and Ephraim Hazan (Jerusalem: Bialik Institute, 2005), 171–178.

10. Hebrew paleographers have established that the Iberian Sephardi style first developed in the southern region of al-Andalus and that the Iberian Jewish communities of the Christian north had a distinct book culture more akin to other northern European Jewish communities, but it was eventually absorbed into the Sephardi style. See, inter alia, Malachi Beit-Arié, "Hebrew Script in Spain: Development, Offshoots, and Vicissitudes," in *Moreshet Sepharad: The Sephardi Legacy*, ed. Haim Beinart (Jerusalem: Magnes, 1992), 282–317; Judith Olszowy-Schlanger, "An Early Palimpsest Scroll of the Book of Kings from the Cairo Geniza," in *"From a Sacred Source": Genizah Studies in Honour of Professor Stefan C. Reif*, ed. Ben Outhwaite and Siam Bhayro (Leiden: Brill, 2010), 237–247; and see the comprehensive survey by Malachi Beit-Arié and Edna Engel, *Specimens of Mediaeval Hebrew Scripts: Volume II, Sefardic Script* (Jerusalem: Israel Academy of Sciences and Humanities, 2002).

11. Beit-Arié, *Hebrew Codicology*, 79–82.

12. This is Beit-Arié's conclusion, "Hebrew Script in Spain," 291.

13. Katrin Kogman-Appel, *Jewish Book Art between Islam and Christianity: The Decoration of Hebrew Bibles in Medieval Spain* (Leiden: Brill, 2004), 47–49; Katrin Kogman-Appel, *Illuminating in Micrography: The Catalan*

Micrography Mahzor—MS Heb 8.6527 in the National Library of Israel (Leiden: Brill, 2013), 86–88.

14. Jonathan Ray, *After Expulsion: 1492 and the Making of Sephardic Jewry* (New York: New York University Press, 2013); Jane Gerber, "Refuge in Morocco after 1492," *Jews and Muslims in Morocco: Their Intersecting Worlds*, ed. Joseph Chetrit, Jane Gerber, and Drora Arussy (Lanham, MD: Lexington Books, 2021), 15–38.

15. From Saba's *Ṣeror ha-mor*, as published by Dan Manor, "Abraham Sabba: His Life and Work," *Jerusalem Studies in Jewish Thought* 2, no. 2 (1983): 208–231.

16. Manor, "Abraham Sabba."

17. Yehuda Ḥayyat, *Minḥat yehuda* on *Ma'arekhet ha-elohut* (Mantua: 1558), as translated by Brian Ogren in *The Posen Library of Jewish Culture and Civilization*, vol. 5, ed. Yosef Kaplan (New Haven, CT: Yale University Press, 2023), 94–95.

18. Menahem Schmelzer, "Hebrew Manuscripts and Printed Books among the Sephardim before and after the Expulsion," in *Crisis and Creativity in the Sephardic World: 1391–1648*, ed. Benjamin R. Gampel (New York: Columbia University Press, 1997), 256–266; Javier del Barco, "Joshua ibn Gaon's Hebrew Bibles and the Circulation of Books in the Late Medieval and Early Modern Periods," in *Patronage, Production, and Transmission of Texts in Medieval and Early Modern Jewish Cultures*, ed. Esperanza Alfonso and Jonathan Decter (Turnhout: Brepols, 2014), 267–297.

19. Inscribed on the first page of a three-volume Masoretic Bible, now in the Royal Danish Library, Copenhagen (RDL Ms. Heb. 7–9); a similar note of Yosef Ben-Ḥanin is also found in a manuscript prayer book (RDL Ms. Hebr. 30).

20. Now NLI RI Yah. A 3. By the eighteenth century, the volumes had migrated to Yemen. See Alexander Gordin, "Hebrew Incunabula in the National Library of Israel as a Source for Early Modern Book History in Europe and Beyond," in *Printing R-Evolution and Society 1450–1500: Fifty Years That Changed Europe*, ed. Cristina Dondi (Venice: Edizioni Ca'Foscari, 2020), 321–338.

21. Avraham Zacuto, *Sefer yuḥasin*, ed. Herschell Filipowski (London: H. Filipowski, 1857), 220.

22. Bodl. Kenn. 5. The chronogram for the year is ambiguous and could be read as either the Hebrew year 5260 or 5255.

23. TCD Ms. 13. See Stefania Silvestri, "Le Bibbie ebraiche della penisola iberica: Committenza, produzione e diffusione tra i secoli XIII e XVI" (PhD diss., Università Ca'Foscari Venezia, 2013), 143–144.

24. ANTT, Chancelaria de Rei Dom Manuel, liv. 17, f. 105, as cited in Elias Lipiner, *Os baptizados em pé: estudos acerca da origem e da luta dos Cristãos-novos em Portugal* (Lisbon: Vega, 1998), 178. Compare the account of a Jew from Massa, on the Atlantic coast of Morocco, who was ransomed from Portuguese captivity in 1510 by a certain Avraham Ben-Zamerro of Safi with "thirty *mithqals* and two large codices [*asfar*] from the books of the Jews": published in Henry de Castries, *Les sources inédites de l'histoire du Maroc: Archives et bibliothèques de Portugal* 1 (Paris: Ernest Leroux, 1934), 233–247, and cf. Lipiner, *Os baptizados em pé*, 178.

25. ANTT Inquisição de Lisboa Processo 12562, "Denúncias contra Vicente Lourenço," 1553: "*que mandasse vir livros de hebraico de Veneza, para vender aos Judeus que estão lá na terra dos mouros.*" See José Alberto Rodrigues da Silva Tavim, *Os judeus na expansão portuguesa em Marrocos durante o século XVI* (Braga: Edições APPACDM, 1997), 325–329.

26. "Mémoire de João Pedro [*sic*] Damtas, 7 juin 1562," published in Henry de Castries, *Les sources inédites de l'histoire du Maroc: Archives et bibliothèques d'Angleterre* 1 (Paris: Ernest Leroux, 1918), 44–49. See José Alberto Rodrigues da Silva Tavim, "Uma 'estranha tolerância' da Inquisição Portuguesa: Belchior Vaz de Azevedo e o interesse das potências europeias por Marrocos (segunda metade do século XVI)," in *Entre el Islam y Occidente: los judíos magrebíes en la edad moderna*, ed. Mercedes García-Arenal (Madrid: Casa de Velázquez, 2003), 101–123.

27. Tavim, *Os judeus*, 328–329.

28. Yosef Frontino's manuscript is BnF Héb. 710, once owned by French Orientalist Gilbert Gaulmin (1585–1665). The Spanish manuscripts copied by the Frontinos are AIU Ms. 101 by Ya'aqov, Seville, 1471; Parm. 2348, by Ya'aqov, Seville, 1474; and Bodl. Opp. Add. Qu. 26, Seville (?), 1480, for which Shmuel copied the Masora. JTS Ms. 10485, signed by "[?] Frontino b. Yehoshua," should probably be added to Ya'aqov's oeuvre.

29. Benjamin Richler, "The Scribe Moses ben Jacob Ibn Zabara of Spain: A Moroccan Saint?," *Jewish Art* 18 (1992): 141–147.

30. Michael Riegler, "Were the Yeshivot in Spain Centers for the Copying of Books?," *Sefarad* 57, no. 2 (1997): 373–398. On the general individual nature of Hebrew manuscript production, see Malachi Beit-Arié, "Ha-im hayyu sifriyyot ṣiburiyyot yehudiyyot bi-ymei ha-benayyim? Ha-ṣivyon ha-individu'ali shel hafaqat ha-sefer ha-'ivri u-ṣrikhato," *Zion* 65 (2000): 441–451.

31. CUL Trinity Ms. R 8 24. See Riegler, "The Distribution of the Jewish Communities in North Africa," 175; Riegler confusingly claims that there were two manuscripts written in Nahon's yeshiva but only references one.

32. BnF Héb. 169.

33. Frankfurt Cod. Hebr. Oct.93, *Midrash shokher ṭov* on Psalms, and RSL Ms. Guenzburg 936, Algiani's commentary on Ecclesiastes.

34. RSL Guenzburg 332, 905, and 910.

35. See, inter alia, Shimon Iakerson, "Unknown Sephardi Incunabula," Adri Offenberg, "What Do We Know about Hebrew Printing in Guadalajara, Híjar, and Zamora?," and Eleazar Gutwirth, "Techne and Culture: Printers and Readers in Fifteenth-Century Hispano-Jewish Communities," in *The Late Medieval Hebrew Book in the Western Mediterranean: Hebrew Manuscripts and Incunabula in Context,* ed. Javier del Barco (Leiden: Brill, 2015), 297–312, 313–337, 338–367.

36. I say "most likely" because although no evidence of earlier presses survives, there are possibilities. According to Hieronymus Münzer (1437–1508), two German printers [*impressores*] went to work in the Kongo kingdom around 1492 but soon returned, "for the region is not healthy for Germans." It is possible that they printed some books while they were there, although no imprints have yet been identified: António Brásio, *Monumenta Missionaria Africana: Africa Ocidental (1469–1599),* vol. 4 (Lisbon: Agencia Geral do Ultramar, 1954), 18–19; Inge Brinkman and Koen Bostoen, "'To Make Book': A Conceptual Historical Approach to Kongo Book Cultures (Sixteenth-Nineteenth Centuries)," in *The Kongo Kingdom: The Origins, Dynamics and Cosmopolitan Culture of an African Polity,* ed. Inge Brinkman and Koen Bostoen (Cambridge: Cambridge University Press, 2018), 216–234.

37. Eliyahu Refael Marṣiano, *Sefer bnei melakhim ve-hu toldot ha-sefer ha-'ivri ba-maroqo mi-shnat 5277 'ad shnat 5749* (Jerusalem: Mekhon haRaShaM, 1989), 11–14; Yosef (Joseph) Tedghi, *Ha-sefer veha-defus ha-'ivri be-fas* (Jerusalem: Ben-Zvi Institute, 1994), 76–83; Marvin Heller, *Further Studies in the Making of the Early Hebrew Book* (Leiden: Brill, 2013), 433–435. Marṣiano and Tedghi also list editions that are believed to have been printed at the Nedivot press but that did not survive, including *Sefer ha-azharot* of Yiṣḥaq b. Reuven al-Barjaloni (Albargeloni) and the *Hilkhot alfasi.*

38. Colophon of *Sefer abudarham* (Fez, 1516), as printed in Tedghi, *Ha-sefer veha-defus,* 79.

39. Haim Zalman Dimitrovsky, *S'ridei Bavli: An Historical and Bibliographical Introduction* (New York: Jewish Theological Seminary of America, 1979), 25, 44–48.

40. The manuscript page is JTS Rab. 2330 [MS 9311]. See Dimitrovsky, *S'ridei Bavli,* 61–70, and cf. Marvin Heller, *Printing the Talmud: A History*

of the Earliest Printed Editions of the Talmud (Brooklyn: Im Hasefer, 1992), 276.

41. Dimitrovsky, *S'ridei Bavli*, 67.

42. Dimitrovsky, *S'ridei Bavli*, 68–69. On the Hebrew press in Guadalajara, see Adri Offenberg, "What Do We Know about Hebrew Printing in Guadalajara, Híjar, and Zamora?," in *The Late Medieval Hebrew Book in the Western Mediterranean: Hebrew Manuscripts and Incunabula in Context*, ed. Javier del Barco (Leiden: Brill, 2015), 313–337.

43. Marvin Heller, *Studies in the Making of the Early Hebrew Book* (Leiden: Brill, 2007), 98.

44. As recorded by Tedghi, *Ha-sefer veha-defus*, 81.

45. Regarding paper, it appears in at least one case that the Nedivot press used Italian paper: the paper used in its printing of *Sefer abudarham*, as checked in the HUC copy, RBR B 2076, carries an Italian watermark of a hand topped with a fleuron: see figure 1.1. The closest match in Briquet's collection is Briquet 10.717, used in Venice, 1498: Charles-Moïse Briquet, *Les Filigranes: Dictionnaire historique des marques du papier dès leur apparition vers 1282 jusqu'en 1600*, vol. 3 (Paris: Picard et fils, 1907), 552.

46. Marṣiano, *Sefer bnei melakhim*, 14, 35; Tedghi, *Ha-sefer veha-defus*, 83.

47. Andrew Pettegree, *The Book in the Renaissance* (New Haven, CT: Yale University Press, 2011), 54–55.

48. Archivio di Stato di Firenze, Carte Strozziane serie I.324 c.46r–47v. I thank my colleagues Martina Mampieri and Francesca Bregoli for their kind assistance with the Italian. Cf. Marino Sanuto, *I Diarii di Marino Sanuto*, vol. 33, ed. Federico Stefani (Venice: F. Visentini, 1892), 576; and the German report of 1523 published in Varela Hervias and Von Waldheim, *Una relación alemana sobre el terremoto de Andalucia, Marruecos, y Azores del año 1522* (Madrid: Comisión de Cultura, 1948). I am grateful to Brad Sabin Hill for drawing my attention to this earthquake and its possible connection with the end of the Nedivot press. This earthquake has not yet been documented in Hebrew or Arabic sources, but it was reported fairly widely by European observers; see Nancy Joe Dyer, "La relación del terremoto en el mediterráneo, 1504–1542," in *España y el mundo mediterráneo a través de las relaciones de sucesos*, ed. Pierre Civil, Françoise Crémoux, and Jacobo S. Sanz Hermida (Salamanca: Ediciones Universidad de Salamanca, 2008), 141–156; Carlos Caracciolo, "Natural Disasters and the European Printed News Network," in *News Networks in Early Modern Europe*, ed. Joad Raymond and Noah Moxham (Leiden: Brill, 2016), 756–778. Modern seismologists have calculated the moment magnitude of this quake, which is believed to have begun in the Gulf of Almería, as 6.5:

José Peláez et al., "A Catalog of Main Moroccan Earthquakes from 1045 to 2005," *Seismological Research Letters* 78, no. 6 (2007): 614–621; Klaus Reicherter and Peter Becker-Heidmann, "Tsunami Deposits in the Western Mediterranean: Remains of the 1522 Almería Earthquake?," *Geological Society Special Publications* 316 (2009): 217–235.

49. I owe this suggestion to David Ruderman.

50. Some backlash to this might also be detected in the insistence by the "native," i.e. non-Sephardi, Jews of Fez on the historical identity of *toshavim* [inhabitants] and the importance of their books and rituals. See, e.g., the note of a certain Avraham Ibn-Danan (there are at least three rabbis with this name, but the writer is probably Avraham b. Menashe Ibn-Danan, 1797–1833; see Yosef Bennaim, *Malkhei rabbanan* (Jerusalem: Ha-ma'arav Press, 1931), 16b–17a) at the end of a sixteenth-century prayer book of the Fez rite: "This [book] is the custom of the *toshavim,* who have [held to this] since before the *megorashim* arrived here in Fez," Leiden UB Or. 4814, fol. 441v. This concern with preserving the textual heritage of the *toshavim* will reappear at the end of the nineteenth century with the *Dovevei Siftei Yeshenim* society, to be examined in chapter 5.

51. Immanuel Aboab, *Nomologia o Discursos Legales* (Amsterdam: s.n., 1629), 220.

52. Perhaps this is the same family as that of Moshe Rosilio of Marrakech (b. 1794) mentioned by Bennaim, *Malkhei rabbanan,* 88b. The manuscript is now HSA B241, Sections I and II; Curiel's acquisition note is on the final flyleaf of the second volume. On Athias's Bible edition, see Theodor Dunkelgrün, "Like a Blind Man Judging Colors: Joseph Athias and Johannes Leusden Defend Their 1667 Hebrew Bible," *Studia Rosenthaliana* 44 (2012): 79–115. Another example of a medieval Iberian Bible purchased by a Portuguese Sephardi from Western Europe in North Africa is BnF Héb. 21, written and decorated in Tudela in 1301 by famed illuminator-scribe Yehoshua Ibn-Gaon, which was purchased in Salé in 1628 from "Abraham Abensur" by a Portuguese-speaking Jew. See del Barco, "Joshua ibn Gaon's Hebrew Bibles," 267–297.

53. Jehosuah da Silva, Semuel Pinto, and Abraham Senior Corronel, "Correctores pio Lectori S.," in *Biblia Hebraica Accuratissima,* ed. Johannes Leusden (Amsterdam: Joseph Athias, 1667).

54. The *mishmarot* are a system of additional extraliturgical readings associated with the weekly parashah; see Ephraim Urbach, "Mishmarot u-ma'amadot," *Tarbiṣ* 42 (1973): 304–327. For candle drippings, see, e.g., RDL Ms. Heb. 8, 151a, and RDL Ms. Heb. 9, 58a.

55. Bodl. Or. 650, acquired in Morocco in 1852 by bookseller Moses Hecht (about whom more follows).

56. Bennaim, *Malkhei rabbanan*, 93a. The Abensur family library will be examined more fully in chapter 6. The current location of Ibn-Zabara's manuscript has not yet been identified; however, there is strong evidence to suggest that it is BL Or. 2286, sold to the British Library by Jacob Sappir in 1880. This manuscript, unfortunately now incomplete, is a Pentateuch with *haftarot* and the *megillot*, exactly as Bennaim describes; it contains a note in an early modern Sephardi hand on 103v that attributes it to Ibn-Zabara and indicates that it should be used as an authorized copy "to correct biblical texts from," exactly as Abensur used it. I thank Judith Olszowy-Schlanger for suggesting this possibility.

57. Bennaim, *Malkhei rabbanan*, 34a.

58. Bodl. Opp. Add. fol. 48, 13v. Neither of the notes appears to be in the handwriting of Ya'aqov Abensur, but the first hand bears a close resemblance to the handwriting of his grandson, Shlomo-Eliyahu Abensur, who sold the manuscript to Eli'ezer Ashkenazi in 1841.

59. Moshe Berdugo, *Rosh mashbir* (Livorno: Moshe Tubiana, 1840), 30b. See Haim Bentov, "Rabbinic Literature in North Africa in the Last 250 Years," *Pe'amim* 86–87 (2001): 216.

60. NLI RIV 71 A 1974, *Sefer ha-shorashim* (Naples, 1491). This note, written in French (with Hebrew initials at the end), is the same hand as the signature on another page by "Ichoua Sultan," Tlemcen, 1887.

61. This was not limited to Hebrew manuscripts but applied to "Oriental" manuscripts in general. See Colin Wakefield, "Arabic Manuscripts in the Bodleian Library: The Seventeenth-Century Collections," in *The 'Arabick' Interest of the Natural Philosophers in Seventeenth-Century England*, ed. G. A. Russell (Leiden: Brill, 1993), 128–146; Gerard Toomer, *Eastern Wisedome and Learning: The Study of Arabic in Seventeenth-Century England* (Oxford: Clarendon, 1996), esp. 93–146.

62. W. B. S. Taylor, *History of the University of Dublin* (London: Cadell and Cumming, 1845), 315. These two manuscripts are now TCD Ms. 13 and 16.

63. They were purchased by Carsten Niebuhr and Frederik Christian von Haven while on the Royal Danish Arabia Expedition (1761–1767). They then entered the Royal Danish Library, where they are now RDL Ms. Heb. 7–9 and 30.

64. It is now Bodl. MS Kenn. 1. On this and other bibles in Kennicott's collection, see Maria Theresa Ortega-Monasterio, "Some Hebrew Bibles in

the Bodleian Library: The Kennicott Collection," *Journal of Semitic Studies* 62, no. 1 (2017): 93–111; and Theodor Dunkelgrün, "The Kennicott Collection," in *Jewish Treasures from Oxford Libraries*, ed. Rebecca Abrams and César Merchán-Hamann (Oxford: Oxford University Press, 2020), 115–158. It was already owned by Chalmers sometime before 1762 since in that year, Kennicott wrote of "the notice lately received of a MS Bible, in the hands of Mr Chalmers of Auld-bar in Scotland; who brought it, some years since, from Gibraltar." Benjamin Kennicott, *The Ten Annual Accounts of the Collation of Hebrew Mss. of the Old Testament Begun in 1760 and Completed in 1769* (Oxford: Fletcher and Prince, 1770), 44–45.

65. Benjamin Kennicott, letter of June 5, 1770, Bodl. MS DD. Radcl. c. 36. Cited in Stanley George Gillam, *The Building Accounts of the Radcliffe Camera* (Oxford: Clarendon, 1958), xxxvii–xxxix.

66. The purchase was recorded in the Minutes of the Radcliffe Trustees, April 5, 1771; it was transferred to the Bodleian Library in 1872. See the companion volume of Bezalel Narkiss and Aliza Cohen-Mushlin to the facsimile edition, *The Kennicott Bible: An Introduction* (London: Facsimile, 1985), 9.

67. Kennicott transcribes the word in Hebrew characters. The genizah was a storage place for worn-out sacred texts, which was regularly emptied, and its contents buried in the Jewish cemetery. On genizah practice among Jews of the Islamic world, see Mark Cohen and Yedida Stillman, "Genizat qahir u-minhagei geniza shel yehudei ha-mizraḥ: ʻiyyun hisṭori ve-etnografi," *Peʻamim* 24, no. 1 (1985): 3–35; Joseph Sadan, "Genizah and Genizah-Like Practices in Islamic and Jewish Traditions," *Bibliotheca Orientalis* 43, no. 1 (1986): 36–58. Kennicott's use of the word, although written in Hebrew script, may be considered its first appearance in English; see Dunkelgrün, "The Kennicott Collection," 145.

68. Bodl. Kenn. 7, 1r. Isaac Netto, or Nieto (1687–1773), was born in Livorno and raised in London, where his father, David, was the *haham* (rabbinic leader) of the Spanish and Portuguese community. He also spent time in Tetouan as a young man, dedicating a *teba* (reading desk) to a newly restored synagogue there in 1720; this was perhaps the occasion of his acquisition of Kenn. 7. Nieto served as a rabbi in London from 1732 to 1741, in Gibraltar from 1749 to 1751, and again in London from 1751 to 1757. See Israel Solomons, "David Nieto and Some of His Contemporaries," *Transactions of the Jewish Historical Society of England* 12 (1928): 1–101.

69. Eva Mroczek, "Batshit Stories: New Tales of Discovering Ancient Texts," *Marginalia Review*, June 22, 2018; and cf. her forthcoming book, *Out of the Cave: The Possibility of a New Scriptural Past.*

70. On the complex history of the Geniza's "discovery" and excavation, see Peter Cole and Adina Hoffman, *Sacred Trash: The Lost and Found World of the Cairo Geniza* (New York: Schocken Books, 2011); Rebecca J. W. Jefferson, "Deconstructing 'the Cairo Genizah': A Fresh Look at Genizah Manuscript Discoveries in Cairo before 1897," *Jewish Quarterly Review* 108, no. 4 (2018): 422–448; and Rebecca J. W. Jefferson, *The Cairo Genizah and the Age of Discovery in Egypt: The History and Provenance of a Jewish Archive* (London: Bloomsbury, 2022).

71. See, e.g., the seventeen manuscripts bought by the Bodleian from Hecht in 1852: Falconer Madan, *A Summary Catalogue of Western Manuscripts in the Bodleian Library at Oxford*, vol. 5 (Oxford: Oxford University Press, 1905), 482. The Leiden manuscripts, bought on Moritz Steinschneider's recommendation, are Leiden Or. 4813 and Or. 4814; see Jan Just Witkam, "Moritz Steinschneider and the Leiden Manuscripts," in *Studies on Steinschneider: Moritz Steinschneider and the Emergence of the Science of Judaism in Nineteenth-Century Germany*, ed. Reimund Leicht and Gad Freudenthal (Leiden: Brill, 2011), 263–275.

72. This manuscript is now Bodl. Or. 604. For Moroccan readers' engagement with the text, not noted in Neubauer's catalog, see, e.g., fol. 31v.

73. Robert (Avraham) Attal, "Les reportages d'Eliézer Ashkenazi: Une source journalistique oubliée sur l'histoire des Juifs de Tunisie à la fin de l'époque pré-coloniale," in *Entre Orient et Occident: Juifs et Musulmans en Tunisie*, ed. Denis Cohen-Tannoudji (Paris: Éditions de l'Éclat, 2007), 335–346. Some of the medieval manuscripts he sold to the British Library include Add. MS 19777, 19779, 19787, 22089, 22090, and 22093.

74. *Sefer ha-zikaron* (Livorno: Jacob Ashkenazi, 1845), 1a. The published text is a supercommentary on Rashi written by Sephardi exile Avraham Halevi Bakrat in Tunis in 1507.

75. Bennaim, *Malkhei rabbanan*, 34a; Anonymous, "Literatur-Berichte," *Literaturblatt des Orients* X (1849) no. 24, 370.

76. *Ḥavaṣelet* 28 (June 10, 1898), 8. For the correspondence with Rabinowich, I am deeply grateful to the late Jacques Soffer (1940–2019) and his son David, Jacob's grandson and great-grandson, for generously sharing material from his family collection with me.

77. E. N. Adler, *Catalogue of Hebrew Manuscripts in the Collection of Elkan Nathan Adler* (Cambridge: Cambridge University Press, 1921), 7. These manuscripts are: JTS Ms. 343 (formerly Adler 1991); JTS Ms. 2450 (Adler 1609); and JTS Ms. 2811 (Adler 837). According to Adler's account, his travels in North Africa included Egypt, 1888; Morocco 1892 and 1894; Algiers and Tunis 1894–1895; Egypt again in 1895–1896, and

1898; Morocco again in 1900; and Algiers and Tunis again in 1905. Adler, *Catalogue*, v.

78. Bennaim, *Malkhei rabbanan*, 34a. According to Aron Freimann, "Typograpisches," *Zeitschrift für hebraeische Bibliographie* (14, 1910), 79, Lipschitz sold the most complete copy of the Fez *Abudarham* to E. N. Adler that same year; it is now HUC RBR B 2076.

79. Bennaim, *Malkhei rabbanan*, 34a. The Fez *Ṭurim* is now JTS RBR BM520.86.A54, a composite of varied provenance, including a penciled note attributing leaves to Schwager. For an account of Schwager's book-buying on a trip to Yemen, see Adam Bin-Nun, "The Ashkenazi Bookdealers in Yemen (1925–1929)," *My Heart Is in the East* 3 (2021): 45–76 (Hebrew).

80. Bennaim, *Malkhei rabbanan*, 34a.

81. The *Avot* commentary is now BnF Ms. hebr. 448, and the Narboni manuscript Ms. hebr. 957. The sales contract, which Bennaim found "among a bundle of letters from Refael [II] Abensur," is summarized in *Malkhei rabbanan* 34a; Bennaim writes that it includes prices, but he unfortunately did not copy them. If the contract is still extant, its current location is unknown to me.

82. Israel Bartal, "The Kinnus Project: Wissenschaft des Judentums and the Fashioning of a 'National Culture' in Palestine," in *Transmitting Jewish Traditions: Orality, Textuality and Cultural Diffusion*, ed. Yaakov Elman and Israel Gershoni (New Haven, CT: Yale University Press, 2000), 310–323; Adam Rubin, "'Like a Necklace of Black Pearls Whose String Has Snapped': Bialik's *Aron ha-sefarim* and the Sacralization of Zionism," *Prooftexts* 28, no. 2 (2008): 157–196.

83. See, e.g., the deep interest in Sephardi literature and history shown by many Jewish intellectuals and Zionist leaders of the late nineteenth and early twentieth centuries (paired with Orientalist and even racist attitudes toward actual living Sephardi communities), including Avraham Meir Habermann, Ḥayyim Naḥman Bialik, Salman Schocken, and Ḥayyim Jefim Schirmann: Sami Shalom Chetrit, "Revisiting Bialik: A Radical Mizrahi Reading of the Jewish National Poet," *Comparative Literature* 62, no. 1 (2010): 1–21; Lital Levy, *Poetic Trespass: Writing between Hebrew and Arabic in Israel/Palestine* (Princeton, NJ: Princeton University Press, 2014), 60–104; S. J. Pearce, "'His (Jewish) Nation and His (Muslim) King': Modern Nationalism Articulated through Medieval Andalusi Poetry," in *'His Pen and Ink Are a Powerful Mirror': Andalusi, Judaeo-Arabic, and Other Near Eastern Studies in Honor of Ross Brann*, ed. Adam Bursi, S. J. Pearce, and Hamza Zafer (Leiden: Brill, 2020), 140–162.

84. The Halevi manuscript is now Bodl. Opp. Add. Qu. 81. The two *Pesiqta* manuscripts are now AIU Ms. 47 and Cambridge Ms. Add. 1497 (purchased from the German bookseller Fischl Hirsch in 1876). On the *Mekitze Nirdamim* Society, see the collected essays in Shulamit Elizur, ed., *From Oblivion to the Bookshelf: The 150th Anniversary of Mekize Nirdamim* (Jerusalem: Mekize Nirdamim, 2013); it also inspired later projects like the *Dovevei Siftei Yeshenim* Society, to be examined in chapter 5.

85. Samuel David Luzzato, "Introduction," in *Virgo Filia Jehudae, sive Excerpta ex inedito . . . Divano* (Prague: M. Landau, 1840), 5.

86. "'Azuva be-shetaḥ meḥqar yehudei ha-mizraḥ," *Ha-boqer* 4871 (October 29, 1951), 4. The urgency of this mission for Ben-Zvi was also due to the mass migration of Jewish communities from the Middle East after the establishment of the State of Israel in 1948, which included the movement of libraries and other cultural property. See Benjamin Richler, "Manuscripts and Manuscript Collections," *Encyclopedia of Jews in the Islamic World*, ed. Noam Stillman (Leiden: Brill, 2010); Noah Gerber, *Anu o sifrei ha-qodesh shebe-yadenu? Ha-gilui ha-tarbuti shel yahadut Teman* (Jerusalem: Ben-Zvi Institute, 2012); Matti Friedman, *The Aleppo Codex: In Pursuit of One of the World's Most Coveted, Sacred, and Mysterious Books* (New York: Workman, 2012); Gish Amit, *Eqs libris: hisṭoria shel gezel, shimur ve-nikus ba-sifriyya ha-le'umit bi-yrushalayim* (Jerusalem: Van Leer, 2014).

87. For similar dynamics among Ladino-speaking Ottoman Sephardi scholars of the same period, see Julia Phillips Cohen and Sarah Abrevaya Stein, "Sephardic Scholarly Worlds: Toward a Novel Geography of Modern Jewish History," *Jewish Quarterly Review* 100, no. 3 (2010): 367–368.

88. Bennaim, *Malkhei rabbanan*, 105b. Two of these volumes survive in NLI Ms. Heb. 8.2085 and 8.4492. Others may have made their way into the Bension Collection, since many of the Bension materials relate to the Abensur family and several even bear the stamp of Refael II Abensur, e.g., BC Pr. 294, a copy of Yishma'el Tanuji's *Sefer ha-zikaron* (Ferrara: Abraham Usque, 1555). See Saul Aranov, *A Descriptive Catalogue of the Bension Collection of Sephardic Manuscripts and Texts* (Edmonton: University of Alberta Press, 1979).

89. Shalom Amar, "Introduction," in *Mishpaṭim yesharim* (Kraków: Josef Fischer, 1891), 1a. *Mishpaṭim yesharim* is the collected responsa of Refael Berdugo of Meknes (1747–1821).

90. Yiṣḥaq Morali, "Sefer ṣafnat paneaḥ," *Koveṣ 'al yad* 7 (1897), 5–6. In his article, Morali presented an edition of liturgical poems by rabbis Yiṣḥaq ben Sheshet (1326–1408) and Shim'on bar Ṣemaḥ Duran

(1361–1444) with his own commentary and a response from the Hungarian Maskilic scholar Haim Brody (1868–1942).

91. In 2002, it was donated to the Musée d'art et d'histoire du judaïsme (mahJ) by Bernard, Jean-Paul, Leon-Georges, and Robert Durand, "following a family consultation meeting in which all family members declared themselves in agreement to the donation." It is now mahJ Inv.2002.36.001.

92. Bodl. Or. 614. For the purchase from Hecht, see Falconer Madan, *A Summary Catalogue of Western Manuscripts in the Bodleian Library at Oxford*, vol. 5 (Oxford: Oxford University Press, 1905), 482, and the inscription on the 3rd inner flyleaf, recto.

93. The quire added by Serfaty comprises fols. 1r–9v, or Gen. 1:1–8:7.

94. Bodl. Or. 614, 1v.

2. SCRIBES, ARTISTS, AND PATRONS OF THE HANDWRITTEN BOOK

1. There is no easy way to calculate exact numbers. A recent search on the KTIV database for manuscripts written in Morocco, Algeria, Tunisia, or "North Africa" between 1600 and 1900 yielded some 2,211 manuscripts; similarly, a search for early modern manuscripts cataloged as being written in "Maghrebi-style" script brought back 3,254 records. No doubt other manuscripts may be hidden by the specific search parameters or not indexed on this site.

2. Emile Schrijver, "Jewish Book Culture since the Invention of Printing," in *The Cambridge History of Judaism: Volume 7, The Early Modern World, 1500–1815*, ed. Jonathan Karp and Adam Sutcliffe (Cambridge: Cambridge University Press, 2017), 291–315.

3. Emile Schrijver, "The Eye of the Beholder: Artistic Sense and Craftsmanship in Eighteenth-Century Jewish Books," *Images* 7 (2015): 35–55.

4. Emile Schrijver, "The Hebraic Book," in *A Companion to the History of the Book*, ed. Simon Eliot and Jonathan Rose (Oxford: Oxford University Press, 2007), 161–162.

5. Shalom Sabar, "Sephardi Elements in North African Hebrew Manuscript Decoration," *Jewish Art* 18 (1992): 169.

6. On the importance of user production for medieval Hebrew manuscripts, see Malachi Beit-Arié, "Ha-'im hayyu sifriyyot ṣiburiyyot yehudiyyot bi-ymei ha-benayyim? Ha-ṣivyon ha-individu'ali shel hafaqat ha-sefer ha-'ivri u-ṣrikhato," *Zion* 65 (2000): 441–451.

7. On the various genres of rabbinic literature in North Africa, see Moshe Bar-Asher, "Ha-sifrut ha-rabbanit bi-ṣfon afriqa 1700–1948," *Pe'amim* 86/87 (2001): 233–257; Hayyim Bentov, "Rabbinic Literature in North Africa in the Last 250 Years," *Pe'amim* 86/87 (2001): 214–232. On the importance of putting down one's own insights in writing for Maghrebi scholars, see Yosef (Joseph) Tedghi, *Ha-sefer veha-defus ha-'ivri be-fas* (Jerusalem: Ben-Zvi Institute, 1994), 9–17.

8. The year is indicated by a chronogram from Zephaniah 3:2, yielding the Hebrew year 5478. Frankfurt University Library, Ms. Oct. 122.

9. NLI Ms. Heb. 8.6551; the date of this inscription is effaced, but it appears to be mid-nineteenth century.

10. On female scribes in other areas of the Jewish world, see Michael Riegler and Judith Baskin, "'May the Writer Be Strong': Medieval Hebrew Manuscripts Copied by and for Women," *Nashim* 16, no. 2 (2008): 9–28.

11. On the development of the cursive Hebrew script used in North Africa, its cultural importance, and the traditional process of learning and using it, see Yael Barouch, "Moallech / nsf qalam: Documentation and Cultural Reflection on Hebrew Cursive Script" (master's thesis, Hebrew University, 2016).

12. Haïm Zafrani, *Pédagogie juive en terre d'Islam: l'enseignement traditionnel de l'hébreu et du judaïsme au Maroc* (Paris: Maisonneuve, 1969), 74. Cf. the remarks on the sofer as an instructor of writing, and the teaching of Hebrew script, in *Pédagogie juive*, 9–11, 31–50.

13. I am relying on the dates given by Yosef Bennaim in *Malkhei rabbanan* (Jerusalem: Ha-ma'arav Press, 1931), 32a, who writes that Toledano died in 1716 at the age of fifty-eight.

14. JTS Ms 6628 (Rab. 805), 8b.

15. JTS Ms 6628 (Rab. 805), 247a.

16. The Talmudic commentary, *Me-harerei nemarim*: Leeds Roth Ms. 313; *Sha'arei shamayyim*: JTS Ms. 361 (Bennaim 110); *Ohel ya'aqov*: Columbia MS X893 T574 (Numbers), and Benayahu Ms. NA 166 (Leviticus-Deuteronomy).

17. Gross 96.

18. NLI Ms. Heb. 8.2144.

19. Bennaim, *Malkhei rabbanan*, 82a.

20. On the legal work of sofrim in Morocco, see Jessica Marglin, *Across Legal Lines: Jews and Muslims in Modern Morocco* (New Haven, CT: Yale University Press, 2016), esp. 30–31.

21. For an example of a Moroccan manuscript of a *tiqqun sofrim*, a model text for the copying of the Torah, see BC Ms. 307, vols. 1–4.

22. On amulet writing among Maghrebi Jews, see Noam Sienna, "Neighbouring Imaginaries: Jews and Demons in the Maghreb" (master's thesis, University of Toronto, 2015), 54–90.

23. *'Eṭ sofer* circulated widely in manuscript and also appeared partially in print in Avraham Ankawa, *Kerem ḥemer* (Livorno: Eliyahu Benamozegh, 1869).

24. Compare, e.g., the anecdote told by Goitein of a learned Yemenite interlocutor, a craftsman by trade who was revealed to be unable to write and who replied contemptuously, "I am not a business clerk." S. D. Goitein, *A Mediterranean Society: The Jewish Communities of the Arab World as Portrayed in the Documents of the Cairo Geniza*, vol. 2 (Oakland: University of California Press, 1971), 179.

25. *Leshon limmudim*, letter 9, as published by David Ovadia, *Fas ve-ḥakhameha: divrei yemei ha-yehudim be-qehillat qodesh fas*, vol. 2 (Jerusalem: Beit Oved, 1979), 265. This passage is a textual interplay with Song of Songs 3:4. See Moshe Amar, "Qavvim li-demuto shel rabbi Ya'aqov Ibn Ṣur," *Mizrah u-ma'arav* 3 (1981): 106–110.

26. JTS Ms. 2187.

27. These are *Sefer ha-kavvanot*, finished at the end of June 1781 for Yiṣḥaq Narboni (JTS Ms. 316 / Ben-Naim 64), and a codex of three other works by Ḥayyim Vital, finished at the end of July 1781 for a patron whose name was erased (NLI Ms. Heb. 8.2803). The first manuscript has a beautifully decorated title page; it is unclear whether this is the work of Bensoussan or another artist.

28. NLI Ms. Yah. Heb. 117.

29. YBZ Ms. 2819, 94v; it was written in Qṣar as-Suq (today Errachidia) in southeastern Morocco, and the second half of the manuscript (written later, by Yehuda Lesri) is dated 1875.

30. Yale MS.1825.0253 (formerly Boesky 64). Bouchoucha began it on the 4th of Av (August 7, 1788) and finished it on the 28th of Elul (September 30), just two days before Rosh Hashanah. In 1806, he wrote himself another mahzor (formerly Sassoon 687) and sold the older one to a certain Ya'aqov Guedj, according to a note on the last page. It was later used in the Old Synagogue of Constantine (Ṣlat l-Qadima) until at least 1918 when it was rebound under the supervision of Joseph Renassia (1879–1962) and the local *consistoire* [Jewish administrative body] of Constantine.

31. Yale MS.1825.0253, 72b.

32. See Moshe Amar, ed., *Sefer minḥat yehuda: mahadura tinyana* (Lod: Orot Yehudei Hamagreb, 2011). Bahlul was copying from a manuscript in the Abensur family library, to be discussed in chapter 6.

33. Not to be confused with the commentary of the same title by Ya'aqov Toledano, this *Ohel ya'aqov* was written by Ya'aqov ben Wolf Kranz (1741–1804) of Dubno, Lithuania, and printed five times by 1865. This manuscript copy is now YBZ 772.

34. YBZ 772, 1v.

35. Unfortunately, the manuscript is missing its final page, which might have contained the scribe's name or the date and place of writing. The manuscript contains Ḥayyim Vital's *Qehillat ya'aqov*, as edited by Ya'aqov Ṣemaḥ, with some additional annotations by the copyist. Once in the collection of Shlomo Moussaieff, it was sold by Sotheby's, sale 9589 (December 15, 2016), lot 157; its current location is unknown, but it was digitized by the IMHM, film no. MSS-D 8669.

36. This note is found on 78v, IMHM film no. MSS-D 8669.

37. Harold Love, *The Culture and Commerce of Texts: Scribal Publication in Seventeenth-Century England*, 2nd ed. (Amherst: University of Massachusetts Press, 1998), 32.

38. Love, *Scribal Publication*, 35–36.

39. Love, *Scribal Publication*, 44–47.

40. Love, *Scribal Publication*, 73.

41. Letter of Ya'aqov Abensur to Menaḥem Serero, 1719 (BC YR MS 105). Abensur explains that these poems, on the theme of tzitzit and tefillin, "were recited on the day of Rosh Ḥodesh Adar, when my son 'Oved was wrapped [for the first time] in public in those three commandments [of tzitzit and tefillin]. . . . They are to educate any young student who is taking on these commandments, and especially when my dear nephew wraps himself [in tzitzit and tefillin] on Rosh Hodesh Nisan, or later.'"

42. NLI Ms. Heb. 8.2062. In fact, this manuscript circulated for well over a century; its cover bears an ownership inscription testifying that "I, Ya'aqov Abensur [Ibn-Ṣur, 1673–1752], purchased it from the inheritors of Levi Toledano," and it continued to be read by the Abensur family; fol. 80b, e.g., bears a correction signed by Shlomo-Eliyahu Abensur (1822–1873), and the cover bears the stamp of the library of Refael Abensur of Fez (1830–1917).

43. This manuscript is now held at the Centre de la culture judéo-marocaine in Brussels (CCJM 30199). The date given on the title page is "Monday, the first of Adar, in the year 'You BLESSED the work of his hands' [5622]," which would yield 1862; however, since Dahan was only born in 1866, I propose also including the word HANDS in the chronogram, yielding 5652 / 1892, in which the first of Adar did indeed fall on a Monday. A complication in this dating is that the manuscript also

mentions Ya'aqov Abuḥaṣira (1806–1880) and follows his name with the phrase "may God protect and guard him," used for living figures, rather than the expected "of blessed memory." However, it is possible (although unlikely) that Dahan had not heard of Abuḥaṣira's death, which happened in Egypt, after Abuḥaṣira's departure from Morocco.

44. *Tehillot adonai* (CCJM 30199), "Introduction."

45. Bennaim records, e.g., that "[Moshe Ibn-Zabara] left behind him a composition on the laws of [writing] a Torah scroll, letter by letter, and this manuscript was kept in Fez by the widow of Rabbi Immanuel Serero: this is known to me from a letter sent by Yiṣḥaq Bengualid to Yedidya Monsonego, asking him to buy the manuscript from this widow, or to hire a scribe to copy it." *Malkhei rabbanan*, 93a. Some examples of surviving letters inquiring about books: Yale MS.1825.0107, 1825.0109, and 1825.0115; Bension BC YR MS 187 and 219, and cf. the many letters between Moroccan rabbis and Jerusalem booksellers: BC YR MS. 32, 54, 135, 145, 232, 238, and 264.

46. *Leshon limmudim*, letter 186, addressed to Moshe Yisrael, *shadar* of Safed in Tunis, as published by Ovadia, *Fas ve-ḥakhameha*, 2:332–333.

47. He collaborated with Shlomo Zarqa to publish a number of important Judeo-Arabic liturgical manuals and rabbinic texts; see Eliyahu Refael Marṣiano, *Sefer malkhei yeshurun* (Jerusalem: Mekhon haRaShaM, 1999), 103. On his correspondent, Shlomo-Eliyahu Abensur, see Bennaim, *Malkhei rabbanan*, 116a.

48. This refers to the Moroccan rabbi Raḥamim Yosef al-Jayani (d. 1891), who authored several books while traveling through Morocco, Tunisia, Algeria, and the Ottoman Empire; see Marṣiano, *Sefer malkhei yeshurun*, 29.

49. This is most likely the historical chronicle of the Ibn-Danan family known as *Divrei ha-yamim* or *al-Tawarikh*, compiled over centuries by the Ibn Danan family and finalized in the early eighteenth century by Shmuel ben Sha'ul Ibn-Danan (1668–ca. 1730); see Yigal Nizri, "Judeo-Moroccan Traditions and the Age of European Expansionism in North Africa," in *The Sephardic Atlantic: Colonial Histories and Postcolonial Perspectives*, ed. Sina Rauschenbach and Jonathan Schorsch (London: Palgrave Macmillan, 2018), 337.

50. Letter of Yehuda Ḍarmon to Shlomo-Eliyahu Abensur, 1866 (BC YR MS 52).

51. In another letter, Abensur told his colleague Levi Toledano—who had apparently copied a book for him in script that he found

displeasing—that the book "was written in letters all twisted together; if any Jewish scholar were to see a Torah scroll written in this type of script, he would immediately tear it up in anger, for [the halakha] demands at least a hairsbreadth of space between each letter, and this has none": *Leshon limmudim*, letter 74 (Ovadia, *Fas ve-ḥakhameha*, 332–333).

52. On medieval Jewish illumination in general, see Marc Michael Epstein, ed., *Skies of Parchment, Seas of Ink: Jewish Illuminated Manuscripts* (Princeton, NJ: Princeton University Press, 2015). On the work of medieval Jewish illuminators, see, inter alia, Vivian Mann, "The Unknown Jewish Artists of Medieval Iberia," in *The Jew in Medieval Iberia, 1100–1500*, ed. Jonathan Ray (Boston: Academic Studies, 2013), 138–175; Suzanne Wijsman, "The Oppenheimer Siddur: Artist and Scribe in a Fifteenth-Century Hebrew Prayer Book," in *Crossing Borders: Hebrew Manuscripts as a Meeting-Place of Cultures*, ed. Piet van Boxel and Sabine Arndt (Oxford: Oxford University Press, 2009), 69–84; Bezalel Narkiss, "A List of Hebrew Books (1330) and a Contract to Illuminate Manuscripts (1335) from Majorca," *Revue des Études Juives* 70 (1961): 297–320; Katrin Kogman-Appel, "Coping with Christian Pictorial Sources: What Did Jewish Miniaturists Not Paint?," *Speculum* 75, no. 4 (2000): 816–858; Yaël Zirlin, "Celui qui se cache derrière l'image: colophons des enlumineurs dans les manuscrits hébraïques," *Revue des Études Juives* 155, no. 1 (1996): 33–53; Katrin Kogman-Appel, "'Elisha ben Abraham, Known as Cresques': Scribe, Illuminator, and Mapmaker in Fourteenth-Century Mallorca," *Ars Judaica* 10 (2014): 27–36.

53. See, e.g., BL Or. 10334 (Gaster 313), a manuscript volume of the songs of Ya'aqov Berdugo, copied in Meknes by Yosef Abensur (Ibn-Ṣur) in 1831.

54. See, e.g., the Hispano-Moresque Haggadah, from Castile, ca. 1300 (BL Or. 2737), and the Second Bible of Yehoshua' Ibn-Gaon, Tudela, 1301 (BNF cod. hébr. 21). See also Sabar, "Sephardi Elements," 168–191; Victor Klagsbald, "À propos de l'illustration du chandelier à sept branches sur un acte de mariage," *Jewish Art* 19/20 (1994): 248–250.

55. Escorial Ms. G-III-13. See Javier del Barco, *Catálogo de manuscritos hebreos de la Comunidad de Madrid, Vol. I: Manuscritos bíblicos, comentarios bíblicos de autor y obras gramaticales en las bibliotecas de El Escorial, Universidad Complutense de Madrid y Palacio Real* (Madrid: CSIC, 2003). I thank Javier del Barco for his assistance with this manuscript.

56. E.g., *Sha'arei shamayyim*, Meknes, 1679 (JTS Ms. 361 / Ben-Naim 110), copied from the printed edition (Prague, 1675); *Mone mispar*,

Tlemcen, 1690 (formerly London Montefiore 421, sold at Sotheby's, 2008). For an example of this illumination style outside of books, see the Algerian ketubah written in 1669 for Aharon Konsino and Simḥa Sasportas from the city of Oran. The ketubah itself was written in the French coastal city of Villefranche-sur-Mer because the Jews of Oran had been expelled that summer by the Spanish governor; see Jonathan Israel, "The Jews of Spanish Oran and Their Expulsion in 1669," *Mediterranean Historical Review* 9, no. 2 (1994): 235–255. The ketubah was in the collection of the late Victor Klagsbald in Paris: Klagsbald, "À propos de l'illustration du chandelier."

57. Columbia MS X893 M6858. I owe this reference to Arielle Korman.

58. For some fine late nineteenth-century examples, see the Moroccan megillah of Braginsky 91, ca. 1880, and Benayahu Ms. NA 30 (Meknes, 1898).

59. Sabar, "Sephardi Elements," 184–189.

60. NLI Heb. 8.3716, compiled by scholar and poet Shlomo Tov-'Elem of Tetouan.

61. Sabar, "Sephardi Elements," 189.

62. Gross Ms. 081.012.024. For other megillot decorated in this style, see Gross Ms. 081.012.013 and 081.012.046 (Essaouira, ca. 1875–1890). For ketubot, see Magnes 71.0.10 (Yehuda Bensultan and Ledisia Nahon, Tetouan, 1828); CCJM 21754 (Yehuda Benguigui and Ḥefṣiba Halevi, Tetouan, 1844).

63. An unusually early example of this style is found in the decorated headings of a manuscript commentary on tractate *Avot*, written in Akka, 1615–1617 (CUL Dd.5.63).

64. Sabar, "Sephardi Elements," 184. On Amazigh crafts, see Cynthia Becker, *Amazigh Arts in Morocco: Women Shaping Berber Identity* (Austin: University of Texas Press, 2007); Lisa Bernasek, *Artistry of the Everyday: Beauty and Craftsmanship in Berber Art* (Cambridge, MA: Peabody Museum, 2008).

65. For examples of books: a prayer book written in southern Morocco, 1791 (Israel Museum Ms. 180/077); *Hekhal ha-shem*, copied by Mas'ud Ben-Ḥamou in Goulmima, 1801 (CCJM 32347); and a mahzor written in Marrakech in 1836 by Shlomo Kohen (Bud. Ms. Kaufmann A 436). For examples of megillot in this style, see Gross Ms. 081.012.016 and 081.012.052, both probably nineteenth-century; for a ketubah, Gross Ms. 035.011.122 (Moshe Ibn-Malka and Buda Ibn-Ilouz, Asfalou, 1880). For an unusual megillah illustrated with birds, fish, lions, and deer, see HUC Scrolls 62 X.5 (Morocco, ca. 1850).

66. Marcelin Beaussier, *Dictionnaire pratique arabe-français* (Algiers: Bouyer, 1871), 414, s.v. *ẓahir*; Moshe Bar-Asher, "Tiqqun pesaḥ mi-tafilalt sheba-maroqo," *Shana Be-shana* 41 (1991): 149.

67. The KTIV database has 134 manuscripts cataloged as a *ḍahir* for Passover, almost all from southern Morocco. One decorated ḍahir has a colophon from Fez, 1845: Benayahu Ms. NA 49. A Passover Haggadah, written and decorated by Mikhael Makhluf ʿAllun (1795–1857), a Marrakech-born scribe who spent most of his life in Italy, shows some interesting hybrid features of Italian and Maghrebi styles (HUC Cincinnati Ms. 284, copied in the Moroccan Rif in 1818). The textual tradition of the ḍahir has been the subject of two articles: Bar-Asher, "Tiqqun pesaḥ mi-tafilalt sheba-maroqo," 147–161, and Shalom Bar-Asher, "Ketav yad shel haggada shel pesaḥ mi-maroqo," in *Shaʿarei lashon: meḥqarim ba-lashon ha-ʿivrit, ba-aramit, uvi-leshonot ha-yehudim mugashim le-moshe bar asher* (Jerusalem: Bialik Institute, 2007), 294–303.

68. A Passover Haggadah and commentary with a decorated title page and illustrations of the matzah and maror appears in a Moroccan manuscript dated 1697, formerly LBD Ms. 121 (current location unknown). For an eighteenth-century example, see HUC Ms. 86, written in 1796 by Moshe Barukh Maṣa. For twentieth-century examples, see NLI Ms. Heb. 38.2618, written by Hayyim Assabag in 1914; Israel Museum B83.0476.a, written in Erfoud in 1927.

69. See, inter alia, Harvard Ms. Heb. 103; NLI Ms. Heb. 8.2144; CCJM 21602; BSB Hebr. Ms. 453; BSB Hebr. Ms. 455; Gross MO.011.009; Gross MO.011.011. For examples of human figures (illustrating the rabbis Elʿazar and Aqiva), see CCJM 22409 (undated); and Hekhal Shlomo Ms. Golinsky 609, written in 1874 by Yaḥya Aṭia.

70. Hekhal Shlomo Ms. Golinsky 609; CCJM 22409; BSB Hebr. 453; Gross MO.011.009; NLI Ms. Heb. 8.2409.

71. For example, NLI Ms. Heb. 8.2409 was written in 1841 for "Yaḥya b. Yosef [illegible], so that he may read it, and his children and grandchildren after him." Two unsigned, decorated, incomplete ḍahirs in the Gross collection, Gross MO.011.011 and MO.011.031, are certainly the work of the same artist. However, since there is no overlap in their text (and they are both bound out of order), they may each be sections of the same original manuscript.

72. JTS Ms. 2187.

73. CCJM 30199.

74. Gross MO.011.18.67. Another predrawn border page, probably also eighteenth-century, is Gross MO.011.048.

75. NLR Ms. Guenzburg 1265, written in Marrakech in the nineteenth century. Other manuscripts with titles squeezed into frames that appear to have been created earlier: NLI 8.4261 (Tlemcen, 1705); Benayahu Ms. G 85 (Algiers, ca. 1730); JTS Ms. 347 / Bennaim 98 (Morocco, ca. 1850).

76. Other sketches of typical frame decorations appear on a flyleaf with eighteenth- and nineteenth-century notes and pen trials; it is unclear whether these are practice attempts from a scribe/artist or whether a reader is simply copying designs they have seen in other books (NLI Heb. 8.5177, 5r-v).

77. Olim Gross MO.011.047, now in the author's personal collection. The name Avraham Kohen is generic enough that it could serve as a placeholder name.

78. *Ḥesed le'avraham* is a common title for Hebrew books, but I cannot find any book with that title that matches the exact language describing it on this title page. The cities of Tinzert and Tagadirt are in southeastern Morocco; on this title page, Tinzert is written in small letters, and Tagadirt in large ones.

79. See the catalogs and the literature cited in them of Vivian Mann, ed., *Morocco: Jews and Art in a Muslim Land* (New York: Jewish Museum, 2000), esp. 126–138; André Goldenberg, *Art and the Jews of Morocco* (Paris: Somogy Éditions d'Art, 2014).

80. Decorated frames were already being used in Hebrew incunabula of the fifteenth century; the first title page in a Hebrew book was likely Soncino's printing of *Sefer ha-roqeaḥ* (Fano, 1505), and the first decorated Hebrew title page, Bomberg's printing of the Rabbinic Bible (Venice, 1517): Marvin Heller, "Behold, You Are Beautiful, My Love: The Use of Ornamental Frames in Hebrew Incunabula," in *Further Studies in the Making of the Early Hebrew Book* (Leiden: Brill, 2013), 3–33; David Stern, *The Jewish Bible: A Material History* (Seattle: University of Washington Press, 2017), 137–158. See also Avraham Meir Habermann, *Sha'arei sefarim 'ivriyyim* (Safed: Museum of the Art of Printing, 1969). On title pages in general, see Margaret Smith, *The Title-Page: Its Early Development, 1460–1510* (London: British Library, 2001); Alastair Fowler, *The Mind of the Book: Pictorial Title-Pages* (Oxford: Oxford University Press, 2017).

81. Elizabeth Eisenstein, *The Printing Press as an Agent of Change: Communications and Cultural Transformations in Early Modern Europe* (Cambridge: Cambridge University Press, 1979), 6.

82. Eisenstein, *The Printing Press*, 66, where she cites the discussion of this scene in Frances Yates, *The Art of Memory* (London: Routledge, 1966), 131.

83. On rethinking Eisenstein's model of the "print revolution," see Adrian Johns, *The Nature of the Book: Print and Knowledge in the Making* (Chicago: University of Chicago Press, 1998); his dialogue with Eisenstein in the AHR Forum: Adrian Johns and Elizabeth Eisenstein, "'An Unacknowledged Revolution Revisited' and 'How to Acknowledge a Revolution,'" *American Historical Review* 107, no. 1 (2002): 87–125; and the collection edited by Sabrina Baron, Eric Lindquist, and Eleanor Shevlin: *Agent of Change: Print Culture Studies after Elizabeth L. Eisenstein* (Amherst: University of Massachusetts Press, 2007).

84. Zeev Gries, *The Book in the Jewish World, 1700–1900* (Liverpool: Littman Library of Jewish Civilization, 2007), 5. This is an English revision of his *Ha-sefer ke-sokhen tarbut, 1700–1900* (*The Book as an Agent of Culture, 1700–1900*), originally published in Hebrew in 2002. Cf. the comments of Arthur Kiron, "Studying the Jewish Book: A Review," *Judaica Librarianship* 14 (2008): 80–87.

85. Nelly Hanna, *In Praise of Books: A Cultural History of Cairo's Middle Class, Sixteenth through the Eighteenth Century* (Syracuse, NY: Syracuse University Press, 2003); Hala Auji, *Printing Arab Modernity: Book Culture and the American Press in Nineteenth-Century Beirut* (Leiden: Brill, 2016); Nir Shafir, "The Road from Damascus: Circulation and the Redefinition of Islam in the Ottoman Empire, 1620–1720" (PhD diss., University of California Los Angeles, 2016); Kathryn A. Schwartz, "Did Ottoman Sultans Ban Print?," *Book History* 20 (2017): 1–39; Orlin Sabev, *Waiting for Müteferrika: Glimpses of Ottoman Print Culture* (Boston: Academic Studies, 2018); Ahmed El Shamsy, *Rediscovering the Islamic Classics: How Editors and Print Culture Transformed an Intellectual Tradition* (Princeton, NJ: Princeton University Press, 2020); Scott Reese, ed., *Manuscript and Print in the Islamic Tradition* (Berlin: De Gruyter, 2022).

86. Robert Darnton, "'What Is the History of Books?' Revisited," *Modern Intellectual History* 4, no. 3 (2007): 495–508.

87. Darnton, "What Is the History of Books?," 504–505.

88. For an example of this methodology applied to Jewish books, see Yaacob Dweck, *The Scandal of Kabbalah: Leon Modena, Jewish Mysticism, Early Modern Venice* (Princeton, NJ: Princeton University Press, 2011). For some recent overviews of studying European manuscripts in the "age of print," see Zeynep Tenger and Paul Trolander, "From Print versus Manuscript to Sociable Authorship and Mixed Media: A Review of Trends in the Scholarship of Early Modern Publication," *Literature Compass* 7/11 (2010): 1035–1048; Mark Mattes, "Toward an Archaeology of Manuscripts,"

Eighteenth-Century Studies 55, no. 4 (2022): 545–552; Steven May, *English Renaissance Manuscript Culture: The Paper Revolution* (Oxford: Oxford University Press, 2023).

89. Yale MS.1825.0253 (formerly Boesky 64), 72b.

90. Yale MS.1825.0253, 96a, and see also his similar remarks on 98a.

3. MAGHREBI JEWS IN EUROPEAN PRINTING HOUSES

1. Since Duran does not give the exact date, I cannot be sure of the weather, but sunny days are good for scribal practice. According to Eliyahu Refael Marṣiano, *Sefer malkhei yeshurun* (Jerusalem: Mekhon haRaShaM, 1999, 94), Ḥayyim Yona Duran lived in Algiers ca. 1730–1800 and copied these manuscripts from the library of his father, Ṣemaḥ ben Binyamin Duran. If Ḥayyim Yona was copying from a manuscript in an Algerian library, however, this does not explain why he signs his colophon in Tunis. Perhaps *Magen avot* was copied in Algiers, and *Qiṣṣur zekher ṣaddiq* in Tunis.

2. See Adolf Neubauer, *Mediaeval Jewish Chronicles and Chronological Notes* (Oxford: Oxford University Press, 1887), xiv. The copy Duran annotated is in the British Library, Add. MS 19785. I thank Zsófi Buda for alerting me to this manuscript and providing me with digital images.

3. BL Add. MS 19785, fol. 153v. Duran uses a chronogram from I Kings 8:57: "May the LORD be with us as with our ancestors," which yields the Hebrew year 5521.

4. Duran's journey, including his stop in Tunis, is described briefly in the introduction to a printing of yet another work of Shim'on bar Ṣemaḥ Duran: *Yakhin u-vo'az* (Livorno: Castello and Saadun, 1782), brought to press by Yona Duran's son Ṣemaḥ.

5. Daniel Schroeter, "The End of the Sephardic World Order," in *From Iberia to Diaspora: Studies in Sephardic History and Culture*, ed. Yedida Stillman and Norman (Noam) Stillman (Leiden: Brill, 1999), 86–101. On this dynamic, see also Daniel Schroeter, *The Sultan's Jew: Morocco and the Sephardi World* (Stanford, CA: Stanford University Press, 2002), esp. 144–158; Yaron Tsur, "Dating the Demise of the Western Sephardi Jewish Diaspora in the Mediterranean," in *Jewish Culture and Society in North Africa*, ed. Emily Gottreich and Daniel Schroeter (Bloomington: Indiana University Press, 2011), 93–106.

6. See, e.g., M. Mitchell Serels, "Sephardic Printings as a Source of Historical Material," *Revue des Études Juives* 138, no. 1 (1979): 147–153; Yosef Tobi and Tsivia Tobi, *Judeo-Arabic Literature in Tunisia, 1850–1950* (Detroit: Wayne State University Press, 2014), 2.

7. See, e.g., the comments of Zeev Gries, quoted in chapter 2, that the Islamic world "paid a heavy price for rejecting printing": Zeev Gries, *The Book in the Jewish World, 1700–1900* (Liverpool: Littman Library of Jewish Civilization, 2007), 5. For a fuller examination of this myth, see Kathryn A. Schwartz, "Did Ottoman Sultans Ban Print?" *Book History* 20 (2017): 1–39.

8. On Ottoman Jewish printing, see Yaron Ben-Naeh, "Hebrew Printing Houses in the Ottoman Empire," in *Jewish Journalism and Printing Houses in the Ottoman Empire and Modern Turkey*, ed. Gad Nassi (Istanbul: Isis, 2001), 73–96. On Armenian, Greek, and other languages in Ottoman printing, see Sebouh Aslanian, *Early Modernity and Mobility: Port Cities and Printers across the Armenian Diaspora, 1512–1800* (New Haven, CT: Yale University Press, 2023), and Nil Pektaş, "The Beginnings of Printing in the Ottoman Capital: Book Production and Circulation in Early Modern Istanbul," *Osmanlı Bilimi Araştırmaları* 16, no. 2 (2015): 3–32. Cf. also Geoffrey Roper, "Printed in Europe, Consumed in Ottoman Lands: European Books in the Middle East, 1514–1842," in *Books in Motion in Early Modern Europe: Beyond Production, Circulation and Consumption*, ed. Daniel Bellingradt, Paul Nelles, and Jeroen Salman (London: Palgrave Macmillan, 2017), 267–288.

9. Metin Coşgel, Thomas Miceli, and Jared Rubin, "The Political Economy of Mass Printing: Legitimacy and Technological Change in the Ottoman Empire," *Journal of Comparative Economics* 40, no. 3 (2012): 357–371; Orlin Sabev, "Waiting for Godot: The Formation of Ottoman Print Culture," in *Historical Aspects of Printing and Publishing in Languages of the Middle East*, ed. Geoffrey Roper (Leiden: Brill, 2014), 101–120.

10. Sabev, "Waiting for Godot," 106–107.

11. Aslanian, *Early Modernity and Mobility*, and see also Sebouh Aslanian, "Port Cities and Printers: Reflections on Early Modern Global Armenian Print," *Book History* 17 (2014): 51–93.

12. Evelyne Oliel-Grausz, "Networks and Communication in the Sephardi Diaspora: An Added Dimension to the Concept of Port Jews and Port Jewries," *Jewish Culture and History* 7 (2004): 62.

13. Noam Sienna, "Rabbis with Inky Fingers: Making an Eighteenth-Century Hebrew Book between North Africa and Amsterdam," *Studia Rosenthaliana* 46, nos. 1/2 (2020): 155–187.

14. Eliyahu Ḥai Guedj, *Ze ha-shulḥan* (Algiers: Ya'aqov Guedj, 1888), "Introduction." The Guedj family and its involvement in the book industry will be discussed later in this chapter.

15. David Cazès, *Notes bibliographiques sur la littérature juive-tunisienne* (Tunis: Imprimerie internationale, 1893), 242. See also the introductory remarks of Ḥayyim Hakohen in *Torat ḥakham* (Venice, 1654). Certainly, the motif of an author's difficult journey to bring their book to press is a literary trope of book introductions, like other motifs discussed in this chapter; see Marvin Heller, "Often Overlooked: Examples of Front-Matter in Early Hebrew Books," *Quntres: An Online Journal for the History of the Jewish Book* 2, no. 1 (2011): 1–21. But this story is also obviously based in familiar material realities.

16. The leading proponent of this stance was Elizabeth Eisenstein; see Elizabeth Eisenstein, *The Printing Press as an Agent of Change: Communications and Cultural Transformations in Early Modern Europe* (Cambridge: Cambridge University Press, 1979), and cf. Adrian Johns, *The Nature of the Book: Print and Knowledge in the Making* (Chicago: University of Chicago Press, 1998), and their dialogue in the AHR Forum: Adrian Johns and Elizabeth Eisenstein, "'An Unacknowledged Revolution Revisited' and 'How to Acknowledge a Revolution,'" *American Historical Review* 107, no. 1 (2002): 87–125.

17. Yosef (Joseph) Tedghi, *Ha-sefer veha-defus ha-'ivri be-fas* (Jerusalem: Ben-Zvi Institute, 1994), 18–27.

18. On Yosef Knafo and his modernizing initiatives in publishing for a popular audience, see Gabriel Abensour, "In Praise of the Multitude: Rabbi Yosef Knafo's Socially Conscious Work in Essaouira at the End of the Nineteenth Century," *Jewish Social Studies* 27, no. 1 (2022): 115–149. A similar articulation of the advantages of printed books can be found in the introduction to *Lev shomea'* (Livorno, 1885) by Hayyim Kohen of Tripoli, which gives twenty reasons why scholars should strive to print their original compositions in their lifetime.

19. Yosef Knafo, *Ot brit qodesh* (Livorno: Elia Benamozegh, 1884). The original source for the commandment to write a Torah scroll is found in b *Sanhedrin* 21b and b *Menaḥ* ot 30a, derived from Deuteronomy 31:19. Already in the medieval period, rabbinic authorities had expanded this commandment to include the creation and acquisition of other religious books: see, e.g., Asher b. Yeḥiel, *Hilkhot sefer torah*, 1.

20. See, e.g., the testimony of Yosef Binyamin Duran (d. 1758) on the Duran family library, which "since the days of my ancestors, has been

hidden away in a place underground where the books will be safe from rot, and they have been there until this day without being taken outside," but "most of the members of my family have drifted away . . . and I feared for myself, since I do not know the day of my death, and there is no-one among the members of my household who knows the ways of guarding material to look after the inheritance which I have received from my father. . . . Therefore I have harvested from the heaps of the books of my ancestor, the RaShBaṢ of blessed memory, which are gathered in my treasure-house, and I chose these two books to publish [i.e., *Yavin shmu'a* and *Ma'amar ḥameṣ*]": Yosef Binyamin Duran, "Introduction," in *Yavin Shmu'a* (Livorno: Abraham Meldola, 1744).

21. Yigal Nizri, "Sharifan Subjects, Rabbinic Texts: Moroccan Halakhic Writing, 1860–1918" (PhD diss., New York University, 2014), 36–42.

22. Yosef Bennaim, *Malkhei Rabbanan* (Jerusalem: Ha-ma'arav Press, 1931), 29b.

23. On the importance of patronage in Mediterranean Jewish publishing, see Sienna, "Rabbis with Inky Fingers," and Francesca Bregoli, "Printing, Fundraising, and Jewish Patronage in Eighteenth-Century Livorno," in *Jewish Culture in Early Modern Europe: Essays in Honor of David B. Ruderman*, ed. Richard I. Cohen, Natalie Dohrmann, Adam Shear, and Elchanan Reiner (Pittsburgh: University of Pittsburgh Press, 2014), 250–259.

24. On Shamama, see Richard Parks, "Scemmama, Nessim," in *Encyclopedia of Jews in the Islamic World*, ed. Noam Stillman (Leiden: Brill, 2010); Jessica Marglin, *The Shamama Case: Contesting Citizenship across the Modern Mediterranean* (Princeton, NJ: Princeton University Press, 2022). On Shamama's role in book publishing, see Robert Attal, *Le Caïd Nessim Samama de Tunis: mécène du livre hebraique* (Jerusalem: R. Attal, 1995); to the thirteen titles listed by Attal, we should also add at least five more: Shlomo Zarka, *Zivḥei tru'a* (Livorno: Salomon Belforte, 1867); Yosef Sedbon, *Ahavat ha-shem* (Livorno: Israel Costa, 1871); a Haggadah with Judeo-Arabic commentary by Eliyahu Ḥai Guedj (Livorno: Israel Costa, 1869), Guedj's *Tokhaḥat megula* (Livorno: Israel Costa, 1872), and his edition of his grandfather's commentary, *Ner david* (Livorno: Israel Costa, 1872).

25. Vat. Neofiti 46, 55v–56r.

26. Anthony Grafton, *Humanists with Inky Fingers: The Culture of Correction in Renaissance Europe* (London: British Library, 2011).

27. Ibn-Adoniyyahu, "Introduction," *Sha'ar adonai he-ḥadash* (Venice: Daniel Bomberg, 1525). On Ibn-Adoniyyahu and his work with Bomberg's press, see Yakov Z. Meir, *Editio Princeps: The 1523 Venice Edition of*

the Palestinian Talmud and the Beginning of Hebrew Printing (Jerusalem: Magnes Press, 2022), 64–81, 174–211. Another Maghrebi Jewish press worker in sixteenth-century Venice was Yaḥya ben Avraham Ben-Ḥamu, from Fez, who edited the third printing of the *Arba'a ṭurim* at the press of Giovanni Di Gara (Venice, 1574).

28. Shmuel Ḥagiz, "Introduction," *Mevaqesh ha-shem* (Venice: Giovanni Di Gara, 1596).

29. Shmuel Ḥagiz, *Dvar shmuel* (Venice, 1596); Hagiz, "Introduction," to Shlomo b. Ṣemaḥ Duran, *Tiferet yisrael* (Venice, ca. 1596); *Maḥzor rosh ha-shana ve-yom ha-kipurim ke-minhag q"q Aljaza'ir* (Venice, 1598), at the request of Moshe and Ṣemaḥ Levi-Ḥazan. The last was printed at the press of Daniel Zanetti, the others by Giovanni di Gara. Hagiz had probably stayed with Duran in Algiers before coming to Venice, as alluded to in a note at the end of a manuscript copied in Algiers in 1593: Montefiore Library Ms. 265, 46v. In the mid-seventeenth century, Hagiz's son Jacob worked extensively with Hebrew presses in Verona and Livorno: Elisheva Carlebach, *The Pursuit of Heresy: Rabbi Moses Hagiz and the Sabbatian Controversies* (New York: Columbia University Press, 1990), 20–25.

30. Ibn-Ḥayyim, "Introduction," *Lev aharon* (Venice: Giovanni di Gara, 1608). He printed a second book of his in Venice, also with Giovanni di Gara: *Qorban aharon* (Venice 1609–1611). See Marvin Heller, *The Seventeenth Century Hebrew Book* (Leiden: Brill, 2011), 217, 241. From Venice, Aharon Ibn-Ḥayyim continued to Egypt and then Ottoman Palestine; he died in Jerusalem in 1632: Joseph Tedghi, "Ibn Ḥayyim, Aaron ben Abraham," *Encyclopedia of Jews in the Islamic World*, ed. Noam Stillman (Leiden: Brill, 2010).

31. The work in question, *Mishpeṭei shmuel*, is a commentary on the Mishnah by Shmuel b. Avraham Hakohen of Fez. Although Ibn-Ḥayyim wrote that "this book is magnificent and worthy of being printed," it was not brought to press: BL Add MS 27049, 75r. See Moshe Amar, "Le-toldot rabi aharon ibn-ḥayyim," *Mi-mizraḥ umi-ma'arav* 4 (1974): 23–36.

32. See, e.g., the list of books by scholars of Fez printed outside of Fez in Tedghi, *Ha-sefer veha-defus ha-'ivri be-fas*, 41–57.

33. On the role of emissaries in Mediterranean Jewish communities and their role in book culture, see Eliyahu Refael Marṣiano, "Terumat rabbanei ereṣ yisrael li-defus ha-'ivri ba-maroqo," in *Meḥqarim be-tarbutam shel yehudei ṣfon afriqa*, ed. Issachar Ben-Ami (Jerusalem: Rubin Mass, 1991), 309–312; Matthias Lehmann, *Emissaries from the Holy Land: The Sephardic Diaspora and the Practice of Pan-Judaism in the Eighteenth Century* (Stanford, CA: Stanford University Press, 2014), esp. 71–118.

34. This was observed in Francesca Bregoli, "Hebrew Printing and Communication Networks between Livorno and North Africa, 1740–1789," in *Report of the Oxford Centre for Hebrew and Jewish Studies 2007–2008* (Oxford: Oxford Centre for Hebrew and Jewish Studies, 2008), 55. The reverse is also occasionally true: in the early eighteenth century, Marrakech-born student Hiyya Cohen Di Lara, studying in Amsterdam, was commissioned by Shlomo Di Miza to transcribe two Kabbalistic works that were "buried in Ashkenazi script, even though the author was Sephardi, and I copied it into the script of Sepharad," now NLR Guenzburg 1095 and Bodl. Mich. 531.

35. In his words: "I endeavoured to seek out and find some student who was expert and learned, in order to bring these writings [of my father's] into order. . . . But the few that I did find who were ready and able to do the work were lacking the ability to understand the writing of my honorable father of blessed memory," Avraham Sasportas, "The Introduction of the Author's Son," in *Ohel ya'aqov* (Amsterdam: Herz Levi Rofe, 1737). Ya'aqov Sasportas was born in Oran and served throughout Algeria and Morocco before traveling to Europe where he held positions as a rabbi and yeshiva head in London, Livorno, and Amsterdam, where he died; see Yaacob Dweck, *Dissident Rabbi: The Life of Jacob Sasportas* (Princeton, NJ: Princeton University Press, 2019). One of his personal notebooks in his own handwriting, including some material published in *Ohel ya'aqov*, is preserved in YUL Ms. 1251.

36. Sasportas, *Ohel ya'aqov*, "Introduction."

37. Sienna, "Rabbis with Inky Fingers," 172.

38. Moshe Meldola, "The Editor's Apology," in *Yavin shmu'a* (Livorno: Abraham Meldola, 1744); Bregoli, "Hebrew Printing and Communication Networks," 55.

39. Abraham Meldola, "The Printer's Introduction," in *Yavin shmu'a* (Livorno: Abraham Meldola, 1744). Decades later, Moshe Meldola was still struggling with this script: he writes in the Editor's Introduction to *Yakhin u-vo'az* (Livorno: Castello and Saadun, 1782) that he "worked night and day, since the manuscript was very old and worn out, and written in Arabic handwriting."

40. Meir b. Yisrael Ya'aqov of Hildesheim, "The Editor's Introduction," in *Ve-zot li-yhuda* (Sulzbach: Aharon ben Meshulam Zalman, 1776). Avraham 'Ayyash also testifies in his introduction that a wealthy patron had to pay to have the manuscript transcribed into Ashkenazi script "since the typesetters cannot understand our script": Avraham 'Ayyash, "Introduction," in *Ve-zot li-yhuda* (Sulzbach: Aharon ben Meshulam Zalman, 1776).

41. In his colophon, al-Fasi indicates that he met Duran in Tunis: Ḥayyim al-Fasi, "Apology," in *Magen avot* (Livorno: Moses Attias, 1762). He also collaborated with his brother Shlomo to edit and expand the work of his father, Mas'ud al-Fasi (d. 1774), which was published posthumously in 1806: *Mishḥa de-revuta* (Livorno: Eliezer Saadun, 1806).

42. Shmuel Adawi, "The Author's Introduction," in *Sefer bnei shmuel* (Livorno: Santini, 1759); translation from Bregoli, "Hebrew Printing and Communication Networks," 55.

43. Yosef Naṭaf, "The Editor's Apology," in *Sefer bnei shmuel* (Livorno: Santini, 1759).

44. Moses Edrehi, "The Editor's Introduction," in *Tehila le-david* (Amsterdam: Proops, 1807). The poems were by Meknessi scholar David Ben-Ḥassin (1727–1792). Compare also Edrehi's remarks in his English work *A Book of Miracles: An Historical Account of the Ten Tribes* (London, s.n., 1836), 140–141.

45. On the environment of the early modern European printing house, see, inter alia, Grafton, *Humanists with Inky Fingers*; Roger Chartier, *The Author's Hand and the Printer's Mind: Transformations of the Written Word in Early Modern Europe* (Boston: Wiley-Blackwell, 2013); Natalie Zemon Davis, *Society and Culture in Early Modern France* (Redwood City, CA: Stanford University Press, 1975); D. F. McKenzie, *Making Meaning: "Printers of the Mind" and Other Essays* (Amherst: University of Massachusetts Press, 2002).

46. David Meldola, "The Editor's Introduction," in *Miqdash melekh* (Amsterdam: Naftali Herz Levi Rofe, 1750). Meldola uses the Hebrew term *ṣura* to refer to the forme, the arrangement of type that has been locked into the wooden or iron frame (chase) ready for printing. On the relationships among Sephardi, Maghrebi, and Ashkenazi workers at Rofe's press, see Sienna, "Rabbis with Inky Fingers," 166–175.

47. Meldola, "The Editor's Apology."

48. These names are taken from the colophons and paratexts of *Iggerot ha-ramaz* (1780); *Oraḥ la-ṣaddiq* (1780); *Divrei shira* (1780); *Zera' emet*, Vol. I (1781); *Leshon ḥakhamim* (1781); *She'elot u-teshuvot le-marana . . . alfasi* (1781); *Yakhin u-vo'az* (1782); *Simḥat ha-regel*, Vol. II (1782); *Oholei ya'aqov* (1783); *Da'at zqenim* (1783); *Sheveṭ yehuda* (1783); *Maṭe yehuda* (1783); *Ṣemaḥ ṣaddiq* (1784); *Geṭ mequshar* (1785); *Migdanot natan*, Vol. II (1785); *Magen avot* (1785); *Divrei mordekhai* (1787); *Ma'amar mordekhai* (1787); *Shufre de-ya'aqov* (1787); *Ḥiddushei ha-riṭva le-masekhet yevamot* (1787); *Yeter ha-baz* (1787); *Imrot ṭehorot* (1787); *Sde ha-areṣ*, Vol. III (1788); *Tiqqunei ha-zohar* (1789).

49. The Grana were Italian Jews (including Italian Sephardi families) living in Tunis. Most but not all were from Livorno, and they distinguished themselves from the Twansa, the native Tunisian Jews. The Lombroso (or Lumbroso) family was of Iberian origin; the Lombrosos of Tunis traced their descent to the Lombrosos of Italy, although it seems that Yiṣḥaq Lombroso was born and raised in Tunis; see Binyamin Refael Kohen, *Sefer malkhei tarshish* (Netivot: B. Kohen, 1986), 201–204.

50. David Cazès, *Notes bibliographiques sur la littérature juive-tunisienne* (Tunis: Imprimerie internationale, 1893), 242.

51. The plate used for the title page of *Zera' yiṣḥaq* is identical to the title page of the last book printed by Ḥazzan's press, *Ne'ot ya'aqov* by Yisrael Ya'aqov al-Gazi (İzmir, 1767). On Ḥazzan, see Avraham Ya'ari, "Ha-defus ha-'ivri be-izmir," *Areshet: sefer ha-shana le-ḥeqer ha-sefer ha-'ivri* 1 (1959): 106.

52. Avraham Lombroso, "The Introduction of the Author's Son," in Yiṣḥaq Lombroso, *Zera' yisḥaq* (Tunis: Yeshu'a Kohen Tanuji, 1768).

53. David Bela'ish, "The Editor's Apology," in *Zera' yiṣḥaq*, ed. Yiṣḥaq Lumbroso (Tunis: Yeshu'a Kohen Tanuji, 1768).

54. Eusèbe Vassel, *La littérature populaire des israélites tunisiens* (Paris: Ernest Leroux, 1907), 17.

55. Nunes-Vais, *'Afar ya'aqov*, a supercommentary published with *Da'at zqenim* (Livorno: Castello and Saadun, 1783).

56. Azulai, *Ma'agal ṭov ha-shalem*, ed. Aron Freimann (Jerusalem: Mekize Nirdamim, 1934), 57. On Azulai's stay in Tunis, see Yaron Tsur, "La culture religieuse à Tunis à la fin du XVIIIe d'après le récit de voyage de Ḥaïm Yossef David Azoulay," in *Entre Orient et Occident: juifs et musulmans en Tunisie*, ed. Denis Cohen-Tannoudji (Paris: Éditions de l'Éclat, 2007), 63–76; Matthias Lehmann, "'Levantinos' and Other Jews: Reading H. Y. D. Azulai's Travel Diary," *Jewish Social Studies* 13, no. 3 (2007): 1–34; and Yaacob Dweck, "A Jew from the East Meets Books from the West," in *Jewish Culture in Early Modern Europe: Essays in Honor of David B. Ruderman*, eds. Richard Cohen, Natalie Dohrmann, Adam Shear, and Elchanan Reiner (Pittsburgh: University of Pittsburgh Press, 2014), 239–249.

57. Yosef Kohen Tanuji, *Bnei yosef*, ed. Yehuda Najjar (Livorno: Eliezer Saadun, 1793), 36a. This work was brought to press by a relative of Yeshu'a Kohen Tanuji, a certain Yehuda Kohen Tanuji; is it possible that more of Lombroso's manuscripts had been given to the family in preparation for printing? Compare Yehuda Kohen Tanuji's remarks in the introduction to *Ereṣ yehuda* (Livorno, 1797).

58. Compare the similar conclusions of Denis Cohen-Tannoudji, "La famille Cohen-Tannoudji de la tradition à la modernité," in *Entre Orient et*

Occident: juifs et musulmans en Tunisie, ed. Denis Cohen-Tannoudji (Paris: Éditions de l'Éclat, 2007), 206.

59. Bernard Dov Cooperman, "Perché gli ebrei furono invitati a Livorno?," *Rassegna Mensile di Israel* 50, no. 9 (1984): 553–566; Benjamin Ravid, "A Tale of Three Cities and Their Raison d'Etat: Ancona, Venice, Livorno, and the Competition for Jewish Merchants in the Sixteenth Century," *Mediterranean Historical Review* 6, no. 2 (1991): 138–162.

60. Francesca Trivellato, *The Familiarity of Strangers: The Sephardic Diaspora, Livorno, and Cross-Cultural Trade in the Early Modern Period* (New Haven, CT: Yale University Press, 2009), 43–69; see also Schroeter, *The Sultan's Jew*, 36–54; Francesca Bregoli, *Mediterranean Enlightenment: Livornese Jews, Tuscan Culture, and Eighteenth-Century Reform* (Redwood City, CA: Stanford University Press, 2014).

61. Trivellato, *The Familiarity of Strangers*; Tsur, "Dating the Demise," 93–106; Alyssa Reiman, "Claiming Livorno: Citizenship, Commerce, and Culture in the Italian Jewish Diaspora: Bridging Europe and the Mediterranean," in *Italian Jewish Networks from the Seventeenth to the Twentieth Century*, ed. Francesca Bregoli, Carlotta Ferrara degli Uberti, and Guri Schwarz (London: Palgrave MacMillan, 2018), 81–100.

62. Schroeter, *The Sultan's Jew*, 41–42.

63. The 1841 census is available to search at https://www.sephardicgen.com/databases/Livorno1841CensusSrchFrm.html (accessed January 9, 2024). It counts a total of 4,771 Jews in 1,261 households, of which 113 households were led by someone born in Morocco, Algeria, Tunisia, or Libya. This is obviously an inexact way to count Maghrebi Jews because by 1841, many Maghrebi Jews had been born in Livorno (or elsewhere, like Gibraltar), and some people born in the Maghreb were Livornese, but it nonetheless captures something of the prominence of the Maghrebi Jewish community in the city.

64. The various agreements between European powers and the Ottoman Porte ("capitulations") allowed Sephardi Jews to negotiate the most advantageous privileges from whichever European consul would "sponsor" them: Jean-Pierre Filippini, "La ballottazione a Livorno nel settecento," *La Rassegna Mensile di Israel* 49 (1983): 199–268; Trivellato, *The Familiarity of Strangers*, 102–131; Sarah Abrevaya Stein, *Extraterritorial Dreams: European Citizenship, Sephardi Jews, and the Ottoman Twentieth Century* (Chicago: University of Chicago Press, 2016).

65. Marvin Heller, "Jedidiah Ben Isaac Gabbai and the First Decade of Hebrew Printing in Livorno," in *Studies in the Making of the Early Hebrew Book* (Leiden: Brill, 2007), 165–177.

66. Francesca Bregoli, "Hebrew Printing in Eighteenth-Century Livorno: From Government Control to a Free Market," in *The Hebrew Book in Early Modern Italy*, ed. Joseph Hacker and Adam Shear (Philadelphia: University of Pennsylvania Press, 2011), 171–196.

67. Bregoli, "Hebrew Printing and Communication Networks," 51–59; Bregoli, "Printing, Fundraising, and Jewish Patronage," 250–259; Clémence Boulouque, "Elia Benamozegh's Printing Presses: Livornese Crossroads and the New Margins of Italian Jewish History," in *Italian Jewish Networks from the Seventeenth to the Twentieth Century*, ed. Francesca Bregoli, Carlotta Ferrara degli Uberti, and Guri Schwarz (London: Palgrave Macmillan, 2018), 65. On the Belforte press in particular, see Arthur Kiron, *The Belforte Publishing House and the Art of Ladino Printing* (Livorno: Salomone Belforte, 2005).

68. *Tosfei ha-rosh* (Livorno: Giovan Vincenzo Falorni, 1776). The introduction is unsigned, and the only named worker is the typesetter, David Ḥayyim b. Ya'aqov Refael Milul. My reading of this introduction differs slightly from Bregoli, "Hebrew Printing and Communication Networks," 56.

69. Bregoli, "Hebrew Printing and Communication Networks," 52–53.

70. Guedj, *Tfila be-khol lashon* (Livorno: Israel Costa, 1883), "The Approbation of the Scholars." The rabbis who signed this haskama were Mordekhai Seror, Eli'ezer Shayish (Chiche), Yosef Seror, Avraham ha-Levi Valensi, Moshe Bu'aziz, Yosef Tabet, Yehuda Loufrani, Shmuel Seror, and Yiṣḥaq Ḥanun (Hanoune).

71. In *Ze ha-shulḥan* (Algiers, 1888), Guedj writes: "I left my home [of Tunis] to collect subscriptions for my edition of the Zohar with commentary [Livorno, 1872] . . . and God led my path to the city of Algiers, where I saw that its citizens were honest and upright. . . . Today, I have been living among them as a resident foreigner for more than a decade, and they have all welcomed me with love."

72. Yosef Guedj, *Pi ha-medaber* (Livorno, 1854); Eliyahu Ḥai Guedj, *Ma'ase sha'ashu'im* (Livorno: Israel Costa, 1868); Eliyahu Ḥai Guedj, *Seder hagada shel pesaḥ ma' tafsir . . . mta tunis* (Livorno: Israel Costa, 1869); Eliyahu Ḥai Guedj, *Seder ve-tiqqun birkat ha-ḥama* (Livorno: Israel Costa, 1869); Ya'aqov Ḥaddad, *Knaf renanim* (Livorno: Israel Costa, 1871); Yosef Guedj, *Zohar 'al ha-tora* (Livorno: Israel Costa, 1872–1886); Eliyahu Ḥai Guedj, *Tokhaḥat megula* (Livorno: Israel Costa, 1872); Yosef Salama, *Shirei zimra* (Livorno: Israel Costa, 1872); David Guedj, *Ner david* (Livorno: Israel Costa, 1872).

73. Yehuda Sitrug (ca. 1840–1913) was a rabbi and companion of Nissim Shamama who had followed Nissim to Paris and then Livorno; his

copublisher, Yosef Shamama, is almost certainly Nissim's nephew Joseph Shamama (1840–1910), who was named as one of Nissim's heirs later that year. See Marglin, *The Shamama Case*, xvi, 69, 79, et passim.

74. Yehuda Sitruk and Yosef Shamama, "The Publishers' Introduction," in *Dinei sheḥiṭa u-vediqa bi-leshon ʿaravi* (Livorno: Israel Costa, 1873), 1.

75. Bregoli, "Hebrew Printing and Communication Networks," 54.

76. As listed in Marṣiano, *Sefer malkhei yeshurun*, 235–249. Ninety-nine of the books were printed in Livorno; the other thirty-three books were printed in Amsterdam (10 books), Berlin (1), Bratislava (1), Ferrara (1), İzmir (2), Istanbul (6), Jerusalem (2), Paris (1), Pisa (1), Venice (5), and Vienna (3).

4. ELIA BENAMOZEGH AND THE MODERN MAGHREBI JEWISH BOOK

1. Alessandro Guetta, *Philosophy and Kabbalah: Elijah Benamozegh and the Reconciliation of Western Thought and Eastern Esotericism*, trans. Helena Kahan (Albany: SUNY Press, 2009); Clémence Boulouque, *Another Modernity: Elia Benamozegh's Jewish Universalism* (Redwood City, CA: Stanford University Press, 2020).

2. Guetta, *Philosophy and Kabbalah*, 5.

3. In addition to Boulouque, *Another Modernity*, see also Clémence Boulouque, "An 'Interior Occident' and the Case for an Oriental Modernity: The Livornese Printing Press and the Mediterranean Publishing Networks of Elia Benamozegh (1823–1900)," *Jewish Social Studies: History, Culture, Society* n.s. 23, no. 2 (2018): 89–95, and Clémence Boulouque, "Elia Benamozegh's Printing Presses: Livornese Crossroads and the New Margins of Italian Jewish History," in *Italian Jewish Networks from the Seventeenth to the Twentieth Century*, ed. Francesca Bregoli, Carlotta Ferrara degli Uberti, and Guri Schwarz (London: Palgrave Macmillan, 2018), 59–80.

4. Boulouque, "An 'Interior Occident,'" 95.

5. Boulouque, *Another Modernity*, 26.

6. Elia Benamozegh, "Ḥeleq ha-mikhtavim / Autobiographien: Eliyahu ben Amozeg be-Livorno," in *Sefer zikaron le-sofrei yisrael ha-ḥayyim itanu ka-yom*, ed. Nahum Sokolow (Warsaw: M. I. Halter, 1889), 128–131. On Benamozegh's life and career, see Boulouque, *Another Modernity*, esp. 15–62.

7. David Ovadia, *Fas ve-ḥakhameha: divrei yemei ha-yehudim be-qehillat qodesh fas* (Jerusalem: Beit Oved, 1979), 261.

8. Benamozegh, "Autobiographien," 128; Boulouque, *Another Modernity*, 4–5.

9. Translation from Boulouque, "Elia Benamozegh's Printing Presses," 73.

10. Samples of Benamozegh's Hebrew handwriting clearly show his ease with writing Maghrebi cursive script; e.g., see his Hebrew correspondence with Ya'aqov Sha'ul Elyashar, NLI Archives Quarto 1271, Box 549.

11. Elia Benamozegh, "Introduction of the Author's Nephew and Student," in *Ma'or va-shemesh*, ed. Yehuda Coriat (Livorno: Eli'ezer Menaḥem Ottolenghi, 1839).

12. Guetta, *Philosophy and Kabbalah*, 101–102.

13. Elia Benamozegh, *Sefer sekhiyyot ha-ḥemda* (Livorno: Salomone Belforte, 1852).

14. Boulouque, "An 'Interior Occident,'" 96.

15. Neither is dated, nor do they have titles. They each have survived in one copy: the first, NLI Ephemera 001117663, and the second, YBZ 296.017. Their dating can be determined not only by the books included but also because the first catalog mentions Benamozegh's name with an epithet reserved for living people ("may God protect and redeem him"), and the second one follows his name with a posthumous epithet ("may his memory be a blessing").

16. NLI Ephemera 001117663.

17. This is from a 1903 broadside advertising the continuation of Benamozegh's press under Emanuel's leadership, in the author's personal collection.

18. Elia Benamozegh, "Thus Says the Compiler and Author," *Sfat emet* (Livorno: Elia Benamozegh, 1855).

19. Boulouque, *Another Modernity*, 135–138.

20. On *Em la-miqra*, see Boulouque, *Another Modernity*, 37–41. I can find only one work in Benamozegh's catalog that is specifically Ashkenazi in origin and orientation: Benamozegh's 1861 edition of *Sha'arei ṣiyyon* by Natan Neta Hannover (1610–1663), first published in Prague in 1662. However, certainly, many of Benamozegh's books would have been of interest to Ashkenazi customers as well.

21. Elia Benamozegh, *La verita svelata ai miei giudici: intorno le tre lettere, prodotte dalla querela Tubiana* (Paris: Minerva, 1861), 77.

22. Benamozegh, *La verita svelata*, 52. See Boulouque, "Elia Benamozegh's Printing Presses," 68–69.

23. See Sharon Liberman Mintz and Elka Deitsch, "From Marrakech to Milan: The Artistic Journey of Makhluf/Michele Allun," in *Windows*

on Jewish Worlds: Essays in Honor of William Gross, Collector Extraordinaire, ed. Shalom Sabar, Emile Schrijver, and Falk Weisemann (Zutphen: Walburg Pers, 2019), 272–285. I thank them for generously sharing their research on ʻAllun.

24. ʻAllun produced a number of *shivitis* [calligraphic devotional sheets] and illustrated amulets, both hand illuminated and engraved; see Mintz and Deitsch, "Marrakech to Milan." An 1824 broadside requests personal assistance for ʻAllun, "trained in the work of the scribe, and in the laws of kosher slaughter, knowledgeable in wisdom and science, and an expert circumciser," signed with rabbinic *haskamot* [approbations] from Morocco and Italy: JTS B (NS) H224. In 1827, he printed a broadside asking for financial assistance to print two of his books, titled *Zevaḥ toda* and *Ma'ane lashon*, neither of which seems to have been published (sold at Winner's Auctions 102, October 24, 2017, lot 126).

25. Mikhael Makhluf ʻAllun, "The Translator's Introduction and Apology," in *Or ne'erav: Bereshit* (Livorno: Elia Benamozegh, 1854).

26. On the *sharḥ* in North Africa, see Moshe Bar-Asher, *Leshon limmudim le-rabbi refael berdugo* (Jerusalem: Bialik, 2001); Joseph (Yosef) Chetrit, "Judeo-Arabic Dialects in North Africa as Communal Languages: Lects, Polylects, and Sociolects," *Journal of Jewish Languages* 10, no. 2 (2014): 202–232; Ofra Tirosh-Becker, "On Dialectical Roots in Judeo-Arabic Texts from Constantine (East Algeria)," *Revue des Études Juives* 170, no. 1 (2011): 227–253.

27. *ʻAseret ha-devarim* (Amsterdam: Joseph Attias, 1737, and Livorno: Jacob Arovas, 1815); David Ḥaliwa, *Ha-pa'am ode* (Amsterdam: Jacob Belinfante, 1838); *Arba'a gevi'im* (Livorno: Moshe Yeshu'a Tubiana, 1839); Eliyahu Sedbon, *Shir ha-shirim* (Livorno: Moshe Yeshu'a Tubiana, 1847).

28. *Sefer ḥanokh la-na'ar* (Livorno, 1866).

29. Mikhael Makhluf ʻAllun, "The Translator's Introduction and Apology," in *Or ne'erav: Bereshit* (Livorno: Elia Benamozegh, 1854).

30. See, e.g., Werner Weinberg, "Language Questions Relating to Moses Mendelssohn's Pentateuch Translation (in Commemoration of the 200th Anniversary of the Biur)," *Hebrew Union College Annual* 55 (1984): 197–242.

31. Shlomo Zarqa and Yehuda Ḍarmon, "Introduction," in *Shay la-mora* (Algiers: Cohen-Solal, 1854).

32. Daniel Newman, "The Arabic Literary Language: The Nahda (and Beyond)," in *The Oxford Handbook of Arabic Linguistics*, edited by Jonathan Owens (Oxford: Oxford University Press, 2013), 472–494.

33. Mikhael Makhluf ʻAllun, "General Note," in *Or neʻerav: Bemidbar* (Livorno: Elia Benamozegh, 1854).

34. ʻAllun, "General Note." Cf. the analysis of Yosef Tobi, "Judaeo-Arabic Printing in North Africa, 1850–1950," in *Historical Aspects of Printing and Publishing in Languages of the Middle East*, ed. Geoffrey Roper (Leiden: Brill, 2014), 144–146.

35. Archivio della Communità Ebraica di Livorno, Minute, filza 29 (1856), "Patti concordati fra gli Ecc. Sigg. Haham Michele Allum e Haham Elia Benamozegh." I am grateful to archivist Barbara Martinelli for making these files available to me, and to Francesca Bregoli for her generous assistance in translating them. It seems that the initial print run did not include the final version of ʻAllun's preface, and the first page was reprinted with the new preface, as approved by Abraham Barukh Piperno, a prominent local rabbi. See also Boulouque, "Elia Benamozegh's Printing Presses," 68–69; Liana Funaro, "A Mediterranean Diaspora: Jews from Leghorn in the Second Half of the Nineteenth Century," in *L'Europe Méditerranéenne*, ed. Marta Petricioli (Brussels: Peter Lang, 2008), 97.

36. Archivio di Stato di Livorno, Governo di Livorno, b. 558, fasc. 210 (March 31, 1857), as cited in Funaro, "A Mediterranean Diaspora," 97.

37. Boulouque, "An 'Interior Occident,'" 100. Decades later, Benamozegh did end up publishing a short-lived Tunisian Judeo-Arabic newspaper titled first *Ha-mevasser* and then *al-Mubashir*, edited by Tunisian-Livornese writer Eliʻezer Farḥi, between 1884 and 1885, which is examined below; the shared titles may be a coincidence or may indicate some connection between these projects.

38. E.g., two of his first publications in 1854 were a volume of selihot and *Tiqqun haṣot* [prayers for a midnight vigil], both published by Moroccan scholar Avraham al-Maliaḥ.

39. Benamozegh, letter of April 28, 1858, published in *Lettere dirette a S.D. Luzzatto da Elia Benamozegh* (Livorno: Elia Benamozegh, 1890), 24–31, as translated in Boulouque, "Elia Benamozegh's Printing Presses," 71.

40. Archivio della Communità Ebraica di Livorno, Minute, filza 29 (1856), "Patti concordati fra gli Ecc. Sigg. Haham Michele Allum e Haham Elia Benamozegh."

41. Boulouque, "Elia Benamozegh's Printing Presses," 70–74; Jessica Marglin, *The Shamama Case: Contesting Citizenship across the Modern Mediterranean* (Princeton, NJ: Princeton University Press, 2022), 191–194.

42. See Norman (Noam) Stillman, *Sephardi Religious Responses to Modernity* (Luxembourg: Harwood, 1995); Boulouque, "Elia Benamozegh's Printing Presses," 78; Gabriel Abensour, "In Praise of the Multitude: Rabbi Yosef Knafo's Socially Conscious Work in Essaouira at the End of the Nineteenth Century," *Jewish Social Studies* 27, no. 1 (2022): 115–149.

43. Isaac Bengualid, *Va-yomer yiṣḥaq* (Livorno: Elia Benamozegh, 1876), siman 99; Boulouque, "An 'Interior Occident,'" 114–115.

44. Eliezer Bashan, "Rabbi eliyahu ḥazzan, rabban shel ṭripoli ve'aleqsandria, ve-yaḥaso la-haskala," in *Hagut 'Ivrit be-arṣot ha-islam*, ed. Menahem Zohori (Jerusalem: Brit 'Ivrit 'Olamit, 1981), 410–418; Stillman, *Sephardi Religious Responses*, 29–48; Zvi Zohar, "Halakhic and Rabbinic Literature in Egypt in the Last Two Centuries," *Pe'amim* 86 (2001): 175–213; Harvey Goldberg, "Sephardi Rabbinic 'Openness' in Nineteenth-Century Tripoli: Examining a Modern Myth in Context," in *Jewish Religious Leadership: Image and Reality*, Vol. 2, ed. Jack Wertheimer (Jewish Theological Seminary Press, 2004), 695–714; Zvi Zohar, *Rabbinic Creativity in the Modern Middle East* (London: Bloomsbury Academic, 2013), 245–246, 280, 360–363.

45. His birth date is uncertain. Estimates in secondary scholarship range from 1840 to 1848; the dates used here are from Zvi Zohar, "Ḥazzan, Elijah Bekhor," in *Encyclopedia of Jews in the Islamic World*, ed. Noam Stillman (Leiden: Brill, 2010). Ḥazzan's brother Aron stayed in İzmir and became an important community leader and journalist, publishing the Judeo-Spanish newspaper *La Buena Esperansa* from 1874 to 1917: Julia Phillips Cohen, "Hazan, Aron de Yosef," in *Encyclopedia of Jews in the Islamic World*, ed. Noam Stillman (Leiden: Brill, 2010).

46. Yisrael Moshe Ḥazzan, *Sha'arei teshuva 'im hagahot iyyei ha-yam* (Livorno: Elia Benamozegh, 1869). Benamozegh also published the first volume of Eliyahu Bekhor Ḥazzan's collected responsa, *Ta'alumot lev*, in 1879; the second volume was published in Livorno by the press of Israel Costa in 1893, and the last two volumes were published in Alexandria (Farag Hayyim Mizrahi, 1903 and 1907).

47. See his published report, "Azien," *Ha-magid* 15, no. 3 (January 18, 1871): 20.

48. Michal Saraf, "Ha-ḥida ha-sifrutit ba-ḥibbur zikhron yerushalayim le-rabbi eliyahu hazzan, shadar yerushalayim bi-ṣfon afriqa," *Proceedings of the World Congress of Jewish Studies* 10 (1989): 89–96.

49. Seyman and Dar'i also sponsored the printing of the responsa of Ḥazzan's great-grandfather a year later in Jerusalem: *Ḥiqrei lev* (Jerusalem: Zvi Hirsch Hakohen, 1875). In the French archives for Annaba/Bône, Seyman appears as "Michel Seyman," and Dar'i as "Frazo Darhé."

50. Eliyahu Bekhor Ḥazzan, *Zikhron yerushalayim* (Livorno: Elia Benamozegh, 1874), 115.

51. Ḥazzan, *Zikhron yerushalayim*, 1–8.

52. Ḥazzan, *Zikhron yerushalayim*, 32.

53. Ḥazzan, *Zikhron yerushalayim*, 112.

54. Ḥazzan, *Zikhron yerushalayim*, 48.

55. Zohar, "Ḥazzan."

56. Gershon Bacon, "The Rabbinical Conference in Kraków (1903) and the Beginnings of Organized Orthodox Jewry," in *Let the Old Make Way for the New: Studies Presented to Immanuel Etkes, Vol. 2: Haskalah, Orthodoxy, and the Opposition to Hasidism*, ed. David Assaf and Ada Rapaport-Albert (Jerusalem: Shazar, 2009), 199–225. One contemporary newspaper report describes the awed reaction Ḥazzan received: "Among [the rabbis] was the great sage, the *hakham-bashi* of Alexandria, who in his reputation and glorious appearance, with his honorable robes adorned with three medals from the Turkish government, inspired many people with desire to see him, such that there was no room to stand outside the synagogue, and so many people gathered on the street . . . that the tramway cars were stopped for half an hour, unable to move." "The Congress of Rabbis in Kraków," *Ha-ṣefira* 176 (August 12, 1903): 2–3.

57. Ḥazzan, *Zikhron yerushalayim*, 57.

58. Ḥazzan, *Zikhron yerushalayim*, 113.

59. See the analyses of Saraf, "Ha-ḥida ha-sifrutit"; Yiṣḥaq Beṣalel, "Pitḥ on pe la-yehudiyya ba-mizraḥ: ha-yaḥas la-isha ba-zikhron yerushalayim le-rabbi eliyahu ḥazzan," in *'Ayin tova: du-siaḥ ve-pulmus be-tarbut yisrael*, ed. Nahem Ilan (Tel Aviv: Hakibbutz Hameuchad, 1999), 197–223.

60. This point is made in Stillman (and others): *Sephardi Religious Responses*, 30; Zohar, *Rabbinic Creativity*, 361; Boulouque, "An 'Interior Occident,'" 114.

61. Eugène Robe, ed., *Journal de la Jurisprudence de la Cour Impériale d'Alger* 11 (1870), 108–136. On the background of the Crémieux Decree in general, see Lisa Leff, *Sacred Bonds of Solidarity: The Rise of Jewish Internationalism in Nineteenth-Century France* (Redwood City, CA: Stanford University Press, 2006), and Joshua Schreier, *Arabs of the Jewish Faith: The Civilizing Mission in Colonial Algeria* (New Brunswick, NJ: Rutgers University Press, 2010).

62. Ḥazzan, *Zikhron yerushalayim*, 80–87.

63. Benjamin Drif, "La communauté juive de Bône (1870–1940): mutations socio-culturelles à l'époque coloniale" (master's thesis, Université Paris 1-Panthéon Sorbonne, 2015), 205–207.

64. Stillman, *Sephardi Religious Responses,* 38.

65. Elia Benamozegh, "Préface de l'Éditeur," in Ḥazzan, *Zikhron yerushalayim.* See Stillman, *Sephardi Religious Responses,* and Zohar, *Rabbinic Creativity;* although cf. the critique of Goldberg, "Sephardi Rabbinic 'Openness,'" who argues that Ḥazzan (and like-minded thinkers) faced much criticism from contemporary Sephardi rabbis who did not subscribe to this philosophy. Indeed, Boulouque observes that Ḥazzan's stance was more conservative than Benamozegh in some areas, such as Ḥazzan's views on science, which "would have put him at odds with Benamozegh's embrace of contemporary science as part of a broad understanding of progressive revelation": Boulouque, "An 'Interior Occident,'" 113–114.

66. Benamozegh, "Préface de l'Éditeur," 1. On the importance of the "Oriental" for Benamozegh, see Boulouque, *Another Modernity,* 135–138.

67. Benamozegh, "Préface de l'Éditeur," 2, 5.

68. In 1852, Benamozegh edited *Sefer sekhiyyot ha-ḥemda* (Livorno: Salomone Belforte, 1852), with instructions for the Passover seder in Maghrebi Judeo-Arabic (43a–52b), which were likely composed by Benamozegh himself. He also served as a Judeo-Arabic translator for the inventory of Nissim Shamama in 1873: Marglin, *The Shamama Case,* 191.

69. Here, I counter the assertion of Clémence Boulouque, who described the publication of Judeo-Arabic folktales and popular stories as "a line that Benamozegh's presses never crossed": Boulouque, "Elia Benamozegh's Printing Presses," 65, no. 17.

70. Quote from Archivio di Stato di Livorno, Governo di Livorno, b. 558, fasc. 210 (March 31, 1857), as cited in Funaro, "A Mediterranean Diaspora," 97.

71. Eusèbe Vassel, *La littérature populaire des israélites tunisiens* (Paris: Ernest Leroux, 1907), 26–27, 46–47; Tsivia Tobi, "Ha-rav ha-maskil eli'ezer farḥi ve-yeṣirotav ha-saṭiriyyot," *Ben 'ever la'arav* 5 (2012): 127–144; Yosef Tobi and Tsivia Tobi, *Judeo-Arabic Literature in Tunisia, 1850–1950* (Detroit: Wayne State University Press, 2014), 245.

72. Vassel, *La litterature populaire,* 27.

73. Eli'ezer Farḥi, *Sirat al-'anqa* (Livorno: Israel Costa, 1886). Farḥi went on to publish several other volumes adapted from classical sirat: Rachel Schine, "A Mirror for the Modern Man: The Siyar Ša'biyya as Advice Literature in Tunisian Judeo-Arabic Editions," *Arabica* 65 (2018): 392–418; Tobi and Tobi, *Judeo-Arabic Literature in Tunisia,* 245.

74. Eli'ezer Farḥi, untitled preface to *Anis al-wujud* (Livorno: Elia Benamozegh, 1885). This is very similar in tone to Farḥi's epilogue to *Sirat al-Azaliyya* (Livorno: Israel Costa, 1887), which is explored at greater length in Schine, "A Mirror for the Modern Man." I am grateful to Dr. Dainy Bernstein for eir assistance in helping me access this rare book.

75. The title page indicates that al-Dahan's translation was done "at the request and with the payment of the publisher." The book presents only the first section of *Yosippon*, and while the introduction suggests that five more volumes were forthcoming, none appeared. On al-Dahan (ca. 1840–1930), see Eliyahu Refael Marṣiano, *Sefer malkhei yeshurun* (Jerusalem: Mekhon haRaShaM, 1999), 30.

76. Schine, "A Mirror for the Modern Man," 406. See also Joshua Picard, "Tunisian Judaeo-Arabic Essays on Religion and Ideology in the Late-Nineteenth Century" (master's thesis, Brandeis University, 2016).

77. Bekache, *Mevasser ṭov* (Livorno, 1884), 13b–14a, and see Avner Ofrath, "*The Harbinger of Good* by Shalom Bekache, 1884," *Absinthe: World Literature in Translation* 29 (2024): 186–194.

78. On the linguistic features of Bekache's Judeo-Arabic, see Ofra Tirosh-Becker, "Linguistic Analysis of an Algerian Judeo-Arabic Text from the Nineteenth Century," *La Linguistique* 55, no. 1 (2019): 193–212.

79. *Piyyut bar yohai bi-sfat 'arav* (Livorno, 1886); *Sefer mahzor qatan* (Livorno, 1886).

80. Tobi and Tobi, *Judeo-Arabic Literature in Tunisia*, 245.

81. Yehuda Jarmon, *Shuva yisrael* (Livorno: Elia Benamozegh, 1886); Eliyahu Allouche, *'Et la-ledet qol sasson* (Livorno: Elia Benamozegh, 1888).

82. Boulouque, "An 'Interior Occident,'" 117–119.

83. Letter to Sabato Morais, August 20, 1869, CAJS Sabato Morais collection, SBM XX FF28, box 1, as cited in Boulouque, "Elia Benamozegh's Printing Presses," 72.

84. Serfaty, *Yaḥas fes*, as edited by David Ovadia, in *Fas ve-ḥakhameha: divrei yemei ha-yehudim be-qehillat qodesh fas*, Vol. 1 (Jerusalem, 1978), 125.

85. This letter was copied by Shlomo b. Refael Abensur (1859–1941) into an anthology of correspondence, now NLI Ms. Heb. 8.5966, 11a. It is undated but appears after another letter seemingly on the same topic, dated 1878–1879 and signed by Matityahu Serero, Avner-Yisrael Serfaty, and Refael Abensur.

86. See, e.g., Guetta's biographical sketch in Guetta, *Philosophy and Kabbalah*, 1–6, and cf. Boulouque, *Another Modernity*.

5. LANDSCAPES OF PRINT IN THE NINETEENTH-CENTURY MAGHREB

1. Auguste Bourget, "Faits divers: Alger," *L'Akhbar: Journal de l'Algérie* no. 1875, October 30 1853, 2. The second book referred to is *Seder havdala bil-'arabi* (Algiers, 1853), but the first book cannot be identified with either of the other two Hebrew books known to have been printed in Algiers that year. See Avraham (Robert) Attal, "'Al ha-defus ha-'ivri ba-magreb," *Mi-mizraḥ umi-ma'arav* 2 (1980): 121–129, and Avraham (Robert) Attal and Meira Harroch, "Ha-defus ha-'ivri be-aljir," *Qiryat sefer* 61 (1986): 561–572. On Jacob's brother and cofounder of their press, Haim Cohen-Solal, see Valérie Assan, "Haïm Cohen-Solal, négociant," *Archives Juives* 45, no. 2 (2012): 143–144.

2. On Bourget and *L'Akhbar*, see Zoulikha Sadaoui, "Un temoin de l'histoire: L'Akhbar, doyen des journaux algeriens de la colonisation" (PhD diss., Université Panthéon-Assas Paris II, 1992); Gavin Murray-Miller, *The Cult of the Modern: Trans-Mediterranean France and the Construction of French Modernity* (Lincoln: University of Nebraska Press, 2017), 209–246; Arthur Asseraf, *Electric News in Colonial Algeria* (Oxford: Oxford University Press, 2019), 27–64. On productivity and industry in the colonial ideology of French Algeria, see Osama Abi-Mershed, *Apostles of Modernity: Saint-Simonians and the Civilizing Mission in Algeria* (Redwood City, CA: Stanford University Press, 2010).

3. Elizabeth le Roux, "Book History in the African World: The State of the Discipline," *Book History* 15 (2012): 248–300 (quote on 250); Ghislaine Lydon and Graziano Krätli, eds., *The Trans-Saharan Book Trade: Manuscript Culture, Arabic Literacy and Intellectual History in Muslim Africa* (Leiden: Brill, 2010); Inge Brinkman and Koen Bostoen, "'To Make Book': A Conceptual Historical Approach to Kongo Book Cultures (Sixteenth-Nineteenth Centuries)," in *The Kongo Kingdom: The Origins, Dynamics and Cosmopolitan Culture of an African Polity*, ed. Inge Brinkman and Koen Bostoen (Cambridge: Cambridge University Press, 2018), 216–234.

4. Moncef Chenoufi, "Le probleme des origines de l'imprimerie et de la presse arabe en Tunisie dans sa relation avec la Renaissance (Nahda) 1847–1887" (PhD diss., Lille III, 1974); Kmar Bendana, "Générations d'imprimeurs et figures d'éditeurs à Tunis entre 1850 et 1950," in *Les mutations du livre et de l'édition dans le monde du XVIIIe siècle à l'an 2000*, ed. Jacques Michon and Jean-Yves Mollier (Paris: Harmattan, 2002), 349–359; Fawzi Abdulrazak, "Printing as an Agent of Change in Morocco,

1864–1912," in *The Book in Africa: Critical Debates,* ed. Caroline Davis and David Johnson (London: Palgrave Macmillan, 2015), 31–43.

5. Asseraf, *Electric News.* Ami Ayalon makes a similar argument for Arabic printing in the Ottoman Levant: *The Arabic Print Revolution: Cultural Production and Mass Readership* (Cambridge: Cambridge University Press, 2016). Cf. Geoffrey Roper, "The Printing Press and Change in the Arab World," in *Agent of Change: Print Culture Studies after Elizabeth L. Eisenstein,* ed. Sabrina Baron, Eric Lindquist, and Eleanor Shevlin (Amherst: University of Massachusetts Press, 2007), 250–267.

6. Asseraf, *Electric News,* 32.

7. Philip Luckombe, *The History and Art of Printing* (London: Philip Luckombe, 1771), 42.

8. For al-Ṣaffar, see Susan Gilson Miller, *Disorienting Encounters: Travels of a Moroccan Scholar in France in 1845–1846* (Oakland: University of California Press, 1992), 201–208. For al-Amrawi, as quoted in Fawzi Abdulrazak: "The Kingdom of the Book: The History of Printing as an Agency of Change in Morocco between 1865 and 1912" (PhD diss., Boston University, 1990), 109.

9. Abdulrazak, "Printing as an Agent of Change," 45–50.

10. Chenoufi, "Le probleme des origines de l'imprimerie"; Jamel Zran, "Aux origines de l'imprimerie et de l'édition en Tunisie: l'imprimerie officielle et le journal al-Râ'id," in *La presse en Tunisie et dans les pays méditerranéens durant un siècle, 1860–1960,* ed. Jamel Zran (Tunis: Université de la Manouba, 2011), 13–36.

11. Asseraf, *Electric News,* 27–64.

12. Abdulrazak, "Printing as an Agent of Change," 46–53.

13. Yosef Tobi, "Judaeo-Arabic Printing in North Africa, 1850–1950," in *Historical Aspects of Printing and Publishing in Languages of the Middle East,* ed. Geoffrey Roper (Leiden: Brill, 2014), 131. It is also considered the first modern play published in Arabic; for more on the play, see Shmuel Moreh, "The Nineteenth-Century Jewish Playwright Abraham Daninos as a Bridge between Muslim and Jewish Theater," in *Judaism and Islam: Boundaries, Communications, and Interaction,* ed. William Brinner and Benjamin Hary (Leiden: Brill, 2000), 409–416. A number of lithographic Arabic printers, as well as French printers, had been operating in Algeria since 1830; see Hermann Fiori, *Bibliographie des ouvrages imprimés à Alger de 1830 à 1850* (Paris: Besson, 1938), 11–16.

14. Avraham Ya'ari, *Sheluḥei ereṣ yisrael: toldot ha-sheliḥut meha-areṣ la-gola me-ḥurban bayit sheni 'ad ha-me'a ha-tesha'-'esrei* (Jerusalem: Mossad Rav Kook, 1977), 860.

15. Impr. Gueymard is not listed in Fiori, *Bibliographie des ouvrages imprimés à Alger,* and the only publications traceable to that press were all published in 1853, including, interestingly, *Réflexions sur l'hypothèque légale de la femme juive,* an anonymous treatise on the rights of Jewish women; see *Bibliographie de la France ou Journal Général de l'Imprimerie et de la Librarie,* no. 8 (1854), 120. However, it is still listed as operating in Algiers in 1855, according to Ferdinand Grimont, *Manuel-annuaire de l'imprimerie, de la librairie et de la presse* (Paris: P. Jannet, 1855), 313.

16. Attal, "'Al ha-defus ha-'ivri ba-magreb," 123–124; Tobi, "Judaeo-Arabic Printing," 134.

17. Isaiah Shachar, *Jewish Tradition in Art: The Feuchtwanger Collection of Judaica* (Jerusalem: Israel Museum, 1981), 188. Another copy of this broadside is in the Gross Collection, 079.011.012.

18. Attal and Harroch, "Ha-defus ha-'ivri be-aljir," 563–564. The second volume of *Shay la-mora* was printed in Livorno by the press of Salomone Belforte in 1864; in the *haskama* [approbation] to that volume, Yosef Burjil (Bourgel) indicates that it was lack of funding that delayed the publication (and presumably spurred the change of press) of the second volume. On Shlomo Zarqa and the language of *Shay la-mora,* see Shlomo Elkayam, "Ḥiddushei lashon be-kitvei rabbi shlomo zarqa," *Pe'amim* 71 (1997): 10–24.

19. Perrier was a printer and journalist from Lorraine, founder and first editor of the important Oranais journal *L'Echo d'Oran* (first issue 1844). In the 1890s, *L'Echo* played an important role in combating antisemitic attacks on the Jews of Oran; Geneviève Dermenjian, *La crise anti-juive oranaise, 1895–1905: l'antisémitisme dans l'Algérie coloniale* (Paris: L'Harmattan, 1986), 18.

20. See the list of their publications in Avraham (Robert) Attal, "Ha-defus ha-'ivri be-wahran," supplement, *Qiryat sefer* 68 (1998): 85–92.

21. Forthcoming article coauthored with Tamir Karkason.

22. *Kitab qanun al-dawla al-tunisiyya* (Tunis: Ḥayyim Ze'ev Ashkenazi, 1861).

23. Eusèbe Vassel, *La littérature populaire des israélites tunisiens* (Paris: Ernest Leroux, 1907), 19. Shamama's other known publications are *Sefinat ma'luf,* a collection of songs for the style of Andalusi malouf music (Livorno: Israel Costa, 1887), and, in collaboration with Eli'ezer Farḥi, *Anis al-wujud,* a collection of short stories (Livorno: Elia Benamozegh, 1885). See also Yosef Tobi, "The Openness of Modern Judeo-Arabic Literature in Tunisia towards Muslim-Arabic Literature," *Pe'amim* 130 (2012): 123.

24. Moshe Shamama, untitled preface to *Kitab qanun al-dawla al-tunisiyya* (Tunis: Ḥayyim Ze'ev Ashkenazi, 1861).

25. Gross 079.011.011 (and 079.011.012) and 027.011.263. The Gross Collection also holds two other similar, unsigned itineraria, perhaps likewise produced in Algiers in the late nineteenth century: 079.011.007 and 079.011.009. Bouyer purchased his lithographic press in 1836 from Italian printer Vaccari (who had opened it in 1831). Perhaps the most well-known book he printed there was Marcelin Beaussier's *Dictionnaire pratique arabe-français* (1871), which is to this day a standard reference for Algerian Arabic. On Bouyer, see Fiori, *Bibliographie des ouvrages imprimés à Alger*, 4–5.

26. These works are popular and frequently reprinted early modern sermon anthologies of Azaria Piccio (1579–1647), Jonathan Eybeschutz (1690–1764), and Ephraim Luntschitz (1550–1619), respectively.

27. *Sefer yosippon* is a medieval chronicle of Jewish history, and *She'erit yisrael* is another historical chronicle, originally composed in Yiddish by Menahem Mann Amelander in Amsterdam in 1743 and marketed as the "second part of *Sefer yosippon*." The edition referred to here is the Hebrew expansion by Abraham Menahem Mendel Mohr, which included a final section with an account of the 1840 Damascus Affair and the Jewish diplomatic mission led by Moses Montefiore and Alphonse Crémieux; it was first printed in L'viv in 1846. The other books mentioned are popular medieval and early modern Hebrew historical and moralistic texts.

28. This is almost certainly the illustrated haggadah with Judeo-Arabic translation prepared by Eliyahu Ḥai Guedj, first printed in Livorno by Israel Costa in 1869; Guedj and his son Ya'aqov would soon become printers and booksellers, first in Algiers and then in Tunis.

29. Advertisement on flyleaf of Mordekhai Seror, *Qol sasson* (Algiers, 1884).

30. *Sefer maḥzor qaṭan* (Livorno: Israel Costa, 1886); *Sefer shavua' ṭov* (Livorno: Israel Costa, 1886); *Hagada ou rituel des deux premieres nuit de Paque* (Livorno: Israel Costa, 1886).

31. The catalog is titled in French and Judeo-Arabic: *Reshimat ha-sefarim alli yinba'u 'ind ribbi avraham bukhabza / Catalogue de Abraham Boukabza*, and a photograph of the cover was printed in Israel Ta-Shma, *The Hebrew Book: An Historical Survey* (Jerusalem: Keter, 1975), 69. Ta-Shma describes it as listing "some 200 books, and from it a great deal can be learned about what books were in demand in Algiers at the end of the nineteenth century, as well as about Hebrew printing there." A photocopy

of the catalog was also in the possession of Robert Attal (Avraham Haṭal, 1927–2011) and listed in the inventory of Attal and Harroch, "Ha-defus ha-ʿivri be-aljir," 565 (no. 16). I was unable to find this photocopy in Attal's papers at the Ben-Zvi Institute or the National Library of Israel. The catalog reproduced in Ta-Shma was sold at Kedem Auction to a book dealer in 2010, and I have been unable to find its current location. I have compiled this inventory from the combined lists, advertisements, and catalogs printed as paratexts in *Qol sasson* (1884), *Maʿasei bustinai* (1886), *Hagada ou rituel* (1886), *Beit pereṣ* (1887), *ʿAseret ha-dibrot* (1887), and *Daniel ha-kuzari* (1887). It comprises some fifty-seven entries, although some clearly refer to more than one title (e.g., "books of the haskala" or "prayerbooks of all types").

32. These are listed in the catalog printed in *Maʿasei bustinai* (1886). Examples of amulets lithographed in gold ink, "sold at [the shop of] Avraham Boukabza in Algiers," are in the Gross Collection: 027.011.401 and 027.011.719 and probably also 027.011.167, 027.011.402, and 027.011.720 (although these are unsigned).

33. Ami Ayalon, "Arab Booksellers and Bookshops in the Age of Printing, 1850–1914," *British Journal of Middle Eastern Studies* 37, no. 1 (2010): 80–81.

34. Ephemera can be defined as any printed material intended to circulate for a temporary period, unbound or not in codex form; it usually refers to single-sheet material, such as posters, broadsides, and postcards, but it can also include booklets, calendars, pamphlets, and other multipage products. Maurice Rickards, the founder of the Ephemera Society, famously termed ephemera "the minor transient documents of everyday life." Maurice Rickards, *Collecting Printed Ephemera* (London: Christie's, 1988), 7. On the study of ephemera in book history, see, inter alia, Cathy Lynn Preston and Michael James Preston, eds., *The Other Print Tradition: Essays on Chapbooks, Broadsides, and Related Ephemera* (London: Routledge, 1995); Maurice Rickards and Michael Twyman, *The Encyclopedia of Ephemera* (London: Routledge, 2000); Martin Andrews, "The Importance of Ephemera," in *A Companion to the History of the Book*, ed. Simon Eliot and Jonathan Rose (Hoboken, NJ: Wiley-Blackwell, 2007), 434–450.

35. Andrew Pettegree, "The Legion of the Lost: Recovering the Lost Books of Early Modern Europe," in *Lost Books: Reconstructing the Print World of Pre-Industrial Europe*, ed. Flavia Bruni and Andrew Pettegree (Leiden: Brill, 2016), 9.

36. Attal, "ʿAl ha-defus ha-ʿivri ba-magreb," 124; Silvia Finzi, "Elia Finzi, imprimeur de père en fils," in *Métiers et professions des Italiens de Tunisie*

(Tunis: Éditions Finzi, 2003), 278–284. Julia Clancy-Smith asserts that Vittorio's father, Giulio Finzi, had "previous experience in Leghorn's printing trade," but I cannot find any record of him working in the Hebrew press (or otherwise) in Livorno: Julia Clancy-Smith, *Mediterraneans: North Africa and Europe in an Age of Migration, c. 1800–1900* (Oakland: University of California Press, 2011), 136.

37. According to Attal ("'Al ha-defus ha-'ivri ba-magreb," 124), the Uzan-Castro press opened in 1891. But the bibliographies of Eusèbe Vassel and Daniel Ḥagège, as well as the listings of the "Bibliography of the Hebrew Book" project at the National Library of Israel, demonstrate that they were printing Hebrew and Judeo-Arabic material starting in 1885. See Vassel, *La littérature populaire*, 104, 242; Michal Saraf, "Daniel Ḥagège ve-ḥiburo 'al toldot ha-sifrut ha-'aravit-yehudit be-tunisia, 1862–1939," *Pe'amim* 30 (1987): 45.

38. Attal, "'Al ha-defus ha-'ivri ba-magreb," 124. Guedj is also mentioned briefly by Daniel Ḥagège; see Yosef Tobi and Tsivia Tobi, *Judeo-Arabic Literature in Tunisia, 1850–1950* (Detroit: Wayne State University Press, 2014), 244. Attal claims that Guedj moved to Tunis in 1890, but numerous examples can be found of books printed by Guedj in Algiers from 1890 to 1895. According to Vassel, Guedj printed a Passover haggada in 1895 that was begun in Algiers but finished in Tunis (Vassel, *La littérature populaire*, 83), although no examples appear to have survived.

39. Vassel, *La littérature populaire.*

40. *Konti di monti kristo* (Tunis: Uzan and Castro, 1889) was translated by Ya'aqov Chemla (1858–1938), and *Ḥikayat robinson krusoi* (Tunis: Uzan and Castro, 1890) by Ḥai (Vita) Sitruk, both of whom were active figures in the literary and journalistic scene of Tunis. On Chemla, Sitruk, Farḥi, and their colleagues, see Tobi and Tobi, *Judeo-Arabic Literature.*

41. Vassel, *La littérature populaire*, 32, 228.

42. Avraham (Robert) Attal, *Kitvei 'et ve-'itonim yehudiyyim bi-ṣfon afriqa* (Tel Aviv: Tel Aviv University, 1996); Jamaâ Baïda, *La presse marocaine d'expression française: des origines à 1956* (Rabat: Faculté des Lettres et des Sciences Humaines de Rabat, 1996); Yosef (Joseph) Chetrit, "Hitgabshutah shel leshon ha-'itonut ha-'aravit-yehudit be-tunis ba-sof ha-me'a ha-19," in *Meḥqarim ba-lashon ha-'ivrit uve-leshonot ha-yehudim*, ed. Moshe Bar-Asher (Jerusalem: Hebrew University, 1996), 523–538; Pierre Cohen, *La presse juive editée au Maroc 1870–1963* (Rabat: Editions Bouregreg, 2007).

43. "Si hasen anonsyos," *Al-Moghreb al-Aksa* 1, no. 18 (May 27, 1883).

44. This broadside survives in the Bar-Ilan Library, Ṣafnat 642.A05 (Rare 309 L). It is also reproduced in Eliyahu Refael Marṣiano, *Sefer bnei*

melakhim ve-hu toldot ha-sefer ha-ʿivri ba-maroqo mi-shnat 5277 ʿad shnat 5749 (Jerusalem: Mekhon haRaShaM, 1989), 34.

45. Attal, "Ha-defus ha-ʿivri be-wahran," 87–88; Baïda, *La presse marocaine*, 189.

46. Marṣiano, *Sefer bnei melakhim*, 39.

47. Eliyahu Ḥai Guedj, *Ḥesed ve-emet* (Algiers: Yaʿaqov Guedj, 1888).

48. See, e.g., the catalog of Eliʿezer Farḥi: *Katalog fi jamiaʿ sdadir* (Tunis, ca. 1894), NLI Rare 8.2011A 5048.

49. Yaʿaqov Moshe Tolédano, *Sarid u-faliṭ* (Tel Aviv: Azriel, 1946), 80.

50. This list was printed as a paratext to Shalom Bekache, *Mi-meqor yisrael* (Algiers: Shalom Bekache, 1892), itself part of the "supplementary" series of Bekache's Judeo-Arabic newspaper *Beit Yisrael / Le Peuple d'Israel.*

51. An exemplar of Soffer's micrographic print of Esther is in the Gross Collection, 078.011.028; the other prints are Jonah on a ship (Gross 078.011.054), Rabbi Shimʿon Bar Yoḥai (Gross 078.011.047), and Judith with the head of Holofernes (in the Soffer family collection). I am deeply grateful to the late Jacques Soffer (1940–2019) and his son David and Jacob's grandson and great-grandson for generously sharing material from his family collection with me.

52. This is held in a binder of loose ephemera in the collection of Paul Dahan, at the CCJM. On the Meshibat Nefesh Society of Essaouira, see Daniel Schroeter, "Anglo-Jewry and Essaouira (Mogador), 1860–1900: The Social Implications of Philanthropy," *Transactions & Miscellanies of the Jewish Historical Society of England* 28 (1982): 73–74.

53. CCJM 3746. On Burjil (Bourgel, d. 1898) and the ʿAmalei Torah society, see his biographical entry in Binyamin Refael Kohen, *Sefer malkhei tarshish* (Netivot, 1986), 121–124.

54. E.g., Burjil helped fund and wrote an introduction for his uncle Yosef Burjil's book *Va-yiqen yosef* (Livorno: Moses Tubiana, 1852), and he contributed a *haskama* [approbation] to his colleague Refael Hakohen's book *Tiferet baḥurim* (Livorno: Israel Costa, 1877).

55. CCJM 4280.

56. This card is now held in a folder labeled "Ephemera" [*dappim bodedim*] among the many boxes of the "Collection Attal" left to the Ben-Zvi Institute by Attal (Avraham Haṭal, 1927–2011) after his death. They are still not fully cataloged, and I am grateful to Ofra Tirosh-Becker and the librarians at YBZ for helping me to access this material.

57. Examples from the Dahan Collection of the CCJM are the letters of Joseph Abergel, 1896 (CCJM 6575); and Salomon Haim Lévy, 1897 (CCJM

6584), both from Safi. There is also printed Moroccan Hebrew stationery from the early twentieth century, still some ten or fifteen years before there were Jewish presses anywhere in Morocco outside of Tangiers: David Samuel Haïm Benharrosh and Refael Ohana of Meknes, 1907 (CCJM 6386); Isaac Asulin Elfasi of Marrakech, 1909 (CCJM 6552).

58. Joseph (Yosef) Chetrit, "Haskala hébraique et haskala judéo-arabe à Tunis à la fin du XIXe siècle," in *Entre orient et occident: Juifs et Musulmans en Tunisie*, ed. Denis Cohen-Tannoudji (Paris: Éditions de l'éclat, 2007), 289–320.

59. Shlomo Zarqa and Yehuda Ḍarmon, *Shay la-mora* (Algiers: Cohen-Solal, 1854), "Introduction."

60. Bekache, *Mi-meqor yisrael*. Cf. his remarks in *Bone yerushalayim*: "I have translated it from the Holy Tongue into the Arabic language, which is common throughout the countries of Algeria, Tunisia, and Morocco." *Bone yerushalayim* (Algiers: Bekache and Cohen-Solal, 1892).

61. The surviving issues of *Adziri* are BNF Jo. 3056; on this journal and its reception, see Avraham (Robert) Attal, "Ha-ʿiṭṭon ha-yehudi ha-rish'on ba-maghreb—L'Israélite Algérien (Adziri), 1870," *Pe'amim* 17 (1983): 88–95.

62. Nessim Benisti, "Réforme, Emancipation, Progrès," *Adziri*, no. 6 (August 26, 1870): 2–3. Emphasis in original.

63. In the original, the two italicized French words are set in Latin type.

64. Mordekhai Seror, *Qol sasson* (Algiers, 1884), "Introduction."

65. Bekache writes *listwaris* in Judeo-Arabic, borrowing from the French *l'histoire* (rather than the Arabic *tawarikh*), which emphasizes Bekache's view of his work in a European model.

66. Shalom Bekache, *Sipurei ha-ṭevaʿ* (Algiers: Shalom Bekache, 1892).

67. Chetrit, "Haskala hébraique et haskala judéo-arabe," 314.

68. Yosef Tobi, "Bekache, Shalom," in *Encyclopedia of Jews in the Islamic World*, ed. Norman Stillman (Leiden: Brill, 2010). Frustratingly, Attal indicates that "a catalog of Bekache's personal library" (presumably in manuscript) was in his personal possession, comprising some six hundred titles, mostly Maskilic books in Hebrew; as with Boukabza's catalog, I have been unable to locate this list. Avraham (Robert) Attal, "Les publications judéo-arabes du rabbin Chalom Bekache, imprimeur et publiciste à Alger," *'Alei Sefer* 2 (1976): 200, no. 6.

69. Norman (Noam) Stillman, *Sephardi Religious Responses to Modernity* (Luxembourg: Harwood, 1995); Daniel Schroeter, "A Different Road to Modernity: Jewish Identity in the Arab World," in *Diasporas and Exiles: Varieties*

of Jewish Identity, ed. Howard Wettstein (Oakland: University of California Press, 2002), 150–163; Zvi Zohar, *Rabbinic Creativity in the Modern Middle East* (London: Bloomsbury Academic, 2013); Yuval Evri and Almog Behar, "Between East and West: Controversies over the Modernization of Hebrew Culture in the Works of Shaul Abdallah Yosef and Ariel Bension," *Journal of Modern Jewish Studies* 16, no. 2 (2017): 295–311; Dov Cohen, "Rabbinic Attitudes towards Manifestations of Modernity and Secularism within Nineteenth-Century Sephardic Society," *Revue des études Juives* 180, no. 1 (2021): 173–192.

70. Michal Saraf, "Daniel Ḥagège ve-ḥiburo ʿal toldot ha-sifrut ha-ʿaravit-yehudit be-tunisia, 1862–1939," *Peʿamim* 30 (1987): 41–59; Tsivia Tobi, "Ha-rav ha-maskil eliʿezer farḥi ve-yeṣirotav ha-saṭiriyyot," *Ben ʿever laʿarav* 5 (2012): 127–144.

71. See, e.g., Yosef Salmon, "David Gordon and *Ha-Maggid*: Changing Attitudes toward Jewish Nationalism, 1860–1882," *Modern Judaism* 17, no. 2 (1997): 109–124.

72. Eliezer Lipman Silberman, *Reshima shel shemot ha-ḥaverim le-ḥevrat meqiṣe nirdamim: shana shenit 625–626* (Ełk: Mekitze Nirdamim, 1866). This list was generously provided to me by Phil Keisman.

73. *Ha-maggid* 9.31 (August 9, 1865), 248.

74. *Ha-maggid* 33.10 (March 7, 1889), 77.

75. Yosef (Joseph) Chetrit, "Moderniyyut le'umit ʿivrit mul moderniyyut ṣarfatit: ha-haskala ha-ʿivrit bi-ṣfon afriqa ba'sof ha-me'a ha-19," *Miqedem u-miyyam* 3 (1990): 26; Michal Ohana, "R. Ḥayyim Bliyyaḥ: maskil ʿivri u-mamshikha shel ha-hagut ha-yehudit ha-sfaradit," *Peʿamim* 154/155 (2018): 163–196.

76. Chetrit, "Haskala hébraique et haskala judéo-arabe," 296–299, and Yosef Chetrit, "Shalom flaḥ u-ma'avaqo le-hora'at ha-ʿivrit be-vatei ha-sefer shel KI"Ḥ be-tunisya," in *Le-sharet et ʿamam be-darkam: KI"Ḥ ve-qidum ha-qehilot ha-yehudiyyot be-arṣot ha-islam,* ed. Haim Saadoun (Jerusalem: Yad Ben Zvi, 2021), 119–141. Flah's textbooks include *Miqra meforash* (Tunis: Uzan and Castro, 1892) and *Shiʿurei ha-ḥinukh / Chiori Ahinnoukh* (Tunis: Sion Uzan, 1899). See also his Hebrew account of the Jewish communities of Tunis, *Sefer ṣedeq ve-shalom* (Tunis: Uzan and Castro, 1897).

77. Daniel Schroeter, "The Politics of Reform in Morocco: The Writings of Yishaq Ben Yaʿis(h) Halewi in Hasfirah (1891)," in *Misgav Yerushalayim Studies in Jewish Literature,* ed. Ephraim Hazan (Jerusalem: Institute for Research on the Sephardi and Oriental Jewish Heritage, 1987), 73–84; Chetrit, "Ha-haskala ha-ʿivrit," and Chetrit, "Haskala hébraique et haskala judéo-arabe."

78. Ofra Tirosh-Becker, "Eli'ezer Ben-Yehuda and Algerian Jews: Relationship and Language," in *Arabic and Semitic Linguistics Contextualized: A Festschrift for Jan Retsö*, ed. Lutz Edzard (Wiesbaden: Harrassowitz, 2015), 430–447.

79. Morali, "Sefer ṣafnat paneaḥ," *Koveṣ 'al yad* 7 (1897): 5–6. On his project, see Ephraim Hazan, "The Literary Activity of R. Isaac Morali and His Plan to Collect the Hebrew Poetry of Algeria," *Pe'amim* 91 (2002): 65–78.

80. Haïm Bliah, *Sha'ar kevod ha-shem* (Tunis: Uzan and Castro, 1902). The manuscript he used was Bodl. Opp. 241.

81. Lital Levy, "Reorienting Hebrew Literary History: The View from the East," *Prooftexts* 29, no. 2 (2009): 127–172; and see Lital Levy, *Global Haskalah: Translation, World Literature, and Jewish Modernity* (forthcoming).

82. The title, taken from Song of Songs 7:9, was commonly used to speak of the posthumous publication of rabbinic works, drawing on the Talmudic dictum that "when anything is said in this world in the name of the [deceased] scholar who taught it, his lips whisper the words in the grave . . . as it is written [Song of Songs 7:9], 'moving the lips of those who sleep.'" See, e.g., p *Sheqalim* 2:5; b *Yevamot* 97a.

83. Zvi Zohar, "Ben-Simeon, Raphael Aaron," in *Encyclopedia of Jews in the Islamic World*, ed. Noam Stillman (Leiden: Brill, 2010).

84. Refael-Aharon Ben-Shim'on, "Introduction," in *Ahavat ha-qadmonim* (Jerusalem: Shmuel Halevi Zuckerman, 1889). This manuscript copy survives in Schocken Ms. 1092.

85. Yigal Nizri, "Sharifan Subjects, Rabbinic Texts: Moroccan Halakhic Writing, 1860–1918" (PhD diss., New York University, 2014), 109–111; Peter Cole and Adina Hoffman, *Sacred Trash: The Lost and Found World of the Cairo Geniza* (New York: Schocken Books, 2011); and Rebecca J. W. Jefferson, *The Cairo Genizah and the Age of Discovery in Egypt: The History and Provenance of a Jewish Archive* (London: Bloomsbury Academic, 2022), 127–142. For an example of a more Schechter-centric narrative, see, e.g., Mark Glickman, *Sacred Treasure—The Cairo Genizah: The Amazing Discoveries of Forgotten History in an Egyptian Synagogue Attic* (Woodstock, VT: Jewish Lights, 2011), 68–69.

86. Nizri, *Sharifan Subjects, Rabbinic Texts*, 145; a similar argument was made by Noam Stillman, who terms Ben-Shim'on a "modern traditionalist": Stillman, *Sephardi Religious Responses*, 29–48.

87. See, e.g., the lists published in Ya'aqov Abensur, *Mishpaṭ u-ṣedaqa be-ya'aqov*, parts 1 and 2 (Alexandria: Farag Mizrahi, 1894 and 1903).

88. Yosef Tedghi, *Ha-sefer veha-defus ha-ʿivri be-fas* (Jerusalem: Ben-Zvi Institute, 1994), 58–68.

89. Nizri, *Sharifan Subjects, Rabbinic Texts,* 111–146; Yigal Nizri, "Writing against Loss: Moroccan Jewish Book Culture in a Time of Disaster," *Jewish Social Studies* 26, no. 1 (2020): 91–100.

90. Ben-Shimʿon, "Introduction," in Abensur, *Mishpaṭ u-ṣedaqa be-yaʿaqov,* part 2. See Moshe Hillel, *Ohel Ra"m: Catalogue of the Manuscripts in the Library of Rabbi Avraham Mordechai Alter of Gur* (Jerusalem: Kehilot Yisrael, 2018), 50–54.

91. Indeed, even lesser distances proved difficult to overcome, as the galley proofs had to be shipped back and forth between Alexandria and Cairo by a daily railway: Ben-Shimʿon, "Introduction," in Abensur, *Mishpaṭ u-Ṣedaqa be-Yaʿaqov,* part 1. As Hillel notes, the connections between Fez and Husiatyn continued over the following decade, leading both to the publication of Moroccan manuscripts in Husiatyn and to the collaboration of Vienna-based bookseller Lipa Schwager with Moroccan booksellers, including Yaʿaqov Moshe Tolédano, in the sale of thousands of rare books from Moroccan collections to European libraries and institutions: *Catalogue,* 54.

92. On the Jewish shift from Judeo-Arabic to French in Tunisia and Morocco, see Keith Walters, "Education for Jewish Girls in Late Nineteenth- and Early Twentieth-Century Tunis and the Spread of French in Tunisia," in *Jewish Culture and Society in North Africa,* ed. Emily Gottreich and Daniel Schroeter (Bloomington: Indiana University Press, 2011), 257–281; Oren Kosansky, "When Jews Speak Arabic: Dialectology and Difference in Colonial Morocco," *Comparative Studies in Society and History* 58, no. 1 (2016): 5–39. The Jewish linguistic landscape in Algeria changed more dramatically due to its earlier colonization and because Jews there were incorporated into the French educational system after receiving citizenship in 1870. On Jewish education in French Algeria, see Joshua Schreier, *Arabs of the Jewish Faith: The Civilizing Mission in Colonial Algeria* (Brunswick, NJ: Rutgers University Press, 2010), 114–142.

93. Michael Laskier, *The Alliance Israélite Universelle and the Jewish Communities of Morocco, 1862–1962* (Albany: SUNY Press, 1983); Aron Rodrigue, *French Jews, Turkish Jews: The Alliance Israélite Universelle and the Politics of Jewish Schooling in Turkey, 1860–1925* (Bloomington: Indiana University Press, 1990); André Kaspi, ed., *Histoire de l'Alliance israélite universelle de 1860 à nos jours* (Paris: Armand Colin, 2010).

94. Susan Gilson Miller, "Moïse Nahon and the Invention of the Modern Maghrebi Jew," in *French Mediterraneans: Transnational and Imperial*

Histories, ed. Patricia Lorcin and Todd Shepard (Lincoln: University of Nebraska Press, 2016), 296.

95. Joy A. Land, "Corresponding Women: Female Educators of the Alliance Israélite Universelle in Tunisia, 1882–1914," in *Jewish Culture and Society in North Africa*, ed. Emily Gottreich and Daniel Schroeter (Bloomington: Indiana University Press, 2011), 239–256; Shalom Bar-Asher, "The Emancipation of North African Jewish Women: The Alliance Israélite Universelle," in *Jews and Muslims in the Islamic World*, ed. Bernard Dov Cooperman and Zvi Zohar (College Park: University of Maryland Press, 2013), 33–50. While the AIU did not run its own schools in Algeria until the twentieth century, it supported the integration of Jewish boys and girls into the French-run public schools, and it did open some "vocational workshops" for Algerian Jewish girls in the late nineteenth century: Michael Laskier, "Aspects of the Activities of the Alliance Israélite Universelle in the Jewish Communities of the Middle East and North Africa: 1860–1918," *Modern Judaism* 3, no. 2 (1983): 147–171.

96. Avraham Laredo and Yiṣḥaq Halevi, *Dat yehudit* (Algiers: Cohen-Solal, 1855), 1. This book was first composed in Maghrebi Judeo-Spanish (*ḥaketía*) and printed in Livorno, 1827. It was translated into Judeo-Arabic by Ya'aqov Ankawa in 1855, and it was this translation that was republished by Guedj. See also Bekache's remarks comparing the literacy of Jewish women in India versus the illiteracy of Jewish women in Algeria: *Mevasser tov* (Livorno, 1884), 13b–14a, and see Avner Ofrath, "*The Harbinger of Good* by Shalom Bekache, 1884," *Absinthe: World Literature in Translation* 29 (2024): 186–194.

97. On orality and textuality among Maghrebi Jewish women, see Edwin Seroussi, "Archivists of Memory: Written Folksong Collections of Twentieth-Century Sephardi Women," in *Music and Gender: Perspectives from the Mediterranean*, ed. Tullia Magrini (Chicago: University of Chicago Press, 2003), 195–214; Joseph (Yosef) Chetrit, "Textual Orality and Knowledge of Illiterate Women: The Textual Performance of Jewish Women in Morocco," in *Women and Knowledge in the Mediterranean*, ed. Fatima Sadiqi (London: Routledge, 2013), 89–107; Vanessa Paloma Elbaz, "Kol b'Isha Erva: The Silencing of Jewish Women's Oral Traditions in Morocco," in *Women and Social Change in North Africa: What Counts as Revolutionary?*, ed. Doris H. Gray and Nadia Sonneveld (Cambridge: Cambridge University Press, 2017), 263–288.

98. Avraham Laredo (ca. 1780–1865) was born in Tetouan, while his son-in-law Yiṣḥaq Halevi (1797–1846) was born in Gibraltar to a Tetouani family. The first edition of *Dat yehudit* was published anonymously in

Maghrebi Judeo-Spanish (Livorno: Eliezer Saadun, 1827). On its language and style, see David Bunis, "The East-West Sephardic La'az (Judeo-Spanish) Dialect Dichotomy as Reflected in Three Editions of Dat Yehudit," in *Estudios sefardíes dedicados a la memoria de Iacob M. Hassán (z"l)*, ed. Elena Romero and Aitor García Moreno (Madrid: CSIC, 2011), 157–190.

99. The *Me'am lo'ez* project, begun by Ya'aqov Kuli in Constantinople, was first published in 1730; it went through many editions in the following century, including an adaptation into Western Judeo-Spanish by Moroccan-Gibraltarian rabbi Avraham Koriat (Livorno, 1822). See Édouard Roditi, "The Me'am Lo'ez and Its Various Editions," *European Judaism* 26, no. 1 (1993): 17–23; Matthias Lehmann, *Ladino Rabbinic Literature and Ottoman Sephardic Culture* (Bloomington: Indiana University Press, 2005), 31–33; Alisa Meyuhas Ginio, "The History of the Me'am Lo'ez: A Ladino Commentary on the Bible," *European Judaism* 43, no. 2 (2010): 117–125.

100. Haïm Zafrani, *Pédagogie juive en terre d'Islam: l'enseignement traditionnel de l'hébreu et du judaïsme au Maroc* (Paris: Maisonneuve, 1969), 79–80.

101. Printed in the margins of *Daniel ha-kuzari* (Algiers: Abraham Boukabza, 1887), 14–20.

102. The first Maghrebi Jewish woman to publish her own work under her own name, to my knowledge, was Adélaïde Bénichou-Azoubib (Algiers, 1850–1924), who published a sermon in a French Jewish journal in 1917, and later a book of reflections on biblical characters in 1922: Adélaïde Bénichou-Azoubib, "Lechana habbaa birouchalaïm," *L'univers israélite* 28 (April 6, 1917), 47–48; *En méditant les livres saintes* (Paris: R. Chiberre, 1922). Her daughter, Berthe-Sultana Bénichou-Aboulker (1888–1942), also published a number of books of poetry and drama: Michele Bitton, "Berthe Bénichou-Aboulker," in *The Shalvi/Hyman Encyclopedia of Jewish Women*, ed. Jennifer Sartori (Newton, MA: Jewish Women's Archive, 2021).

103. Chalom Flah, "Ha-ṣofe et penei tunis," *He-asif* vol. 6 (Warsaw: Halter and Eisenstadt, 1893), 78–94 (quote on 93–94).

104. Martin [Mordekhai] Seror, *Hagada, ou rituel des deux premières nuit [sic] de Paque* (Livorno: Israel Costa, 1886).

105. Isaac Bloch, *haskama* [approbation] to Eliyahu Ḥai Guedj, *Ḥesed veemet* (Algiers: Ya'aqov Guedj, 1888).

106. Isaac Bloch, *Inscriptions tumulaires des anciens cimetières israélites d'Alger* (Paris: Armand Durlacher, 1888); Henri-Delmas de Grammont, "Bibliographie: Inscriptions tumulaires des anciens cimetières israélites

d'Alger, par Isaac Bloch, Grand Rabbin d'Alger," *Revue Africaine* 190 (1888): 320.

107. *Neṣaḥ yisrael* (Tunis: Uzan and Castro, 1888), 42–43, as translated by Joshua Picard, "Tunisian Judaeo-Arabic Essays on Religion and Ideology in the Late-Nineteenth Century" (Master's thesis, Brandeis University, 2016), 30. See also Tobi and Tobi, *Judeo-Arabic Literature*, 184–194.

108. Tamir Karkason, "Between 'Pure Faith' and 'Faithful Enlightenment': The Thought of Shalom Flah (1855–1936) against the Background of the Transformations in Tunisian Jewry," in *Beyond Cultural Identities: The Jews of Polyphony, Relationality and Translation in Muslim Contexts*, ed. Ottfried Fraisse (Berlin: De Gruyter, forthcoming). I am grateful to Dr. Karkason for sharing an advance copy of this work.

109. David Cazès, *Notes bibliographiques sur la littérature juive-tunisienne* (Tunis: Imprimerie Internationale, 1893), 17. On Cazès, see Colette Zytnicki, "David Cazès (1850–1913), historien des Juifs de Tunisie: un métis culturel?," *Outre-Mers Revue d'histoire* 352 (2006): 97–106.

110. Jacqueline Fraenkel, "L'Imprimerie Hébraique à Djerba" (PhD diss., University of Paris, 1982).

111. Marṣiano, *Sefer bnei melakhim*; Tedghi, *Ha-sefer veha-defus.*

112. Attal, "'Al ha-defus ha-'ivri ba-magreb," 128–129.

113. David Guedj, "Judeo-Arabic Popular Nonfiction in Morocco during the First Half of the Twentieth Century," *Quest: Issues in Contemporary Jewish History* 22 (2022): 78–108.

114. Moïse Nahon, "La communauté israélite de Tlemcen," *Revue des Écoles* 8 (1903): 34–35. On Nahon, see Miller, "The Invention of the Modern Maghrebi Jew."

115. Lisa Moses Leff, *Sacred Bonds of Solidarity: The Rise of Jewish Internationalism in Nineteenth-Century France* (Redwood City, CA: Stanford University Press, 2006).

116. Nahon, "La communauté israélite," 48.

117. Nahum Slouschz, *Travels in North Africa* (Philadelphia: Jewish Publication Society, 1927), 237–238.

118. Marcel Cohen, *Le Parler Arabe des Juifs d'Alger* (Paris: Librarie Ancienne, 1912), 13–15. Interestingly, one of his informants was Maurice Bekache, son of printer and translator Shalom Bekache.

119. Tobi, "Judaeo-Arabic Printing," 140. For an example, see the booklets of song lyrics produced by Kiki Guetta with Latin transliteration in the early twentieth century, such as *Ghnaïet Bibia, Aadabna fi Bissah,* or *Tebkaou Aâla khaïr besslama* (Tunis: Imprimerie Phénix).

120. Tobi, "Judaeo-Arabic Printing," 140.

121. On the immigration of Maghrebi Jews to Israel, see Michael Laskier, *North African Jewry in the Twentieth Century: The Jews of Morocco, Tunisia, and Algeria* (New York: New York University Press, 1994), 117–344.

122. Tobi and Tobi, *Judeo-Arabic Literature*, 222.

6. EARLY MODERN AND MODERN MAGHREBI JEWISH LIBRARIES

1. NLI Ms. Heb. 8.3466, 3a.

2. Reid Byers, *The Private Library: The History of the Architecture and Furnishing of the Domestic Bookroom* (New Castle, DE: Oak Knoll, 2021). See also Andrew Pettegree and Arthur der Weduwen, *The Library: A Fragile History* (London: Profile Books, 2021).

3. Joshua Teplitsky, *Prince of the Press: How One Collector Built History's Most Enduring and Remarkable Jewish Library* (New Haven, CT: Yale University Press, 2019), 5.

4. Moshe Amar, "Sifriyyat yeshivat eṣ ḥayyim: aspaqlarya le-ʿolamam ha-ruḥani shel ha-ḥakhamim be-tunis be-shilhei ha-me'a ha-teshaʿ-ʿesrei," in *Jews of Tunisia: Heritage, History, Literature*, ed. Ephraim Hazan and Haim Saadon (Ramat Gan: Bar Ilan University Press, 2009), 109–146.

5. He is probably the same as the David Buenos-Ombres who signed a legal document in Rabat in 1847: NLI Ms. Heb. 8.2085, 114b. The surname Buenos-Ombres was used as an equivalent of the Arabic surname al-Maliaḥ (Elmaleh): see Eliyahu Elmaleh, *Beqa la-gulgolet* (Jerusalem: S. Zukerman, 1911), 11. Members of this family are well documented in Morocco as well as among the Moroccan diaspora in Gibraltar, London, and Jerusalem.

6. As is typical in halakhic literature, the responsum anonymizes the case study by using the hypothetical names Reuven and Shimʿon.

7. Avraham Ankawa, *Kerem ḥemer*, vol. 1 (Livorno: Elia Benamozegh, 1869), *Yore Deʿa* 20, 19b–20a.

8. In early modern Europe, the *studio* or *studiolo* emerged among humanists as "[a] specific room set aside for a book collector's literary activities": Pettegree and der Weduwen, *The Library*, 61–63, and compare Byers, *The Private Library*, 120–126, and Andrew Hui, *The Study: The Inner Life of Renaissance Libraries* (Princeton, NJ: Princeton University Press, 2024). In Judeo-Spanish, however, the term *estudyo* generally referred to a

room where one worked; it did not designate a book collection specifically. The use of *estudyo* to refer to a library may be a unique Maghrebi development. Ḥayyim Yosef David Azulai used the term *estudyo* to describe the University of Padua in 1775: *Ma'agal ṭov*, ed. Aron Freimann (Jerusalem: Mekize Nirdamim, 1934), 82. I thank Bryan Kirschen, Ora Schwarzwald, Jacob Bentolila, and David Bunis for their input on this terminology.

9. Sasportas, *Ohel ya'aqov* (Amsterdam: Naftali Herz Levi Rofe, 1737), no. 11, 12b–13a; and see also Yaacob Dweck, *Dissident Rabbi: The Life of Jacob Sasportas* (Princeton, NJ: Princeton University Press, 2019), 72–73.

10. *Tosfei ha-rosh* (Livorno: Giovan Vincenzo Falorni, 1776), "Introduction."

11. *Leshon limmudim*, letter 185 (David Ovadia, *Fes ve-ḥakhameha: divrei yemei ha-yehudim be-qehillat qodesh fes*, vol. 2 [Jerusalem: Beit Oved, 1979], 422). For another instance of Abensur describing his library as his *estudyo*, see JTS Ms. 384 (Bennaim 133), 77a, to be discussed later in this chapter.

12. There are several book collections, primarily in France and Israel, which have a Maghrebi provenance of the early twentieth century; but they are generally not accessible to researchers, nor can it be ascertained what percentage of the collections is original to the library as it was assembled in North Africa. One prominent example is the library of the Porat Yosef Yeshiva in Jerusalem, which includes the collection of Ḥayyim David Serero (1884–1968) of Fez; another is the book collection of Yosef Bennaim himself, which was purchased by the Jewish Theological Seminary in New York in 1961. Unfortunately, many of the manuscripts were badly damaged or destroyed in a 1965 fire, and Bennaim's printed books were absorbed into the general collection of JTS' rare books without a clear indication of their provenance. See Yosef Tedghi, *Ha-sefer veha-defus ha-'ivri be-fas* (Jerusalem: Ben-Zvi Institute, 1994), 69–75.

13. I borrow the term "footprints," meaning notes, ownership inscriptions, or other indications that document the material presence of a specific book copy at a particular time and place, from the collaborative digital humanities project "Footprints: Jewish Books through Time and Place" (footprints.ctl.columbia.edu). See Michelle Margolis, Marjorie Lehman, Adam Shear, and Joshua Teplitsky, "Footprints: A Digital Approach to (Jewish) Book History," *European Journal of Jewish Studies* 17 (2023): 1–30.

14. On Jewish libraries in the world of medieval Cairo, see Nehemiah Allony, *The Jewish Library in the Middle Ages: Book Lists from the Cairo Genizah* (Jerusalem: Ben-Zvi Institute, 2006). On medieval Sephardi

libraries: Joseph Hacker, "Jewish Book Owners and Their Libraries in the Iberian Peninsula, Fourteenth-Fifteenth Centuries," in *The Late Medieval Hebrew Book in the Western Mediterranean: Hebrew Manuscripts and Incunabula in Context*, ed. Javier del Barco (Leiden: Brill, 2015), 70–104; S. J. Pearce, *The Andalusi Literary and Intellectual Tradition: The Role of Arabic in Judah Ibn Tibbon's Ethical Will* (Bloomington: Indiana University Press, 2017).

15. Pier Francesco Fumagalli, "Hebrew Books in Italian Libraries of the Modern Age," *Aevum* 85, no. 3 (2011): 819–834. See also Shifra Baruchson, *Books and Readers: Reading Culture of Italian Jews at the End of the Renaissance* (Tel Aviv: Bar-Ilan University Press, 1993); Joseph Hacker and Adam Shear, eds., *The Hebrew Book in Early Modern Italy* (Philadelphia: University of Pennsylvania Press, 2011).

16. Joshua Teplitsky, *Prince of the Press: How One Collector Built History's Most Enduring and Remarkable Jewish Library* (New Haven, CT: Yale University Press, 2019).

17. Avriel Bar-Levav, "Amsterdam and the Inception of the Jewish Republic of Letters," in *The Dutch Intersection: The Jews and the Netherlands in Modern History*, ed. Yosef Kaplan (Leiden: Brill, 2008), 225–237. See also Yosef Kaplan, "The Libraries of Three Sephardi Rabbis in Early Modern Western Europe," in *Libraries and Book Collections*, ed. Yosef Kaplan and Moshe Sluhovsky (Jerusalem: Shazar, 2006), 225–260; David Sclar, "A Communal Tree of Life: Western Sephardic Jewry and the Library of the Ets Haim Yesiba in Early Modern Amsterdam," *Book History* 22 (2019): 43–65; Benjamin Fisher, "From Boxes and Cabinets to the *Bibliotheca*: Building the Jewish Library of the Ex-Conversos in Amsterdam, 1620–1665," *European Journal of Jewish Studies* 13, no. 1 (2019): 43–76; Anna de Wilde, "Sales Catalogues of Jewish-Owned Private Libraries in the Dutch Republic during the Long Eighteenth Century: A Preliminary Overview," in *Book Trade Catalogues in Early Modern Europe*, ed. Arthur der Weduwen, Andrew Pettegree, and Graeme Kemp (Leiden: Brill, 2021), 212–248.

18. Dan Rabinowitz, *The Lost Library: The Legacy of Vilna's Strashun Library in the Aftermath of the Holocaust* (Waltham, MA: Brandeis University Press, 2019); Robert Singerman, "Books Weeping for Someone to Visit and Admire Them: Jewish Library Culture in the United States, 1850–1910," *Studies in Bibliography and Booklore* 20 (1998): 99–144; Dov Schidorsky, "Libraries in Late Ottoman Palestine between the Orient and the Occident," *Libraries & Culture* 33, no. 3 (1998): 260–276.

19. See, e.g., the work of Konrad Hirschler, especially *A Monument to Medieval Syrian Book Culture: The Library of Ibn ʿAbd Al-Hādī* (Edinburgh: Edinburgh University Press, 2021); Shamil Jeppie and Souleymane Bachir Diagne, eds., *The Meanings of Timbuktu* (Cape Town: Human Sciences Research Council, 2008); Ghislaine Lydon and Graziano Krätli, eds., *The Trans-Saharan Book Trade: Manuscript Culture, Arabic Literacy and Intellectual History in Muslim Africa* (Leiden: Brill, 2011); Boris Liebrenz, "The Library of Ahmad al-Rabbat: Books and Their Audience in 12th to 13th/18th to 19th Century Syria," in *Marginal Perspectives on Early Modern Ottoman Culture: Missionaries, Travellers, Booksellers*, ed. Ralf Elger and Ute Pietruschka (Halle: Zentrum für Interdisziplinäre Regionalstudien, 2013), 17–59; Daniel Hershenzon, "Traveling Libraries: The Arabic Manuscripts of Muley Zidan and the Escorial Library," *Journal of Early Modern History* 18, no. 6 (2014): 535–558; Doris Behrens-Abouseif, *The Book in Mamluk Egypt and Syria, 1250–1517* (Leiden: Brill, 2019).

20. Liebrenz, "The Library of Ahmad al-Rabbat," 33–38.

21. François Déroche and Lbachir Tahali, "Collecting Books in Eighteenth-Century Morocco: The Bannani Library in Fez," *Studies in Manuscript Cultures* 29 (2023): 63–106.

22. Déroche and Tahali, "The Bannani Library," 95.

23. Of ten Maghrebi booklists from the eighteenth and nineteenth centuries, the number of recorded titles ranges from 13 to 122, with an average collection size of 44 books: Columbia Ms X 893 P21 (Meknes, ca. 1735); BZI 275 (Morocco, ca. 1750); Gross MS MO.011.18.67 (Morocco, 1785); JTS Ms 1999 (Tunis, ca. 1794); Vat. Neofiti 46 (Meknes, 1811); BZI 738 (Tunis, ca. 1815); BZI 228 (Tunis, ca. 1820); BZI Ms. 2888 (Morocco, ca. 1850); BL Or. 9994 (Morocco, ca. 1850); NLI 38.7797 (Morocco, ca. 1850).

24. Technically speaking, he should be Yaʿaqov II since his grandfather was also Yaʿaqov Abensur. But in this chapter, I am concerned with the Yaʿaveṣ and his descendants, so I begin my accounting of the family from him. The biography that follows is based on Moshe Amar, "Qavvim li-demuto shel rabbi yaʿaqov ibn ṣur," *Mizrah u-maʿarav* 3 (1981): 89–124, and Shalom Bar-Asher, "Aben Ṣur, Jacob," in *Encyclopedia of Jewish in the Islamic World* (Leiden: Brill, 2010). In other sources, his birthplace is given as Fez: e.g., Yehuda Nini, "Lettres choisies de R. Yaʿaqov Ibn Tsur," *Michael: On the History of the Jews in the Diaspora* 5 (1978): 192–214.

25. Netanel Avital, *Pinqas qehilat fes* (Elʿad: N. Avital, 2018), 114–117.

26. Yitzhak Zuzot, "R. refaʿel berdugo: ha-ish ve-tequfato" (master's thesis, Touro College, 1995), 71–114.

27. Yosef Messas, "Introduction," in *Ner ha-ma'arav*, ed. Ya'aqov Moshe Tolédano, 2nd ed. (Jerusalem: Abécassis Brothers, 1973), ii; see also the remarks of Yosef Bennaim, *Malkhei rabbanan* (Jerusalem: Ha-ma'arav Press, 1931), 4b and 60b.

28. This copy is now in the Chabad Collection, 112-M, no. 11902.

29. Leeds Roth Ms. 737, 51v. See also Amar, "Qavvim," 94.

30. This manuscript, now in a private collection, served as the copy for the printed edition of Raphaël-Baruk Toledano (Meknes, 1940); see also the introduction of Moshe Amar to his edition, *Sefer minḥat yehuda: mahadura tinyana* (Lod: Orot Yehudei Hamagreb, 2011).

31. JTS Ms. 3138. This book was indeed continued by his descendants, including Shlomo-Eliyahu Abensur, and appeared in print in Avraham Ankawa, *Kerem ḥemer*, vol. 2 (Livorno: Eliyahu Benamozegh, 1869).

32. JTS Ms. 384 (Bennaim 133), 77a. In a responsum written around this time, Ya'aqov I again laments the inaccessibility of his library: "The light of my eyes, namely my books, which I left in Fez and came here like a body separated from its soul": *Mishpaṭ u-ṣedaqa be-ya'aqov*, vol. 2 (Alexandria: Farag Mizrahi, 1903), siman 139, 77b.

33. Recorded on the flyleaf of *Ta'ava la-'einayim* (Sulzbach, 1687), Chabad Collection, 113-T, no. 18199.

34. Klagsbald Ms. 21.

35. *Leshon limmudim*, letter 186, as published by Ovadia, *Fes ve-ḥakhameha*, 423–424.

36. *Peruta* is a Talmudic term for a small coin; it likely refers here to the copper *flus* (ninety-six of which made one *uqiyya*). If so, the 111-page manuscript cost three and a half *uqiyya* in total.

37. Klagsbald Ms. 8. This manuscript was copied from the printed edition, *Me'orot natan* (Frankfurt, 1709), and is dated "Tuesday, the 19th of Av," but the year cannot be read. It is probably either 1738 or 1741, when the 19th of Av fell on a Tuesday.

38. See, e.g., Klagsbald Ms. 11.

39. André Elbaz, "Tefuṣat ha-sefarim ha-'ivriyyim be-qerev ḥakhmei fes ba-me'a ha-18," *Mi-kedem umi-yam* 9 (2006): 41; cf. the similar remarks of Amar, "Qavvim," 103–106.

40. E.g., NLI Ms. Heb. 8.2062, an anthology compiled by El'azar Bahlul in 1712, which Ya'aqov I purchased "from the inheritors of Levi Toledano," or Bodleian Opp. Add. Qu. IV.442, an incunabula volume of *Sefer halikhot 'olam* (Leiria, ca. 1492–1496), which Ya'aqov I purchased "from the estate of the grandson of [illegible]."

41. BC YR MS 135.

42. *Leshon limmudim,* letter 182 (Ovadia, *Fes ve-ḥakhameha,* 420); see also Nini, "Lettres choisies," 213.

43. *Leshon limmudim,* letter 181 (Ovadia, *Fes ve-ḥakhameha,* 419). *Leḥem setarim,* a Talmudic commentary of Shlomo al-Gazi, was printed in Venice in 1664.

44. *Leshon limmudim,* letter 184 (Ovadia, *Fes ve-ḥakhameha,* 421–422). *Knesset ha-gedola,* a halakhic work of Hayyim Benveniste, was published in several parts: Livorno, 1657; İzmir, 1660; Constantinople, 1711 and 1716; and İzmir, 1731 and 1734.

45. Matthias Lehmann, *Emissaries from the Holy Land: The Sephardic Diaspora and the Practice of Pan-Judaism in the Eighteenth Century* (Redwood City, CA: Stanford University Press, 2014).

46. In the Chabad Collection, edited in Shalom-Dovber Levin, *Mibeis Hagenozim: Treasures from the Chabad Library* (New York: Kehot, 2009), 208. A second letter from the following week, also in Levin, *Mibeis Hagenozim,* mentions the purchase of these two books. The first book is probably the edition of Sirkis's responsa printed in Frankfurt in 1697. The second book, the responsa of seventeenth-century Egyptian rabbi Avraham Halevi, was printed in Constantinople in 1715.

47. *Mishpaṭ u-ṣedaqa be-ya'aqov,* vol. 1 (Alexandria: Farag Mizrahi, 1894), siman 8, 24b. The book mentioned is *Bnei ya'aqov* (Constantinople, 1714) by Ya'aqov Sasson.

48. Levin, *Mibeis Hagenozim,* 121.

49. *Leshon limmudim,* letter 45 (Ovadia, *Fes ve-ḥakhameha,* 310). Cf. his letter to Avraham 'Abo regarding this same issue: *Leshon limmudim,* letter 184 (Ovadia, *Fes ve-ḥakhameha,* 420–421).

50. The relative value of these coins and their terminology changed frequently in the eighteenth and nineteenth centuries. For this estimate, I have used the system of 96 *flus* to 1 *uqiyya,* 10 *uqiyya* to 1 *mithqal,* and 2 *mithqal* to 1 *riyal.* On currencies in early modern North Africa, see Haim Zafrani, *Études et recherches sur la vie intellectuelle juive au Maroc* (Paris: Geuthner, 1972), 150–151; Aomar Boum and Thomas Park, *Historical Dictionary of Morocco,* 2nd ed. (Oxford: Scarecrow, 2006), "Currency, Accounting" and "Currency, Historic."

51. *Leshon limmudim,* letter 183 (Ovadia, *Fes ve-ḥakhameha,* 420).

52. *Leshon limmudim,* letter 97 (Ovadia, *Fes ve-ḥakhameha,* 341–342).

53. Letters to various members of the Abensur family survive in the Bension Collection at the University of Alberta; see Saul Aranov, *A*

Descriptive Catalogue of the Bension Collection of Sephardic Manuscripts and Texts (Edmonton: University of Alberta Press, 1979). Another group of letters is today held by CAHJP, box 18 MA F; I have used the edition of Netanel Avital, in the appendix to *Pinqas qehilat fes* (2018). The earliest dated letters are from the 1830s, while the latest are from the 1880s.

54. For Ibn-Yuli's letters to Shlomo I Abensur regarding books, see Avital, *Pinqas*, 114, 124. For manuscripts owned by Ibn-Yuli, see, inter alia, BnF hébr. 842; NLI Heb. 4.639; JTS Ms. 6225; and NLI Heb. 8.843. See also JTS Ms. 7029 and Harvard Heb. 34, which he copied. The work he published is *Hadar zeqenim* (Livorno: Moshe Tubiana, 1840); while he was in Livorno, he also helped bring to press a manuscript of Moshe Birdugo on the Talmud, *Rosh mashbir* (Livorno: Moshe Tubiana, 1840), and a collection of Maghrebi liturgical poetry, *Shir shevaḥa* (Livorno: Moshe Tubiana, 1841). On Ibn-Yuli and his family in general, see Haim Bentov, "The Ha-Levi ibn Yuli Family," *East and Maghreb: Researches in the History of the Jews in the Orient and North Africa* 2 (1980): 131–158 (Hebrew).

55. BC YR MS 54, 101, 145, 221, 232, 238, and 264. David Ben-Shim'on's son was Refael-Aharon Ben-Shim'on (1847–1928), discussed in chapter 5. I cannot definitively identify Yosef Sassoon; he may be Yosef Sassoon (d. 1892), a Jerusalem-born descendant of the Baghdadi Sassoon family who founded a *tamḥui* [community fund] for Sephardim in Jerusalem in 1859: Yishaq-Yehezqel Yehuda, "Ha-tamḥui la-'adat ha-sefardim bi-yrushalayim," *Reshumot: me'asef le-divrei zikhronot* 6 (1930): 544–548; Moshe-David Gaon, *Yehudei ha-mizraḥ be-ereṣ yisrael*, vol. 2 (Jerusalem: Azriel, 1938), 692–693.

56. Avital, *Pinqas*, 130. On this book, see David Ruderman, *A Best-Selling Hebrew Book of the Modern Era: The* Book of the Covenant *of Pinhas Hurwitz and Its Remarkable Legacy* (Seattle: University of Washington Press, 2014).

57. Two incunabula are listed as having been purchased from the Abensur family by Eliezer Ashkenazi in 1841 (Bennaim, *Malkhei rabbanan*, 1931, 34a): the Former and Latter Prophets with David Qimhi's commentary. Their current whereabouts are unknown. A third incunabulum, *Sefer halikhot 'olam* (Leiria, ca. 1492–1496), bears an ownership inscription from Ya'aqov I Abensur and a note indicating that it was sold to the Bodleian by a certain Abraham Acher in 1848: it is now Bodleian Opp. Add. Qu. IV.442. A copy of the Lisbon printing of *Sefer abudarham* (1489), currently in the Bension Collection, is almost certainly also from the Abensur library; it is now BC Pr. 297. BC Pr. 294, *Sefer ha-zikaron* by Yishma'el

Kohen-Tanuji of Tunis (Ferrara, 1555), also bears the library stamp of Refael II Abensur.

58. Shalom-Dovber Levin, *Mibeis Hagenozim: Treasures from the Chabad Library* (New York: Kehot, 2009), 116–121, and are cataloged online at chabadlibrary.org. The Klagsbald manuscripts are described in Victor Klagsbald, *Catalogue des manuscrits marocains de la collection Klagsbald* (Paris: Editions du Centre national de la recherche scientifique, 1980).

59. *Leshon limmudim*, haskama of November 1751 (Ovadia, *Fes ve-ḥakhameha*, 251). Bennaim recorded of Ya'aqov I that "he frequently wrote in the margins of all his books at length, and he wrote many sermons in manuscript that are still in the hands of his descendants": Bennaim, *Malkhei rabbanan*, 64b.

60. Klagsbald Ms. 38; see Klagsbald, *Catalogue des manuscrits marocains*, 82–83, and cf. Lehmann Ms. 215, a copy of these same notes.

61. BC YR MS 66. Abensur's copy of the 1585 edition of *Midrash shmuel* has also survived in the Chabad Collection, 113-M, no. 9856.

62. *Mishpaṭ u-ṣedaqa be-ya'aqov*, vol. 1 (Alexandria: Farag Mizrahi, 1894), siman 33, 46a.

63. For material copied from Bacharach and Lonzano, see Leeds Roth Ms. 737, 93b and 217b–218a (and there can be no doubt that he is copying from the printed edition since he copies the details of their title pages); for the *qundrisim* of Dayyan, see, e.g., 90a–102b. For anonymous texts, see, e.g., 109a–113b. Ya'aqov once asked a *shadar* for help acquiring *Shtei yadot* "since no trace of it can be found in this city": *Leshon limmudim*, letter 187 (Ovadia, *Fes ve-ḥakhameha*, 422). Apparently, he found it!

64. This manuscript was written in 1478 and was owned by Shlomo-Shmuel Abensur (d. 1792). It is now Bodl. Opp. Add. Qu. 19.

65. Bodl. Opp. Add. fol. 48–49.

66. See, e.g., the letters cited in Elbaz, "Tefuṣat ha-sefarim," 39–43.

67. Letter of Yehuda Ḍarmon to Shlomo-Eliyahu Abensur (1866), BC YR MS 52.

68. BC YR Ms. 197.

69. Eli'ezer Bahlul, *Mar'e 'enayyim*: NLI Ms. Heb. 8.2062, 2a.

70. See Amar, *Sefer minḥat yehuda*.

71. This pinqas is now JTS Ms. 8287; see Haim Bentov, "Jewish Artisans in Fez during the 17th and 18th Centuries," *Sefunot* 10 (1966): 314–483. The four books were a book of sermons, probably in manuscript; *Ta'amei miṣvot* (perhaps of Menahem b. Moshe Ha-bavli, printed in Lublin, 1571, and

Hamburg, 1707); a commentary on the tractate *Kallah*; and a book of the commentary of Rashi.

72. BC YR Ms. 132.

73. See, inter alia, JTS Ms. 289 (Meknes, 1809), and BZI Ms. 738 (Tunis, ca. 1815).

74. This manuscript, which at the time belonged to Immanu'el Serero (b. 1705), is now BnF héb Ms. 714, 7v.

75. This is probably the Kabbalistic work of Avraham Halevi, either as printed in the book *Ma'or va-shemesh* (Livorno, 1839) or in manuscript.

76. Avital, *Pinqas*, 115.

77. Elbaz, "Tefuṣat ha-sefarim," 43.

78. Elbaz, "Tefuṣat ha-sefarim," 45.

79. Avital, *Pinqas*, 120–121. Ibn-Yuli's instructions to burn the letter were thankfully ignored.

80. Avital, *Pinqas*, 129. Indeed, the Serero family library had once contained such a manuscript since El'azar Bahlul borrowed it in 1711.

81. The term *rishonim*, literally "early [authorities]," refers to rabbinic scholars of the medieval period, usually starting with the close of the geonic period in the mid-eleventh century and ending with the composition of the *Shulḥan 'arukh* in 1563.

82. Avital, *Pinqas*, 131. The manuscript he is referring to is presumably the one he published as *Hadar zeqenim* (Livorno: Moshe Tubiana, 1840).

83. JTS Ms. 6063.

84. The stamp of Refael II, made in Jerusalem and bearing an image of the Temple Mount, reads "Refael Aben Sur, Fes" in French and Hebrew; I have found it stamped on at least a dozen books. Shlomo II had a similar stamp, now preserved in the Gross Family Collection (041.002.001), but I have only found its imprint stamped on one book: *'Et le-khol ḥefeṣ* (Alexandria: Farag Mizrahi, 1893), NLI R.1025 (formerly Valmadonna 9483): see figures 6.1 and 6.2. One book in the Gross Collection has a different stamp imprint of "Salomon Abensour," with his name in Hebrew, French, and Arabic, along with the stamp of Refael II: *Yisa berakha* (Livorno: Ya'aqov Tubiana, 1822), Gross B.893. Another stamp, reading simply "Shlomo Abensur" in Hebrew, is also in the Gross Collection, 041.002.002; this may be the stamp of Shlomo I (1805–1843).

85. Bennaim, *Malkhei rabbanan*, 105b.

86. NLI Ms. Heb. 8.2085 and 8.4492.

87. This manuscript was purchased by Moses Hecht along with a number of others, including at least one other manuscript owned by the Serfaty

family—perhaps even from Avner-Yisrael I Serfaty directly—and sold to Leiden University in 1854, where it is now Or. 4814.

88. These books are now held in the Bension Collection of Sephardic Texts at the University of Alberta; see Aranov, *The Bension Collection,* and Jonatan Meir, *Kabbalistic Circles in Jerusalem, 1896–1948* (Leiden: Brill, 2016), 1–23. They may have been acquired ca. 1927, when Bension traveled through Morocco as a Zionist agent of the Jewish Foundation Fund.

89. See, e.g., Bennaim, *Malkhei rabbanan,* 8a, regarding autograph manuscripts of Avraham Monsano (1719–1781) in the Abensur library.

90. E.g., in addition to those already cited, see the Abensur library copies of *Dameseq eli'ezer* (Lublin: Zvi Yaffe, 1646), sold by Kestenbaum, March 23, 2006, auction 32, lot 93; *Halakhot qeṭanot* (Venice: Bragadin, 1704), sold by Kadmon Auctions, February 4, 2020, auction 21, lot 152; and the manuscript registers of Refael II Abensur, covering 1891–1908, sold by Refaeli Auctions, October 30 2019, auction 10, lot 32. An edition of *Mishpeṭei shmuel* (Venice: Daniel Zanetti, 1600) with Refael II's stamp imprint and notations from Shlomo-Eliyahu and Shlomo II Abensur was sold by Asset Auctions in 2022 and is now in my possession.

91. Their family name is romanized in a variety of ways, including Hassarfaty, Serfaty, and Sarfati. I have chosen Serfaty on the basis of Avner-Yisrael I's personal stamp, which reads "*R. Y. Abener Serfaty, Fes,*" and the fact that this is the spelling used by most of his contemporary descendants.

92. In fact, the family claimed roots extending back to eleventh-century France (hence the name *Ha-ṣarfati,* literally "the Frenchman"), including the famed exegete Shlomo ben Yiṣḥaq of Troyes (Rashi). See Vidal Serfaty, "La communauté de Fès et la famille Hassarfati," *Etsi: revue de généalogie et d'histoire séfarades* 29 (2005): 5–10, and Shalom Bar-Asher, "Ṣarfati Family," in *Encyclopedia of Jews in the Islamic World,* ed. Noam Stillman (Leiden: Brill, 2010).

93. Eliezer Bashan, *Yehudei fes 1873–1900 'al pi te'udot hadashot* (Jerusalem: Yad Harav Nissim, 2002), 51–58; Paul Fenton and David Littman, *Exile in the Maghreb: Jews under Islam, Sources and Documents, 997–1912* (Lanham, MD: Rowman & Littlefield, 2016), 389–390 (documents B30–31).

94. See Hay's letters to Granville in *Correspondence Relative to the Conference Held at Madrid in 1880 Respecting the Right of Protection of Moorish Subjects by the Diplomatic and Consular Representatives of Foreign Powers in Morocco* (London: House of Commons, 1880), 137–139, and cf. the account in Philip Durham Trotter, *Our Mission to the Court of Marocco in 1880: Under Sir John Drummond Hay* (Edinburgh: David Douglas, 1881), 176–178.

Hay's response to the petition was to suggest that this measure might provoke anti-Jewish violence and recommended that the Jews "should continue to bear with patience their long sufferings."

95. Charles de Foucauld, *Reconnaissance au Maroc 1883–1884* (Paris: Librairie coloniale, 1888), 395.

96. Narcisse Leven, *Cinquante ans d'histoire: L'Alliance israélite universelle (1860–1910), Vol. II* (Paris: Félix Alcan, 1920), 94; Michael Laskier, *The* Alliance Israélite Universelle *and the Jewish Communities of Morocco, 1862–1962* (Albany: SUNY Press, 1983), 87, 198; and cf. the letters of Vidal V reproduced in documents B160 and B173, Fenton and Littman, *Exile in the Maghreb*, 549, 563–564.

97. Bennaim, *Malkhei rabbanan*, 18b.

98. Colette Zytnicki, *Les Juifs du Maghreb: naissance d'une historiographie coloniale* (Paris: Presses de l'Universite Paris-Sorbonne, 2011), 214.

99. The three manuscripts from 1879 are AIU Ms. 84; London School of Jewish Studies Library Ms. 1; and a copy in the private possession of Moshe Serfaty, microfilmed by the IMHM, NLI 8.5974.

100. "The Late Rabbi Abner of Fez," *Jewish Chronicle*, no. 813 (October 24, 1884): 6.

101. Auguste Mouliéras, *Fez: ouvrage illustré de 12 photographies prises au cours de la mission de l'auteur à Fez* (Paris: A. Challamel, 1902), 291.

102. Eugène Aubin, *Le Maroc d'aujourd'hui* (Paris: Armand Colin, 1904), 376; Louis Brunot and Elie Malka, *Textes judéo-arabes de Fès* (Rabat: Institut des hautes études marocaines, 1939), 287; Issachar Ben-Ami, *Saint Veneration among the Jews in Morocco* (Detroit: Wayne State University Press, 1998), 201–202 et passim.

103. Yomtob Sémach, "Une chronique juive de Fès: le 'Yahas Fès' de Ribbi Abner Hassarfaty," *Hésperis* 19 (1934): 79–94.

104. Serfaty, "La famille Hassarfati," 5.

105. Aharon Serfaty, "Introduction," in Vidal I Serfaty, *Ṣuf devash* (Amsterdam: Proops, 1718).

106. According to Avner-Yisrael I's comments in *Yaḥas fes*, his parents were first cousins: his mother Simḥa (d. 1871) was the daughter of Yehuda b. Mattityahu Serero (1755–1835), and his father Vidal IV Serfaty (1797–1856) was the son of Yehuda's sister Zahra b. Mattityahu Serero. See also M. Mitchell Serels, who claims that "[Avner-Yisrael I] amassed an amazing library which remains a major inheritance of the Serero family": Serels, "The Hahamim of the Serero Family," *Sephardic Scholar* 4 (1982): 106.

107. The first manuscript, the Pentateuch, was sold by Hecht to the Bodleian Library in 1852, where it is now Bodl. Or. 614. The second, the

mahzor, was sold two years later to Leiden University, where it is now Or. 4814.

108. Yosef Tedghi, "The Jewish Cemetery in Fez," *Mi-qedem umi-yam* 9 (2006): 122.

109. Shlomo-Moshe Suzin (d. 1898) was a Palestinian *shadar* and grandson of the *Rishon le-zion* [Chief Rabbi of Ottoman Palestine] of the same name; see Avraham Ya'ari, *Sheluḥei ereṣ yisrael: toldot ha-sheliḥut meha-areṣ la-gola me-ḥurban bayit sheni 'ad ha-me'a ha-tesha'-'esrei* (Jerusalem: Mossad Rav Kook, 1977), 743. The books for Avner-Yisrael I were the two volumes of Refael-Asher Kovo's responsa, *Sha'ar asher* (Salonica, 1877), and a book "by Rabbi Rosen, the name of which I have forgotten": BC YR Ms. 232.

110. *Yaḥas fes*, as edited by Ovadia, *Fas ve-ḥakhameha*, 87–171.

111. BZI Ms. 2856, fols. 34–43, and Benayahu Ms. NA 194, fol. 2a–23a, both written in Avner-Yisrael I's hand. The BZI inventory, comprising a continuous nineteen pages, lists the books organized by theme, followed by a single page of the arrangement of their shelf numbers; it is bound with two later inventories of the library, ca. 1930. The Benayahu inventory has a listing of the books by theme (2a–8b) followed by a list of books alphabetized by title, starting with the letter *he* (9a–16a) and then ordered by number (16b–22b) and finally the arrangement of the books by shelf. This inventory appears to be later than the BZI inventory (e.g., some books in the BZI inventory are crossed out or added in an interlinear correction, while the Benayahu inventory is a neater copy), but they contain the same books. It has been bound with six pages of a halakhic manuscript, also in Avner-Yisrael I's hand.

112. Amar, "Sifriyyat yeshivat eṣ ḥayyim," 109–146.

113. Amar, "Sifriyyat yeshivat eṣ ḥayyim," 116–119.

114. On Benamozegh and *Em la-miqra*, see Yaron Harel, "The Edict to Destroy Em Lamikra—Aleppo, 1865," *Hebrew Union College Annual* 64 (1993): 27–36; Zvi Zohar, *Rabbinic Creativity in the Modern Middle East* (London: Bloomsbury Academic, 2013), 97–101; Clémence Boulouque, *Another Modernity: Elia Benamozegh's Jewish Universalism* (Redwood City, CA: Stanford University Press, 2020).

115. Amar, "Sifriyyat yeshivat eṣ ḥayyim." Similar proportions also hold for the library of Moïse Sebaoun, as cataloged by Gérard Nahon: "D'où venaient les livres hebreux étudiés dans les communautés juives d'Algérie au XVIIe et au XVIIIe siècle?" in *International Conference on Jewish Communities in Muslim Lands* (Jerusalem: Ben-Zvi Institute, 1974), 1–28; Gérard Nahon, "Livres anciens du Tribunal rabbinique d'Oran," in *Présence juive au*

Maghreb: hommage à Haïm Zafrani, ed. Joseph Tedghi and Nicole Serfaty (Saint-Denis: Éditions Bouchène, 2004), 143–146.

116. Amar, "Sifriyyat yeshivat eṣḥayyim," 144–146.

117. NLI ARC. 4.1537.2.21. The book in question covers "the principles of the science of magnetism, in all its laws, actions, observations, and effects." See Eliyahu Hakohen, "Ḥokhmat ha-magnetismus," *'Et-mol* 12, no. 3 (1987): 10–11.

118. Bennaim, *Malkhei rabbanan*, 18b.

119. Avner-Yisrael I describes these circumstances himself in the beginning of *Yaḥas fes*. See also Sémach, "Une chronique juive de Fès," 79–80.

120. *Yaḥas fes* (as printed in Ovadia, *Fas ve-ḥakhameha*, 1979), 87.

121. *Yaḥas fes*, 106. *Mikhlal yofi* is cited in the Serfaty catalog, no. 27.

122. *Yaḥas fes*, 94. This is true, e.g., of the printing of *Sefer rav alfas* (Venice: Daniel Bomberg, 1522).

123. *Yaḥas fes*, 93. See Rapoport's introduction, *Maḥberet ha-'arukh* (Presberg: Anton Edler von Schmid, 1844), x. Two copies of *Ha-'arukh* are listed in the Serfaty catalog, nos. 420 and 586.

124. *Yaḥas fes*, 95.

125. *Yaḥas fes*, 114.

126. *Yaḥas fes*, 141.

127. *Yaḥas fes*, 121.

128. *Yaḥas fes*, 138–141.

129. *Yaḥas fes*, 92.

130. Maya Shatzmiller, *L'historiographie mérinide: Ibn Khaldoun et ses contemporains* (Leiden: Brill, 1982), 18–29; Miguel Ángel Manzano Rodríguez, "Ibn Abī Zar'," in *Encyclopaedia of Islam*, 3rd edition (Leiden: Brill, 2007).

131. The first work, by Czech astronomer David Gans (1541–1613), published in Jessnitz in 1743, is not listed in the Serfaty catalog, but he clearly must have seen a copy since he alludes to the diagram (which is found on page 71b). The second work, by eighteenth-century scholar Yonatan ben Yosef of Ruzhany (Frankfurt, 1720), is cataloged as no. 104; the diagram in question is found on 3b.

132. *Yaḥas fes*, 152.

133. NLI Ms. Heb. 4.1089, 4a–b. The letter is concerned with a legal question relating to the sale of property.

134. Book no. 582 in the Serfaty catalog, *Sefer maspiq* (Vienna, 1857), is an Arabic textbook by Orientalist Jacob Goldenthal (1815–1868) written in Hebrew "for the use of the Jews of the Orient."

135. Benayahu Ms. NA 194, 33a. This page is titled "The register [*zimam*] of people who still have books with them as of 7 Nisan [5]652 [= April 4, 1892]," although the list was clearly edited and updated over time.

136. The rabbinic books were David-Shlomo Eybeschutz's *'Arvei naḥal* (printed in many editions); Yosef Albo's *Sefer ha-'iqqarim* (also in many editions); and *Shmena laḥmo* (Dessau, 1701). The geography book was *Be'er ha-gola* (Mainz, 1877). The medical book is titled *Darkei ha-refu'a*; there are at least two nineteenth-century printed books with this title, but neither appears in any of the Serfaty inventories, so perhaps the note refers more generally to a different medical book that was in the collection. Yiṣḥaq Maymaran is mentioned by Refael-Aharon Ben-Shim'on as one of the founders of the *Dovevei Siftei Yeshenim* Society discussed in chapter 5: *Mishpaṭ u-ṣedaqa be-ya'aqov*, vol. 1 (Alexandria: Farag Mizrahi, 1894), i.

137. The borrowers were Aharon Aflalo, Shlomo II Abensur, Shlomo Haroun, and a certain Ya'aqov. It is unclear whether this is the same manuscript in all cases, or whether the library had multiple copies.

138. Refael-Aharon Ben-Shim'on, *Ahavat ha-qadmonim* (Jerusalem, 1889), viii.

139. Ya'aqov Moshe Tolédano, *Ner ha-ma'arav* (Jerusalem: Abraham Lunz, 1911), ii, 207.

140. *Malkhei rabbanan* 18b; for a reference to a manuscript he consulted in the Serfaty library, see 119b. A manuscript copy of *Yaḥas fes* that Bennaim wrote for himself in 1923 is today BZI Ms. 1743.

141. BZI Ms. 2856, fol. 18b.

142. Simha Assaf, "Le-toldot ha-yehudim be-fas," in *Mizrah Oumaarav* [*Mizraḥ u-ma'arav*] vol. 4 (1930), 259–266, 383–390; vol. 5 (1931), 55–62, 198–201; Sémach, "Une chronique juive de Fès," 79–94.

143. Serfaty, "La famille Hassarfati," 9. The two were Rahamim Serfaty (1903–1972), great-grandson of Avner-Yisrael I, and Vidal Serfaty (d. 1976), a descendant of another branch of the Serfaty family, who immigrated to Israel the following year. In a conversation with the family of Rahamim's son, they confirmed that they knew of the family's library but no longer held any significant material from it. Vidal's son Moshe Serfaty still holds several manuscripts and books, including an autograph manuscript of *Yaḥas fes,* although whether their original provenance is all from the library of Avner-Yisrael I is not clear. Moshe Serfaty, personal communication, August 2021.

144. The Ben-Amozeg manuscript is now in the library of a yeshiva in El'ad, Yad Harav Zrihan (Ms. 5), which also owns several volumes

of Avner-Yisrael I's correspondence (Ms. 4 and 74), a manuscript of his responsa (Ms. 76), and a manuscript of the responsa of Eliyahu I Serfaty (Ms. 6). The mahzor, which is actually a manuscript quire bound together with a printed liturgical booklet, *Tiqqun ḥaṣot* (Livorno, 1800), is now Benayahu Ms. Z 48.

145. See the sale of *Ḥinukh beit yehuda* (Frankfurt, 1705) and *Melo ha-ro'im* (Warsaw, 1880), both with ownership inscriptions and the stamp of Avner-Yisrael I: Moreshet Auctions, auction 9 (2016), lot 394. These books are listed in his inventory, nos. 312 and 185. Books with the Serfaty stamp deaccessioned from Bar-Ilan and sold at public auction (now in the author's personal collection) include *Shema' shlomo* (Amsterdam, 1710), Serfaty no. 132; *Yakhin u-vo'az* (Livorno, 1782), Serfaty no. 240; and *Shevitat yom ṭov* (Salonica, 1788), Serfaty no. 235.

146. On Halewi: Daniel Schroeter, "The Politics of Reform in Morocco: The Writings of Yishaq Ben Ya'is(h) Halewi in Hasfirah (1891)," in *Misgav Yerushalayim Studies in Jewish Literature* (Jerusalem, 1987), 73–84. On 'Abo: Clémence Boulouque, "An 'Interior Occident' and the Case for an Oriental Modernity: The Livornese Printing Press and the Mediterranean Publishing Networks of Elia Benamozegh (1823–1900)," *Jewish Social Studies: History, Culture, Society* n.s. 23, no. 2 (2018): 99, 116, 134, 156–161.

147. Robert Attal, "Les publications judéo-arabes du rabbin Chalom Bekache, imprimeur et publiciste à Alger," *'Alei Sefer* 2 (1976): 219–228; Joseph Chetrit, "Haskala hébraique et haskala judéo-arabe à Tunis à la fin du XIXe siècle," in *Entre orient et occident: Juifs et Musulmans en Tunisie*, ed. Denis Cohen-Tannoudji (Paris: Éditions de l'éclat, 2007), 289–320; Tsivia Tobi, "Ha-rav ha-maskil eli'ezer farḥi ve-yeṣirotav ha-saṭiriyyot," *Ben 'ever la-'arav* 5 (2012): 127–144.

148. Julia Phillips Cohen and Sarah Abravaya Stein, "Sephardic Scholarly Worlds: Toward a Novel Geography of Modern Jewish History," *Jewish Quarterly Review* 100, no. 3 (2010): 351. See also Devin Naar, "Fashioning the 'Mother of Israel': The Ottoman Jewish Historical Narrative and the Image of Jewish Salonica," *Jewish History* 28 (2014): 337–372; Tamir Karkason, "Between Two Poles: Barukh Mitrani between Moderate Haskalah and Jewish Nationalism," *Zutot* 18 (2021): 14–25.

149. James Budgett Meakin, "The Jews of Morocco," *Jewish Quarterly Review* 4, no. 3 (1892): 371.

150. Nahon, "Livres anciens," 157.

CONCLUSION

1. The records of the Yehoash Folkshule (named for famed Yiddish writer and poet Solomon Blumgarten, 1872–1927, who wrote under the pen name Yehoash) are in the Ottawa Jewish Archives, E0004. A photograph of Sam and Katie at the 1923 meeting of the Yiddish Literary and Dramatic Society of Ottawa is in the OJA, 7-045. Reports on the Poliskys' participation in the Yehoash Folkshule and the Yiddish Literary and Dramatic Society of Ottawa can also be found in the *Ottawa Citizen* for October 22, 1924; June 2, 1925; February 23, 1926; February 19, 1927; November 5, 1928; and October 29, 1931.

2. Montreal Circuit Court, Citizenship Registration Records, Vol. 891, file 4671: "Naturalization of Samuel Polisky, 1909."

3. Alexander Harkavy, *Der amerikanisher lehrer: a praktishes lehr-bikhel fir yeden eingevanderten yiden vos vil kenen english un veren bekant mit amerika—The American Teacher: Practical Manual of the English Language and American Institutions* (New York: J. Katzenelenbogen, 1897). I am grateful to Raphael Halff for directing me to this work and sharing it with me.

4. "I wish to learn the art of printing," and "I know the art of printing very well," Harkavy, *Der amerikanisher lehrer,* 100–105. Harkavy was intimately familiar with the Yiddish terminology of the printing house, having worked as a teenager at the famed Romm Press in Vilna, owned by his cousin Dvora Harkavy-Romm; a 1926 biography describes him as having been a *bukhshtabnshlayfer*; literally, a "letter-polisher," presumably referring to brushing the type to clean it before and after printing: Zalmen Reyzen, *Leksikon fun yidisher literatur* (Vilna: Wilner, 1926), 793–796.

5. On the technological and mechanical shifts in printing in the nineteenth century, see Rob Bantham, "The Industrialization of the Book, 1800–1970," in *A Companion to the History of the Book,* ed. Simon Eliot and Jonathan Rose (Boston: Wiley-Blackwell, 2007), 273–290.

6. William Kelly, *Presswork: A Practical Handbook for the Use of Pressmen and Their Apprentices,* 2nd ed. (Chicago: Inland Printing Company, 1902).

7. J. M. Wright, "Uncle Sam's Pressrooms," *American Pressman* 11, no. 1 (December 1900): 5–7.

8. I borrow this phrase from Julia Phillips Cohen and Sarah Abravaya Stein, "Sephardic Scholarly Worlds: Toward a Novel Geography of Modern Jewish History," *Jewish Quarterly Review* 100, no. 3 (2010): 384.

9. Refael-Aharon Ben-Shim'on, "Introduction," in *Mishpaṭ u-ṣedaqa be-ya'aqov*, vol. 2 ed. Ya'aqov Abensur, (Alexandria: Farag Mizrahi, 1903).

10. On geniza practice among Jews of the Islamic world, see Mark Cohen and Yedida Stillman, "Genizat qahir u-minhagei geniza shel yehudei ha-mizraḥ: 'iyyun hisṭori ve-etnografi," *Pe'amim* 24, no. 1 (1985): 3–35; Joseph Sadan, "Genizah and Genizah-Like Practices in Islamic and Jewish Traditions," *Bibliotheca Orientalis* 43, no. 1 (1986): 36–58.

11. For the documents of a collection of genizot from Rabat spanning the nineteenth to mid-twentieth centuries, see the Rabat Genizah Project, managed by Oren Kosansky, online at http://library.lclark.edu/rabatgenizahproject. For a similar nineteenth- and twentieth-century collection discovered in Cairo, see Mark Cohen, "Geniza for Islamicists, Islamic Geniza, and the New Cairo Geniza," *Harvard Middle Eastern and Islamic Review* 7 (2006): 129–145.

12. D. F. McKenzie, *Bibliography and the Sociology of Texts* (Cambridge: Cambridge University Press, 1999), 9–29.

13. McKenzie, *Bibliography and the Sociology of Texts* (Cambridge: Cambridge University Press, 1999), 13–15.

14. Simon Eliot and Jonathan Rose, "Introduction," in *A Companion to the History of the Book*, ed. Simon Eliot and Jonathan Rose (Boston: Wiley-Blackwell, 2007), 1.

15. Angus Phillips, "Coda: Does the Book Have a Future?," in *A Companion to the History of the Book*, ed. Simon Eliot and Jonathan Rose (Boston: Wiley-Blackwell, 2007), 547–559.

16. Bridget Whearty, *Digital Codicology: Medieval Books and Modern Labor* (Redwood City, CA: Stanford University Press, 2022).

17. Yale MS.1825.2170. The document is dated to the beginning of Tevet 5640, which falls in December 1879.

18. The *duro* was another term for the Spanish "hard dollar," or piastre, which was one of the main currencies in nineteenth-century Morocco. See Daniel Schroeter, *The Sultan's Jew: Morocco and the Sephardi World* (Redwood City, CA: Stanford University Press, 2002), xxi. The rabbis who signed this document—Moshe bar Yosef Hakohen-Sqali and Avraham bar Ya'aqov Hakohen-Sqali—are well known as rabbinic leaders in Debdou, as is the Barmalil family; see Eliyahu Refael Marṣiano, *Yaḥas debdu he-ḥadash: toldoteha shel qehilat debdu ve-yiḥus mishpeḥoteha* (Jerusalem: Mekhon haRaShaM, 1997).

19. CCJM 23987; see also José Alberto Rodrigues da Silva Tavim, "Adibe Family," in *Encyclopedia of Jews in the Islamic World*, ed. Noam Stillman (Leiden: Brill, 2010). Interestingly, the sole example of a Jewish

woman in North Africa known to compose Hebrew poetry was also from the Adibe family: learned scholar and poet Freḥa bat Avraham Bar-Adibe, who moved from Morocco to Tunis in the mid-eighteenth century. See Yosef (Joseph) Chetrit, "Freḥa bat rabbi avraham: nosafot ʿal meshorreret ʿivriyya mi-maroqo ba-me'a 18," *Peʿamim* 55 (1993): 124–130, and Yosef (Joseph) Chetrit, "Piyyuṭei freḥa bat yosef teʿu-da ḥadasha ʿal ḥayyehah ve-motah," *Deḥaq le-sifrut tova* 1 (2011): 36–42.

20. See, e.g., many of the objects in Nitza Behrouzi, *From the Remotest West: Ritual Articles from Synagogues in Spanish Morocco* (Tel Aviv: Eretz Yisrael Museum, 1989), and Vivian Mann, ed., *Morocco: Jews and Art in a Muslim Land* (New York: Jewish Museum, 2000).

21. Eliezer Bashan, *Jewish Women in Morocco: From the Time of the Exile from Spain until the Twentieth Century* (Tel Aviv: Bar-Ilan University Press, 2003), 89–98. For female book sponsors, see, e.g., Yosef Knafo's tribute to ʿAisha Abitbol of Essaouira, whose parents Yiṣḥaq and Zohra had initially sponsored Knafo's work *Ot brit qodesh* but died before the book was finished; ʿAisha continued to support the book's publication and also took it upon herself "to establish a yeshiva for scholars in [her father's house], and gave of her own money to furnish it," as well as sponsoring the writing of two Torah scrolls in her parents' memory: Yosef Knafo, *Ot brit qodesh* (Livorno: Elia Benamozegh, 1884), 4a–b.

22. Many Jews from Debdou did have commercial and social ties with the larger city of Oran; e.g., Debdou-born rabbi David Hakohen-Sqali (1862–1949) served as a judge and community leader in Oran, and many young Jews from Debdou migrated to Oran in search of work: Shlomo Glicksberg, "R. David Hakohen-Sqali: pesiqa mesortit be-ʿidan shel temurot," in *Yehudei aljiria ve-luv*, ed. Moshe Halamish, Moshe Amar, and Maurice Roumani (Tel Aviv: Bar-Ilan University Press, 2014), 134–155; Joshua Schreier, *The Merchants of Oran: A Jewish Port at the Dawn of Empire* (Redwood City, CA: Stanford University Press, 2017), 7.

23. Samuel Meir Feigensohn, "Le-toldot defus rom," in *Yahadut lita*, ed. Natan Goren (Tel Aviv: Am Ha-sefer, 1959), 268–302; Michael Stanislawski, "The 'Vilna Shas' and East European Jewry," in *Printing the Talmud: From Bomberg to Schottenstein*, ed. Sharon Liberman Mintz and Gabriel Goldstein (New York: Yeshiva University Museum, 2005), 97–102.

24. Yale MS.1825.2170.

BIBLIOGRAPHY

PRIMARY SOURCES

Abensur, Ya'aqov. *Mishpaṭ u-ṣedaqa be-ya'aqov*, vol. 1. Alexandria: Farag Mizrahi, 1894.
Abensur, Ya'aqov. *Mishpaṭ u-ṣedaqa be-ya'aqov*, vol. 2. Alexandria: Farag Mizrahi, 1903.
Aboab, Immanuel. *Nomologia o Discursos Legales.* Amsterdam, s.n., 1629.
Abudarham, David. *Sefer abudarham.* Fez: Shmuel and Yiṣḥaq Nedivot, 1516.
'Adawi, Shmuel. *Sefer bnei shmuel.* Livorno: Antonio Santini, 1759.
Allouche, Eliyahu. *'Et la-ledet qol sasson.* Livorno: Elia Benamozegh, 1888.
'Allun, Mikhael Makhluf, ed. and trans. *Or ne'erav.* Livorno: Elia Benamozegh, 1854.
Ankawa, Avraham. *Kerem ḥemer.* Livorno: Elia Benamozegh, 1869.
Asher ben Yeḥiel. *Tosfei ha-rosh.* Livorno: Giovan Vincenzo Falorni, 1776.
'Ayyash, Yehuda. *Beit yehuda.* Livorno: Abraham Meldola, 1746.
'Ayyash, Yehuda. *Ve-zot li-yhuda.* Sulzbach: Aharon ben Meshulam Zalman, 1776.
Azulai, Ḥayyim Yosef David. *Ma'agal ṭov ha-shalem.* Edited by Aron Freimann. Jerusalem: Mekize Nirdamim, 1934.
Bekache, Shalom. *Bone yerushalayim.* Algiers: Bekache and Cohen-Solal, 1892.
Bekache, Shalom. *Daniel ha-kuzari.* Algiers: Avraham Boukabza, 1887.
Bekache, Shalom. *Mevasser ṭov.* Livorno: Elia Benamozegh, 1884.

Bekache, Shalom. *Mi-meqor yisrael.* Algiers: Shalom Bekache, 1892.

Bekache, Shalom, ed. *Piyut bar yohai bi-sfat 'arav.* Livorno: Elia Benamozegh, 1886.

Bakrat, Avraham Halevi. *Sefer ha-zikaron.* Edited by Eli'ezer Ashkenazi. Livorno: Jacob Ashkenazi, 1845.

Bekache, Shalom, ed. *Sefer mahzor qaṭan.* Livorno: Elia Benamozegh, 1886.

Bekache, Shalom. *Sipurei ha-ṭeva'.* Algiers: Shalom Bekache, 1892.

Ben-Ḥassin, David. *Tehila le-david.* Amsterdam: Proops, 1807.

Ben-Shim'on, Refael-Aharon, ed. *Ahavat ha-qadmonim.* Jerusalem: Shmuel Halevi Zuckerman, 1889.

Benamozegh, Elia. *La verita svelata ai miei giudici: intorno le tre lettere, prodotte dalla querela Tubiana.* Paris: Minerva, 1861.

Benamozegh, Elia, ed. *Sefer ḥanokh la-na'ar.* Livorno: Elia Benamozegh, 1866.

Benamozegh, Elia, ed. *Sefer sekhiyot ha-ḥemda.* Livorno: Salomone Belforte, 1852.

Benamozegh, Elia, ed. *Sfat emet.* Livorno: Elia Benamozegh, 1855.

Bengualid, Isaac. *Va-yomer yiṣḥaq.* Livorno: Elia Benamozegh, 1876.

Benisti, Nessim. "Réforme, Emancipation, Progrès." *Adziri,* no. 6 (August 26, 1870): 2–3.

Berdugo, Refael. *Mishpaṭim yesharim.* Edited by Shalom Amar. Kraków: Josef Fischer, 1891.

Berdugo, Moshe. *Rosh mashbir.* Livorno: Moshe Tubiana, 1840.

Bibliographie de la France ou Journal Général de l'Imprimerie et de la Librarie, vol. 8 (Paris: Pillet, February 25, 1854).

Bliah, Haïm. *Sha'ar kevod ha-shem.* Tunis: Uzan and Castro, 1902.

Bloch, Isaac. *Inscriptions tumulaires des anciens cimetières israélites d'Alger.* Paris: Armand Durlacher, 1888.

Boukabza, Abraham, ed. *Sefer maḥzor qaṭan.* Livorno: Israel Costa, 1886.

Boukabza, Abraham, ed. *Sefer shavua' ṭov.* Livorno: Israel Costa, 1886.

Bourget, Auguste. "Faits divers: Alger." *L'Akhbar: Journal de l'Algérie* 13, no. 1875 (October 30, 1853): 2.

Buzaglo, Shalom. *Miqdash melekh.* Amsterdam: Naftali Herz Levi Rofe, 1750.

Coriat, Yehuda, ed. *Ma'or va-shemesh.* Livorno: Eli'ezer Menaḥem Ottolenghi, 1839.

Duran, Ṣemaḥ. *Yakhin u-vo'az.* Livorno: Castello and Saadun, 1782.

Duran, Shim'on. *Magen avot.* Livorno: Moses Attias, 1762.

Duran, Shim'on. *Sefer ha-tashbeṣ.* Amsterdam: Naftali Herz Levi Rofe, 1739.

Duran, Shim'on. *Yavin shmu'a.* Livorno: Abraham Meldola, 1744.

Duran, Shlomo. *Tiferet yisrael*. Venice: Giovanni di Gara, 1596.
Edrehi, Moses. *A Book of Miracles: An Historical Account of the Ten Tribes*. London, s.n., 1836.
Elmaleh, Eliyahu. *Beqa la-gulgolet*. Jerusalem: S. Zukerman, 1911.
Farḥi, Eli'ezer, ed. *Anis al-wujud*. Livorno: Elia Benamozegh, 1885.
Farḥi, Eli'ezer, ed. *Sirat al-azaliyya*. Livorno: Israel Costa, 1887.
al-Fasi, Mas'ud. *Mishḥa de-revuta*. Livorno: Eliezer Saadun, 1806.
Flah, Chalom. "Ha-ṣofe et penei tunis." *He-asif* vol. 6: 78–94. Warsaw: Halter and Eisenstadt, 1893.
de Grammont, Henri-Delmas. "Bibliographie: Inscriptions tumulaires des anciens cimetières israélites d'Alger, par Isaac Bloch, Grand Rabbin d'Alger." *Revue Africaine* 190 (1888): 320.
Grimont, Ferdinand. *Manuel-annuaire de l'imprimerie, de la librairie et de la presse*. Paris: P. Jannet, 1855.
Guedj, David. *Ner david*. Livorno: Israel Costa, 1872.
Guedj Eliyahu Ḥai. *Ḥesed ve-emet*. Algiers: Ya'aqov Guedj, 1888.
Guedj, Eliyahu Ḥai. *Ma'ase sha'ashu'im*. Livorno: Israel Costa, 1868.
Guedj, Eliyahu Ḥai, ed. *Seder hagada shel pesaḥ ma' tafsir . . . mta tunis*. Livorno: Israel Costa, 1869.
Guedj, Eliyahu Ḥai, ed. *Seder ve-tiqqun birkat ha-ḥama*. Livorno: Israel Costa, 1869.
Guedj, Eliyahu Ḥai, ed. *Tfila be-khol lashon*. Livorno: Israel Costa, 1883.
Guedj Eliyahu Ḥai. *Tokhaḥat megula*. Livorno: Israel Costa, 1872.
Guedj, Eliyahu Ḥai. *Ze ha-shulḥan*. Algiers: Ya'aqov Guedj, 1888.
Guedj, Yosef. *Pi ha-medaber*. Livorno: Moshe Yeshu'a Tubiana, 1854.
Guedj, Yosef. *Zohar 'al ha-tora*. Livorno: Israel Costa, 1872–1886.
Ḥaddad, Ya'aqov. *Kenaf renanim*. Livorno: Israel Costa, 1871.
Ḥagiz, Shmuel. *Dvar shmuel*. Venice: Giovanni di Gara, 1596.
Ḥagiz, Shmuel, ed. *Maḥzor rosh ha-shana ve-yom ha-kipurim ke-minhag q"q Aljaza'ir*. Venice: Daniel Zanetti, 1598.
Ḥagiz, Shmuel. *Mevaqesh ha-shem*. Venice: Giovanni di Gara, 1596.
Ḥaliwa, David. *Ha-pa'am ode*. Amsterdam: Jacob Belinfante, 1838.
Ḥazzan, Eliyahu Bekhor. *Ta'alumot lev*. Livorno: Elia Benamozegh, 1879.
Ḥazzan, Eliyahu Bekhor. *Zikhron yerushalayim*. Livorno: Elia Benamozegh, 1874.
Ḥazzan, Refael Yosef. *Ḥiqrei lev*. Jerusalem: Zvi Hirsch Hakohen, 1875.
Ḥazzan, Yisrael Moshe. *Sha'arei teshuva 'im hagahot iyyei ha-yam*. Livorno: Elia Benamozegh, 1869.
Ibn-Adoniyyahu, Ya'aqov, ed. *Sha'ar adonai he-ḥadash*. Venice: Daniel Bomberg, 1525.

Ibn-Ḥayyim, Aharon. *Lev aharon*. Venice: Giovanni di Gara, 1608.
Jarmon, Yehuda. *Shuva yisrael*. Livorno: Elia Benamozegh, 1886.
Kennicott, Benjamin. *The Ten Annual Accounts of the Collation of Hebrew Mss. of the Old Testament Begun in 1760 and Completed in 1769*. Oxford: Fletcher and Prince, 1770.
Kohen Tanuji, Yehuda. *Ereṣ yehuda*. Livorno: Eliezer Saadun, 1797.
Kohen Tanuji, Yosef. *Bnei yosef*. Livorno: Eliezer Saadun, 1793.
Knafo, Yosef. *Ot brit qodesh*. Livorno: Elia Benamozegh, 1884.
Laredo, Avraham, and Yiṣḥaq Halevi. *Dat yehudit*. Algiers: Cohen-Solal, 1855.
Leusden, Johannes (editor). *Biblia Hebraica Accuratissima*. Amsterdam: Joseph Athias, 1667.
Luckombe, Philip. *The History and Art of Printing*. London: Philip Luckombe, 1771.
Lumbroso, Yiṣḥaq. *Zera' yiṣḥaq*. Tunis: Yeshu'a Kohen Tanuji, 1768.
Luzzato, Samuel David, ed. *Virgo Filia Jehudae, sive Excerpta ex inedito . . . Divano*. Prague: M. Landau, 1840.
Ma'arek, Ya'aqov. *Shufre de-ya'aqov*. Livorno: Castello and Saadun, 1787.
Morali, Yiṣḥaq. "Sefer ṣafnat paneaḥ." *Koveṣ 'al yad (Sammelband kleiner Beiträge aus Handschriften)* 7 (1897): 5–47.
Nahon, Moïse. "La communauté israélite de Tlemcen." *Revue des Écoles* 8: 34–35. 1903.
Najjar, Yehuda. *Limudei ha-shem*. Livorno: Castello and Saadun, 1787.
Nunes-Vais, Ya'aqov (editor). *Da'at zqenim*. Livorno: Castello and Saadun, 1783.
Pereṣ, Yehuda, ed. *'Aseret ha-devarim*. Amsterdam: Joseph Attias, 1737.
Pereṣ, Yehuda, ed. *'Aseret ha-devarim*. Livorno: Jacob Arovas, 1815.
Robe, Eugène, ed. *Journal de la Jurisprudence de la Cour Impériale d'Alger* 12, no. 1, (1870).
Salama, Yosef. *Shirei zimra*. Livorno: Israel Costa, 1872.
Sasportas, Ya'aqov. *Ohel ya'aqov*. Amsterdam: Herz Levi Rofe, 1737.
Sedbon, Eliyahu, ed. *Shir ha-shirim*. Livorno: Moshe Yeshu'a Tubiana, 1847.
Sedbon, Yosef. *Ahavat ha-shem*. Livorno: Israel Costa, 1871.
Seror, Martin (Mordekhai). *Hagada ou rituel des deux premieres nuit de Paque*. Livorno: Israel Costa, 1886.
Seror, Mordekhai. *Qol sasson*. Algiers: Avraham Boukabza, 1884.
Shamama, Moshe, ed. *Kitab qanun al-dawla al-tunisiyya*. Tunis: Ḥayyim Ze'ev Ashkenazi, 1861.
Silberman, Eliezer Lipman. *Reshima shel shemot ha-ḥaverim le-ḥevrat meqiṣe nirdamim: shana shenit 625–626*. Ełk: Mekitze Nirdamim, 1866.

da Silva, Jehosuah, Semuel Pinto, and Abraham Senior Corronel. "Correctores pio Lectori S." In *Biblia Hebraica Accuratissima*, eds Johannes Leusden. Amsterdam: Joseph Athias, 1667.

Sitruk, Yehuda, and Yosef Shamama. *Dinei sheḥiṭa u-vediqa bi-leshon ʿaravi*. Livorno: Israel Costa, 1873.

Sokolow, Nahum, ed. *Sefer zikaron le-sofrei yisrael ha-ḥayyim itanu ka-yom*. Warsaw: M. I. Halter, 1889.

Tubiana, Moshe Yeshuʿa, ed. *Arbaʿa gevi'im*. Livorno: Moshe Yeshuʿa Tubiana, 1839.

Vassel, Eusèbe. *La littérature populaire des israélites tunisiens*. Paris: Leroux, 1907.

Wright, J. M. "Uncle Sam's Pressrooms." *American Pressman* 11, no. 1 (December 1900): 5–7.

Zacuto, Avraham. *Sefer yuḥasin: Liber Juchassin sive Lexicon Biographical et historicum*. Edited by Herschell Filipowski. London: H. Filipowski, 1857.

Zarqa, Shlomo. *Zivḥei truʿa*. Livorno: Salomon Belforte, 1867.

Zarqa, Shlomo, and Yehuda Ḍarmon, ed. *Shay la-mora*. Algiers: Cohen-Solal, 1854.

SECONDARY SOURCES

Abdulrazak, Fawzi. "The Kingdom of the Book: The History of Printing as an Agency of Change in Morocco between 1865 and 1912." PhD diss., Boston University, 1990.

Abdulrazak, Fawzi. "Printing as an Agent of Change in Morocco, 1864–1912." In *The Book in Africa: Critical Debates*, edited by Caroline Davis and David Johnson, 31–43. London: Palgrave Macmillan, 2015.

Abensour, Gabriel. "In Praise of the Multitude: Rabbi Yosef Knafo's Socially Conscious Work in Essaouira at the End of the Nineteenth Century." *Jewish Social Studies* 27, no. 1 (2022): 115–149.

Abi-Mershed, Osama. *Apostles of Modernity: Saint-Simonians and the Civilizing Mission in Algeria*. Redwood City, CA: Stanford University Press, 2010.

Adler, Elkan Nathan. *Catalogue of Hebrew Manuscripts in the Collection of Elkan Nathan Adler*. Cambridge: Cambridge University Press, 1921.

Akkerman, Olly. *A Neo-Fatimid Treasury of Books: Arabic Manuscripts among the Alawi Bohras of South Asia*. Edinburgh: Edinburgh University Press, 2022.

Alcalay, Ammiel. "Intellectual Life." In *The Jews of the Middle East and North Africa in Modern Times*, edited by Reeva Spector Simon, Michael Menachem Laskier, and Sara Reguer, 85–112. New York: Columbia University Press, 2002.

Allony, Nehemiah. *The Jewish Library in the Middle Ages: Book Lists from the Cairo Genizah.* Jerusalem: Ben-Zvi Institute, 2006.

Amar, Moshe. "Le-toldot rabbi aharon ibn-ḥayyim." *Mi-mizraḥ umi-ma'arav* 4 (1984): 23–36.

Amar, Moshe. "Qavvim li-demuto shel rabbi ya'aqov ibn ṣur." *Mi-mizraḥ umi-ma'arav* 3 (1981): 89–124.

Amar, Moshe. "Sifriyyat yeshivat eṣ ḥayyim: aspaqlarya le-'olamam ha-ruḥani shel ha-ḥakhamim be-tunis be-shilhei ha-me'a ha-tesha'-'esrei." In *Jews of Tunisia: Heritage, History, Literature,* edited by Ephraim Hazan and Haim Saadon, 109–146. Ramat Gan: Bar Ilan University Press, 2009.

Amar, Moshe, ed. *Sefer minḥat yehuda: mahadura tinyana.* Lod: Orot Yehudei Hamagreb, 2011.

Amit, Gish. *Eqs libris: hisṭoria shel gezel, shimur ve-nikus ba-sifriyya ha-le'umit bi-yrushalayim.* Jerusalem: Van Leer, 2014.

Amory, Hugh. "The Trout and the Milk: An Ethnobibliographical Talk." *Harvard Library Bulletin* 7 (1996): 51–65.

Andrews, Martin. "The Importance of Ephemera." In *A Companion to the History of the Book,* edited by Simon Eliot and Jonathan Rose, 434–450. Hoboken, NJ: Wiley-Blackwell, 2007.

Anonymous. "'Azuva be-shetaḥ meḥqar yehudei ha-mizraḥ." *Ha-boqer* 4871 (October 1951): 4.

Anonymous. "Les obsèques du grand rabbin Seboun." *L'Univers Israélite* 44 (1889): 173–176.

Anonymous. "Literatur-Berichte." *Literaturblatt des Orients* 10, no. 24 (1849): 370.

Aranov, Saul. *A Descriptive Catalogue of the Bension Collection of Sephardic Manuscripts and Texts.* Edmonton: University of Alberta Press, 1979.

Arkin, Kimberly. *Rhinestones, Religion, and the Republic: Fashioning Jewishness in France.* Redwood City, CA: Stanford University Press, 2014.

Aslanian, Sebouh. *Early Modernity and Mobility: Port Cities and Printers across the Armenian Diaspora, 1512–1800.* New Haven, CT: Yale University Press, 2023.

Aslanian, Sebouh. "Port Cities and Printers: Reflections on Early Modern Global Armenian Print." *Book History* 17 (2014): 51–93.

Assaf, Simha. "Le-toldot ha-yehudim be-fas." *Mizrah Oumaarav [Mizrah U-maarav],* no. 4 (1930): 259–266, 383–390; no. 5 (1931): 55–62, 198–201.

Assan, Valérie. "Haïm Cohen-Solal, négociant." *Archives Juives* 45, no. 2 (2012): 143–144.

Assan, Valérie. *Les consistoires israélites d'Algérie au XIXe siècle: l'alliance de la civilisation et la religion.* Paris: Armand Colin, 2012.

Assan, Valérie. "Les synagogues dans l'Algérie coloniale du XIXe siècle." *Archives juives* 37, no. 1 (2004): 70–85.

Asseraf, Arthur. *Electric News in Colonial Algeria*. Oxford: Oxford University Press, 2019.

Attal, Avraham (Robert). "'Al ha-defus ha-'ivri ba-magreb." *Mi-mizraḥ umi-ma'arav* 2 (1980): 121–129.

Attal, Avraham (Robert). "Ha-defus ha-'ivri be-wahran." Supplement, *Qiryat Sefer* 68 (1998): 85–92.

Attal, Avraham (Robert). "Ha-'iṭṭon ha-yehudi ha-rish'on ba-maghreb—L'Israélite Algérien (Adziri), 1870." *Pe'amim* 17 (1983): 88–95.

Attal, Avraham (Robert). *Kitvei 'et ve-'itonim yehudiyyim bi-ṣfon afriqa*. Tel Aviv: Tel Aviv University, 1996.

Attal, Avraham (Robert). "Les publications judéo-arabes du rabbin Chalom Bekache, imprimeur et publiciste à Alger." *'Alei Sefer* 2 (1976): 219–228.

Attal, Robert (Avraham). "Les reportages d'Eliézer Ashkenazi: Une source journalistique oubliée sur l'histoire des Juifs de Tunisie à la fin de l'époque pré-coloniale." In *Entre Orient et Occident: Juifs et Musulmans en Tunisie*, edited by Denis Cohen-Tannoudji, 335–346. Paris: Éditions de l'Éclat, 2007.

Attal, Avraham (Robert), and Meira Harroch. "Ha-defus ha-'ivri be-aljir." *Qiryat sefer* 61 (1986): 561–572.

Attal, Robert (Avraham). *Le Caïd Nessim Samama de Tunis: mécène du livre hebraique*. Jerusalem: R. Attal, 1995.

Auji, Hala. *Printing Arab Modernity: Book Culture and the American Press in Nineteenth-Century Beirut*. Leiden: Brill, 2016.

Avital, Netanel, ed. *Pinqas qehilat fes*. El'ad: N. Avital, 2018.

Ayalon, Ami. "Arab Booksellers and Bookshops in the Age of Printing, 1850–1914." *British Journal of Middle Eastern Studies* 37, no. 1 (2010): 73–93.

Ayalon, Ami. *The Arabic Print Revolution: Cultural Production and Mass Readership*. Cambridge: Cambridge University Press, 2016.

Ayoun, Richard. "Le grand rabbin d'Algérie David Askénazi." *Revue Européenne des Études Hébraïques* 7 (2002): 103–108.

Ayoun, Richard. "Samuel Aboulker (Abulher), rabbin, juge du tribunal rabbinique et chohet (abatteur rituel) (Alger 1814 - Jérusalem vers 1895)." *Revue Européenne des Études Hébraïques: À la Mémoire de Richard Ayoun*, Hors-Serie (2008): 195–198.

Bacon, Gershon. "The Rabbinical Conference in Kraków (1903) and the Beginnings of Organized Orthodox Jewry." In *Let the Old Make Way for the New: Studies Presented to Immanuel Etkes, Vol. 2: Haskalah, Orthodoxy, and the Opposition to Hasidism*, edited by David Assaf and Ada Rapaport-Albert, 199–225. Jerusalem: Shazar, 2009.

Baïda, Jamaâ. *La presse marocaine d'expression française: des origines à 1956*. Rabat: Faculté des Lettres et des Sciences Humaines de Rabat, 1996.

Bantham, Rob. "The Industrialization of the Book, 1800–1970." In *A Companion to the History of the Book*, edited by Simon Eliot and Jonathan Rose, 273–290. Boston: Wiley-Blackwell, 2007.

Bar-Asher, Moshe. "Ha-sifrut ha-rabbanit bi-ṣfon afriqa 1700–1948." *Pe'amim* 86/87 (2001): 233–257.

Bar-Asher, Moshe. *Leshon limmudim le-rabbi refael berdugo*. Jerusalem: Bialik, 2001.

Bar-Asher, Moshe. "Tiqqun pesaḥ mi-tafilalt sheba-maroqo." *Shana be-shana* 41 (1991): 147–161.

Bar-Asher, Shalom. "Aben Ṣur, Jacob." In *Encyclopedia of Jewish in the Islamic World*, edited by Noam Stillman. Leiden: Brill, 2010.

Bar-Asher, Shalom. "The Emancipation of North African Jewish Women: The Alliance Israélite Universelle." In *Jews and Muslims in the Islamic World*, edited by Bernard Dov Cooperman and Zvi Zohar, 33–50. College Park: University of Maryland Press, 2013.

Bar-Asher, Shalom. "Ketav yad shel haggada shel pesaḥ mi-maroqo." In *Sha'arei lashon: meḥqarim ba-lashon ha-'ivrit, ba-aramit, uvi-leshonot ha-yehudim mugashim le-moshe bar asher*, 294–303. Jerusalem: Bialik Institute, 2007.

Bar-Asher, Shalom. "Ṣarfati Family." In *Encyclopedia of Jews in the Islamic World*, edited by Noam Stillman. Leiden: Brill, 2010.

Bar-Levav, Avriel. "Amsterdam and the Inception of the Jewish Republic of Letters." In *The Dutch Intersection: The Jews and the Netherlands in Modern History*, edited by Yosef Kaplan, 225–237. Leiden: Brill, 2008.

Baron, Sabrina, Eric Lindquist, and Eleanor Shevlin, eds. *Agent of Change: Print Culture Studies after Elizabeth L. Eisenstein*. Amherst: University of Massachusetts Press, 2007.

Barouch, Yael. "Moallech / nsf qalam: Documentation and Cultural Reflection on Hebrew Cursive Script." Master's thesis, Hebrew University, 2016.

Bartal, Israel. "The Kinnus Project: Wissenschaft des Judentums and the Fashioning of a 'National Culture' in Palestine." In *Transmitting Jewish Traditions: Orality, Textuality and Cultural Diffusion*, edited by Yaakov Elman and Israel Gershoni, 310–323. New Haven, CT: Yale University Press, 2000.

Baruchson, Shifra. *Books and Readers: Reading Culture of Italian Jews at the End of the Renaissance*. Tel Aviv: Bar-Ilan University Press, 1993.

Bashan, Eliezer. *Jewish Women in Morocco: From the Time of the Exile from Spain until the Twentieth Century*. Tel Aviv: Bar-Ilan University Press, 2003.

Bashan, Eliezer. "Prof. Ḥ. Z. Hirshberg z"l." *Cathedra* 2 (1976): 173–175.

Bashan, Eliezer. "Rabbi eliyahu ḥazzan, rabban shel ṭripoli ve-aleqsandria, ve-yaḥaso la-haskala." In *Hagut '-ivrit be-arṣot ha-islam*, edited by Menahem Zohori, 410–418. Jerusalem: Brit 'Ivrit 'Olamit, 1981.

Bashan, Eliezer. *Yehudei fes 1873–1900 'al pi te'udot ḥadashot*. Jerusalem: Yad Harav Nissim, 2002.

Beaussier, Marcelin. *Dictionnaire pratique arabe-français*. Algiers: Bouyer, 1871.

Becker, Cynthia. *Amazigh Arts in Morocco: Women Shaping Berber Identity*. Austin: University of Texas Press, 2007.

Behrens-Abouseif, Doris. *The Book in Mamluk Egypt and Syria, 1250–1517*. Leiden: Brill, 2019.

Behrouzi, Nitza. *From the Remotest West: Ritual Articles from Synagogues in Spanish Morocco*. Tel Aviv: Eretz Yisrael Museum, 1989.

Beit-Arié, Malachi. "Ha-im hayyu sifriyyot ṣiburiyyot yehudiyyot bi-ymei ha-benayyim? Ha-ṣivyon ha-individu'ali shel hafaqat ha-sefer ha-'ivri u-ṣrikhato." *Zion* 65 (2000): 441–451.

Beit-Arié, Malachi. *Hebrew Codicology: Historical and Comparative Typology of Medieval Hebrew Codices*. Jerusalem: Israel Academy of Sciences and Humanities, 2021.

Beit-Arié, Malachi. "Hebrew Script in Spain: Development, Offshoots, and Vicissitudes." In *Moreshet Sepharad: The Sephardi Legacy*, edited by Haim Beinart, 282–317. Jerusalem: Magnes, 1992.

Beit-Arié, Malachi. "Introduction." In *Specimens of Mediaeval Hebrew Scripts, Vol. II: Sefardic Script*, edited by Malachi Beit-Arié and Edna Engel, 9–20. Jerusalem: Israel Academy of Sciences and Humanities, 2002.

Beit-Arié, Malachi, and Edna Engel. *Specimens of Mediaeval Hebrew Scripts: Volume II, Sefardic Script*. Jerusalem: Israel Academy of Sciences and Humanities, 2002.

Bellingradt, Daniel, and Jeroen Salman. "Books and Book History in Motion: Materiality, Sociality, and Spatiality." In *Books in Motion in Early Modern Europe: Beyond Production, Circulation and Consumption*, edited by Daniel Bellingradt, Paul Nelles, and Jeroen Salman, 1–14. London: Palgrave Macmillan, 2017.

Ben-Ami, Issachar. *Saint Veneration among the Jews in Morocco.* Detroit: Wayne State University Press, 1998.

Bendana, Kmar. "Générations d'imprimeurs et figures d'éditeurs à Tunis entre 1850 et 1950." In *Les mutations du livre et de l'édition dans le monde du XVIIIe siècle à l'an 2000,* edited by Jacques Michon and Jean-Yves Mollier, 349–359. Paris: Harmattan, 2002.

Ben-Naeh, Yaron. "Hebrew Printing Houses in the Ottoman Empire." In *Jewish Journalism and Printing Houses in the Ottoman Empire and Modern Turkey,* edited by Gad Nassi, 73–96. Istanbul: Isis, 2001.

Bennaim, Yosef. *Malkhei rabbanan.* Jerusalem: Ha-ma'arav Press, 1931.

Ben-Sasson, Menahem. *Ṣemiḥat ha-qehila ha-yehudit be-arṣot ha-islam: qayrawan 800–1057.* Jerusalem: Magnes, 1996.

Bentov, Haim. "The Ha-Levi ibn Yuli Family." *East and Maghreb: Researches in the History of the Jews in the Orient and North Africa* 2 (1980): 131–158.

Bentov, Haim. "Jewish Artisans in Fez during the 17th and 18th Centuries." *Sefunot* 10 (1966): 314–483.

Bentov, Haim. "Rabbinic Literature in North Africa in the Last 250 Years." *Pe'amim* 86/87 (2001): 214–232.

Bernasek, Lisa. *Artistry of the Everyday: Beauty and Craftsmanship in Berber Art.* Cambridge, MA: Peabody Museum, 2008.

Beṣalel, Yiṣḥaq. "Pitḥon pe la-yehudiyya ba-mizraḥ: ha-yaḥas la-isha ba-zikhron yerushalayim le-rabbi eliyahu ḥazzan." In *'Ayin tova: du-siaḥ ve-pulmus be-tarbut yisrael,* edited by Nahem Ilan, 197–223. Tel Aviv: Hakibbutz Hameuchad, 1999.

Bevilacqua, Alexander. "Beyond East and West." In *New Horizons for Early Modern European Scholarship,* edited by Ann Blair and Nicholas Popper, 72–92. Baltimore: Johns Hopkins University Press, 2021.

Bin-Nun, Adam. "The Ashkenazi Bookdealers in Yemen (1925–1929)." *My Heart Is in the East* 3 (2021): 45–76 (Hebrew).

Bitton, Michele. "Berthe Bénichou-Aboulker." In *The Shalvi/Hyman Encyclopedia of Jewish Women,* edited by Jennifer Sartori. Newton, MA: Jewish Women's Archive, 2021.

Borovaya, Olga. *Modern Ladino Culture: Press, Belles Lettres, and Theater in the Late Ottoman Empire.* Bloomington: Indiana University Press, 2012.

Boulouque, Clémence. *Another Modernity: Elia Benamozegh's Jewish Universalism.* Redwood City, CA: Stanford University Press, 2020.

Boulouque, Clémence. "Elia Benamozegh's Printing Presses: Livornese Crossroads and the New Margins of Italian Jewish History." In *Italian*

Jewish Networks from the Seventeenth to the Twentieth Century, edited by Francesca Bregoli, Carlotta Ferrara degli Uberti, and Guri Schwarz, 59–80. London: Palgrave Macmillan, 2018.

Boulouque, Clémence. "An 'Interior Occident' and the Case for an Oriental Modernity: The Livornese Printing Press and the Mediterranean Publishing Networks of Elia Benamozegh (1823–1900)." *Jewish Social Studies: History, Culture, Society* n.s. 23, no. 2 (2018): 89–95.

Boum, Aomar. *Memories of Absence: How Muslims Remember Jews in Morocco*. Redwood City, CA: Stanford University Press, 2013.

Boum, Aomar, and Thomas Park. *Historical Dictionary of Morocco*, 2nd ed. Oxford: Scarecrow, 2006.

Brásio, António. *Monumenta Missionaria Africana: Africa Ocidental (1469–1599)*. Vol. 4. Lisbon: Agencia Geral do Ultramar, 1954.

Bregoli, Francesca. "Hebrew Printing and Communication Networks between Livorno and North Africa, 1740–1789." In *Report of the Oxford Centre for Hebrew and Jewish Studies 2007–2008*, 51–59. Oxford: Oxford Centre for Hebrew and Jewish Studies, 2008.

Bregoli, Francesca. "Hebrew Printing in Eighteenth-Century Livorno: From Government Control to a Free Market." In *The Hebrew Book in Early Modern Italy*, edited by Joseph Hacker and Adam Shear, 171–196. Philadelphia: University of Pennsylvania Press, 2011.

Bregoli, Francesca. *Mediterranean Enlightenment: Livornese Jews, Tuscan Culture, and Eighteenth-Century Reform*. Redwood City, CA: Stanford University Press, 2014.

Bregoli, Francesca. "Printing, Fundraising, and Jewish Patronage in Eighteenth-Century Livorno." In *Jewish Culture in Early Modern Europe: Essays in Honor of David B. Ruderman*, edited by Richard I. Cohen, Natalie B. Dohrmann, Adam Shear, and Elchanan Reiner, 250–259. Philadelphia: University of Pittsburgh Press, 2014.

Brinkman, Inge, and Koen Bostoen, "'To Make Book': A Conceptual Historical Approach to Kongo Book Cultures (Sixteenth-Nineteenth Centuries)." In *The Kongo Kingdom: The Origins, Dynamics and Cosmopolitan Culture of an African Polity*, edited by Inge Brinkman and Koen Bostoen, 216–234. Cambridge: Cambridge University Press, 2018.

Briquet, Charles-Moïse. *Les Filigranes: Dictionnaire historique des marques du papier dès leur apparition vers 1282 jusqu'en 1600*. Vol. 3. Paris: Picard et fils, 1907.

Bronner, Simon. *American Material Culture and Folklife*. Ann Arbor: University of Michigan Research Press, 1985.

Brunot, Louis, and Elie Malka. *Textes judéo-arabes de Fès*. Rabat: Institut des hautes études marocaines, 1939.

Bunis, David. "The East-West Sephardic La'az (Judeo-Spanish) Dialect Dichotomy as Reflected in Three Editions of Dat Yehudit." In *Estudios sefardíes dedicados a la memoria de Iacob M. Hassán (z"l)*, edited by Elena Romero and Aitor García Moreno, 157–190. Madrid: CSIC, 2011.

Byers, Reid. *The Private Library: The History of the Architecture and Furnishing of the Domestic Bookroom*. New Castle, DE: Oak Knoll, 2021.

Cahen, Abraham. *Les juifs dans l'Afrique septentrionale*. Constantine: L. Arnolet, 1867.

Caracciolo, Carlos. "Natural Disasters and the European Printed News Network." In *News Networks in Early Modern Europe*, edited by Joad Raymond and Noah Moxham, 756–778. Leiden: Brill, 2016.

Carlebach, Elisheva. *The Pursuit of Heresy: Rabbi Moses Hagiz and the Sabbatian Controversies*. New York: Columbia University Press, 1990.

Cazès, David. *Notes bibliographiques sur la littérature juive-tunisienne*. Tunis: Imprimerie internationale, 1893.

Chartier, Roger. *The Author's Hand and the Printer's Mind: Transformations of the Written Word in Early Modern Europe*. Boston: Wiley-Blackwell, 2013.

Chartier, Roger. *The Order of Books: Readers, Authors, and Libraries in Europe between the Fourteenth and Eighteenth Centuries*. Redwood City, CA: Stanford University Press, 1994.

Chartier, Roger, and Peter Stallybrass. "What Is a Book?" In *The Cambridge Companion to Textual Scholarship*, edited by Neil Fraistat and Julia Flanders, 188–204. Cambridge: Cambridge University Press, 2015.

Chenoufi, Moncef. "Le probleme des origines de l'imprimerie et de la presse arabe en Tunisie dans sa relation avec la Renaissance (Nahda) 1847–1887." PhD diss., Lille III, 1974.

Chetrit, Joseph (Yosef). "Haskala hébraique et haskala judéo-arabe à Tunis à la fin du XIXe siècle." In *Entre orient et occident: Juifs et Musulmans en Tunisie*, edited by Denis Cohen-Tannoudji, 289–320. Paris: Éditions de l'éclat, 2007.

Chetrit, Joseph (Yosef). "Judeo-Arabic Dialects in North Africa as Communal Languages: Lects, Polylects, and Sociolects." *Journal of Jewish Languages* 10, no. 2 (2014): 202–232.

Chetrit, Joseph (Yosef). "Textual Orality and Knowledge of Illiterate Women: The Textual Performance of Jewish Women in Morocco." In *Women and Knowledge in the Mediterranean*, edited by Fatima Sadiqi, 89–107. London: Routledge, 2013.

Chetrit, Sami Shalom. "Revisiting Bialik: A Radical Mizrahi Reading of the Jewish National Poet." *Comparative Literature* 62, no. 1 (2010): 1–21.

Chetrit, Yosef (Joseph). "Freḥa bat rabbi avraham: nosafot ʿal meshorreret ʿivriyya mi-maroqo ba-me'a ha18." *Pe'amim* 55 (1993): 124–130.

Chetrit, Yosef (Joseph). "Hitgabshutah shel leshon ha-ʿitonut ha-ʿaravit-yehudit be-tunis ba-sof ha-me'a ha-19." In *Meḥqarim ba-lashon ha-ʿivrit uve-leshonot ha-yehudim*, edited by Moshe Bar-Asher, 523–538. Jerusalem: Hebrew University, 1996.

Chetrit, Yosef (Joseph). "Moderniyyut le'umit ʿivrit mul moderniyyut ṣarfatit: ha-haskala ha-ʿivrit bi-ṣfon afriqa ba-sof ha-me'a ha-19." *Mi-qedem u-miyyam* 3 (1990): 11–76.

Chetrit, Yosef (Joseph). "Piyyuṭei freḥa bat yosef ve-te'uda ḥadasha ʿal ḥayyehah ve-motah." *Deḥaq le-sifrut tova* 1 (2011): 36–42.

Chetrit, Yosef (Joseph). "Shalom flaḥ u-ma'avaqo le-hora'at ha-ʿivrit be-vatei ha-sefer shel KI"Ḥ be-tunisya." In *Le-sharet et ʿamam be-darkam: KI"Ḥ ve-qidum ha-qehilot ha-yehudiyyot be-arṣot ha-islam*, edited by Haim Saadoun, 119–141. Jerusalem: Yad Ben Zvi, 2021.

Chouraqui, André. *Les juifs d'Afrique du Nord: Marche vers l'occident*. Paris: Presses universitaires de france, 1952.

Clancy-Smith, Julia. *Mediterraneans: North Africa and Europe in an Age of Migration, c. 1800–1900*. Oakland: University of California Press, 2011.

Cohen, Dov. "Rabbinic Attitudes towards Manifestations of Modernity and Secularism within Nineteenth-Century Sephardic Society." *Revue des études Juives* 180, no. 1 (2021): 173–192.

Cohen, Julia Phillips. "Hazan, Aron de Yosef." In *Encyclopedia of Jews in the Islamic World*, edited by Noam Stillman. Leiden: Brill, 2010.

Cohen, Julia Phillips, and Sarah Abravaya Stein. "Sephardic Scholarly Worlds: Toward a Novel Geography of Modern Jewish History." *Jewish Quarterly Review* 100, no. 3 (2010): 349–384.

Cohen, Marcel. *Le Parler Arabe des Juifs d'Alger*. Paris: Librarie Ancienne, 1912.

Cohen, Mark. "Geniza for Islamicists, Islamic Geniza, and the New Cairo Geniza." *Harvard Middle Eastern and Islamic Review* 7 (2006): 129–145.

Cohen, Mark, and Yedida Stillman. "Genizat qahir u-minhagei geniza shel yehudei ha-mizraḥ: ʿiyyun hisṭori ve-etnografi." *Pe'amim* 24, no. 1 (1985): 3–35.

Cohen, Pierre. *La presse juive editée au Maroc 1870–1963*. Rabat: Editions Bouregreg, 2007.

Cohen-Tannoudji, Denis. "La famille Cohen-Tannoudji de la tradition à la modernité." In *Entre Orient et Occident: juifs et musulmans en Tunisie,* edited by Denis Cohen-Tannoudji, 196–215. Paris: Éditions de l'éclat, 2007.

Cole, Peter, and Adina Hoffman. *Sacred Trash: The Lost and Found World of the Cairo Geniza*. New York: Schocken Books, 2011.

Cooperman, Bernard Dov. "Perché gli ebrei furono invitati a Livorno?" *Rassegna Mensile di Israel* 50, no. 9 (1984): 553–566.

Coşgel, Metin, Thomas Miceli, and Jared Rubin, "The Political Economy of Mass Printing: Legitimacy and Technological Change in the Ottoman Empire." *Journal of Comparative Economics* 40, no. 3 (2012): 357–371.

Danet, Brenda. "Books, Letters, Documents: The Changing Aesthetics of Texts in Late Print Culture." *Journal of Material Culture* 2, no. 1 (1997): 5–6.

Darnton, Robert. "'What Is the History of Books?' Revisited." *Modern Intellectual History* 4, no. 3 (2007): 495–508.

Davis, Natalie Zemon. *Society and Culture in Early Modern France*. Redwood City, CA: Stanford University Press, 1975.

Davis, Natalie Lemon. *Trickster Travels: A Sixteenth-Century Muslim between Worlds*. New York: Macmillan, 2007.

de Castries, Henry. *Les sources inédites de l'histoire du Maroc: Archives et bibliothèques d'Angleterre* 1. Paris: Ernest Leroux, 1918.

de Castries, Henry. *Les sources inédites de l'histoire du Maroc: Archives et bibliothèques de Portugal* 1. Paris: Ernest Leroux, 1934.

del Barco, Javier. *Catálogo de manuscritos hebreos de la Comunidad de Madrid, Vol. I: Manuscritos bíblicos, comentarios bíblicos de autor y obras gramaticales en las bibliotecas de El Escorial, Universidad Complutense de Madrid y Palacio Real*. Madrid: CSIC, 2003.

del Barco, Javier. "Joshua ibn Gaon's Hebrew Bibles and the Circulation of Books in the Late Medieval and Early Modern Periods." In *Patronage, Production, and Transmission of Texts in Medieval and Early Modern Jewish Cultures*, edited by Esperanza Alfonso and Jonathan Decter, 267–297. Turnhout: Brepols, 2014.

Dermenjian, Geneviève. *La crise anti-juive oranaise, 1895–1905: l'antisémitisme dans l'Algérie coloniale*. Paris: L'Harmattan, 1986.

Déroche, François, and Lbachir Tahali. "Collecting Books in Eighteenth-Century Morocco: The Bannani Library in Fez." *Studies in Manuscript Cultures* 29 (2023): 63–106.

Deshen, Shlomo. *The Mellah Society: Jewish Community Life in Sherifian Morocco*. Chicago: University of Chicago Press, 1989.

de Wilde, Anna. "Sales Catalogues of Jewish-Owned Private Libraries in the Dutch Republic during the Long Eighteenth Century: A Preliminary

Overview." In *Book Trade Catalogues in Early Modern Europe*, edited by Arthur der Weduwen, Andrew Pettegree, and Graeme Kemp, 212–248. Leiden: Brill, 2021.

Dimitrovsky, Haim Zalman. *S'ridei Bavli: An Historical and Bibliographical Introduction*. New York: Jewish Theological Seminary of America, 1979.

Drif, Benjamin. "La communauté juive de Bône (1870–1940): mutations socio-culturelles à l'époque coloniale." Master's thesis, Université Paris 1-Panthéon Sorbonne, 2015.

Dunkelgrün, Theodor. "The Kennicott Collection." In *Jewish Treasures from Oxford Libraries*, edited by Rebecca Abrams and César Merchán-Hamann, 115–158. Oxford: Oxford University Press, 2020.

Dunkelgrün, Theodor. "Like a Blind Man Judging Colors: Joseph Athias and Johannes Leusden Defend Their 1667 Hebrew Bible." *Studia Rosenthaliana* 44 (2012): 79–115.

Dweck, Yaacob. "A Jew from the East Meets Books from the West." In *Jewish Culture in Early Modern Europe: Essays in Honor of David B. Ruderman*, edited by Richard Cohen, Natalie Dohrmann, Adam Shear, and Elchanan Reiner, 239–249. Pittsburgh: University of Pittsburgh Press, 2014.

Dweck, Yaacob. *Dissident Rabbi: The Life of Jacob Sasportas*. Princeton, NJ: Princeton University Press, 2019.

Dweck, Yaacob. *The Scandal of Kabbalah: Leon Modena, Jewish Mysticism, Early Modern Venice*. Princeton, NJ: Princeton University Press, 2011.

Dweck, Yaacob. "What Is a Jewish Book?" *AJS Review* 34, no. 2 (2010): 367–375.

Dyer, Nancy Joe. "La relación del terremoto en el mediterráneo, 1504–1542." In *España y el mundo mediterráneo a través de las relaciones de sucesos*, edited by Pierre Civil, Françoise Crémoux, and Jacobo S. Sanz Hermida, 141–156. Salamanca: Ediciones Universidad de Salamanca, 2008.

Eisenstein, Elizabeth. *The Printing Press as an Agent of Change: Communications and Cultural Transformations in Early Modern Europe*. Cambridge: Cambridge University Press, 1979.

Elbaz, André. "Tefuṣat ha-sefarim ha-ʿivriyyim be-qerev ḥakhmei fes ba-me'a ha-18." *Mi-kedem umi-yam* 9 (2006): 37–46.

Elbaz, Vanessa Paloma. "Kol b'Isha Erva: The Silencing of Jewish Women's Oral Traditions in Morocco." In *Women and Social Change in North Africa: What Counts as Revolutionary?*, edited by Doris H. Gray and Nadia Sonneveld, 263–288. Cambridge: Cambridge University Press, 2017.

Eliot, Simon, and Jonathan Rose. "Introduction." In *A Companion to the History of the Book*, edited by Simon Eliot and Jonathan Rose, 1–6. Boston: Wiley-Blackwell, 2007.

Elizur, Shulamit, ed. *From Oblivion to the Bookshelf: The 150th Anniversary of Mekize Nirdamim*. Jerusalem: Mekize Nirdamim, 2013.

Elkayam, Shlomo. "Ḥiddushei lashon be-kitvei rabbi shlomo zarqa." *Pe'amim* 71 (1997): 10–24.

El Shamsy, Ahmed. *Rediscovering the Islamic Classics: How Editors and Print Culture Transformed an Intellectual Tradition*. Princeton, NJ: Princeton University Press, 2020.

Epstein, Marc Michael, ed. *Skies of Parchment, Seas of Ink: Jewish Illuminated Manuscripts*. Princeton, NJ: Princeton University Press, 2015.

Evri, Yuval, and Almog Behar. "Between East and West: Controversies over the Modernization of Hebrew Culture in the Works of Shaul Abdallah Yosef and Ariel Bension." *Journal of Modern Jewish Studies* 16, no. 2 (2017): 295–311.

Feigensohn, Samuel Meir. "Le-toldot defus rom." In *Yahadut lita*, edited by Natan Goren, 268–302. Tel Aviv: Am Ha-sefer, 1959.

Fenton, Paul, and David Littman, *Exile in the Maghreb: Jews under Islam, Sources and Documents, 997–1912*. Lanham, MD: Rowman & Littlefield, 2016.

Filippini, Jean-Pierre. "La ballottazione a Livorno nel settecento." *La Rassegna Mensile di Israel* 49 (1983): 199–268.

Finzi, Silvia. "Elia Finzi, imprimeur de père en fils." In *Métiers et professions des Italiens de Tunisie*, edited by Silvia Finzi, 278–284. Tunis: Éditions Finzi, 2003.

Fiori, Hermann. *Bibliographie des ouvrages imprimés à Alger de 1830 à 1850*. Paris: Besson, 1938.

Fisher, Benjamin. "From Boxes and Cabinets to the *Bibliotheca*: Building the Jewish Library of the Ex-Conversos in Amsterdam, 1620–1665." *European Journal of Jewish Studies* 13, no. 1 (2019): 43–76.

Fishman, Talya. *Becoming the People of the Talmud: Oral Torah as Written Tradition in Medieval Jewish Cultures*. Philadelphia: University of Pennsylvania Press, 2011.

Fowler, Alastair. *The Mind of the Book: Pictorial Title-Pages*. Oxford: Oxford University Press, 2017.

Fraenkel, Jacqueline. "L'Imprimerie Hébraique à Djerba." PhD diss., University of Paris, 1982.

Freimann, Aron. "Typograpisches." *Zeitschrift fuür hebraeische Bibliographie* 14 (1910): 79.

Friedman, Matti. *The Aleppo Codex: In Pursuit of One of the World's Most Coveted, Sacred, and Mysterious Books*. New York: Workman, 2012.

Fumagalli, Pier Francesco. "Hebrew Books in Italian Libraries of the Modern Age." *Aevum* 85, no. 3 (2011): 819–834.

Funaro, Liana. "A Mediterranean Diaspora: Jews from Leghorn in the Second Half of the Nineteenth Century." In *L'Europe Méditerranéenne*, edited by Marta Petricioli, 95–110. Brussels: Peter Lang, 2008.

Gaon, Moshe-David. *Yehudei ha-mizrah be-ereṣ yisrael*. Vol. 2. Jerusalem: Azriel, 1938.

Gerber, Jane. *Jewish Society in Fez 1450–1700: Studies in Communal and Economic Life*. Leiden: Brill, 1980.

Gerber, Jane. "Refuge in Morocco after 1492." In *Jews and Muslims in Morocco: Their Intersecting Worlds*, edited by Joseph Chetrit, Jane Gerber, and Drora Arussy, 15–38. Lanham, MD: Lexington Books, 2021.

Gerber, Noah. *Anu o sifrei ha-qodesh shebe-yadenu? Ha-gilui ha-tarbuti shel yahadut teman*. Jerusalem: Ben-Zvi Institute, 2012.

Gillam, Stanley George. *The Building Accounts of the Radcliffe Camera*. Oxford: Clarendon, 1958.

Ginio, Alisa Meyuhas. "The History of the Me'am Lo'ez: A Ladino Commentary on the Bible." *European Judaism* 43, no. 2 (2010): 117–125.

Glickman, Mark. *Sacred Treasure—the Cairo Genizah: The Amazing Discoveries of Forgotten History in an Egyptian Synagogue Attic*. Woodstock, VT: Jewish Lights, 2011.

Glicksberg, Shlomo. "Rabbi david hakohen-sqali: pesiqa mesortit be-'idan shel temurot." In *Yehudei aljiria ve-luv*, edited by Moshe Halamish, Moshe Amar, and Maurice Roumani, 134–155. Tel Aviv: Bar-Ilan University Press, 2014.

Goitein, S. D. *A Mediterranean Society: The Jewish Communities of the Arab World as Portrayed in the Documents of the Cairo Geniza*. Oakland: University of California Press, 1967–1993.

Goldberg, Harvey. "Sephardi Rabbinic 'Openness' in Nineteenth-Century Tripoli: Examining a Modern Myth in Context." In *Jewish Religious Leadership: Image and Reality*, edited by Jack Wertheimer, vol. 2, 695–714. Jewish Theological Seminary Press, 2004.

Goldberg, Harvey. "Some Cautionary Tales from an Anthropological Romance with Jews from Libya." In *Serendipity in Anthropological Research: The Nomadic Turn*, edited by Haim Hazan and Esther Hertzog, 109–122. London: Routledge, 2012.

Goldenberg, André. *Art and the Jews of Morocco*. Paris: Somogy Éditions d'Art, 2014.

Gordin, Alexander. "Hebrew Incunabula in the National Library of Israel as a Source for Early Modern Book History in Europe and Beyond." In *Printing R-Evolution and Society 1450–1500: Fifty Years That Changed Europe*, edited by Cristina Dondi, 321–338. Venice: Edizioni Ca'Foscari, 2020.

Gottreich, Emily. *Jewish Morocco: A History from Pre-Islamic to Postcolonial Times*. London: I.B. Tauris, 2020.

Gottreich, Emily. *The Mellah of Marrakech: Jewish and Muslim Space in Morocco's Red City*. Bloomington: Indiana University Press, 2007.

Gottreich, Emily. "Of Messiahs and Sultans: Shabbetai Zevi and Early Modernity in Morocco." *Journal of Modern Jewish Studies* 12, no. 2 (2013): 184–209.

Gottreich, Emily, and Daniel Schroeter. "Introduction: Rethinking Jewish Culture and Society in North Africa." In *Jewish Culture and Society in North Africa*, edited by Emily Gottreich and Daniel Schroeter, 3–23. Bloomington: Indiana University Press, 2011.

Grafton, Anthony. *Humanists with Inky Fingers: The Culture of Correction in Renaissance Europe*. London: British Library, 2011.

Gries, Zeev. *The Book in the Jewish World, 1700–1900*. Liverpool: Littman Library of Jewish Civilization, 2007.

Guedj, David. "Judeo-Arabic Popular Nonfiction in Morocco during the First Half of the Twentieth Century." *Quest: Issues in Contemporary Jewish History* 22 (2022): 78–108.

Guetta, Alessandro. *Philosophy and Kabbalah: Elijah Benamozegh and the Reconciliation of Western Thought and Eastern Esotericism*. Translated by Helena Kahan. Albany: SUNY Press, 2009.

Gutwirth, Eleazar. "Techne and Culture: Printers and Readers in Fifteenth-Century Hispano-Jewish Communities." In *The Late Medieval Hebrew Book in the Western Mediterranean: Hebrew Manuscripts and Incunabula in Context*, edited by Javier del Barco, 338–367. Leiden: Brill, 2015.

Habermann, Avraham Meir. *Sha'arei sefarim 'ivriyyim*. Safed: Museum of the Art of Printing, 1969.

Hacker, Joseph. "Jewish Book Owners and Their Libraries in the Iberian Peninsula, Fourteenth-Fifteenth Centuries." In *The Late Medieval Hebrew Book in the Western Mediterranean: Hebrew Manuscripts and Incunabula in Context*, edited by Javier del Barco, 70–104. Leiden: Brill, 2015.

Hacker, Joseph, and Adam Shear, eds. *The Hebrew Book in Early Modern Italy*. Philadelphia: University of Pennsylvania Press, 2011.

Ḥagège, Daniel. *Intishar al-ktayib al-yahudiyya al-barbariyya al-tunisiyya*. Sousse: Makhlouf Nadjar, 1939.

Hakohen, Eliyahu. "Ḥokhmat ha-magnetismus." *'Et-mol* 12, no. 3 (1987): 10–11.

Halbertal, Moshe. *People of the Book: Canon, Meaning, and Authority*. Cambridge, MA: Harvard University Press, 1997.

Hanna, Nelly. *In Praise of Books: A Cultural History of Cairo's Middle Class, Sixteenth through the Eighteenth Century*. Syracuse, NY: Syracuse University Press, 2003.

Hannoum, Abdelmajid. *The Invention of the Maghreb: Between Africa and the Middle East*. Cambridge: Cambridge University Press, 2021.

Harel, Yaron. "The Edict to Destroy *Em Lamikra*—Aleppo, 1865." *Hebrew Union College Annual* 64 (1993): 27–36.

Harkavy, Alexander. *Der amerikanisher lehrer: A praktishes lehr-bikhel fir yeden eingevanderten yiden vos vil kenen english un veren bekant mit amerika—The American Teacher: Practical Manual of the English Language and American Institutions*. New York: J. Katzenelenbogen, 1897.

Hazan, Ephraim. "The Literary Activity of R. Isaac Morali and His Plan to Collect the Hebrew Poetry of Algeria." *Pe'amim* 91 (2002): 65–78.

Heckman, Alma. *The Sultan's Communists: Moroccan Jews and the Politics of Belonging*. Redwood City, CA: Stanford University Press, 2020.

Heller, Marvin. *Further Studies in the Making of the Early Hebrew Book*. Leiden: Brill, 2013.

Heller, Marvin. "Often Overlooked: Examples of Front-Matter in Early Hebrew Books." *Quntres: An Online Journal for the History of the Jewish Book* 2, no. 1 (2011): 1–21.

Heller, Marvin. *Printing the Talmud: A History of the Earliest Printed Editions of the Talmud*. Brooklyn: Im Hasefer, 1992.

Heller, Marvin. *The Seventeenth Century Hebrew Book*. Leiden: Brill, 2011.

Heller, Marvin. *Studies in the Making of the Early Hebrew Book*. Leiden: Brill, 2007.

Hershenzon, Daniel. "Traveling Libraries: The Arabic Manuscripts of Muley Zidan and the Escorial Library." *Journal of Early Modern History* 18, no. 6 (2014): 535–558.

Hervias, Varela, and Von Waldheim. *Una relación alemana sobre el terremoto de Andalucia, Marruecos, y Azores del año 1522*. Madrid: Comisión de Cultura, 1948.

Hillel, Moshe. *Ohel Ra"m: Catalogue of the Manuscripts in the Library of Rabbi Avraham Mordechai Alter of Gur*. Jerusalem: Kehilot Yisrael, 2018.

Hirschberg, Haim Zeev. *A History of the Jews in North Africa*. Leiden: Brill, 1974.

Hirschberg, Haim Zeev. *Me-ereṣ mevo ha-shemesh: 'im yehudei afriqa ha-ṣfonit be-arṣotehem*. Jerusalem: Jewish Agency, 1957.

Hirschberg, Haim Zeev. *Toldot ha-yehudim be-afriqa ha-ṣfonit*. Jerusalem: Bialik, 1965.

Hirschler, Konrad. *A Monument to Medieval Syrian Book Culture: The Library of Ibn ʿAbd Al-Hādī*. Edinburgh: Edinburgh University Press, 2021.

Hoffman, Eva. "Pathways of Portability: Islamic and Christian Interchange from the Tenth to the Twelfth Century." *Art History* 24, no. 1 (2001): 17–50.

Howsam, Leslie. *Old Books and New Histories: An Orientation to Studies in Book and Print Culture*. Toronto: University of Toronto Press, 2006.

Howsam, Leslie. "The Study of Book History." In *The Cambridge Companion to the History of the Book*, edited by Leslie Howsam, 1–16. Cambridge: Cambridge University Press, 2015.

Hui, Andrew. *The Study: The Inner Life of Renaissance Libraries*. Princeton, NJ: Princeton University Press, 2024.

Iakerson, Shimon. "Unknown Sephardi Incunabula." In *The Late Medieval Hebrew Book in the Western Mediterranean: Hebrew Manuscripts and Incunabula in Context*, edited by Javier del Barco, 297–312. Leiden: Brill, 2015.

Israel, Jonathan. "The Jews of Spanish Oran and Their Expulsion in 1669." *Mediterranean Historical Review* 9, no. 2 (1994): 235–255.

Jefferson, Rebecca J. W. *The Cairo Genizah and the Age of Discovery in Egypt: The History and Provenance of a Jewish Archive*. London: Bloomsbury Academic, 2022.

Jefferson, Rebecca J. W. "Deconstructing 'the Cairo Genizah': A Fresh Look at Genizah Manuscript Discoveries in Cairo before 1897." *Jewish Quarterly Review* 108, no. 4 (2018): 422–448.

Jeppie, Shamil, and Souleymane Bachir Diagne, eds. *The Meanings of Timbuktu*. Cape Town: Human Sciences Research Council, 2008.

Johns, Adrian. *The Nature of the Book: Print and Knowledge in the Making*. Chicago: University of Chicago Press, 1998.

Johns, Adrian, and Elizabeth Eisenstein. "'An Unacknowledged Revolution Revisited' and 'How to Acknowledge a Revolution.'" *American Historical Review* 107, no. 1 (2002): 87–125.

Kalman, Julie. *The Kings of Algiers: How Two Jewish Families Shaped the Mediterranean World During the Napoleonic Wars and Beyond*. Princeton, NJ: Princeton University Press, 2023.

Kaplan, Yosef. "The Libraries of Three Sephardi Rabbis in Early Modern Western Europe." In *Libraries and Book Collections*, edited by Yosef Kaplan and Moshe Sluhovsky, 225–260. Jerusalem: Shazar, 2006.

Karkason, Tamir. "Between 'Pure Faith' and 'Faithful Enlightenment': The Thought of Shalom Flah (1855–1936) against the Background of the Transformations in Tunisian Jewry." In *Beyond Cultural Identity: The Jews of Polyphony, Relationality and Translation in Muslim Contexts*, edited by Ottfried Fraisse. Berlin: De Gruyter, forthcoming.

Karkason, Tamir. "Between Two Poles: Barukh Mitrani between Moderate Haskalah and Jewish Nationalism." *Zutot* 18 (2021): 14–25.

Kaspi, André, ed. *Histoire de l'Alliance israélite universelle de 1860 à nos jours*. Paris: Armand Colin, 2010.

Katz, Ethan. *The Burdens of Brotherhood: Jews and Muslims from North Africa to France*. Cambridge, MA: Harvard University Press, 2015.

Kelly, William. *Presswork: A Practical Handbook for the Use of Pressmen and Their Apprentices*. 2nd ed. Chicago: Inland, 1902.

Kiron, Arthur. *The Belforte Publishing House and the Art of Ladino Printing*. Livorno: Salomone Belforte, 2005.

Kiron, Arthur. "Studying the Jewish Book: A Review." *Judaica Librarianship* 14 (2008): 80–87.

Klagsbald, Victor. *Catalogue des manuscrits marocains de la collection Klagsbald*. Paris: Editions du Centre national de la recherche scientifique, 1980.

Klagsbald, Victor. "À propos de l'illustration du chandelier à sept branches sur un acte de mariage." *Jewish Art* 19/20 (1994): 248–250.

Kogman-Appel, Katrin. "Coping with Christian Pictorial Sources: What Did Jewish Miniaturists Not Paint?" *Speculum* 75, no. 4 (2000): 816–858.

Kogman-Appel, Katrin. "'Elisha ben Abraham, Known as Cresques': Scribe, Illuminator, and Mapmaker in Fourteenth-Century Mallorca." *Ars Judaica* 10 (2014): 27–36.

Kogman-Appel, Katrin. *Illuminating in Micrography: The Catalan Micrography Mahzor—MS Heb 8.6527 in the National Library of Israel*. Leiden: Brill, 2013.

Kogman-Appel, Katrin. *Jewish Book Art between Islam and Christianity: The Decoration of Hebrew Bibles in Medieval Spain*. Leiden: Brill, 2004.

Kohen, Binyamin Refael. *Sefer malkhei tarshish*. Netivot: B. Kohen, 1986.

Kosansky, Oren. "When Jews Speak Arabic: Dialectology and Difference in Colonial Morocco." *Comparative Studies in Society and History* 58, no. 1 (2016): 5–39.

Lambourn, Elizabeth. *Abraham's Luggage: A Social Life of Things in the Medieval Indian Ocean World*. Cambridge: Cambridge University Press, 2018.

Land, Joy A. "Corresponding Women: Female Educators of the Alliance Israélite Universelle in Tunisia, 1882–1914." In *Jewish Culture and*

Society in North Africa, edited by Emily Gottreich and Daniel Schroeter, 239–256. Bloomington: Indiana University Press, 2011.

Laskier, Michael. *The* Alliance Israélite Universelle *and the Jewish Communities of Morocco, 1862–1962*. Albany: SUNY Press, 1983.

Laskier, Michael. "Aspects of the Activities of the Alliance Israélite Universelle in the Jewish Communities of the Middle East and North Africa: 1860–1918." *Modern Judaism* 3, no. 2 (1983): 147–171.

Laskier, Michael. *North African Jewry in the Twentieth Century: The Jews of Morocco, Tunisia, and Algeria*. New York: New York University Press, 1994.

Leff, Lisa Moses. *Sacred Bonds of Solidarity: The Rise of Jewish Internationalism in Nineteenth-Century France*. Redwood City, CA: Stanford University Press, 2006.

Le Gall, Michel, and Kenneth Perkins, eds. *The Maghrib in Question: Essays in History and Historiography*. Austin: University of Texas Press, 1997.

Lehmann, Matthias. *Emissaries from the Holy Land: The Sephardic Diaspora and the Practice of Pan-Judaism in the Eighteenth Century*. Redwood City, CA: Stanford University Press, 2014.

Lehmann, Matthias. "Introduction: Sephardi Identities." *Jewish Social Studies* 15, no. 1 (2008): 1–9.

Lehmann, Matthias. *Ladino Rabbinic Literature and Ottoman Sephardic Culture*. Bloomington: Indiana University Press, 2005.

Lehmann, Matthias. "'Levantinos' and Other Jews: Reading H. Y. D. Azulai's Travel Diary." *Jewish Social Studies* 13, no. 3 (2007): 1–34.

le Roux, Elizabeth. "Book History in the African World: The State of the Discipline." *Book History* 15 (2012): 248–300.

Leven, Narcisse. *Cinquante ans d'histoire: L'Alliance israélite universelle (1860–1910), Vol. II*. Paris: Félix Alcan, 1920.

Levin, Shalom-Dovber. *Mibeis Hagenozim: Treasures from the Chabad Library*. New York: Kehot, 2009.

Levy, Lital. *Global Haskalah: Translation, World Literature, and Jewish Modernity*. Forthcoming.

Levy, Lital. *Poetic Trespass: Writing between Hebrew and Arabic in Israel/Palestine*. Princeton, NJ: Princeton University Press, 2014.

Levy, Lital. "Reorienting Hebrew Literary History: The View from the East." *Prooftexts* 29, no. 2 (2009): 127–172.

Liebrenz, Boris. "The Library of Ahmad al-Rabbat: Books and Their Audience in 12th to 13th/18th to 19th Century Syria." In *Marginal Perspectives on Early Modern Ottoman Culture: Missionaries, Travellers, Booksellers*, edited by Ralf Elger and Ute Pietruschka, 17–59. Halle: Zentrum für Interdisziplinäre Regionalstudien, 2013.

Lipiner, Elias. *Os baptizados em pé: estudos acerca da origem e da luta dos Cristãos-novos em Portugal*. Lisbon: Vega, 1998.

Love, Harold. *The Culture and Commerce of Texts: Scribal Publication in Seventeenth-Century England*. 2nd ed. Amherst: University of Massachusetts Press, 1998.

Love, Harold. "Early Modern Print Culture: Assessing the Models." *Parergon* 20, no. 1 (2003): 45–64.

Lydon, Ghislaine, and Graziano Krätli, eds. *The Trans-Saharan Book Trade: Manuscript Culture, Arabic Literacy and Intellectual History in Muslim Africa*. Leiden: Brill, 2011.

Madan, Falconer. *A Summary Catalogue of Western Manuscripts in the Bodleian Library at Oxford*. Vol. 5. Oxford: Oxford University Press, 1905.

Mandel, Maud. *Muslims and Jews in France: History of a Conflict*. Princeton, NJ: Princeton University Press, 2014.

Mann, Vivian, ed. *Morocco: Jews and Art in a Muslim Land*. New York: Jewish Museum, 2000.

Mann, Vivian. "The Unknown Jewish Artists of Medieval Iberia." In *The Jew in Medieval Iberia, 1100–1500*, edited by Jonathan Ray, 138–175. Boston: Academic Studies, 2013.

Manor, Dan. "Abraham Sabba: His Life and Work." *Jerusalem Studies in Jewish Thought* 2, no. 2 (1983): 208–231.

Mansouri, Mabrouk. "The Image of the Jews among Ibadi Imazighen in North Africa before the Tenth Century." In *Jewish Culture and Society in North Africa*, edited by Emily Gottreich and Daniel Schroeter, 45–58. Bloomington: Indiana University Press, 2011.

Marglin, Jessica. *Across Legal Lines: Jews and Muslims in Modern Morocco*. New Haven, CT: Yale University Press, 2016.

Marglin, Jessica. *The Shamama Case: Contesting Citizenship across the Modern Mediterranean*. Princeton, NJ: Princeton University Press, 2022.

Margolis, Michelle, Marjorie Lehman, Adam Shear, and Joshua Teplitsky. "Footprints: A Digital Approach to (Jewish) Book History." *European Journal of Jewish Studies* 17 (2023): 1–30.

Marṣiano, Eliyahu Refael. *Sefer bnei melakhim: ve-hu toldot ha-sefer ha-ʿivri ba-maroqo mi-shnat 5277 ʿad shnat 5749*. Jerusalem: Mekhon haRaShaM, 1989.

Marṣiano, Eliyahu Refael. *Sefer malkhei yeshurun*. Jerusalem: Mekhon haRaShaM, 1999.

Marṣiano, Eliyahu Refael. "Terumat rabbanei ereṣ yisrael li-defus ha-ʿivri ba-maroqo." In *Meḥqarim be-tarbutam shel yehudei ṣfon afriqa*, edited by Issachar Ben-Ami, 309–312. Jerusalem: Rubin Mass, 1991.

Marṣiano, Eliyahu Refael. *Yaḥas debdu he-ḥadash: toldoteha shel qehilat debdu ve-yiḥus mishpeḥoteha*. Jerusalem: Mekhon haRaShaM, 1997.

Mattes, Mark. "Toward an Archaeology of Manuscripts." *Eighteenth-Century Studies* 55, no. 4 (2022): 545–552.

May, Steven. *English Renaissance Manuscript Culture: The Paper Revolution*. Oxford: Oxford University Press, 2023.

McKenzie, D. F. *Bibliography and the Sociology of Texts*. Cambridge: Cambridge University Press, 1999.

McKenzie, D. F. *Making Meaning: "Printers of the Mind" and Other Essays*. Amherst: University of Massachusetts Press, 2002.

Meakin, James Budgett. "The Jews of Morocco." *Jewish Quarterly Review* 4, no. 3 (1892): 369–396.

Meir, Jonatan. *Kabbalistic Circles in Jerusalem, 1896–1948*. Leiden: Brill, 2016.

Meir, Yakov Z. *Editio Princeps: The 1523 Venice Edition of the Palestinian Talmud and the Beginning of Hebrew Printing*. Jerusalem: Magnes, 2022.

Messas, Yosef. "Introduction." In *Ner ha-maʿarav*, ed. Yaʿaqov Moshe Tolédano, 2nd ed, i–iv. Jerusalem: Abécassis Brothers, 1973.

Miller, Susan Gilson. *Disorienting Encounters: Travels of a Moroccan Scholar in France in 1845–1846*. Oakland: University of California Press, 1992.

Miller, Susan Gilson. "Moïse Nahon and the Invention of the Modern Maghrebi Jew." In *French Mediterraneans: Transnational and Imperial Histories*, edited by Patricia Lorcin and Todd Shepard, 293–319. Lincoln: University of Nebraska Press, 2016.

Mintz, Sharon Liberman, and Elka Deitsch. "From Marrakech to Milan: The Artistic Journey of Makhluf/Michele Allun." In *Windows on Jewish Worlds: Essays in Honor of William Gross, Collector Extraordinaire*, edited by Shalom Sabar, Emile Schrijver, and Falk Weisemann, 272–285. Zutphen: Walburg Pers, 2019.

Moreh, Shmuel. "The Nineteenth-Century Jewish Playwright Abraham Daninos as a Bridge between Muslim and Jewish Theater." In *Judaism and Islam: Boundaries, Communications, and Interaction*, edited by William Brinner and Benjamin Hary, 409–416. Leiden: Brill, 2000.

Mouliéras, Auguste. *Fez: ouvrage illustré de 12 photographies prises au cours de la mission de l'auteur à Fez*. Paris: A. Challamel, 1902.

Mroczek, Eva. "Batshit Stories: New Tales of Discovering Ancient Texts." *Marginalia Review*, June 22, 2018.

Mroczek, Eva. *Out of the Cave: The Possibility of a New Scriptural Past*. Forthcoming.

Murray-Miller, Gavin. *The Cult of the Modern: Trans-Mediterranean France and the Construction of French Modernity*. Lincoln: University of Nebraska Press, 2017.

Naar, Devin. "Fashioning the 'Mother of Israel': The Ottoman Jewish Historical Narrative and the Image of Jewish Salonica." *Jewish History* 28 (2014): 337–372.

Nahon, Gérard. "D'où venaient les livres hebreux étudiés dans les communautés juives d'Algérie au XVIIe et au XVIIIe siècle?" In *International Conference on Jewish Communities in Muslim Lands*, 1–28. Jerusalem: Ben-Zvi Institute, 1974.

Nahon, Gérard. "Livres anciens du Tribunal rabbinique d'Oran." In *Présence juive au Maghreb: hommage à Haïm Zafrani*, edited by Joseph Tedghi and Nicole Serfaty, 143–146. Saint-Denis: Éditions Bouchène, 2004.

Narkiss, Bezalel. "A List of Hebrew Books (1330) and a Contract to Illuminate Manuscripts (1335) from Majorca." *Revue des Études Juives* 70 (1961): 297–320.

Narkiss, Bezalel, and Aliza Cohen-Mushlin. *The Kennicott Bible: An Introduction*. London: Facsimile, 1985.

Neubauer, Adolf. *Mediaeval Jewish Chronicles and Chronological Notes*. Oxford: Oxford University Press, 1887.

Newman, Daniel. "The Arabic Literary Language: The Nahda (and Beyond)." In *The Oxford Handbook of Arabic Linguistics*, edited by Jonathan Owens, 472–494. Oxford: Oxford University Press, 2013.

Nini, Yehuda. "Lettres choisies de R. Ya'aqov Ibn Tsur." *Michael: On the History of the Jews in the Diaspora* 5 (1978): 192–214.

Nizri, Yigal. "Judeo-Moroccan Traditions and the Age of European Expansionism in North Africa." In *The Sephardic Atlantic: Colonial Histories and Postcolonial Perspectives*, edited by Sina Rauschenbach and Jonathan Schorsch, 333–360. London: Palgrave Macmillan, 2018.

Nizri, Yigal. "Sharifan Subjects, Rabbinic Texts: Moroccan Halakhic Writing, 1860–1918." PhD diss., New York University, 2014.

Nizri, Yigal. "Writing against Loss: Moroccan Jewish Book Culture in a Time of Disaster." *Jewish Social Studies* 26, no. 1 (2020): 91–100.

Offenberg, Adri. "What Do We Know about Hebrew Printing in Guadalajara, Híjar, and Zamora?" In *The Late Medieval Hebrew Book in the*

Western Mediterranean: Hebrew Manuscripts and Incunabula in Context, edited by Javier del Barco, 313–337. Leiden: Brill, 2015.

Ofrath, Avner. "*The Harbinger of Good* by Shalom Bekache, 1884." *Absinthe: World Literature in Translation* 29 (2024): 186–194.

Ogren, Brian, trans. "*Minḥat Yehudah* (The Offering of Judah): Commentary on *Ma'arekhet ha-elohut* (The Divine Hierarchy), 1558." In *The Posen Library of Jewish Culture and Civilization,* vol. 5, edited by Yosef Kaplan, 94–95. New Haven, CT: Yale University Press, 2023.

Ohana, Michal. "Rabbi ḥayyim bliyyaḥ: maskil 'ivri u-mamshikha shel ha-hagut ha-yehudit ha-sfaradit." *Pe'amim* 154/155 (2018): 163–196.

Oliel-Grausz, Evelyne. "Networks and Communication in the Sephardi Diaspora: An Added Dimension to the Concept of Port Jews and Port Jewries." *Jewish Culture and History* 7 (2004): 61–76.

Oliel, Jacob. *Les Juifs au Sahara: le Touat au moyen âge*. Paris: CNRS Éditions, 1994.

Olszowy-Schlanger, Judith. "An Early Palimpsest Scroll of the Book of Kings from the Cairo Geniza." In *"From a Sacred Source": Genizah Studies in Honour of Professor Stefan C. Reif,* edited by Ben Outhwaite and Siam Bhayro, 237–247. Leiden: Brill, 2010.

Ortega-Monasterio, Maria Theresa. "Some Hebrew Bibles in the Bodleian Library: The Kennicott Collection." *Journal of Semitic Studies* 62, no. 1 (2017): 93–111.

Ovadia, David. *Fes ve-ḥakhameha: divrei yemei ha-yehudim be-qehillat qodesh fes*. Jerusalem: Beit Oved, 1978–1979.

Parks, Richard. "Scemmama, Nessim." In *Encyclopedia of Jews in the Islamic World,* edited by Noam Stillman. Leiden: Brill, 2010.

Parush, Iris. *Reading Jewish Women: Marginality and Modernization in Nineteenth-Century Eastern European Jewish Society*. Waltham, MA: Brandeis University Press, 2004.

Pearce, S. J. *The Andalusi Literary and Intellectual Tradition: The Role of Arabic in Judah Ibn Tibbon's Ethical Will*. Bloomington: Indiana University Press, 2017.

Pearce, S. J. "'His (Jewish) Nation and His (Muslim) King': Modern Nationalism Articulated through Medieval Andalusi Poetry." In *'His Pen and Ink Are a Powerful Mirror': Andalusi, Judaeo-Arabic, and Other Near Eastern Studies in Honor of Ross Brann,* edited by Adam Bursi, S. J. Pearce, and Hamza Zafer, 140–162. Leiden: Brill, 2020.

Pektaş, Nil. "The Beginnings of Printing in the Ottoman Capital: Book Production and Circulation in Early Modern Istanbul." *Osmanlı Bilimi Araştırmaları* 16, no. 2 (2015): 3–32.

Peláez, José, M. Chourak, B. A. Tadili, L. Aït Brahim, M. Hamdache, C. López Casado, and J. M. Martínez Solares. "A Catalog of Main Moroccan Earthquakes from 1045 to 2005." *Seismological Research Letters* 78, no. 6 (2007): 614–621.

Pettegree, Andrew. *The Book in the Renaissance*. New Haven, CT: Yale University Press, 2011.

Pettegree, Andrew. "The Legion of the Lost: Recovering the Lost Books of Early Modern Europe." In *Lost Books: Reconstructing the Print World of Pre-Industrial Europe*, edited by Flavia Bruni and Andrew Pettegree, 1–27. Leiden: Brill, 2016.

Pettegree, Andrew, and Arthur der Weduwen. *The Library: A Fragile History*. London: Profile Books, 2021.

Phillips, Angus. "Coda: Does the Book Have a Future?" In *A Companion to the History of the Book*, edited by Simon Eliot and Jonathan Rose, 547–559. Boston: Wiley-Blackwell, 2007.

Picard, Joshua. "Tunisian Judaeo-Arabic Essays on Religion and Ideology in the Late-Nineteenth Century." Master's thesis, Brandeis University, 2016.

Preston, Cathy Lynn, and Michael James Preston, eds. *The Other Print Tradition: Essays on Chapbooks, Broadsides, and Related Ephemera*. London: Routledge, 1995.

Price, Leah. *How to Do Things with Books in Victorian Britain*. Princeton, NJ: Princeton University Press, 2012.

Rabinowitz, Dan. *The Lost Library: The Legacy of Vilna's Strashun Library in the Aftermath of the Holocaust*. Waltham, MA: Brandeis University Press, 2019.

Ravid, Benjamin. "A Tale of Three Cities and Their Raison d'Etat: Ancona, Venice, Livorno, and the Competition for Jewish Merchants in the Sixteenth Century." *Mediterranean Historical Review* 6, no. 2 (1991): 138–162.

Ray, Jonathan. *After Expulsion: 1492 and the Making of Sephardic Jewry*. New York: New York University Press, 2013.

Raz-Krakotzkin, Amnon. *The Censor, the Editor, and the Text: The Catholic Church and the Shaping of the Jewish Canon in the Sixteenth Century*. Philadelphia: University of Pennsylvania Press, 2007.

Reese, Scott, ed. *Manuscript and Print in the Islamic Tradition*. Berlin: De Gruyter, 2022.

Reicherter, Klaus, and Peter Becker-Heidmann. "Tsunami Deposits in the Western Mediterranean: Remains of the 1522 Almería Earthquake?" *Geological Society Special Publications* 316 (2009): 217–235.

Reif, Stefan. "A Centennial Assessment of Genizah Studies." In *The Cambridge Genizah Collections: Their Contents and Significance*, edited by Stefan Reif, 1–35. Cambridge: Cambridge University Press, 2002.

Reiman, Alyssa. "Claiming Livorno: Citizenship, Commerce, and Culture in the Italian Jewish Diaspora: Bridging Europe and the Mediterranean." In *Italian Jewish Networks from the Seventeenth to the Twentieth Century*, edited by Francesca Bregoli, Carlotta Ferrara degli Uberti, and Guri Schwarz, 81–100. London: Palgrave Macmillan, 2018.

Reyzen, Zalmen. *Leksikon fun yidisher literatur*. Vilna: Wilner, 1926.

Richler, Benjamin. "Manuscripts and Manuscript Collections." In *Encyclopedia of Jews in the Islamic World*, edited by Noam Stillman. Leiden: Brill, 2010.

Richler, Benjamin. "The Scribe Moses ben Jacob Ibn Zabara of Spain: A Moroccan Saint?" *Jewish Art* 18 (1992): 141–147.

Rickards, Maurice. *Collecting Printed Ephemera*. London: Christie's, 1988.

Rickards, Maurice, and Michael Twyman. *The Encyclopedia of Ephemera*. London: Routledge, 2000.

Riegler, Michael. "The Distribution of the Jewish Communities in North Africa according to the Medieval Hebrew Manuscripts Copied There." In *Progress and Tradition: Creativity, Leadership and Acculturation Processes among the Jews of North Africa*, edited by Moises Orfali and Ephraim Hazan, 171–178. Jerusalem: Bialik Institute, 2005.

Riegler, Michael. "Ma'atiqei sefarim mi-megorashei sfarad ve-hemshekh pe'ilotam be-arṣot qeliṭatam." In *Ḥevra ve-tarbut: yehudei sfarad le-aḥar ha-gerush*, edited by Michael Abitbol, Galit Hasan-Rokem, and Yom-Tov Assis, 188–201. Jerusalem: Misgav Yerushalayim, 1997.

Riegler, Michael. "Were the Yeshivot in Spain Centers for the Copying of Books?" *Sefarad* 57, no. 2 (1997): 373–398.

Riegler, Michael, and Judith Baskin. "'May the Writer Be Strong': Medieval Hebrew Manuscripts Copied by and for Women." *Nashim* 16, no. 2 (2008): 9–28.

Roditi, Édouard. "The Me'am Lo'ez and Its Various Editions." *European Judaism* 26, no. 1 (1993): 17–23.

Rodrigue, Aron. *French Jews, Turkish Jews: The Alliance Israélite Universelle and the Politics of Jewish Schooling in Turkey, 1860–1925*. Bloomington: Indiana University Press, 1990.

Rodríguez, Miguel Ángel Manzano. "Ibn Abī Zar'." In *Encyclopaedia of Islam*, 3rd ed. Leiden: Brill, 2007.

Roper, Geoffrey. "Printed in Europe, Consumed in Ottoman Lands: European Books in the Middle East, 1514–1842." In *Books in Motion in Early Modern Europe: Beyond Production, Circulation and Consumption*, edited by Daniel Bellingradt, Paul Nelles, and Jeroen Salman, 267–288. London: Palgrave Macmillan, 2017.

Roper, Geoffrey. "The Printing Press and Change in the Arab World." In *Agent of Change: Print Culture Studies after Elizabeth L. Eisenstein*, edited by Sabrina Baron, Eric Lindquist, and Eleanor Shevlin, 250–267. Amherst: University of Massachusetts Press, 2007.

Rubin, Adam. "'Like a Necklace of Black Pearls Whose String Has Snapped': Bialik's *Aron ha-sefarim* and the Sacralization of Zionism." *Prooftexts* 28, no. 2 (2008): 157–196.

Ruderman, David. *A Best-Selling Hebrew Book of the Modern Era: The* Book of the Covenant *of Pinhas Hurwitz and Its Remarkable Legacy*. Seattle: University of Washington Press, 2014.

Rudy, Kathryn. *Postcards on Parchment: The Social Lives of Medieval Books*. New Haven, CT: Yale University Press, 2015.

Sabar, Shalom. "The Preservation and Continuation of Sephardi Art in Morocco." *European Judaism* 52, no. 2 (2019): 59–81.

Sabar, Shalom. "Sephardi Elements in North African Hebrew Manuscript Decoration." *Jewish Art* 18 (1992): 168–191.

Sabev, Orlin. "Waiting for Godot: The Formation of Ottoman Print Culture." In *Historical Aspects of Printing and Publishing in Languages of the Middle East*, edited by Geoffrey Roper, 101–120. Leiden: Brill, 2014.

Sabev, Orlin. *Waiting for Müteferrika: Glimpses of Ottoman Print Culture*. Boston: Academic Studies, 2018.

Sadan, Joseph. "Genizah and Genizah-Like Practices in Islamic and Jewish Traditions." *Bibliotheca Orientalis* 43, no. 1 (1986): 36–58.

Sadaoui, Zoulikha. "Un temoin de l'histoire: L'Akhbar, doyen des journaux algeriens de la colonisation." PhD diss., Université Panthéon-Assas Paris II, 1992.

Salmon, Yosef. "David Gordon and *Ha-Maggid*: Changing Attitudes toward Jewish Nationalism, 1860–1882." *Modern Judaism* 17, no. 2 (1997): 109–124.

Sanuto, Marino. *I Diarii di Marino Sanuto*. Vol. 33, edited by Federico Stefani. Venice: F. Visentini, 1892.

Saraf, Michal. "Daniel Ḥagège ve-ḥiburo ʻal toldot ha-sifrut ha-ʻaravit-yehudit be-tunisia, 1862–1939." *Peʻamim* 30 (1987): 41–59.

Saraf, Michal. "Ha-ḥida ha-sifrutit ba-ḥibbur zikhron yerushalayim le-rabbi eliyahu ḥazzan, shadar yerushalayim bi-ṣfon afriqa." *Proceedings of the World Congress of Jewish Studies* 10 (1989): 89–96.

Schidorsky, Dov. "Libraries in Late Ottoman Palestine between the Orient and the Occident." *Libraries & Culture* 33, no. 3 (1998): 260–276.

Schine, Rachel. "A Mirror for the Modern Man: The Siyar Šaʻbiyya as Advice Literature in Tunisian Judeo-Arabic Editions." *Arabica* 65 (2018): 392–418.

Schmelzer, Menahem. "Hebrew Manuscripts and Printed Books among the Sephardim before and after the Expulsion." In *Crisis and Creativity in the Sephardic World: 1391–1648*, edited by Benjamin R. Gampel, 256–266. New York: Columbia University Press, 1997.

Schreier, Joshua. *Arabs of the Jewish Faith: The Civilizing Mission in Colonial Algeria*. New Brunswick, NJ: Rutgers University Press, 2010.

Schreier, Joshua. *The Merchants of Oran: A Jewish Port at the Dawn of Empire*. Redwood City, CA: Stanford University Press, 2017.

Schrijver, Emile. "The Eye of the Beholder: Artistic Sense and Craftsmanship in Eighteenth-Century Jewish Books." *Images* 7 (2015): 35–55.

Schrijver, Emile. "The Hebraic Book." In *A Companion to the History of the Book*, edited by Simon Eliot and Jonathan Rose, 161–162. Oxford: Oxford University Press, 2007.

Schrijver, Emile. "Jewish Book Culture since the Invention of Printing." In *The Cambridge History of Judaism: Volume 7, The Early Modern World, 1500–1815*, edited by Jonathan Karp and Adam Sutcliffe, 291–315. Cambridge: Cambridge University Press, 2017.

Schroeter, Daniel. "Anglo-Jewry and Essaouira (Mogador), 1860–1900: The Social Implications of Philanthropy." *Transactions & Miscellanies of the Jewish Historical Society of England* 28 (1982): 73–74.

Schroeter, Daniel. "A Different Road to Modernity: Jewish Identity in the Arab World." In *Diasporas and Exiles: Varieties of Jewish Identity*, edited by Howard Wettstein, 150–163. Oakland: University of California Press, 2002.

Schroeter, Daniel. "The End of the Sephardic World Order." In *From Iberia to Diaspora: Studies in Sephardic History and Culture*, edited by Yedida Stillman and Norman (Noam) Stillman, 86–101. Leiden: Brill, 1999.

Schroeter, Daniel. "From Sephardi to Oriental: The 'Decline' Theory of Jewish Civilization in the Middle East and North Africa." In *The Jewish Contribution to Civilization: Reassessing an Idea*, edited by Richard Cohen and Jeremy Cohen, 125–148. Liverpool: Littman Library of Jewish Civilization, 2007.

Schroeter, Daniel. *Merchants of Essaouira: Urban Society and Imperialism in Southwestern Morocco, 1844–1886*. Cambridge: Cambridge University Press, 1988.

Schroeter, Daniel. "Moroccan Jewish Studies in Israel." *Hésperis-Tamuda* 51, no. 2 (2016): 84–85.

Schroeter, Daniel. "The Politics of Reform in Morocco: The Writings of Yishaq Ben Ya'is(h) Halewi in Hasfirah (1891)." In *Misgav Yerushalayim*

Studies in Jewish Literature, edited by Ephraim Hazan, 73–84. Jerusalem: Institute for Research on the Sephardi and Oriental Jewish Heritage, 1987.

Schroeter, Daniel. "The Shifting Boundaries of Moroccan Jewish Identities." *Jewish Social Studies* 15, no. 1 (2008): 145–164.

Schroeter, Daniel. *The Sultan's Jew: Morocco and the Sephardi World*. Redwood City, CA: Stanford University Press, 2002.

Schroeter, Daniel, and Joseph Chetrit. "Emancipation and Its Discontents: Jews at the Formative Period of Colonial Rule in Morocco." *Jewish Social Studies* 13, no. 1 (2006): 170–206.

Schwartz, Kathryn A. "Did Ottoman Sultans Ban Print?" *Book History* 20 (2017): 1–39.

Sclar, David. "A Communal Tree of Life: Western Sephardic Jewry and the Library of the Ets Haim Yesiba in Early Modern Amsterdam." *Book History* 22 (2019): 43–65.

Sémach, Yomtob. "Une chronique juive de Fès: le 'Yahas Fès' de Ribbi Abner Hassarfaty." *Hésperis* 19 (1934): 79–94.

Serels, M. Mitchell. "The Hahamim of the Serero Family." *Sephardic Scholar* 4 (1982): 102–110.

Serels, M. Mitchell. "Sephardic Printings as a Source of Historical Material." *Revue des Études Juives* 138, no. 1 (1979): 147–153.

Serfaty, Vidal. "La communauté de Fès et la famille Hassarfati." *Etsi: revue de généalogie et d'histoire séfarades* 29 (2005): 5–10.

Seroussi, Edwin. "Archivists of Memory: Written Folksong Collections of Twentieth-Century Sephardi Women." In *Music and Gender: Perspectives from the Mediterranean*, edited by Tullia Magrini, 195–214. Chicago: University of Chicago Press, 2003.

Shachar, Isaiah. *Jewish Tradition in Art: The Feuchtwanger Collection of Judaica*. Jerusalem: Israel Museum, 1981.

Shafir, Nir. "The Road from Damascus: Circulation and the Redefinition of Islam in the Ottoman Empire, 1620–1720." PhD diss., University of California Los Angeles, 2016.

Shatzmiller, Maya. *L'historiographie mérinide: Ibn Khaldoun et ses contemporains*. Leiden: Brill, 1982.

Shmidman, Michael. "Radical Theology in Defense of the Faith: A Fourteenth-Century Example." *Tradition: A Journal of Orthodox Jewish Thought* 41, no. 2 (2008): 245–255.

Sienna, Noam. "Neighbouring Imaginaries: Jews and Demons in the Maghreb." Master's thesis, University of Toronto, 2015.

Sienna, Noam. "Rabbis with Inky Fingers: Making an Eighteenth-Century Hebrew Book between North Africa and Amsterdam." *Studia Rosenthaliana* 46, nos. 1/2 (2020): 155–187.

Silvestri, Stefania. "Le Bibbie ebraiche della penisola iberica: Committenza, produzione e diffusione tra i secoli XIII e XVI." PhD diss., Università Ca'Foscari Venezia, 2013.

Singerman, Robert. "Books Weeping for Someone to Visit and Admire Them: Jewish Library Culture in the United States, 1850–1910." *Studies in Bibliography and Booklore* 20 (1998): 99–144.

Skloot, Joseph. *First Impressions: Sefer Hasidim and Early Modern Hebrew Printing*. Waltham, MA: Brandeis University Press, 2023.

Slouschz, Nahum. "Études sur l'histoire des Juifs au Maroc." *Archives Marocaines* 4 (1905): 345–411 and 5 (1906): 1–167.

Slouschz, Nahum. *Travels in North Africa*. Philadelphia: Jewish Publication Society, 1927.

Smith, Margaret. *The Title-Page: Its Early Development, 1460–1510*. London: British Library, 2001.

Solomons, Israel. "David Nieto and Some of His Contemporaries." *Transactions of the Jewish Historical Society of England* 12 (1928): 1–101.

Stanislawski, Michael. "The 'Vilna Shas' and East European Jewry." In *Printing the Talmud: From Bomberg to Schottenstein*, edited by Sharon Liberman Mintz and Gabriel Goldstein, 97–102. New York: Yeshiva University Museum, 2005.

Stein, Sarah Abrevaya. *Extraterritorial Dreams: European Citizenship, Sephardi Jews, and the Ottoman Twentieth Century*. Chicago: University of Chicago Press, 2016.

Stein, Sarah Abrevaya. *Making Jews Modern: The Yiddish and Ladino Press in the Russian and Ottoman Empires*. Bloomington: Indiana University Press, 2004.

Stern, David. *The Jewish Bible: A Material History*. Seattle: University of Washington Press, 2017.

Stern, Karen. *Inscribing Devotion and Death: Archaeological Evidence for Jewish Populations of North Africa*. Leiden: Brill, 2008.

Stillman, Norman (Noam). *Sephardi Religious Responses to Modernity*. Luxembourg: Harwood, 1995.

Stillman, Yedida Khalfon. "Hashpa'ot sefardiyyot al ha-tarbut ha-ḥomrit shel yehudei maroqo." In *The Sephardi and Oriental Jewish Heritage*, edited by Issachar Ben-Ami, 359–366. Jerusalem: Magnes, 1992.

Taïeb, Jacques. "Les juifs Livournais de 1600 à 1881." In *Histoire communautaire, histoire plurielle: La communauté juive de Tunisie*, edited by

Abdelhamid Larguèche, 153–164. Tunis: Centre de publication universitaire, 1999.

Ta-Shma, Israel. *The Hebrew Book: An Historical Survey.* Jerusalem: Keter, 1975.

Tavim, José Alberto Rodrigues da Silva. "Adibe Family." In *Encyclopedia of Jews in the Islamic World,* edited by Noam Stillman. Leiden: Brill, 2010.

Tavim, José Alberto Rodrigues da Silva. *Os judeus na expansão portuguesa em Marrocos durante o século XVI.* Braga: Edições APPACDM, 1997.

Tavim, José Alberto Rodrigues da Silva. "Uma 'estranha tolerância' da Inquisição Portuguesa: Belchior Vaz de Azevedo e o interesse das potências europeias por Marrocos (segunda metade do século XVI)." In *Entre el Islam y Occidente: los judíos magrebíes en la edad moderna,* edited by Mercedes García-Arenal, 101–123. Madrid: Casa de Velázquez, 2003.

Taylor, W. B. S. *History of the University of Dublin.* London: Cadell and Cumming, 1845.

Tedghi, Joseph (Yosef). "Ibn Ḥayyim, Aaron ben Abraham." In *Encyclopedia of Jews in the Islamic World,* edited by Noam Stillman. Leiden: Brill, 2010.

Tedghi, Yosef (Joseph). *Ha-sefer veha-defus ha-'ivri be-fas.* Jerusalem: Ben-Zvi Institute, 1994.

Tedghi, Yosef (Joseph). "The Jewish Cemetery in Fez." *Mi-qedem umi-yam* 9 (2006): 93–140.

Tenger, Zeynep, and Paul Trolander. "From Print versus Manuscript to Sociable Authorship and Mixed Media: A Review of Trends in the Scholarship of Early Modern Publication." *Literature Compass* 7/11 (2010): 1035–1048.

Teplitsky, Joshua. *Prince of the Press: How One Collector Built History's Most Enduring and Remarkable Jewish Library.* New Haven, CT: Yale University Press, 2019.

Tirosh-Becker, Ofra. "Eli'ezer Ben-Yehuda and Algerian Jews: Relationship and Language." In *Arabic and Semitic Linguistics Contextualized: A Festschrift for Jan Retsö,* edited by Lutz Edzard, 430–447. Wiesbaden: Harrassowitz, 2015.

Tirosh-Becker, Ofra. "Linguistic Analysis of an Algerian Judeo-Arabic Text from the Nineteenth Century." *La Linguistique* 55, no. 1 (2019): 193–212.

Tirosh-Becker, Ofra. "On Dialectical Roots in Judeo-Arabic Texts from Constantine (East Algeria)." *Revue des Études Juives* 170, no. 1 (2011): 227–253.

Tobi, Tsivia. "Ha-rav ha-maskil eli'ezer farḥi ve-yeṣirotav ha-saṭiriyyot." *Ben 'ever la-'arav* 5 (2012): 127–144.

Tobi, Yosef. "Bekache, Shalom." In *Encyclopedia of Jews in the Islamic World,* edited by Norman Stillman. Leiden: Brill, 2010.

Tobi, Yosef. "Judaeo-Arabic Printing in North Africa, 1850–1950." In *Historical Aspects of Printing and Publishing in Languages of the Middle East,* edited by Geoffrey Roper, 129–150. Leiden: Brill, 2014.

Tobi, Yosef. "The Openness of Modern Judeo-Arabic Literature in Tunisia towards Muslim-Arabic Literature." *Pe'amim* 130 (2012): 117–140.

Tobi, Yosef, and Tsivia Tobi. *Judeo-Arabic Literature in Tunisia, 1850–1950.* Detroit: Wayne State University Press, 2014.

Tolédano, Ya'aqov Moshe. *Ner ha-ma'arav.* Jerusalem: Abraham Lunz, 1911.

Tolédano, Ya'aqov Moshe. *Sarid u-faliṭ.* Tel Aviv: Azriel, 1946.

Toomer, Gerard. *Eastern Wisedome and Learning: The Study of Arabic in Seventeenth-Century England.* Oxford: Clarendon, 1996.

Toukabri, Hmida. *Les Juifs dans la Tunisie médiévale, 909–1057: d'après les documents de la Geniza de Caire.* Paris: Romillat, 2002.

Trivellato, Francesca. *The Familiarity of Strangers: The Sephardic Diaspora, Livorno, and Cross-Cultural Trade in the Early Modern Period.* New Haven, CT: Yale University Press, 2009.

Tsur, Yaron. "Dating the Demise of the Western Sephardi Jewish Diaspora in the Mediterranean." In *Jewish Culture and Society in North Africa,* edited by Emily Gottreich and Daniel Schroeter, 93–106. Bloomington: Indiana University Press, 2011.

Tsur, Yaron. "Haskala in a Sectional Colonial Society: Mahdia (Tunisia) 1884." In *Sephardi and Middle Eastern Jewries: History and Culture in the Modern Era,* edited by Harvey E. Goldberg, 146–167. Bloomington: Indiana University Press, 1996.

Tsur, Yaron. "La culture religieuse à Tunis à la fin du XVIIIe d'après le récit de voyage de Ḥaïm Yossef David Azoulay." In *Entre Orient et Occident: juifs et musulmans en Tunisie,* edited by Denis Cohen-Tannoudji, 63–76. Paris: Éditions de l'Éclat, 2007.

Urbach, Ephraim. "Mishmarot u-ma'amadot." *Tarbiṣ* 42 (1973): 304–327.

Vajda, Georges. "Ahl al-Kitab." In *Encyclopaedia of Islam,* 2nd ed. Leiden: Brill, 1960.

van Orden, Kate. *Materialities: Books, Readers, and the Chanson in Sixteenth-Century Europe.* Oxford: Oxford University Press, 2015.

Wacks, David. *Double Diaspora in Sephardic Literature: Jewish Cultural Production before and after 1492.* Bloomington: Indiana University Press, 2015.

Wakefield, Colin. "Arabic Manuscripts in the Bodleian Library: The Seventeenth-Century Collections." In *The 'Arabick' Interest of the*

Natural Philosophers in Seventeenth-Century England, edited by G. A. Russell, 128–146. Leiden: Brill, 1993.

Walters, Keith. "Education for Jewish Girls in Late Nineteenth- and Early Twentieth-Century Tunis and the Spread of French in Tunisia." In *Jewish Culture and Society in North Africa,* edited by Emily Gottreich and Daniel Schroeter, 257–281. Bloomington: Indiana University Press, 2011.

Weinberg, Werner. "Language Questions Relating to Moses Mendelssohn's Pentateuch Translation (in Commemoration of the 200th Anniversary of the Biur)." *Hebrew Union College Annual* 55 (1984): 197–242.

Whearty, Bridget. *Digital Codicology: Medieval Books and Modern Labor.* Redwood City, CA: Stanford University Press, 2022.

Wijsman, Suzanne. "The Oppenheimer Siddur: Artist and Scribe in a Fifteenth-Century Hebrew Prayer Book." In *Crossing Borders: Hebrew Manuscripts as a Meeting-Place of Cultures,* edited by Piet van Boxel and Sabine Arndt, 69–84. Oxford: Oxford University Press, 2009.

Witkam, Jan Just. "Moritz Steinschneider and the Leiden Manuscripts." In *Studies on Steinschneider: Moritz Steinschneider and the Emergence of the Science of Judaism in Nineteenth-Century Germany,* edited by Reimund Leicht and Gad Freudenthal, 263–275. Leiden: Brill, 2011.

Ya'ari, Avraham. *Ha-defus ha-'ivri be-arṣot ha-mizraḥ.* Jerusalem: Magnes, 1936.

Ya'ari, Avraham. "Ha-defus ha-'ivri be-izmir." *Areshet: sefer ha-shana le-ḥeqer ha-sefer ha-'ivri* 1 (1959): 106.

Ya'ari, Avraham. *Sheluḥei ereṣ yisrael: toldot ha-sheliḥut meha-areṣ la-gola me-ḥurban bayit sheni 'ad ha-me'a ha-tesha'-'esrei.* Jerusalem: Mossad Rav Kook, 1977.

Yates, Frances. *The Art of Memory.* London: Routledge, 1966.

Yehuda, Yishaq-Yehezqel. "Ha-tamḥui la-'adat ha-sefardim bi-yrushalayim." *Reshumot: me'asef le-divrei zikhronot* 6 (1930): 544–548.

Zafrani, Haim. *Études et recherches sur la vie intellectuelle juive au Maroc.* Paris: Geuthner, 1972.

Zafrani, Haim. *Pédagogie juive en terre d'Islam: l'enseignement traditionnel de l'hébreu et du judaïsme au Maroc.* Paris: Maisonneuve, 1969.

Zirlin, Yaël. "Celui qui se cache derrière l'image: colophons des enlumineurs dans les manuscrits hébraïques." *Revue des Études Juives* 155, no. 1 (1996): 33–53.

Zohar, Zvi. "Ben-Simeon, Raphael Aaron." In *Encyclopedia of Jews in the Islamic World,* edited by Noam Stillman. Leiden: Brill, 2010.

Zohar, Zvi. "Halakhic and Rabbinic Literature in Egypt in the Last Two Centuries." *Pe'amim* 86 (2001): 175–213.

Zohar, Zvi. "Ḥazzan, Elijah Bekhor." In *Encyclopedia of Jews in the Islamic World,* edited by Noam Stillman. Leiden: Brill, 2010.

Zohar, Zvi. *Rabbinic Creativity in the Modern Middle East.* London: Bloomsbury Academic, 2013.

Zran, Jamel. "Aux origines de l'imprimerie et de l'édition en Tunisie: l'imprimerie officielle et le journal al-Râ'id." In *La presse en Tunisie et dans les pays méditerranéens durant un siècle, 1860–1960,* edited by Jamel Zran, 13–36. Tunis: Université de la Manouba, 2011.

Zuzot, Yitzhak. "R. refa'el berdugo: ha-ish ve-tequfato." Master's thesis, Touro College, 1995.

Zytnicki, Colette. "David Cazès (1850–1913), historien des Juifs de Tunisie: un métis culturel?" *Outre-Mers Revue d'histoire* 352 (2006): 97–106.

Zytnicki, Colette. *Les Juifs du Maghreb: naissance d'une historiographie coloniale.* Paris: Presses de l'Universite Paris-Sorbonne, 2011.

INDEX

Abensur, Ya'aqov, 29–30, 47–48, 51, 53–54, 154–169, 190–192, 217n56, 225nn41–42
al-Qṣar al-Kbir (Ksar el Kbir), 19–20
Alexandria, 85, 99, 102, 141, 162–163, 260n91
Algeria, *see individual cities*
Algiers, 37, 48, 72, 76, 98, 99, 109, 111, 113, 115–116, 119–120, 123–126, 128, 134–135, 138–139, 144–146, 148, 162, 164
Alliance Israélite Universelle (AIU), 4, 142–145, 174–175, 183, 197, 261n95
Amsterdam, 29, 72, 75, 77, 79, 156, 237n34
Ashkenazi Jews, in Europe, 7, 77–78, 138, 193, 196; in North Africa, 32–36, 104, 141–142; *see also* Haskalah, modernity

Ben-Shim'on, Refael-Aharon, 36, 139–141, 188, 196, 270n55, 277n136
Bibles and biblical texts, 12–13, 21–22, 29–30, 39–41, *40*, 97–101, 124, 165–166, 176, 178–180, 217n56
bookstores and booksellers, 14, 32–34, 87, 94–95, 117, 123–126, 131, 138, 161, 177

Cairo Geniza, 8, 17, 32, 140, 155, 207n23; *see also* genizot
Cairo, 20, 23, 139–141, 196, 260n91
Chefchaouen, 20
Constantine, 8, 48, 66–67, 100, 102, 106, 148
conversos (New Christians), 21–22, 85
Crémieux, Adolphe and the Crémieux Decree, 105–106, 124, 142

Ḍarmon, Yehuda, 54–55, 121, 132–133, 137–138
Debdou, 141, 185, 198–200

Egypt, *see individual cities*
Essaouira (Mogador), 58–59, 62, 101, 130, 148, 189
European Jews, *see* Ashkenazi Jews
Exile from Spain, 9, 15–16, 18–24, 54, 86, 148, 160, 210n1

Fez, 2, 8, 9, 16, 22, 23, 24–28, 29, 30, 34, 36, 39–41, 54, 57–58, 76, 86, 93, 140, 148, 154, 156–157, 158–190, 216n50, 236n27
French language, 103, 132–135, 138, 142–150, 154, 155–192

genizot, 1, 32, 37–38, 197, 204n10, 218n67; *see also* Cairo Geniza
Gibraltar, 31, 58, 75, 99, 127, 164, 218n64

Haggadah, 46, 47, 60–62, 88, 112, 120, 124, 144
haketía, *see* Judeo-Spanish
Haskalah, 106–107, 110, 124, 132, 136–142, 175–190, 192

illumination and book decoration, 18, 22, 31–34, 39–41, 42–44, 55–64, 166, 244n24
incunabula, 20, 23, 26, 31, 33, 34, 165, 230n80, 270n57
Islamic literature, 5, 156–157, 185–187
Istanbul (Constantinople), xvi, 9, 20, 76, 242n76
Italy, *see individual cities*
İzmir (Smyrna), 81–82, 102

Jerusalem, xvi, 9, 74, 76, 87, 102–103, 107, 119, 140, 149, 161, 162–163, 164, 177
Jewish quarter, 9, 22, 34, 174
Judeo-Arabic, x, xiv, xvii, 29, 60, 75, 86, 87–89, 92, 95–101, 107–114, 115–116, 120–137, 143–150, 190, 197–198, 248n68, 261n96
Judeo-Spanish, 11–12, 75, 86, 95–96, 112, 114, 120, 121, 127, 143–144, 246n45, 261n96

Kabbalistic texts, 19, 23, 49, 62, 161, 165, 170, 178, 179, 210n1

Ladino, *see* Judeo-Spanish
libraries and librarians, xiv, 1–4, 8, 14, 29–30, 138–139, 151–192, 198–201, 234–235n20, 256n56, 260n91, 265n12
lithography, 117–119, 123, 125, 129–130, 253n25, 254n32

Livorno, ix–x, 1, 9, 69, 72, 75, 77–80, 81, 83, 84–90, 91–114, 115–116, 123–125, 126, 130, 145, 197

manuscripts, *see* scribes and scribal practice
Marrakech, 9, 59, 97, 148, 237n34
Mediterranean world, 8–9, 14–16, 20–22, 68–69, 84–86, 96, 112, 190
Meknes, 22, 51, 75, 79, 141, 151, 158, 159, 160, 162, 221n89
mellah, *see* Jewish quarter
modernity and modernization, 4–5, 7–8, 10, 90, 91–114, 132–150, 174–190, 197–198
Morocco, *see individual cities*
Mostaganem, 101, 137, 139, 189

newspapers and journalism, 37, 99–100, 108–114, 115–116, 126–127, 133–134, 137–138, 189, 197

Oran (Wahran), 1–4, 9, 33, 54, 97, 99, 113, 121, 127–128, 137–138, 148, 191, 199–200
Ottoman Empire, 70–71, 85, 233nn7–9; Jews from, 7, 49, 80–81, 102, 119–120, 140, 162, 176; *see also individual cities*

printing and print culture, 13–14, 17, 23–28, 69–90, 91–114, 115–150, 194–195

rabbinic leadership and authority, 2, 3, 29, 37, 40–41, 45–48, 74, 81, 101–107, 112–114, 136–137, 145–146, 148, 157–158, 175, 190–192

Safi, 21, 31, 213n24, 256n57
scribes and scribal practice, 22–23, 39, 42–67, 68–69, 157–158, 160–161, 167–171, 183–185
Sebaoun, Moïse (Moshe Sib'on), 2–4, 3, 8, 137, 159, 191, 200, 204n3, 275n115

Sefrou, 2, 54, 154, 162, 167, 182, 185, 187
Sephardi identity, 6–9, 17–20, 22–23, 26–27, 60, 77–78, 85–86, 91–96, 104–106, 112–114, 138, 148, 191, 197–198
Serfaty, Avner-Yisrael, 36, 39–41, 53, 112, 155, 174–190, 192, 197, 249n85, 274n106
Shamama, Nissim, 9, 74, 101, 241n73, 248n68

Tafilalt, 45, 52, 59–61
Talmud, 20, 24–26, 33, 46, 120, 153, 160, 165, 167, 170, 178–180, 198–200
Tangiers, 2, 113, 127–128, 141, 143, 190
Tetouan, 2, 32, 58, 93, 101, 127, 143, 158, 161, 168, 218n68
Thessaloniki (Salonica), 20, 29, 119–120
Tlemcen, 21, 31, 100, 130–131, 138, 148
translation, xvii–xviii, 29, 60, 87–88, 97–101, 108–111, 120–124, 126–127, 132–136, 143–145, 149, 189–190; *see also individual languages*
Tunis, 9, 15, 20, 21, 29, 33, 35, 48, 53–54, 62, 68, 71, 78, 81–84, 88–89, 99, 102–103, 108, 110–111, 113, 121–123, 126–128, 130, 138–139, 143–146, 153, 161, 162, 180, 210n4, 219n74

Venice, 20, 21, 75–76

women, literacy of, 45, 134, 143–144, 154, 198–200, 261n96

Zionism, 1, 10, 35–36, 101–107, 273n88
Zohar, 19, 53, 88, 94, 120. *See also* Kabbalistic texts

NOAM SIENNA is a scholar of Jewish culture in the Islamic world, focusing on book history and material culture. He is currently a Postdoctoral Research Fellow with the University of Toronto, where he studies Jewish books in the medieval and early modern Mediterranean as part of the interdisciplinary project Hidden Stories: New Approaches to the Local and Global History of the Book.

For Indiana University Press

Tony Brewer, Artist and Book Designer
Dan Crissman, Acquisitions Editor
Anna Francis, Assistant Acquisitions Editor
Anna Garnai, Production Coordinator
Katie Huggins, Production Manager
Darja Malcolm-Clarke, Project Manager/Editor
Dan Pyle, Online Publishing Manager
Michael Regoli, Director of Publishing Operations
Stephen Williams, Assistant Director of Marketing
Jennifer Witzke, Senior Artist and Book Designer